ENGAGEMENT & EMPLOYABILITY

NASPA®
Student Affairs Administrators
in Higher Education

ADAM PECK

Editor

ENGAGEMENT & EMPLOYABILITY

*Integrating **Career Learning***
*Through **Cocurricular Experiences***
in Postsecondary Education

NASPA®
Student Affairs Administrators
in Higher Education

Engagement and Employability:
Integrating Career Learning Through Cocurricular Experiences
in Postsecondary Education

Published by
NASPA–Student Affairs Administrators in Higher Education
111 K Street, NE
10th Floor
Washington, DC 20002
www.naspa.org

Additional copies may be purchased by contacting the NASPA publications department at 202-265-7500 or visiting http://bookstore.naspa.org.

NASPA does not discriminate on the basis of race, color, national origin, religion, sex, age, gender identity, gender expression, affectional or sexual orientation, or disability in any of its policies, programs, and services.

Library of Congress Cataloging-in-Publication Data

Names: Peck, Adam (Student affairs administrator), editor.
Title: Engagement and employability : integrating career learning through
  cocurricular experiences in postsecondary education / Adam Peck, editor.
Description: First edition. | Washington, DC : NASPA-Student Affairs
  Administrators in Higher Education, [2017]
Identifiers: LCCN 2016050568 (print) | LCCN 2017000059 (ebook) | ISBN
    9780931654626 | ISBN 9780931654626 (hardcover) | ISBN 9780931654725
(eBook (mobi)) | ISBN 9780931654718 (eBook (e-pub))
Subjects: LCSH: Career education--United States. | Student activities--United
  States. | Employability--Study and teaching (Higher)--United States.
Classification: LCC LC1037.5 .E58 2017 (print) | LCC LC1037.5 (ebook) | DDC
  370.1130973--dc23
LC record available at https://lccn.loc.gov/2016050568

Printed and bound in the United States of America

FIRST EDITION

CONTENTS

SECTION II
In Practice: Developing Employability Skills
Through Cocurricular Experiences

Disruption, Change, and Telling the Story of Student Affairs
An Introduction

Kevin Kruger and Adam Peck

Anyone who has worked in the field of student affairs has likely observed how difficult it can be to explain to others the nature of our work. Even those closest to us—spouses, children, parents, and so forth—may have a basic idea of our day-to-day work without completely understanding the big picture of why our jobs exist in the first place.

For many practitioners, their own college experiences strongly influence their perception of the purpose of student affairs. Those who lived in a residence hall may see the role of student affairs as providing students housing and perhaps some activities to help residents get to know each other. Those who participated in intramurals may see the purpose as helping students engage in physical activity and pursue their personal wellness. Those who needed assistance with a disability may see student affairs in terms of helping students succeed. There are potentially as many perspectives as there are programs and services in student affairs.

Of course, it is equally likely that students aren't aware of the field of student affairs as any sort of collective whole. Student affairs appears to them as individual programs and services provided by the institution that students either use or do not use. The mission of student affairs is to personalize and humanize the collegiate experience, to create intentional environments that support learning, to help students overcome obstacles to their success, and to provide opportunities for students to learn through involvement. This mission may be entirely lost on even deeply involved students. And yet, there is frequently a common understanding among those who attended college as traditional-aged students that they learned as much from their experiences outside the classroom in the rich milieu of the college experience than they did attending classes—even courses within their major.

Some skeptics may ask, why does it matter whether students are aware of the existence of student affairs and how it contributes to students' personal growth and development in college? First, if students do not understand the purpose of student affairs, it will be harder for them to derive meaning from their cocurricular experiences, nor will they be able to fully engage with the programs. Second, today's students are tomorrow's leaders and policy makers. Konnikova (2014) reported that 18 U.S. presidents were members of fraternities while in college, as well as 85% of U.S. Supreme Court justices, 76% of U.S. senators, and 85% of Fortune 500 executives. If we as student affairs educators are to improve our ability to articulate our purpose, it would make sense to start with those who already engage with us in some way.

PURPOSES OF THE BOOK

This book is intended to serve two important purposes. First, it demonstrates the critical role that student affairs can play in helping students gain and articulate career skills through cocurricular experiences. In pursuit of this goal, chapters are offered that focus on how this kind of learning can be developed through experiences outside of the classroom. Featuring contributions from six higher education professional association executives, the book charts a course for student affairs colleagues.

A second, but no less important goal, is to help those outside of student affairs understand the work of student affairs professionals. Each chapter in Section II highlights common experiences that demonstrate how students can gain important skills. These chapters specifically focus on the outcomes that matter most to stakeholders—the top skills that employers demand when seeking to hire recent college graduates.

The timing of this book is also imperative. There is little doubt that higher education is in a time of great (some would suggest disruptive) change. New content delivery models promise increased efficiency, lower cost, and the ability to expand the reach of higher education both geographically and demographically. That is to say that these new models can reach potential students who might not have had access to traditional forms of college education for any number of reasons. For student affairs to participate fully in these new models of higher education, the profession must be prepared to speak with one voice and explain clearly how student affairs can contribute, while being mindful of the guidance of Eric Hoffer (1982), who wrote, "In times of change learners inherit the earth; while the learned find themselves beautifully equipped to deal with a world that no longer exists" (p. 30).

COCURRICULAR EXPERIENCES AND EMPLOYABILITY SKILLS

This book is organized around the top skills desired by employers as determined by the National Association of Colleges and Employers (NACE; 2015). The alignment between these skills and the kinds of learning outcomes already pursued in student affairs is clear. The positive effect that cocurricular experiences have on students' verbal and written communication skills—their ability to influence others, to work as a member of a team, or to plan and organize initiatives—is already commonly known. Other topics, such as whether cocurricular experiences help students develop computer skills or quantitative reasoning skills, may be initially dismissed as non-germane to experiential educators or may be seen as areas of untapped potential in which student affairs can help students develop skills they may be less likely to develop otherwise. This latter approach deserves consideration as educators imagine what might be possible.

In Chapter 3, Peck, Griffin, and LaCount share the data from Project CEO (Cocurricular Experience Outcomes), a national effort to collect learning outcomes data from 40 institutions and more than 15,000 college students. The data are compelling and suggest that a myriad of experiences are embedded in cocurricular learning that can help develop the skills on which this book is based. Subsequent chapters offer guidance on turning this potential learning into actual learning and are framed in the terms and definitions that were used in Project CEO.

CRISIS, DANGER, AND OPPORTUNITY IN STUDENT AFFAIRS

John F. Kennedy is quoted as saying, "When written in Chinese, the word crisis is composed of two characters. One represents danger and the other represents opportunity" (Howell, 2014, para 1). While experts in the Chinese language assert that Kennedy's quote is not entirely accurate (Nguyen, 2014), the wide reporting of and acceptance for the premise on which it is based are likely driven by the eternal truth that is embedded within it. We can choose how we experience change: We can see it as danger, or we can see it as opportunity.

Much has been made of "disruptive innovation" in a variety of industries. The application of this concept to higher education distorts the theory somewhat (as it was created to describe business), but many key concepts apply. For instance, those institutions that find a way to deliver what their customers want while increasing efficiency and cutting costs will not only become more successful but also have the potential to change the ways these products or services are offered even by the established industry leaders (Christensen, Raynor, & McDonald, 2015). It stands to reason that as the expanding potential of technology is applied to the field of higher education, change will naturally result. Change can be disconcerting to many. But what if this change isn't disruptive? A case can be made that some of the most significant changes in higher education have enhanced the mission of student affairs.

Consider what was arguably the single greatest catalyst for growth in higher education and expansion of the role of student affairs on college and university campuses: the passage of the G.I. Bill (Bound & Turner, 2002). The bill was a sea change of massive proportions. It increased enrollment in higher education by more than 50% and resulted in considerable degree attainment for World War II veterans (Bound & Turner, 2002). It also changed the structure of higher education institutions, creating a need for new services to meet the demands of the college students of the day (Rhatigan, 2009). This innovation was paradigm changing but also productive.

A more contemporary example can be found in the growth of the behavioral intervention role of student affairs. With the passage of the Americans with Disabilities Act in 1990 (Mayerson, 1992), institutions of higher education substantially changed their approach to providing mental health services on campus. The classification of mental illness as a disability resulted in a reinterpretation of Section 504 of the 1973 Rehabilitation Act and gave new rights to students with mental health concerns (Mayerson, 1992). When considered along with the tragic shootings at Virginia Tech in April 2007, the assessment and evaluation of potential threats from students with mental illness took on new relevance. In its 2007 report on the mass shootings, the Virginia Tech Review Panel recommended that "institutions of higher learning should have a threat assessment team that includes representatives from law enforcement, human resources, student and academic affairs, legal counsel, and mental health functions" (p. 19). While these approaches required broad buy-in from a variety of constituencies on college campuses (Sokolow & Lewis, 2009), on many (if not most) campuses student affairs took the lead. A qualitative study conducted by Greenstein (2014) looked at the perspectives of faculty and staff regarding behavioral assessment teams and determined that those studied had a favorable impression of the impact of such efforts on the overall safety of their campus. An argument could be made that the need for and impact of behavioral intervention efforts have helped demonstrate the purpose of student affairs on college campuses. Faculty in particular gained perspective on how students experiencing mental illness could often be assisted on campus and how the engagement of student affairs staff could benefit students. So, rather than being a source of disruption, the increase in awareness of mental health issues has improved student affairs' practice through the development of new functions that provide more effective frameworks for addressing students of concern.

CHALLENGES AND OPPORTUNITIES

Today, higher education is facing many challenges and opportunities, including:

- the growth of online education and the increase in the percentage of students whose class experience is either entirely online or a hybridized experience of online and in-person classes;

- the growing number of credit hours that students are bringing to campus with them from early college programs or dual enrollment;
- the expansion of competency-based approaches to teaching and learning in which students are awarded credit for their ability to prove competency in the subject through ways other than completion of a college course; and
- the development of new credentials that address employers' critical in-demand skills.

Perhaps these challenges present new opportunities as well. Any of these changes could diminish the role of student affairs on campus. With regard to online education, it makes intuitive sense that online students have very different needs than students in face-to-face classes, and many of the programs and services offered by student affairs are hard to duplicate for online and distance learners. But the opportunity may lie in the ability of student affairs educators to affect these student populations. For example, completion rates for online students are considerably lower than those for students who take courses on campus (Pierrakeas, Xenos, Panagiotakopoulos, & Vergidis, 2004). Perhaps this results from the difficulty of engaging students in an online environment. In his theory of student departure, Vincent Tinto (1987) famously pointed to students' academic and social integration into the life of the university as important factors in persistence. In his more recent work, Tinto (2012) reinforced the idea that student retention is strongly influenced by "social forces internal and external to the campus, especially those that influence students' sense of belonging and membership in the social communities of the institution" (p. 27). Creating engagement with students is part of the charge of student affairs professionals on campus. As online learning continues to expand, improving the ability of colleges and universities to connect with students will become more critical, and student affairs can lead the way.

Additionally, changes that shorten the time to completion affect the way that programs are administered and services are delivered. But the faster pace of higher education being driven by early college and dual enrollment programs can present advantages. The faster pace of programs can sharpen the focus on career development, putting it on students' radar much earlier in their college experience. Compressed enrollment can also reduce overall cost and, potentially, the loans needed to support attendance. Lower costs may provide greater access points for low-income students. However, the loss of the traditional freshman year may also spur developmental challenges. Improvements in academic advising for students in this faster-paced trajectory will likely require competent guidance from professional advisors; consequently, the services and developmental opportunities currently offered by student affairs will need to be integrated into the student experience in meaningful ways. The more effectively we are able to articulate the contributions of student affairs to these new structures, the more likely the role of student affairs professionals will be enhanced rather than diminished.

Finally, competency-based models arguably represent the most disruptive innovation in higher education in that they may completely change the way education is delivered. In 2015, Southern New Hampshire University's College for America began offering "online, self-paced, competency-based degrees that do not feature formal instruction and are completely untethered from the credit-hour standard" (Fain, 2015, p. 2). This format not only removes the traditional college classroom environment and structure but also changes the way online instruction is offered. Once a student can demonstrate proficiency in the course matter, the course is over and the student receives credit for completion. Some preliminary indications reported by

Fain (2015) indicate that students who are participating in College for America performed comparably to (and occasionally better than) students in more traditional educational environments. Experiments in microcredentials as an alternative to 2- or 4-year degrees also raise important questions about opportunities for psychosocial development, particularly for traditional-aged and first-generation students who may seek alternative credentials. What will student affairs look like within a competency-based or microcredential model? It is hard to imagine. But the question deserves consideration as it is likely that many will be called on to answer it.

ADDRESSING CRITICS

Growing demands from the business sector, lawmakers, and the general public for accountability and return on investment in higher education present additional challenges. A further complication lies in the perceptions of business leaders with regard to how well prepared they perceive college graduates to be for the challenges of the workforce.

State law and policy makers often predicate their support of higher education on the notion that their investment will lead to students becoming gainfully employed and thus contributors to their state's economy. This justification is used for the subsidy of tuition and fees provided by state appropriations. It can result in a viewpoint that is heavily influenced by a desire to see a return on the state's investment rather than a desire to produce educated citizens for the state. It can pressure institutions to produce more diplomas as a way of stimulating the economy rather than focusing on producing students who have been prepared with the skills and abilities necessary for success in the workforce.

The narrative that colleges and universities aren't adequately preparing students for their careers appears to be gaining traction. For example, Florida governor Rick Scott, who has made improving the employment rates of college graduates a cornerstone of his efforts to reduce unemployment within his state, said, "Too many university students are graduating today, some after spending years of their family's savings and others after taking on decades of debt, not able to find a job. Our state-funded universities can and must do more to help graduates get a good paying job" (States News Service, 2015, para. 3). Fellow Floridian and 2016 presidential candidate U.S. Senator Marco Rubio also questioned students' career choices. In an *Inside Higher Education* editorial, Lynn Pasquerella (2016), president of Mount Holyoke College, wrote,

> Following the fourth round of the [2016] Republican presidential debates, a flurry of media attention focused on Florida Senator Marco Rubio's assertion that 'we need more welders, less philosophers.' In addition to noting the grammatical error in his statement, defenders of the liberal arts leaped to prove Rubio wrong by producing data from the Bureau of Labor Statistics indicating that the median salary of philosophers in fact exceeds that of welders. (para. 1)

This rhetoric creates dissonance between higher education institutions and law and policy makers, and it also suggests a false dichotomy between higher education and vocational education.

Business leaders have become more vocal in their skepticism as well. A survey conducted by Gallup found that just 11% of business leaders and 14% of the general public believe that college prepares students for success in the workplace (Lumina Foundation, 2013). Additionally, a 2015 report produced by the Association of American Colleges and Universities (AAC&U) found that students tend to think of themselves as far more prepared for their first job than do their employers (Jaschik, 2015). It is impossible to determine if higher education as a whole is doing a poor job in preparing students, or if this example is just an apt illustration of the significant difference in perception between higher education and its stakeholders as to how students should be prepared for day one on the job. Certainly in difficult economic times, companies look for ways to cut their costs. One popular approach is to spend less on employee training and development. When this happens, companies expect more from higher education. This can prompt unreasonable expectations, which can lead to disappointment.

Rising costs in higher education have no doubt exacerbated and amplified the criticism student affairs is currently facing. Among the explanations for rising costs has been *administrative bloat*, a term made prominent by Robert Hiltonsmith (2015) in a report published by the Washington, D.C., think tank Demos. In this report, administrative bloat was defined as "excessive spending beyond what is necessary to support the core academic functions of a university," identifying such experiences as "spending on student services" (Hiltonsmith, 2015, para. 5). This explanation confirms a popular perception of higher education as elitist and uncaring about the impact of increased expenses on students. New campus recreation centers, student unions, and athletic facilities are identified as the expenditures driving increased costs.

However, a recent initiative called the Delta Cost Project has found that the median expenditures on non-teaching staff labeled "administration" explain only about 6% of the change in price for higher education (Hiltonsmith, 2015). Student affairs is among the lowest expenditures. It isn't accurate or fair to place such a large share of the blame for rising costs on such a low percentage of the generation of this cost. In this atmosphere, new student services become proxies for the public's frustration with increases in tuition and fees. New residence halls, recreation centers, climbing walls, and lazy rivers are often used as a proxy for the public concern about the rising costs of higher education. But these rising costs are more likely a result of the dis-investment by states in public higher education, accounting for 79% of tuition hikes at public universities (Hiltonsmith, 2015). Increasingly, the massive reduction in state support is making college attendance a private good versus its historical place in American society as a public good. The financial burden of college has now shifted heavily toward families and the students themselves.

It is not well known that while costs continue to rise in higher education, in the majority of cases, budgets continue to shrink. For example, in 2015, Arizona governor Doug Ducey and the Arizona legislature cut $99 million from state university funding, promoting significant hikes in tuition and fees by the Arizona Board of Regents (Rau, 2015). As Chokshi (2015) pointed out, "Spending per student remains below—in some cases well below—pre-recession levels in 47 states, reflecting years of cuts to public colleges and universities that have yet to be undone" (para. 2). These cuts can create an environment in which various programs within the institution compete for these scarce resources rather than collaborate in holistically educating students.

Student affairs also faces criticism on college and university campuses from faculty, academic administration, and even senior leadership outside of student affairs. On the academic side, perhaps many faculty members were so focused on their courses when they themselves were students that they did not participate in student organizations or other cocurricular experiences. To these faculty, student affairs work may appear frivolous because they see only the public side: the carnivals and movie series and free ice cream. In an environment in which faculty may struggle to secure funding to attend a conference or support their research and without much knowledge of the importance of student engagement in the retention and success of students, it may be tempting to doubt the important role of student affairs. The importance of telling the student affairs story to faculty is magnified when we consider that many provosts and presidents begin as faculty and may develop and retain a mindset that undervalues the contributions that student affairs makes.

CHALLENGING THE NARRATIVE: TELLING THE STORY OF STUDENT AFFAIRS

This brings us to the definitive consideration of this introduction: How can we as student affairs professionals tell our story in order to capitalize on the opportunities presented by potentially disruptive innovations in higher education? How can we demonstrate our impact on student engagement and our ability to help students succeed both in college and throughout their lives?

We must first begin by acknowledging why we have struggled in this regard. Identifying credible data that underscore the role student affairs plays in key learning outcomes has proven challenging. Even the notion of learning and learning outcomes is not universally understood to be a part of student affairs, despite decades of literature that supports the role of the whole student experience in student learning through such documents as the *Student Learning Imperative* (ACPA–College Student Educators International, 1996) and *Learning Reconsidered* (Keeling, 2004). Adding to the problem, some of the most compelling and comprehensive data about what students are learning from their participation in cocurricular experiences have been gathered during assessment activities on individual campuses and are never published or shared.

To overcome these limitations, we must not only demonstrate the impact that student affairs makes on students in general but articulate the impact student affairs makes on the specific outcomes that stakeholders care about most. These outcomes include the ability to attract, retain, and graduate students. As the funding mix for colleges and universities continues to shift, these important considerations become even more so for both public and private institutions. Changes in enrollment can be particularly devastating for private institutions, especially those without substantial endowments. The number of students paying tuition and fees are the primary (and frequently the only significant) source of funds with which to operate the institution. As funding by state legislatures trends toward dwindling support, state institutions are finding themselves in a similar predicament. As a result, maintaining a consistent enrollment is very important. When we show that student affairs helps attract, retain, and graduate students, we are demonstrating the value of student affairs work.

We must also embrace an outcome that can be surprisingly controversial, namely how student affairs contributes to the employment of students after college. A major source of tension inherent in this goal is disagreement about the purpose of higher education. While most acknowledge that a college degree should result in employment, many argue that this is an output of college—not the input. In other words, the college needs to provide transformative experiences that help prepare students not just for a job but for a career and for lifelong learning. This distinction may seem esoteric, but it is extremely important. It is the difference between the instrumental view of college as the pathway to securing a job versus the developmental view of college as the pathway to creating a meaningful life. The instrumental approach argues that higher education may be able to prepare students for careers in accountancy much more quickly if they didn't have to take classes in philosophy or English, or if they didn't have to learn a foreign language or take a class on government. These classes often seem superfluous to those outside the field of higher education. But the developmental view argues that it is through such core curriculum courses that students learn more than just the skills to be an entry-level accountant—they gain critical thinking skills that they can adapt to an ever-changing job and an ever-changing world.

THE DECLINING PROMINENCE OF LIBERAL EDUCATION: AN OPPORTUNITY?

Two trends have converged that may relate to each other and inform this conversation. During the same period that employers have been openly voicing their skepticism for how well colleges and universities are preparing students for the workforce, appreciation for the value of a liberal education has been declining. AAC&U produced a "Statement on Liberal Learning" in 1998 that articulates the benefits of this kind of education, noting,

> A truly liberal education is one that prepares us to live responsible, productive, and creative lives in a dramatically changing world. It is an education that fosters a well-grounded intellectual resilience, a disposition toward lifelong learning, and an acceptance of responsibility for the ethical consequences of our ideas and actions. (para. 1)

According to Pasquerella (2016), "For many people in America, a liberal arts education seems reserved for those within the ivory tower, reflecting a willful disconnect from the practical matters of everyday life" (para. 7). Kimball (2014) discussed the perceptions of decline in the liberal arts ideal. He concluded that perhaps this decline is overestimated, but also acknowledged that "notwithstanding this shift, however, the historical enrollment in the collegiate liberal arts may not endure" (p. 245).

Within this philosophical divide, could we find yet another opportunity disguised as a danger? As we increase our focus on initiatives that link education from preschool through undergraduate degrees (often called p–16 initiatives) with a focus on speeding up college completion, it can be difficult to figure out how to integrate transformative experiences into the curriculum. The cocurriculum can present a solution to this problem. If experiences outside the classroom can provide the opportunity to develop those skills that matter most to employers through participation in experiential education, student affairs can expand learning opportunities and develop better learning outcomes for students. Student affairs can also improve the accuracy of the perceptions of stakeholders with regard to the quality of graduates and provide a more realistic picture of the developmental purpose of student affairs as a whole.

The impact of student affairs on career development is not well studied; consequently, it is not well known. It is important to consider more than just the programs sponsored by offices of career development and career services. As the research that provides a foundation for this book suggests, many more experiences contribute to the impact. Internships, for example, do appear to be an excellent source of career knowledge, but so does participation in a student organization. Additionally, while students learn a considerable amount about their careers from jobs on campus, they see their off-campus job as being at least equally impactful (Peck et al., 2016).

Considering how students develop career skills through a variety of experiences on campus serves many purposes. First, it provides student affairs educators with a road map for integrating cocurricular learning into a student's entire experience at the institution. Second, it makes cocurricular learning more salient to the students themselves, which can, in time, help them articulate what they are learning to potential employers. This can help student affairs to change perceptions about the purpose of cocurricular experiences and, consequently, change perceptions about the value these experiences offer as well as the value student affairs provides as a whole.

The learning potential for jobs on and off campus presents yet another danger/opportunity in the well-established fact that students have to work more hours than ever before while in college. Perna (2010) reported that about one in five full-time, traditional-aged college students work between 20 and 35 hours per week. This number has increased in the past decade (Perna, 2010). Additionally, 8% now work 35 hours or more (Perna, 2010). There is more than sufficient research to suggest that these work responsibilities can and do negatively affect student persistence, academic performance, and participation in cocurricular experiences (see, e.g., Astin, 1975; Furr & Elling, 2000; Orszag, Orszag, & Whitmore, 2001). But they also present a largely untapped opportunity. As colleges and universities find ways to help students become aware of how their jobs on and off campus can play a role in developing career skills, it is possible to increase the impact that can be made on career readiness. It stands to reason that students who must work more hours are more likely to receive less financial support from their families and, thus, are more economically disadvantaged. It also seems most plausible that students who come from lower-income families face challenges that their wealthier peers do not. These challenges can place them at a competitive disadvantage when it comes time to start their career and find their first job. Targeting transformative career experiences to these students has potential to close this gap.

Institutions that can demonstrate a connection between the programs they offer and the ability for students to get a job should see a decided advantage in recruiting students. This is especially true when considering the preferences of the next generation of college students. Preliminary research into this group conducted by Northeastern University (n.d.) suggests that they may be more fiscally conservative and career-minded then previous generations. They also strongly desire the integration of practical experiences into their education (Northeastern University, n.d.). Colleges and universities that adopt this approach could broaden how students define what constitutes a learning experience.

LEARNING TO ARTICULATE SKILLS

Realizing the full potential of learning inside and outside the classroom will require more than just providing meaningful learning experiences that help students develop necessary skills and abilities. It also requires that students recognize these new abilities in themselves and articulate to others what they are learning. This last aspect could easily be overlooked, but it is far and away the most important. Without the ability to demonstrate what they are learning to others, students are in the same position as if they did not develop these skills at all.

Several chapters in this book discuss in depth how student affairs professionals can help students articulate what they are learning. But, in general, there are several emerging initiatives that can support this worthy goal. Among the most promising can be found in building on the established practice of cocurricular transcripts. According to Coven (2015), "A co-curricular transcript program is a system designed to increase intentional involvement among students, and produces a document of their involvement in activities outside of curricular requirements" (p. 2). The concept of what was then called "student development transcripts" was initiated by Robert Brown at the University of Nebraska in 1977 (Coven, 2015). This approach appears to have fallen out of favor in 1996, as publishing pertaining to this concept dropped off suddenly at that time (Coven, 2015).

In October 2015, the American Association of Collegiate Registrars and Admissions Officers (AACRAO) and NASPA–Student Affairs Administrators in Higher Education announced a joint project supported by the Lumina Foundation to "develop models for a more comprehensive student record" (AACRAO Consulting, 2015, para. 1). The associations selected eight institutions to develop pilot projects that could identify ways for students to record, and institutions to authenticate, the range of experiences students engage in outside the classroom. The results may or may not look like traditional transcripts. But, importantly, these records could be put in a format that employers would find useful during the hiring process. The associations hope these records will also increase the intentionality with which students approach their selection of cocurricular experiences, and that by recording these experiences with the same level of rigor applied to classroom learning, a variety of key stakeholders (including the students themselves) can recognize the important role these learning experiences have in student learning and development.

CONCLUSION

Robert C. Gallagher is quoted as saying, "Change is inevitable, except from a vending machine" (Brandreth, 2015, p. 212). This is especially true on a college campus. Higher education is grounded in centuries of tradition, which can make innovation difficult—innovation and tradition lie at opposite ends of a continuum.

It is impossible to ignore the tremendous change occurring within higher education. Changes in technology raise questions about how content is delivered. Changes in state and federal financial support of higher education affect both public and private institutions and encourage a model that can value the speed of completion over the quality of learning.

For student affairs to thrive (and perhaps even survive, at least as we know it now), we as student affairs professionals must prove our value to students and institutions. We need to increase our focus on career-related outcomes and provide resources that can be used by contemporary practitioners to put this philosophy in action.

REFERENCES

AACRAO Consulting. (2015, October 21). *AACRAO and NASPA name comprehensive student record implementation institutions.* Retrieved from http://consulting.aacrao.org/aacrao-and-naspa-name-student-record-institutions

ACPA–College Student Educators International. (1996). *The student learning imperative: Implications for student affairs.* Retrieved from http://co.myacpa.org/wp-content/uploads/2015/01/acpas_student_learning_imperative.pdf

Association of American Colleges and Universities. (1998, October 1). *Statement on liberal learning.* Retrieved from https://www.aacu.org/about/statements/liberal-learning

Astin, A. W. (1975). *Preventing students from dropping out.* San Francisco, CA: Jossey-Bass.

Bound, J., & Turner, S. (2002). Going to war and going to college: Did World War II and the G.I. Bill increase educational attainment for returning veterans? *Journal of Labor Economics, 20*(4), 784–815.

Brandreth, G. (2015). *Oxford dictionary of humorous quotations* (5th ed.). Oxford, United Kingdom: Oxford University Press.

Chokshi, N. (2015, May 13). The economy's bouncing back. But higher education funding isn't. *The Washington Post.* Retrieved from https://www.washingtonpost.com/blogs/govbeat/wp/2015/05/13/the-economys-bouncing-back-higher-education-funding-isnt

Christensen, C. M., Raynor, M. E., & McDonald, R. (2015, December). What is disruptive innovation? *Harvard Business Review,* 44–53.

Coven, C. M. (2015). *History and development of co-curricular transcripts* (Master's thesis). Retrieved from http://purl.flvc.org/fsu/fd/FSU_migr_etd-9316

Fain, P. (2015, November 25). Measuring competency. *Inside Higher Ed.* Retrieved from https://www.insidehighered.com/news/2015/11/25/early-glimpse-student-achievement-college-america-competency-based-degree-provider

Furr, S. R., & Elling, T. W. (2000). The influence of work on college student development. *NASPA Journal, 37*(2), 454–470.

Greenstein, K. (2014). Faculty and staff perspectives of a behavior assessment team: A case study evaluation (Doctoral dissertation). Retrieved from http://digitalcommons.georgiasouthern.edu/cgi/viewcontent.cgi?article=2239&context=etd

Hiltonsmith, R. (2015, May). *Pulling up the higher-ed ladder: Myth and reality of college affordability.* Retrieved from http://www.demos.org/publication/pulling-higher-ed-ladder-myth-and-reality-crisis-college-affordability

Hoffer, E. (1982). *Between the devil and the dragon: The best essays and aphorisms of Eric Hoffer.* New York, NY: Harper & Row.

Howell, D. (2014). *John F. Kennedy and the meaning of crisis in Chinese.* Retrieved from http://americanreviewmag.com/blogs/John-F.-Kennedy-and-the-meaning-of-crisis-in-Chinese

Jaschik, S. (2015, January 20). Study finds big gaps between student and employer perceptions. *Inside Higher Ed.* Retrieved from https://www. insidehighered.com/news/2015/01/20/study-finds-big-gaps-between-studentand-employer-perceptions

Keeling, R. P. (Ed.) (2004). *Learning reconsidered: A campus-wide focus on the student experience.* Washington, D.C: ACPA–College Student Educators International & NASPA–Student Affairs Administrators in Higher Education.

Kimball, B. (2014). Revising the declension narrative: Liberal arts colleges, universities, and honors programs, 1870s–2010s. *Harvard Educational Review, 84*(2), 243–264.

Konnikova, M. (2014, February 21). 18 U.S. presidents were in college fraternities: Do frats create future leaders, or simply attract them? *The Atlantic.* Retrieved from http://www.theatlantic.com/education/archive/2014/02/18-us-presidents-were-in-college-fraternities/283997

Lumina Foundation. (2013). *The 2013 Lumina study of the American public's opinion on higher education and U.S. business leader's poll on higher education.* Indianapolis, IN: Author.

Mayerson, A. (1992). *The history of the ADA: A movement perspective.* Retrieved from http://dredf.org/news/publications/the-history-of-the-ada

National Association of Colleges and Employers. (2015). *Job outlook 2016.* Bethlehem, PA: Author.

Nguyen, S. (2014, August 10). In Chinese: Crisis does not mean danger and opportunity. *Workplace Psychology.* Retrieved from https://workplacepsychology.net/2014/08/10/in-chinese-crisis-does-not-mean-danger-and-opportunity

Northeastern University. (n.d.). *Innovation imperative: Meet generation Z.* Retrieved from http://www.northeastern.edu/news/2014/11/innovation-imperative-meet-generation-z

Orszag, J. M, Orszag, P. R., & Whitmore D. M. (2001). *Learning and earning: Working in college.* Retrieved from https://www.brockport.edu/academics/career/supervisors/upromise.html

Pasquerella, L. (2016, January 21). Philosophers, welders and the public trust. *Inside Higher Ed.* Retrieved from https://www.insidehighered.com/views/2016/01/21/liberal-arts-education-should-be-public-good-people-all-socioeconomic-backgrounds

Peck, A., Hall, D., Cramp, C., Lawhead, J., Fehring, K., & Simpson, T. (2016). The co-curricular connection: The impact of experiences beyond the classroom on soft skills. *NACE Journal, 76*(3), 30–34.

Perna, L. W. (2010). Understanding the working college student. *Academe, 96*(4), 30–33.

Pierrakeas, C., Xenos, M., Panagiotakopoulos, C., & Vergidis, D. (2004). A comparative study of dropout rates and causes for two different distance education courses. *International Review of Research in Open and Distance Learning, 5*(2), 1–15. doi: 10.19173/irrodl.v5i2.183

Rau, A. (2015, May 13). Arizona tops nation in college cuts, tuition hikes. *The Arizona Republic.* Retrieved from http://www.azcentral.com

Rhatigan, J. J. (2009). From the people up: A brief history of student affairs administration. In G. S. McClellan & J. Stringer (Eds.), *The handbook of student affairs administration* (3rd ed., pp. 3–20). San Francisco, CA: Jossey-Bass.

Sokolow, B. A., & Lewis, W. S. (2009). *2nd generation behavioral intervention best practices.* Retrieved from http://www.nabita.org/docs/2009NCHERMwhitepaper.pdf

States News Service. (2015, December 2). Governor Rick Scott issues "Ready, Set, Work" university challenge [Press release]. Retrieved from http://www.highbeam.com/doc/1G1-436276805.html

Tinto, V. (1987). *Leaving college: Rethinking the causes and cures of student attrition.* Chicago, IL: University of Chicago Press.

Tinto, V. (2012). *Completing college: Rethinking institutional action.* Chicago, IL: University of Chicago Press.

Virginia Tech Review Panel. (2007). Mass shootings at Virginia Tech: Report of the review panel. Retrieved from https://governor.virginia.gov/media/3772/fullreport.pdf

I

THE SKILLS
EMPLOYERS WANT

The first section of this book takes a comprehensive look at the topic of helping students develop the skills that employers want from new college graduates. Framed by the work of the National Association of Colleges and Employers, which annually studies what skills are most sought after, the authors consider some of the ways in which institutions can respond to this demand. This section also examines how special populations, such as first-generation students, can benefit from intentional efforts to engage them in cocurricular experiences. An analysis of the political landscape in which this work is pursued is included.

1

Employer-Preferred Skills and Attributes

Marilyn Mackes

Consider the life of a college graduate 90 days post-graduation. The graduate's degree is probably framed or tucked away in a safe place as a reminder of his or her hard work and accomplishments. The graduate may or may not have moved away from home to work, to gain additional certifications, to pursue an advanced degree, to volunteer or become involved in some form of community service, or to travel or study different cultures. Numerous national research studies conducted by the National Association of Colleges and Employers (NACE)[1] and others indicate that, for the vast majority of college graduates, some type of professional employment is their preferred long-term objective.

Since the 1950s, NACE has been collecting, tracking, analyzing, and reporting data about the career expectations of college graduates, the job outlook for each graduating class, hiring forecasts and recruiting

---

[1] Established in 1956, the National Association of Colleges and Employers (NACE) connects more than 6,700 college career services professionals at nearly 2,000 colleges and universities and more than 2,900 university relations and recruiting professionals from the employment sector. NACE is the leading source of information on the employment of the college educated. It forecasts hiring and trends in the job market; tracks starting salaries, recruiting and hiring practices, and student attitudes and outcomes; and identifies best practices and benchmarks.

trends, and employer preferences when hiring new college graduates. These data have captured the attention of higher education stakeholders, leaders in business and industry, policy makers, prospective students and parents, and the general public as we consider implications for the higher education experience and the student's preparation for the future workforce.

A core outcome of NACE's research points to the critical value of soft skills and attributes that college graduates, regardless of academic major, type of institution, or type of employer, can apply in portable fashion to achieve their life and professional goals.

DEFINITIONS OF HARD SKILLS AND SOFT SKILLS

Hard skills are most often associated with knowledge-based and occupational skills that are quantifiable and measureable. These skills might include computer programming, accounting, or subject matter expertise. Most often, employers will look to academic major or task-focused projects to reveal a candidate's ability to fulfill a job's requirements. The traditional college transcript and GPA are typically considered as measures of knowledge and capacity to perform the hard skills required.

In contrast, *soft skills* are related to EQ (the Emotional Intelligence Quotient), the range of character traits and interpersonal skills engaged in people relationships. These skills describe more how individuals act and interact than what they know. Soft skills include a cluster of capabilities that relate to communication, social interaction, leading others, and influencing outcomes. Unlike an academic transcript, there are no traditional measurements to determine soft skill capabilities. Consequently, college students entering the job market often find it challenging to demonstrate their soft skills on applications and résumés and in interviews. Yet it is the acquisition and application of these soft skills that can make all the difference for success in the workplace.

NACE RESEARCH FINDINGS

For more than two decades, global, national, and regional employers have responded to the NACE *Job Outlook* survey for each graduating class. First released in the early 1990s, this survey asks employers to identify those skills most preferred when hiring new college graduates. A breakdown of these responses provides a more detailed view of how employers view these preferences over time. As noted in the charts provided in this chapter, certain skills and attributes have consistently appeared on the list, reinforcing the fact that these are not short-lived trends.

From 2006 until 2011, survey results revealed a relatively stable list of 20 skills and attributes ranked by employers in terms of importance for new job candidates. Throughout this period, and in the 8 years preceding this period, communication skills topped the list as the most important skill or attribute, followed by work ethic, teamwork, initiative, and ability to problem solve. Despite minor variations from one year to the next, there was no clear trend in the ratings of the individual skills and attributes.

For its *Job Outlook 2012* survey, NACE adopted a significantly different approach to assessing the importance of attributes and skills in job candidates. NACE took the list of attributes from its previous research and asked respondents to identify the attributes they seek on a candidate's résumé. It then ranked the attributes based on the percentage of respondents who stated they looked for the attribute on the candidate's résumé. Table 1.1 shows the attributes employers seek on a candidate's résumé by percentage of respondents for the years 2012–2016. NACE also added a more defined list of skills and asked respondents to rate how important a particular skill is to success in the employer's organization. Respondents rated these skills on a five-point scale ranging from 1 (*not at all important*) to 5 (*extremely important*); see Table 1.2.

Table 1.1. Attributes Employers Seek on a Candidate's Résumé, By Percentage of Respondents

	2012	2013	2014	2015	2016
Leadership	77.2%	80.6%	76.0%	77.8%	80.1%
Ability to work in a team	79.8%	74.2%	71.4%	77.8%	78.9%
Communication–written	75.6%	74.7%	76.6%	73.4%	70.2%
Problem solving	74.1%	75.3%	70.3%	70.9%	70.2%
Work ethic	73.1%	73.1%	72.0%	70.4%	68.9%
Analytical/quantitative	72.0%	72.0%	73.1%	68.0%	62.7%
Communication–verbal	67.4%	67.2%	68.6%	67.0%	68.9%
Initiative	65.3%	66.7%	68.6%	66.5%	65.8%
Technical skills	61.1%	64.0%	61.1%	67.5%	59.6%
Computer skills	55.4%	64.5%	62.9%	62.6%	55.3%
Flexibility	56.0%	57.5%	59.4%	62.1%	60.9%
Detail-oriented	57.5%	57.5%	65.7%	57.6%	52.8%
Interpersonal skills	54.9%	57.0%	58.3%	60.6%	58.4%
Organizational ability	50.8%	49.5%	42.9%	42.4%	48.4%
Friendly	29.0%	33.3%	32.6%	29.1%	35.4%
Strategic planning	29.0%	32.8%	33.7%	35.0%	26.7%
Entrepreneurial	21.8%	25.8%	23.4%	25.1%	18.6%
Creativity	22.3%	25.8%	21.7%	18.2%	23.6%
Tact	21.2%	23.7%	22.9%	23.2%	20.5%

Note. Data compiled from NACE *Job Outlook* reports, 2011–2015, by the National Association of Colleges and Employers.

Table 1.2. **Candidate Skills Rated in Importance to Success in an Employer's Organization**

	2012	2013	2014	2015	2016
Ability to work in a team structure	4.60	4.60	4.55	4.61	4.62
Ability to verbally communicate with persons inside and outside the organization	4.59	4.63	4.48	4.60	4.63
Ability to make decisions and solve problems	4.49	4.51	4.50	4.61	4.49
Ability to plan, organize, and prioritize work	4.45	4.46	4.48	4.59	4.41
Ability to obtain and process information	4.46	4.43	4.37	4.57	4.34
Ability to analyze quantitative data	4.23	4.30	4.25	4.32	4.21
Technical knowledge related to the job	4.23	3.99	4.01	4.19	3.99
Proficiency with computer software programs	4.04	3.95	3.94	4.03	3.86
Ability to create and/or edit written reports	3.65	3.56	3.62	3.75	3.60
Ability to sell or influence others	3.51	3.55	3.54	3.56	3.55

Note. 5-point scale: 1 = not at all important; 5 = extremely important. Data compiled from NACE *Job Outlook* reports, 2011–2015, by the National Association of Colleges and Employers.

For its *Job Outlook 2013* survey, NACE added an additional component that asked respondents to grade their new employees on a series of attributes and skills that were consistently viewed as important. Respondents were asked to grade their recent employee hires on a scale from A (*extraordinarily capable in that skill*) to F (*completely lacking in that skill*); see Table 1.3.

Table 1.3. **Grades for New Graduate Employees on Selected Skills and Attributes**

	2013	2014	2015	2016
Ability to work in a team structure	A-	A-	B	A-
Ability to verbally communicate with persons inside and outside the organization	B+	B+	B+	B+
Ability to make decisions and solve problems	B+	B+	A-	B+
Initiative	B+	B+	A-	B+
Work ethic	B+	B+	B	B+
Ability to analyze quantitative data	A-	A-	B+	B+
Leadership	B+	B+	B+	B+
Ability to create and/ or edit written reports	B	B+	B-	B

Note. Data compiled from NACE *Job Outlook* reports, 2012–2015, by the National Association of Colleges and Employers.

More than 70% of employers have consistently identified leadership, teamwork, written communication ability, problem solving, and work ethic as key résumé attributes. Teamwork, verbal communication skills, and problem solving are the skills employers consider important for success. An interesting finding is that neither proficiency with computer software nor written communication skills are rated particularly high as factors for success even though respondents have consistently rated them as important in getting hired.

Overall, employers have given new employees high grades. Teamwork is the skill that seems to be consistently fulfilled. By contrast, written communication skills appear to be the one attribute most consistently lacking in new recruits. The research clearly indicates that soft skills greatly affect the employer selection process and their views on candidate performance once hired.

EMPLOYER PERSPECTIVE

Dan Black, director of recruiting at EY Americas, has sourced thousands of college graduates from a broad range of institutions and across multiple disciplines for more than two decades. In 2013–2014, he served as president of NACE. The following paragraphs are excerpts from an e-mail interview in which Black provided an employer perspective on the importance of soft skills.

The Timeless Value of Soft Skills

Although the nature of work has evolved through major changes in technology, globalization, process automation, and other advances, soft skills have remained remarkably consistent in their applicability and importance to career success. In contrast, many of the technical skills required in the workforce have undergone significant changes over the past two decades. Think about what a newly minted consultant needs to know today from a technical standpoint versus 20 years ago. Technological advancements, knowledge of global regulations and geopolitical influences, the impact of social media on corporate brand, and the effect of climate change on raw material supplies are all critical technical skills needed today, which was certainly not the case in the early 1990s. However, the ability to communicate effectively, work in a team structure, and organize and prioritize work—all generally classified as soft skills—are as important today, if not more so, than they were two or three decades ago. As a result, employers have consistently sought to assess these skills using various tools and methods that continue to mature and evolve over time. (D. Black, personal communication, December 4, 2015)

Critical Skills That Matter

Given the dynamics of today's workforce, several skills stand out as critical for success. Interpersonal skills, including the ability to work well in teams, influence others, and communicate ideas effectively, are more important than ever, despite the hyper-availability of means by which individuals can interact via technology. Teams are more diverse than ever before, and successful employees must understand and embrace the value that differences bring.

At EY, we say we need 212,000 inclusive leaders who can effectively interact and work with people who have different backgrounds, skills, preferences, and experiences. In other words, the ability to recognize and embrace differences is not enough. We need leaders who think and act inclusively to truly unlock the potential of the whole organization. Most organizations today expect employees to have a global mindset. At EY, we define global mindset as the intellectual, psychological, and social attributes that allow a person to function capably anywhere in the world. As companies and markets become more global, students who are comfortable in—and seek out—different environments, settings, and cultures will be highly sought after for their talent. (D. Black, personal communication, December 4, 2015)

Examples of Workforce Attributes Needed

I recently spoke with a student athlete who described her schedule as follows: morning run, team workout, classes, studying, afternoon practice, group project work, evening workout, and finally a student council meeting. Interestingly enough, that was just Monday! This young woman was already managing a demanding schedule that involved frequent changes, travel, multiple deliverables, and fluctuating demands from a host of counterparts. After speaking with her, I was confident that she would be able to succeed in the EY environment, which sounded uncannily familiar!

As I interviewed a student at a large campus, I noted that he was certainly bright and well spoken, but he did not stand out as extraordinary or exceptional in any particular area until he started talking about his volunteer work. He was one of the team leaders for a dance-a-thon that raised a sizable amount of money for a national charity. As he discussed his responsibilities and his numerous accomplishments, I picked up on a whole host of competencies that I had not yet seen, including motivating others and overcoming setbacks. (D. Black, personal communication, December 4, 2015)

Marketing Soft Skills to Employers

For as long as I've worked in talent acquisition, students have struggled to find the best way to highlight their unique talents to potential employers. Often bereft of relevant work experience, many students that I speak with fear that they don't have the skills employers are looking for. In reality, students often have more experiences and skills to offer than they realize, and it's simply a matter of showcasing transferable skills and highlighting accomplishments in multiple contexts.

For example, let's look at inclusive leadership skills. Most students will not have had the opportunity to lead a team of employees on a large corporate project. But the college environment presents endless opportunities to shine in this regard. Students volunteer to take leadership roles in student organizations, become resident advisors, or even head up intramural sports teams. The students who stand out are those who find something they are passionate about and truly engaged in, regardless of whether they find it in their communities, their fraternities or sororities, their jobs, their internships, or somewhere else.

I tell students all the time that it's not just about being involved, it's about being deeply engaged and passionate about what you are doing, taking on a leadership role, and truly making a difference. In the job interview, these experiences translate extremely well and have excellent predictive validity for future on-the-job success. Employer recruiting teams are trained to ask behavioral questions that will uncover these skills through the exploration of experiences in a multitude of environments. Students need to be aware of the opportunity to highlight these skills on their résumés, in conversations, and during networking activities. (D. Black, personal communication, December 4, 2015)

PREPARING STUDENTS FOR WORKFORCE EXPECTATIONS

Workforce Trends

NACE research reports based on input from employers, campus career services offices, and graduating students underscore significant trends that relate to preparing students for the demands they can expect in the workplace.

- **People skills are essential at the onset.** Although job knowledge is important, employers recognize that jobs and employee knowledge will evolve over time. What is needed from the onset is the demonstration that employees can interact effectively with colleagues, managers, and customers.
- **Business relies heavily on the use of project teams to accomplish goals.** As noted by Assistant Vice President and Executive Director of New York University's Wasserman Center for Career Development Trudy Steinfeld (personal communication, December 4, 2015):

  Employers putting together project teams with different perspectives, backgrounds, and skills is becoming the new 'norm.' Students who participate in a sports team, club, or student government organization will undoubtedly develop many skills that can translate positively to this type of work environment, including preparedness, teamwork, motivation, and strategic thinking.

- **Words and data matter.** Every career field needs people who have the capacity to communicate effectively and to apply data in making good decisions. Steinfeld (personal communication, December 4, 2015) shared these observations:

Information, in both written and verbal forms, can be misconstrued if not expressed appropriately. Today's students are so used to texting and abbreviating that they sometimes don't understand the importance of including and communicating information that could be vital to interpreting a report or situation appropriately. In addition, we can't go through a day without hearing or reading about 'data-driven decisions.' Analyzing data has become a critical skill for students to master.

As an example of how both words and data matter, students should be aware that recruiters from diverse industries are using case interviews to assess job candidates, asking them to apply their communication and analytical skills during the interview process.

- **Focus to strengthen results.** Employers value a student's ability to focus interests and energy when engaged in campus activities. Black (personal communication, December 4, 2015) noted:

Students need to find a balance that affords them the opportunity to showcase their full range of interests and abilities. In most cases, this means taking enough time to make meaningful contributions outside the classroom, while still maintaining a competitive academic profile that is attractive to employers. One of the best strategies in this regard is for students to focus on a smaller number of cocurricular activities and go deeper with their involvement in them. Rather than participating in seven to eight clubs and organizations, students should pick two or three and put their energy into making a difference through regular activity, leadership roles, and so forth. This approach will give students the best chance of being holistically successful.

And once the student becomes the career professional, focus will continue to play a vital part in their success on the job.

- **Preparation strengthens competitive advantage.** In today's employment marketplace, new college graduates have found that an early start in developing soft skills and hands-on applications of these skills through various experiences strengthens their competitive position when looking for that first job. By starting earlier in their academic careers, students will have more time to find those activities, opportunities, and experiences, which will be both meaningful and fulfilling. In addition, the practice of developing oneself through preparation for the future is a lifelong skill that successful professionals will practice throughout their careers.

In considering the implications of these workforce trends, it is important to keep in mind that student preparation for their future careers is a shared responsibility. Steinfeld (personal communication, December 4, 2015) stated it this way:

One of the keys necessary for students to acquire critical skills and attributes is creating a culture that embraces the development of the whole student. This is not just the responsibility of the career center. It's important that colleges and universities create an ecosystem that views career services and student outcomes as an important value and part of the institution's strategic vision. In other words, academic advisors, faculty, college administrators engaged in student development, as well as employer partners must collaborate to provide opportunities for students to develop a variety of skills and attributes that will be critical in their working life.

SOFT SKILLS AND CAREER READINESS: IMPLICATIONS FOR THE FUTURE

The strong foundation of research data combined with insights from those actively engaged in assisting students with transitions to the workforce reinforces the value and need for collaboration among all stakeholders engaged as educators in students' learning experiences. No single constituency owns the development of soft skills. Indeed, as noted above, higher education professionals share in an institutional ecosystem that values the preparation of students to achieve their professional goals, and are called to integrate this preparation into the strategic direction and actions for all who engage with students.

NACE will continue to capture and report data, benchmarks, and best practices related to the role of soft skills and their importance to employers; this encourages and supports institutional commitments to develop a strong and productive future workforce. In addition, NACE is committed to clarifying the definition and competencies related to career readiness.

The career readiness of college graduates is an important issue in higher education, in the labor market, and in the public arena. Yet, until recently, career readiness was undefined, making it difficult for leaders in higher education, workforce development, and public policy to work together effectively to ensure the career readiness of today's graduates.

In accordance with NACE's mission to lead the community that is focused on the employment of the new college graduate, a task force of college career services and corporate human resources professionals developed a career readiness definition based on extensive research among more than 600 employers in 20 different industries, and identified seven competencies associated with career readiness for the new college graduate. In 2015, the NACE Board of Directors approved the definition and competencies and released them publicly to a range of higher education, corporate, and policy-making stakeholders.

Definition of Career Readiness

Career readiness is "...the attainment and demonstration of requisite competencies that broadly prepare college graduates for a successful transition into the workforce" (NACE, 2015a, para 3). These competencies are as follows:

- **Critical Thinking/Problem Solving:** Exercise sound reasoning to analyze issues, make decisions, and overcome problems. The individual can obtain, interpret, and use knowledge, facts, and data to solve problems, and may demonstrate originality and inventiveness.

- **Oral/Written Communication:** Articulate thoughts and ideas clearly and effectively in written and oral forms to persons inside and outside the organization. The individual possesses public speaking skills; can express ideas to others; and can write and edit memos, letters, and complex technical reports clearly and effectively.

- **Teamwork/Collaboration:** Build collaborative relationships with colleagues and customers representing diverse cultures, races, ages, genders, religions, lifestyles, and viewpoints. The individual can work within a team structure, and can negotiate and manage conflict.

- **Information Technology Application:** Select and use appropriate technology to accomplish a given task. The individual can apply computing skills to solve problems.

- **Leadership:** Leverage the strengths of others to achieve common goals, and use interpersonal skills to coach and develop others. The individual can assess and manage his or her emotions and those of others; use empathetic skills to guide and motivate; and organize, prioritize, and delegate work.

- **Professionalism/Work Ethic:** Demonstrate personal accountability and effective work habits (e.g., punctuality, working productively with others, and time–workload management), and understand the impact of nonverbal communication on professional work image. The individual demonstrates integrity and ethical behavior, acts responsibly with the interests of the larger community in mind, and can learn from his or her mistakes.

- **Career Management:** Identify and articulate one's skills, strengths, knowledge, and experiences relevant to the position desired and career goals, and identify areas necessary for professional growth. The individual can navigate and explore job options, understands and can take the steps necessary to pursue opportunities, and understands how to self-advocate for opportunities in the workplace. (NACE, 2015a, para. 4–10)

The definition and competencies provide for the development of strategies and tactics that will close the gap between higher education and the world of work. They lay the foundation for the effort needed to prepare college students for successful entry into the workforce by

- providing a common vocabulary and framework to use when discussing career-readiness metrics on campus, within employing organizations, and as part of national public policy;
- establishing defined competencies as guidelines when educating and advising students; and
- establishing defined competencies to identify and assess when hiring the college educated.

CONCLUSION

Currently, NACE is developing career-readiness tool kits that campus career centers can use in their work with students and that hiring organizations can use in their efforts to identify preferred job candidates. NACE is also actively engaged in discussions with the Department of Education, the Department of Labor, the White House, policy makers, and national higher education association leaders regarding the definition of career readiness, requisite competencies, and the implications for sharing respective insights and collaborating on this issue of national importance.

Looking ahead, NACE encourages those engaged as student affairs educators to share their thoughts and suggestions as it continues its efforts to clarify career readiness and identify how today's students can prepare for their professional roles in the future.

REFERENCES

National Association of Colleges and Employers. (2011). *Job outlook 2012.* Bethlehem, PA: National Association of Colleges and Employers.

National Association of Colleges and Employers. (2012). *Job outlook 2013.* Bethlehem, PA: National Association of Colleges and Employers.

National Association of Colleges and Employers. (2013). *Job outlook 2014.* Bethlehem, PA: National Association of Colleges and Employers.

National Association of Colleges and Employers. (2014). *Job outlook 2015.* Bethlehem, PA: National Association of Colleges and Employers.

National Association of Colleges and Employers. (2015a). *Career readiness defined.* Retrieved from http://www.naceweb.org/knowledge/career-readiness-competencies.aspx

National Association of Colleges and Employers. (2015b). *Job outlook 2016.* Bethlehem, PA: National Association of Colleges and Employers.

2

Developing Career-Ready Skills
A Review of the Literature

Amy Swan and Jan Arminio

The role of *soft skills* in academic and career success has in recent years garnered increased attention from scholars and policy makers (Hart Research Associates, 2013; Kyllonen, 2013; Tough, 2013). These "personal qualities other than cognitive ability that determine success" (Duckworth & Yeager, 2015, p. 239)—alternately referred to as "noncognitive skills," "21st century skills," or "new basic skills" (Murnane & Levy, 1996; Pellegrino & Hilton, 2012; Soland, Hamilton, & Stecher, 2013)—are unfortunately very challenging to identify, measure, and assess (Heckman & Kautz, 2012; Naemi, Burrus, Kyllonen, & Roberts, 2012; Stecher & Hamilton, 2014).

The difficulties associated with identifying, measuring, and assessing these skills may be due, in part, to the variety of terms used to refer to this skill set as well as confusion about the terminology used to describe individual skills (Duckworth & Yeager, 2015; Farrington et al., 2012; Pellegrino & Hilton, 2012; Robbins et al., 2004; Shechtman, DeBarger, Dornsife, Rosier, & Yarnall, 2013; Snipes, Fancsali, & Stoker, 2012). For example, one analysis of the soft skills literature found that the terms *adaptability* and *flexibility* were both commonly used to describe the same skill, defined as "the ability to understand

and respond effectively to unexpected changes or challenges" (Savitz-Romer, Rowan-Kenyon, Ott, Liu, & Swan, 2015, p. 47). Likewise, *goal commitment*, defined as "the ability to persist toward a goal despite challenges or obstacles," is often referred to as *determination, tenacity*, or *drive* (Savitz-Romer et al., 2015, p. 47). Some researchers posited that this confusion over terminology is partly to blame for the perception that college graduates lack the skills they need to succeed in the workforce (Savitz-Romer et al., 2015). More problematic is that, according to Capelli (2012), employers are unwilling to offer the training they insist their workforce needs.

This perceived misalignment in the college-to-career pipeline is based on reports from graduates and employers (Fallows & Steven, 2000; Stevens, 2005), as well as research that reveals a mismatch between the skills acquired within fields of study and the skills required by jobs (Evers & Rush, 1996; Robst, 2007). Studies show, for example, that employers believe recent college graduates lack such soft skills as public speaking, decision making, and leadership (Casner-Lotto, 2006; Harris Interactive, 2013; Maguire Associates, Inc., 2012; Miller & Malandra, 2006; Stevens, 2005; Tanyel, Mitchell, & McAlum, 1999). Further, 45% of workers reported that their job was either partially related or unrelated to their field of study (Robst, 2007). Indeed, in an attempt to bridge this gap between graduate skills and employer expectations, some universities have developed programs or curricula that aim to enhance students' soft skills (Bembenutty, 2009; Navarro, 2012). Research also suggests that functional areas of student affairs do provide opportunities for students to gain some of the soft skills that employers are seeking. With that in mind, traditional student affairs units or departments are encouraged to use outcomes research to refine their programs and increase soft skills development (Kuh, 2009).

Unfortunately, not all research of soft skills outcomes is consistent, with some research meriting more attention than other research.

Besides the definitional difficulties mentioned earlier, other challenges in identifying, measuring, and assessing outcomes include pinpointing the specific gains a particular involvement activity offers. Also, many measures include students' self-perceptions of gains without taking into consideration whether this approach is appropriate to the topic being studied. Self-reported data have been deemed appropriate if five conditions are met: (1) the information being requested is known to those being surveyed, (2) survey questions are unambiguous and understandable, (3) survey items refer to recent events, (4) survey takers believe the survey has a worthy purpose, and (5) survey items are not deemed too private (Pike, 2003). This has come into question recently, as evidence of pressure to be culturally appropriate has been found to compromise self-reported data (Hottell & Rowan-Kenyon, 2015). Self-reported data currently remain an appropriate means of learning outcomes measurement.

This chapter highlights rigorous empirical outcomes research that describes the soft skills potentially gained from opportunities provided by student affairs cocurricular programs and services. Note that much of this research is multi-institutional, using findings from large data sets involving thousands of students. As described earlier, the researchers conducting these studies do not necessarily use the same soft skills terms as employers. As described in Chapter 1, according to the National Association of Colleges and Employers (NACE; 2015), the skills that employers seek include:

- Critical thinking/problem solving
- Oral/written communication
- Teamwork/collaboration
- Information technology application
- Leadership
- Professionalism/work ethic
- Career management

When possible, outcomes research of these skills is highlighted, but also included is outcomes research that focuses on such other soft skills as self-efficacy, personal development, career development, and the ability to promote social justice and establish interracial friendships.

This chapter intends to connect outcomes research to specific student affairs areas. However, because some outcomes research spans several student affairs areas in a single study, some of these student affairs areas have been grouped together. The chapter begins with a general discussion of involvement and engagement. Then, it examines outcomes research that is closely associated with the NACE-identified soft skills. It then turns to outcomes research of other soft skills. The chapter concludes with a summary of the soft skills research and offers cautions about the research's limitations and suggests future directions.

STUDENT INVOLVEMENT IN STRUCTURED GROUPS AND ACTIVITIES

Although student involvement is a relatively recent term, structural efforts to encourage and enhance student involvement began in earnest in the late 1700s and early 1800s with the founding of literary and debate societies, the Phi Beta Kappa honorary society, and the student unions at Cambridge (1815), Oxford (1823), and Harvard (1823) (Council for the Advancement of Standards in Higher Education, 2015; Dungy & Gordon, 2011). At its essence, the College Union Idea (Butts, 1971) is a vision of a facility and organizational structure to bring students from various groups and interests together for an open discussion to promote collegiality. This vision would today be considered the facility of the college union and its programs and services that typically house student organizations, including programming boards, cultural centers, student government, fraternities and sororities, and, to some degree, recreational facilities.

Most readers will recognize the differentiation of involvement and engagement. Whereas Astin's (1984) theory of involvement emphasized the elements of time on task and the quality of effort of involvement, Kuh (2009) popularized the institutional goal of engagement, in which through institutional initiatives, students devote time and effort to educationally purposeful endeavors. The former invites students to participate in opportunities that they devote time and effort to, and the latter calls on institutions to create structures that prompt students to achieve educational gains. Engagement is an obligation of the institution, whereas involvement is more of a student responsibility. These gains potentially include both cognitive and noncognitive skills. It is estimated that by the end of their senior year, 80% of students participate in at least one college organization (Dugan & Komives, 2007). But not all clubs and organizations are alike. For example, there appears to be what Dugan (2013) called "gateway experiences" (p. 244) that influence students to become even more involved. In other words, involvement in academic groups, intramurals, and honor societies appears to subsequently encourage students to become involved in other ways on campus.

Structure of the activity matters. In a study of five Canadian institutions, researchers found that students involved in highly structured cocurricular activities had a smoother transition into the college experience (Tieu, Pancer, & Pratt, 2010). Highly structured means that the activity is led by an experienced student, faculty, or staff member; occurrences are regular; the activity has a purpose that leads to the expansion of at least one skill; participation requires effort or attention; and participants receive critical feedback on their participation. Such highly structured activities include residence hall council, athletics, and participation in religious groups. Structure has also been found to increase outcomes of student participation in U.S. collegiate organizations. In a single institution study, Zúñiga, Williams, and Berger (2005)

found that students involved in "intentionally structured involvement and engagement" (p. 671) were more likely to challenge their
own biases and promote inclusion and social justice. More specifically,
involvement in "general activities" (recreation, academic clubs, arts and
media, religious and spiritual involvement, and volunteering) "is positively correlated with participation in ethnic/cultural activities and
cross-group interactions" (Zúñiga, Williams, & Berger, 2005, p. 671).

SOFT SKILLS OUTCOMES RESEARCH

Soft skills outcomes research has been conducted in many specific
student affairs areas, including recreation, identity development
groups and programs, developmental leadership, community service
and service–learning programs, and student clubs and organizations including fraternities and sororities. The following paragraphs
discuss research that shows that indeed, students involved in these
areas gain important skills, many of which align with those described
throughout this book.

Collegiate Recreation

A cocurricular area in which students have been shown to acquire
soft skills is collegiate recreation. Research shows that recreation
departments provide soft skills to students through participation in
programs and activities (Forrester, 2014), as well as through employment experiences (Hall, 2013). Of the soft skills identified as outcomes
of participation in collegiate recreation, several correspond with those
identified by NACE, including the ability to work in a team structure
(Forrester, 2014); the ability to make decisions and solve problems
(Forrester, 2014; Schuh, 1999); the ability to plan, organize, and prioritize work (Forrester, 2014; Kerr-Downs Research, 2003; Schuh, 1999);
the ability to verbally communicate with persons inside and outside

the organization (Forrester, 2014; Hall, 2013; Schuh, 1999); the ability to create and edit written reports (Hall, 2013); and the ability to sell or influence others (Hall, 2013; Kerr-Downs Research, 2003; Schuh, 1999).

Students participate in recreation programs and activities through the use of recreation facilities and programs (e.g., weight training, wellness classes) as well as through involvement in recreational sports (e.g., sport clubs, outdoor adventure activities) (Forrester, 2014). In typical college recreational sports settings, the latter form of participation offers a range of volunteer student leadership opportunities (Hall, Forrester, & Borsz, 2008). Such opportunities, which include governance boards, committees, or club sport officer roles, provide responsibilities that can contribute to the development of soft skills (Hall et al., 2008). For example, Hall et al. (2008) found that students serving in leadership roles within the context of collegiate recreation gained organizing, planning, and delegating skills through coordinating meetings and events. Students also enhanced their writing skills by composing e-mails, editing newsletters, and developing websites (Hall et al., 2008).

Indeed, two national studies conducted on behalf of NIRSA: Leaders in Collegiate Recreation provide evidence of the impact of collegiate recreation on soft skills outcomes related to career success. The first study was completed in 2003 and included data from a survey of more than 2,600 students at 16 public and private colleges of varying sizes (Kerr-Downs Research, 2003). Findings showed that similar percentages of students at public and private colleges said that recreational sports participation helped them manage their time, improved their leadership abilities, and taught them important team-building skills (Kerr-Downs Research, 2003). The second study, completed in 2014, included data collected from more than 33,500 students at 38 colleges and universities (Forrester, 2014). Sixty-four percent of study participants reported that increased participation in campus recreation had provided them with skills or abilities that they anticipated using after college (Forrester, 2014). Further, students reported an increase in the following soft skills as a result of participation in campus recreation facilities, programs, or services: "time management skills" (75%), "ability to multi-task" (66%), "group cooperation skills" (60%), "communication skills" (59%), and "problem-solving skills" (55%) (Forrester, 2014, p. 23).

With respect to soft skills associated with employment experiences, recreation departments rely heavily on students to handle much of the work associated with managing recreation facilities and programs (Turner, Jordan, & DuBord, 2005), a trend that is likely to continue given many institutions' investment in the construction or renovation of campus recreation facilities (Bower, Hums, & Keedy, 2005; Fehring, 2013). While many students may begin their work in recreation for financial reasons (Schuh, 1999), research reveals that students develop a host of soft skills through their work, particularly because they are often asked to assume supervisory roles that require them to direct the work activities of peer employees (Turner et al., 2005). In a single-institution study by Hall (2013), for example, students reported that working for the campus recreation department provided opportunities to "gain skills for their career, such as working with people, leadership skills, and communication skills" (p. 143). Similarly, a study of student intramural officials (Schuh, 1999) showed that officiating involved preparation and organization prior to games or events, as well as making decisions on the field and navigating problems related to player and fan behavior.

IDENTITY DEVELOPMENT GROUPS AND PROGRAMS

A dearth of literature specifically examines career-related or soft skills outcomes associated with participation in identity development programs, which include programs related to such specific elements of psychosocial identity as race, ethnicity, gender, and sexual orientation

(Renn & Ozaki, 2010). However, research on students' experiences with these programs and student organizations connected to these programs suggests that they foster the development of soft skills that are variations of those identified by NACE. Soft skills associated with identity development programs and organizations include the ability to work in a team structure (Patton, 2006); the ability to make decisions and solve problems (Renn, 2007); the ability to plan, organize, and prioritize work (Renn, 2007); the ability to communicate verbally with persons inside and outside the organization (Patton, 2006; Renn & Ozaki, 2010); and the ability to sell or influence others (Renn, 2007).

Among students involved in lesbian, gay, bisexual, and transgender (LGBT) organizations and activism, Renn and Ozaki (2010) found that those involved in leadership roles engaged in such tasks as representing their group to peers, administrators, or the media. In another study (Renn, 2007), LGBT student leaders and queer activists described engagement in a variety of tasks including serving on committees, recruiting younger students to take on responsibilities or leadership roles, and organizing conferences or rallies. Similarly, research on first-year student participation in programs sponsored by Black culture centers (Patton, 2006) showed that students learned such skills as "public speaking, planning and promoting events, and teamwork" (p. 6).

In addition to soft skills that students acquire through their involvement in identity-development programs or organizations, and activism associated with them, research also suggests that identity development programs may help connect students with opportunities for soft skills development. Byrne (2000), for example, noted that an independent field experience supervised by one on-campus women's center serves as a direct link between theory and practice. Students who participate in the field experience identify skills they hope to gain from it, and their site supervisors are required to submit performance appraisals that

assess students' soft skills such as "dependability, punctuality and attendance, and their attitude and initiative" (Byrne, 2000, p. 60).

Concerns often arise that students who participate in identity-
related organizations and initiatives will segregate themselves and not
initiate or maintain acquaintances and friendships across differences.
Outcomes research indicates that this is not the case. The change in
interracial friendships from high school through college was measured
by Kim, Park, and Koo (2015) in a study conducted at 28 selective institutions. They found that greater involvement in identity-based student
organizations did not inhibit cross-racial friendships. Beyond cross-
racial friendships, in a longitudinal study that included data collection
six years after graduation, Bowman, Park, and Denson (2015) found
that involvement in ethnic student organizations predicted involvement in community leadership, discussions of racial issues, money
donations, news consumption, and volunteer work after graduation.

Developmental Leadership

Although the empirical study of college student leadership is a
relatively recent phenomenon, a wide body of research over the past 20
years has explored the ways in which college informs leadership development among students (Komives, Dugan, Owen, Slack, & Wagner,
2011). However, little of this research has examined soft skills outcomes
associated with participation in leadership development programs.
Further, developmental leadership research that has identified soft
skills outcomes has largely done so in the context of identifying a more
general range of educational outcomes or outcomes specifically related
to leadership capacity (Cress, Astin, Zimmerman-Oster, & Burkhardt,
2001; Dugan et al., 2011; Komives et al., 2011; Zimmerman-Oster &
Burkhardt, 2000). Among the soft skills outcomes that have been identified, some align with those identified by NACE, including the ability
to work in a team structure (Dugan & Komives, 2007); the ability to

make decisions and solve problems (Cress et al., 2001; Zimmerman-Oster & Burkhardt, 2001); the ability to plan, organize, and prioritize work (Cress et al., 2001); and the ability to verbally communicate with persons inside and outside the organization (Cress et al., 2001; Zimmerman-Oster & Burkhardt, 2001).

Two frequently cited studies of leadership development program outcomes are those conducted by Cress et al. (2001) and Zimmerman-Oster and Burkhardt (2001). Cress et al. (2001) analyzed longitudinal student survey data from 10 institutions and found that participants in leadership activities were more likely than nonparticipants to report growth in such outcomes as "conflict resolution skills," "ability to plan and implement programs and activities," and "ability to set goals" (p. 18); leadership activity participants also showed increased gains in skill areas including "decision-making abilities" (p. 18). Similarly, Zimmerman-Oster and Burkhardt (2001) evaluated 31 leadership development programs for college-age adults and found that outcomes reported by at least 50% of the programs included "improved communication skills," "improved problem-solving ability," and "improved conflict resolution skills" (pp. 8–9).

Research that uses the social change model of leadership development (SCM) is one example of work that focuses more specifically on outcomes associated with leadership capacity (Dugan & Komives, 2007). The leadership theory most often applied in the context of collegiate leadership development programs (Kezar, Carducci, & Contreras-McGavin, 2006; Owen, 2008), the SCM includes *group values* that are similar in nature to NACE skills related to teamwork, decision making, and problem solving. According to the SCM, *collaboration* is defined as "working with others in a common effort, sharing responsibility, authority, and accountability" and "multiplying group effectiveness by capitalizing on various perspectives and talents" (Komives et al., 2011, p. 46). Using a survey instrument based on the SCM, a national study found that student participation in formal leadership programs resulted in slightly higher effect sizes for outcomes including collaboration (Dugan & Komives, 2007).

Community Service and Service-Learning Programs

Research on community service programs, including service–learning, shows that participation in such programs contributes to students' career development by providing them with skills and knowledge that they can use outside the college environment and that can influence their career choice process (Conway, Amel, & Gerwien, 2009; Eyler, Giles, Stenson, & Gray, 2001; Niehaus & Inkelas, 2015; Simons & Cleary, 2006; Vogelsang & Astin, 2000). While this body of literature does not discuss outcomes in terms of soft skills specifically, it does identify outcomes comparable to the soft skills set forth by NACE. In particular, studies have shown that community service participation contributes to students' ability to work in a team structure (Astin, Vogelsang, Ikeda, & Yee, 2000; Conway et al., 2009; Simons & Cleary, 2006) and make decisions and solve problems (Chesbrough, 2011; Levesque-Bristol, Knapp, & Fisher, 2010; Simons & Cleary, 2006).

With regard to working in a team structure, community service research often frames this skill in terms of interpersonal interaction (Astin et al., 2000; Conway et al., 2009). For example, Simons and Cleary (2006) found that among students who completed service–learning courses, the majority reported that their experiences with service "allowed them to work well with others" (p. 315) and thus contributed to their interpersonal development. Similarly, a meta-analysis of the effect of service–learning on a variety of outcomes showed that community service participation had a significant effect on social outcomes including "interacting or working well with others" (Conway et al., 2009, p. 234).

Findings on the impact of community service programs on students' decision-making and problem-solving skills are more straightforward.

One study, for example, showed that students whose service–learning courses provided them with the opportunity to discuss their experiences had higher levels of problem-solving skills (Levesque-Bristol et al., 2010). Likewise, Chesbrough (2011) identified a strong and positive relationship between hours of service participation and "sense of autonomy in decision-making" (p. 701).

Intuitively, in a study of 46 public institutions, researchers found that the most significant effect of students who engaged in service–learning was social responsibility. Such programs increase students' desire to make a difference. This is particularly the case for men, as well as Native American, Asian, and White students (Endberg & Fox, 2011).

Student Organizations

Several studies investigated the outcomes associated with involvement in a variety of college cocurricular endeavors (Gellin, 2003; Flowers, 2004), often including resident councils, student union programming boards, student government, identity-related organizations, student media, and an entire host of student clubs and organizations. Sometimes fraternities and sororities are included in this general examination (Gellin, 2003), but other studies examine these groups separately (Hevel, Martin, Weeden, & Pascarella, 2015; Pike, 2003; Saville & Johnson, 2007). In a meta-analysis, Gellin (2003) found that students who lived on campus, participated in clubs and organizations, and interacted with peers achieved gains in critical thinking.

Critical thinking, which is arguably an element of the NACE soft skill of decision making and problem solving, is also an outcome central to several studies of fraternity and sorority participation. However, one of the hallmarks of studies on Greek life is the inconsistency in the findings, particularly those using data from single institutions. Differences in outcomes by class year and race complicate educators' understanding of findings. Using data from the Wabash National Study of Liberal Arts

Education of 17 institutions, Hevel et al. (2015) found in their fourth year, White students had a disadvantage in critical thinking compared with their independent peers, whereas Greek students of color were found to have a positive but not statistically significant advantage in critical thinking skills. Surprisingly, these researchers found that those students who entered college in the low two-thirds distribution of precollege critical thinking skills and then became members of Greek life were linked to significant disadvantages in critical thinking. However, those who scored in the highest one third in critical thinking in precollege skills were unaffected by affiliation. Hence, the researchers found that "fraternal membership has different influences on specific groups" (p. 466).

Fraternities and sororities are one of the oldest, and perhaps most controversial, institution-sponsored means of involvement. To address the concern that students who participate in Greek life may segregate themselves, Pike (2003) found that seniors who were involved in Greek life were more engaged than those who were not Greek. Also, first-year and senior Greek students reported more gains in personal development than non-Greek students. However, personal development was not defined. Moreover, Pike noted that there were greater positive effects for seniors who were Greek than there were for first-year students. This finding mirrors the class-year differences that Hevel et al. (2015) reported. It is important to note though that Hevel et al. found that Greek affiliation had no direct deleterious effect on students' educational outcomes.

Several studies addressed self-esteem and self-efficacy outcomes associated with Greek membership. Two single-institution studies found conflicting results. Saville and Johnson (2007) found no differences between Greek and independent students' sense of self-esteem. However, Thompson, Oberle, and Lilley (2011) found that Greek affiliation does lead to greater self-efficacy and academic effort, but it does not lead to improved academic performance. Although self-efficacy is not a NACE soft skill, it could be argued that self-esteem and self-efficacy are important attributes to influencing others.

A thorough examination of the outcomes of involvement for African American students comes from Flowers's (2004) study of students at 192 institutions. Flowers used the College Student Experience Questionnaire to determine self-perceptions about outcome gains of African American students involved in the student union and campus organizations. He found that involvement in the student union and student clubs increased personal and social skills. Specifically, this occurs when students discuss with other students the nature of conflict and collaboration. Also, outcomes of personal and social skills, including communication, are enhanced when African American students can identify with a key figure at an event. Even notices in the student newspaper about events and student organizations increase personal and social skills outcomes. Flowers found that African American students were only moderately involved in student clubs and organizations. Institutions must thus ensure that they provide incentives and opportunities to enhance student engagement.

CONCLUSION

This chapter presents evidence that student involvement in programs and services provided by student affairs can offer students gains in the soft skills desired by employers. This is particularly the case when such events are structured and purposeful. However, connecting these outcomes to the skills desired by employers can be difficult owing to differences in terminology and inconsistent definitions for terms. That said, the NACE soft skills that seem most addressed by student affairs programs and services include the ability to work in a team structure, make decisions and solve problems, communicate, influence others, and organize work. Soft skills noted in the literature but not identified by NACE that are frequently noted as cocurricular learning outcomes are critical thinking, personal and social skills, and establishing cross-racial relationships. Hence, it behooves student affairs professionals to pay attention to such research so that purposeful cocurricular educational experiences can evolve and continually offer greater benefits to all students as they move through college and into the workplace. Continued research in the area of outcomes of cocurricular activities, especially research that is beyond self-report data, is recommended. Also, efforts to align the definition of terms associated with soft skills and their consistent use in research could prove beneficial to both students and employers.

REFERENCES

Astin, A. W. (1984). Student involvement: A developmental theory for higher education. *Journal of College Student Development, 25,* 297–308.

Astin, A. W., Vogelsang, L. J., Ikeda, E. K., & Yee, J. A. (2000). *How service learning affects students.* Retrieved from Higher Education Research Institute website: http://heri.ucla.edu/PDFs/HSLAS/HSLAS.PDF

Bembenutty, H. (2009). Academic delay of gratification, self-efficacy, and time-management among academically unprepared college students. *Psychological Reports, 55,* 613–623.

Bower, G. G., Hums, M. A., & Keedy, J. L. (2005). Factors influencing the willingness to mentor students within campus recreation. *Recreational Sports Journal, 29*(1), 59–77.

Bowman, N. A., Park, J., & Denson, N. (2015). Student involvement in ethnic student organizations: Examining civic outcomes 6 years after graduation. *Research in Higher Education, 56,* 127–145. doi: 10.1007/s1162-014-9353-8

Butts, P. (1971). *The college union idea.* Bloomington, IN: Association of College Unions-International.

Byrne, K. Z. (2000). The roles of campus-based women's centers. *Feminist Teacher, 13*(1), 48–60.

Capelli, P. (2012). *"Why good people can't get good jobs": The skills gap and what companies can do about it.* Philadelphia, PA: Wharton Digital Press.

Casner-Lotto, J. (2006). *Are they really ready to work? Employers' perspectives on the basic knowledge and applied skills of new entrants to the 21st century.* Retrieved from http://www.p21.org/storage/documents/FINAL_REPORT_PDF09-29-06.pdf

Chesbrough, R. D. (2011). College students and service: A mixed methods exploration of motivations, choices, and learning outcomes. *Journal of College Student Development, 52*(6), 687–705.

Conway, J. M., Amel, E. L., & Gerwien, D. P. (2009). Teaching and learning in the social context: A meta-analysis of service learning's effects on academic, personal, social, and citizenship outcomes. *Teaching of Psychology, 36,* 233–245.

Council for the Advancement of Standards in Higher Education. (2015). *CAS professional standards for higher education* (9th ed.). Washington, DC: Author.

Cress, C. M., Astin, H. S., Zimmerman-Oster, K., & Burkhardt, J. C. (2001). Developmental outcomes of college students' involvement in leadership activities. *Journal of College Student Development, 42*(1), 15–27.

Duckworth, A. L., & Yeager, D. S. (2015). Measurement matters: Assessing personal qualities other than cognitive ability for educational purposes. *Educational Researcher, 44*(4), 237–251. doi: 10.3102/0013189X15584327

Dugan, J. P. (2013). Patterns in group involvement experiences during college: Identifying a taxonomy. *Journal of College Student Development, 54,* 229–246. doi: 10.1353/csd.2013.0028

Dugan, J. P., Bohle, C. W., Gebhardt, M., Hofert, M., Wilk, E., & Cooney, M. A. (2011). Influences of leadership program participation on students' capacities for socially responsible leadership. *Journal of Student Affairs Research and Practice, 48*(1), 65–84. doi: 10.2202/1949-6605.6206

Dugan, J. P., & Komives, S. R. (2007). *Developing leadership capacity in college students: Findings from a national study.* Retrieved from https://nclp.umd.edu/include/pdfs/mslreport-final.pdf

Dungy, G., & Gordon, S. A. (2011). The development of student affairs. In J. H. Schuh, S. R. Jones, & S. R. Harper (Eds.), *Student services: A handbook for the profession* (pp. 61–79). San Francisco, CA: Jossey-Bass.

Endberg, M. E., & Fox, K. (2011). Exploring the relationship between undergraduate service-learning experiences and global perspective-taking. *Journal of Student Affairs Research and Practice, 48,* 85–105. doi: 10.2202/1949-6605.6192

Evers, F. T., & Rush, J. C. (1996). The bases of competence skill development during the transition from university to work. *Management Learning, 27*(3), 275–299.

Eyler, J., Giles, D. E., Stenson, C. M., & Gray, C. J. (2001). *At a glance: What we know about the effects of service-learning on college students, faculty, institutions and communities, 1993–2000* (3rd ed.). Retrieved from http://www.compact.org/wp-content/uploads/resources/downloads/aag.pdf

Fallows, S., & Steven, C. (2000). Building employability skills into the higher education curriculum: A university-wide initiative. *Education & Training, 42*(2), 75–83.

Farrington, C. A., Roderick, M., Allensworth, E., Nagaoka, J., Keyes, T. S., Johnson, D. W., & Beechum, N. O. (2012). *Teaching adolescents to become learners: The role of noncognitive factors in shaping school performance: A critical literature review*. Retrieved from https://ccsr.uchicago.edu/publications/teaching-adolescents-become-learners-role-noncognitive-factors-shaping-school

Fehring, K. (2013, April 25). *Results from the NIRSA facility construction and renovation report (2013–2018)*. Retrieved from https://www.nirsa.org/wcm/_Discover/News/stories_1304/130425_01.aspx

Flowers, L. A. (2004). Examining the effects of student involvement on African American college student development. *Journal of College Student Development, 45*, 633–654.

Forrester, S. A. (2014). *The benefits of campus recreation*. Retrieved from http://rfc.wayne.edu/mort-harris/forrester_2014-report.pdf

Gellin, A. (2003). The effect of undergraduate student involvement on critical thinking: A meta-analysis of the literature 1991–2000. *Journal of College Student Development, 44*, 746–762.

Hall, S. L. (2013). Influence of campus recreation employment on student learning. *Recreational Sports Journal, 37*(2), 136–146.

Hall, S. L., Forrester, S., & Borsz, M. (2008). A constructivist case study examining the leadership development of undergraduate students in campus recreational sports. *Journal of College Student Development, 49*(2), 125–140.

Harris Interactive. (2013). *Bridge that gap: Analyzing the Student Skill Index*. Retrieved from Chegg website: http://www.chegg.com/pulse

Hart Research Associates. (2013). It takes more than a major: Employer priorities for college learning and student success. *Liberal Education, 99*(2), 22–29.

Heckman, J. J., & Kautz, T. D. (2012). Hard evidence on soft skills. *Labour Economics, 19*(4), 451–464.

Hevel, M. S., Martin, G. L., Weeden, D. D., & Pascarella, E. T. (2015). The effects of fraternity and sorority membership in the fourth year of college: A detrimental or value-added component of undergraduate education? *Journal of College Student Development, 56*, 456–470.

Hottell, D., & Rowan-Kenyon, H. (2015). *What tale do surveys tell?: Understanding the rise of self-reported surveys in higher education research and exploring alternative data interpretations*. Paper presented at the annual meeting of the Association for the Study of Higher Education Annual Conference, Denver, CO.

Kerr-Downs Research. (2003). Benefits of recreational sports. *Recreational Sports Journal, 27*(1), 44–54.

Kezar, A., Carducci, R., & Contreras-McGavin, M. (2006). Rethinking the "L" word in higher education: The revolution in research on leadership. *ASHE Higher Education Report, 31*(6). San Francisco, CA: Jossey-Bass.

Kim, Y. K., Park, J. J., & Koo, K. K. (2015). Testing self-segregation: Multiple-group structural modeling of college students' interracial friendship by race. *Research in Higher Education, 56*, 57–77. doi: 10.1007/s1162-014-9337-8

Komives, S. R., Dugan, J. P., Owen, J. E., Slack, C., & Wagner. (Eds.). (2011). *The handbook for student leadership development* (2nd ed.). San Francisco, CA: Jossey-Bass.

Kuh, G. D. (2009). What student affairs professionals need to know about student engagement. *Journal of College Student Development, 50*, 683–699.

Kyllonen, P. C. (2013). Soft skills for the workplace. *Change: The Magazine of Higher Learning, 45*(6), 16–23.

Levesque-Bristol, C., Knapp, T. D., & Fisher, B. J. (2010). The effectiveness of service-learning: It's not always what you think. *Journal of Experiential Education, 33*(3), 208–224.

Maguire Associates, Inc. (2012). *The role of higher education in career development: Employer perceptions*. Retrieved from http://www.chronicle.com/items/biz/pdf/Employers%20Survey.pdf

Miller, C., & Malandra, G. (2006). *The Secretary of Education's Commission on the Future of Higher Education, issue paper: Accountability/assessment*. Retrieved from http://www.ed.gov/about/bdscomm/list/hiedfuture/reports/miller-malandra.pdf

Murnane, R. J., & Levy, F. (1996). *Teaching the new basic skills: Principles for educating children to thrive in a changing economy.* New York, NY: Free Press.

Naemi, B., Burrus, J., Kyllonen, P. C., & Roberts, R. D. (2012). *Building a case to develop noncognitive assessment products and services targeting workforce readiness at ETS.* Retrieved from https://www.ets.org/s/workforce_readiness/pdf/rm_12_23.pdf

Navarro, D. (2012). Supporting the students of the future. *Change: The Magazine of Higher Learning, 44*(1), 43–51.

National Association of Colleges and Employers. (2015). *Job outlook 2016.* Bethlehem, PA: National Association of Colleges and Employers.

Niehaus, E., & Inkelas, K. K. (2015). Exploring the role of alternative break programs in student's career development. *Journal of Student Affairs Research and Practice, 52,* 134–146. doi: 10.108019495591.2015.1020247

Owen, J. E. (2008). *Towards an empirical typology of collegiate leadership development programs: Examining effects on student self-efficacy and leadership for social change* (Doctoral dissertation). Retrieved from ProQuest: Dissertations & Theses. (3324779)

Patton, L. D. (2006, May–June). Black culture centers: Still central to student learning. *About Campus,* 2–8.

Pellegrino, J. W., & Hilton, M. L. (2012). *Education for life and work: Developing transferable knowledge and skills in the 21st century.* Retrieved from http://www.nap.edu/catalog/13398/education-for-life-and-work-developing-transferable-knowledge-and-skills

Pike, G. R. (2003). Membership in a fraternity or sorority, student engagement, and educational outcomes at AAU public research universities. *Journal of College Student Development, 44,* 369–382.

Renn, K. A. (2007). LGBT student leaders and queer activists: Identities of lesbian, gay, bisexual, transgender, and queer identified college student leaders and activists. *Journal of College Student Development, 48*(3), 311–330.

Renn, K. A., & Ozaki, C. C. (2010). Psychosocial and leadership identities among leaders of identity-based campus organizations. *Journal of Diversity in Higher Education, 3*(1), 14–26. doi: 10.1037/a0018564

Robbins, S., Lauver, K., Le, H., Davis, D., Langley, R., & Carlstrom, A. (2004). Do psychosocial and study skill factors predict college outcomes? A meta-analysis. *Psychological Bulletin, 130,* 261–288.

Robst, J. (2007). Education and job match: The relatedness of college major and work. *Economics of Education Review, 26*(4), 397–407.

Saville, B. K., & Johnson, K. B. (2007). Year in college and sorority membership in predicting self-esteem of a sample of college women. *Psychological Reports, 101,* 907–912. doi: 10.2466/PRO.101.3.907-912

Savitz-Romer, M., Rowan-Kenyon, H. T., Ott, M. W., Liu, P., & Swan, A. K. (2015, November). *Moving towards coherence: A review of the literature describing noncognitive skills and their role in college success and career readiness.* Research paper presented at the Association for the Study of Higher Education Annual Conference, Denver, CO.

Schuh, J. H. (1999). Student learning and growth resulting from service as an intramural official. *NIRSA Journal, 23*(2), 51–61.

Shechtman, N., DeBarger, A. H., Dornsife, C., Rosier, S., & Yarnall, L. (2013). *Promoting grit, tenacity, and perseverance: Critical factors for success in the 21st century.* Washington, DC: U.S. Department of Education Office of Educational Technology.

Simons, L., & Cleary, B. (2006). The influence of service learning on students' personal and social development. *College Teaching, 54*(4), 307–319.

Snipes, J., Fancsali, C., & Stoker, G. (2012). *Student academic mindset interventions: A review of the current landscape.* Retrieved from http://www.impaqint.com/work/case-studies/student-academic-mindset-interventions-critical-review

Soland, J., Hamilton, L. S., & Stecher, B. M. (2013). *Measuring 21st century competencies: Guidance for* *educators*. Retrieved from http://asiasociety.org/files/gcen-measuring21cskills.pdf

Stecher, B. M., & Hamilton, L. S. (2014). *Measuring hard-to-measure student competencies: A research and development plan*. Retrieved from http://www.rand.org/pubs/research_reports/RR863.html

Stevens, B. (2005). What communication skills do employers want? Silicon Valley recruiters respond. *Journal of Employment Counseling, 42*(1), 2–9.

Tanyel, F., Mitchell, M. A., & McAlum, H. G. (1999). The skill set for success of new business school graduates: Do prospective employers and university faculty agree? *Journal of Education for Business, 75*(1), 33–37.

Thompson, J. G., Oberle, C. D., & Lilley, J. L. (2011). Self-efficacy and learning in sorority and fraternity students. *Journal of College Student Development, 52*, 749–753.

Tieu, T., Pancer, S. M., & Pratt, M. W. (2010). Helping out or hanging out: The features of involvement and how it relates to university adjustment. *Research in Higher Education, 60*, 343–355. doi: 10.1007/s10734-0009-0

Tough, P. (2013). *How children succeed: Grit, curiosity, and the hidden power of character*. New York, NY: Houghton Mifflin Harcourt.

Turner, B. A., Jordan, J. S., & DuBord, R. R. (2005). Retaining student workers: The importance of organizational commitment. *Recreational Sports Journal, 29*(2), 117–126.

Vogelsang, L. J., & Astin, A. W. (2000, Fall). Comparing the effects of community service and service-learning. *Michigan Journal of Community Service Learning*, 25–34.

Zimmerman-Oster, K., & Burkhardt, J. C. (2000). *Leadership in the making: Impact and insights from leadership development programs in U.S. colleges and universities*. Retrieved from http://www.wkkf.org/resource-directory/resource/2004/01/leadership-in-the-making-impact-and-insights-from-leadership-development-programs-in-us-colleges-and

Zúñiga, X., Williams, E. A., & Berger, J. (2005). Action-oriented democratic outcomes: The impact of student involvement with campus diversity. *Journal of College Student Development, 46*, 660–678.

3

How Students Gain Employability Skills
Data From Project CEO

Kate Griffin, Adam Peck, and Shannon LaCount

This chapter presents data from Project CEO (Cocurricular Experience Outcomes), whose findings can help higher education professionals explore the question: How can institutions better prepare students to make the transition from campus to career marketplace? Using the *Job Outlook 2015* survey from the National Association of Colleges and Employers (NACE; 2014) as a starting point for data collection, Project CEO focused on student perceptions of skill development and attainment, especially in relation to cocurricular experiences. The research also considered the impact of off-campus employment, on-campus employment, internships and practical experiences, and the first-generation student experience.

ABOUT PROJECT CEO

Project CEO was started at Stephen F. Austin State University (SFA) in Nacogdoches, Texas, in the spring of 2012. The first version highlighted the 10 most desirable skills for new college graduates to possess, as identified by NACE (2014) in its *Job Outlook 2015* survey. For Project CEO, students were asked to self-report on two key questions:

1. Did they feel as if they were learning these skills?
2. How and where, in their opinion, was the learning taking place—through classes, cocurricular programs, or both?

After looking at their own data, SFA administrators were curious to see how students at other institutions across the United States were reporting skills development. In spring 2014, the university partnered with Campus Labs to offer this study to other Campus Labs member campuses. A review of the data collected in this benchmark indicated a relationship between how involved students are on campus and how likely they are to believe they are developing the employability skills identified in the NACE *Job Outlook* survey. To gain greater insight into the self-reporting of these skills, a working group of student affairs assessment professionals from across the country, as well as a consultant from Campus Labs, reviewed the project scope and method to identify areas for improvement. In 2015, an updated version of Project CEO was launched. More than 15,000 students from 40 colleges and universities nationwide participated in the expanded survey. It should be noted that the second most desirable skill from the NACE *Job Outlook* survey was broken into two distinct skills, resulting in a total of 11 skills for Project CEO (see Table 3.1).

Table 3.1. **Skills Desired by Employers**

NACE Job Outlook (10 skills)	Project CEO (11 skills)	Definition
The ability to work in a team structure	Teamwork	Working together as a group to accomplish the group's goals, effectively using the strengths of individuals within the group
The ability to make decisions and solve problems	Decision making	Choosing between different options to best help the group to meet their goals
	Problem solving	Finding solutions to issues that threaten the ability of the group to meet their goals
The ability to plan, organize, and prioritize work	Workflow planning	Structuring the work of a group so there is a shared understanding among members of the group about their objectives and goals; establishing priorities for the group
The ability to verbally communicate with people inside and outside the organization	Verbal communication	Speaking to others effectively in large or small groups, putting abstract ideas into language others can understand
The ability to obtain and process information	Information processing	Knowing where to find information and to apply critical thinking skills to evaluate this information in order to determine its credibility
The ability to analyze quantitative data	Quantitative analysis	Understanding the meaning of numbers in a variety of contexts from managing budgets to evaluating data collected by the group
Technical knowledge related to the job	Career-specific knowledge	Developing skills that are necessary for one's chosen profession. This also involves identifying gaps in their skill set and identifying strategies for gaining the needed experience.
Proficiency with computer software programs	Computer software skills	Learning to use common applications such as word processing, spreadsheets, and presentation software as well as complex or technical software applications specific to a future career
The ability to write and edit reports	Writing and editing reports	Putting thoughts in writing such that others can easily understand it. The ability to write in engaging ways that make others want to read. This includes the ability to write without technical or grammatical mistakes.
The ability to sell to, achieve buy-in from, or influence others	Selling and influencing	Motivating a group to do something, convincing or persuading others

In addition to identifying whether students felt they were gaining career competencies, Project CEO measured the experiences that students found most effective in developing these skills, as well as the level of development they felt they had achieved. The survey considered the following experiences: classes, internships and practical experiences, cocurricular activities and events, on-campus employment, and off-campus employment. If a student reported gaining a skill in one of these areas, the student was asked to rate his or her ability using the scale in Table 3.2. Their responses could be used to illustrate how participation in certain activities related to students' self-rated competency in each of the skills studied.

Table 3.2. Student Rating Scale

Beginner: I am just now beginning to acquire this skill.
Developing: I am improving in this area.
Competent: I do this skill pretty well.
Advanced: I am above average at this skill.
Expert: Others look to me to teach them this skill.

INSTITUTIONS AND PARTICIPANTS

Participating institutions were solicited through outreach by Campus Labs as well as presentations at the annual conferences of four professional associations: NASPA–Student Affairs Administrators in Higher Education, ACPA–College Student Educators International, NIRSA: Leaders in Collegiate Recreation, and National Association for Campus Activities. All of the participating schools were 4-year institutions. Eleven percent were small institutions (enrollments of 1,000 to 2,999), 28% were medium-sized institutions (enrollments of 3,000 to 9,999 students) and 61% were large institutions (enrollments of 10,000 students or more). Seventy percent were public institutions. See Figures 3.1 and 3.2.

Sampling procedures were intended to promote equal representation of a variety of groups in the sample. For the most part, the sample is comparable with the characteristics of all college students as provided by the Integrated Postsecondary Education Data System, with a few notable examples. In terms of race and ethnicity, as shown in Figure 3.3, African American students were underrepresented in the sample while Caucasian students were overrepresented. Asian and Hispanic representation was fairly similar to the population as a whole. Women were somewhat overrepresented in the sample (see Figure 3.4).

Figure 3.1. Participant Representation, By Institution Size

All were 4-year institutions, with large, public universities comprising the majority.

Question for further reflection: How do you think your institution's type and size affect the overall learning and skill development of your students?

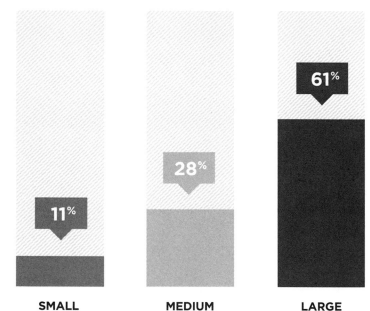

SMALL	MEDIUM	LARGE
Full Time Enrollment of 1,000–2,999	Full Time Enrollment of 3,000–9,999	Full Time Enrollment of at least 10,000

Figure 3.2. Participant Representation, By Institution Type

Figure 3.3. Participant Representation, By Race and Ethnicity

Although the data sets are comparable, there are significant differences for two of the student groupings. Project CEO yielded a much smaller sample of African American/Black students and a much greater sample of Caucasian/White students.

Questions for further reflection:
How diverse is the student body at your institution?
What steps can you take to capture the voices of a diverse student body?

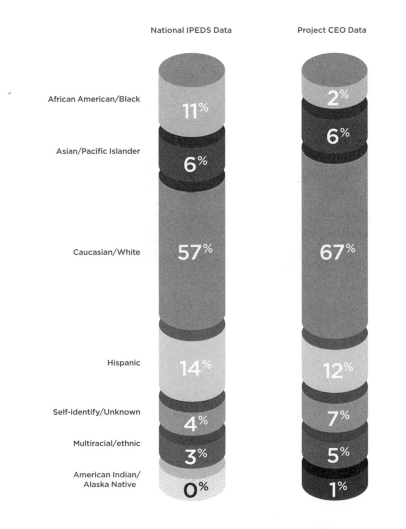

National IPEDS Data	Project CEO Data
African American/Black — 11%	2%
Asian/Pacific Islander — 6%	6%
Caucasian/White — 57%	67%
Hispanic — 14%	12%
Self-identify/Unknown — 4%	7%
Multiracial/ethnic — 3%	5%
American Indian/Alaska Native — 0%	1%

Note. IPEDS data do not add to 100%. In IPEDS, students can identify as nonresident alien; however, nonresident alien was not an option in the race/ethnicity category in the Project CEO survey. This figure excludes nonresident alien data.

Figure 3.4. Participant Representation, By Gender

Compared to national IPEDS data, Project CEO had a higher rate of female respondents.

Question for further reflection: How can your institution increase junior- and senior-year access to experiences that will help prepare students for the post-graduation job search?

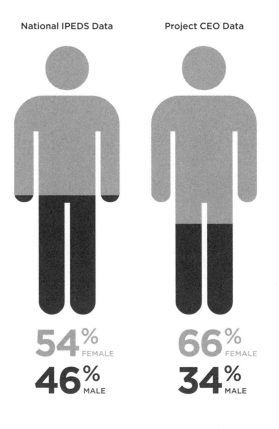

National IPEDS Data | Project CEO Data

54% FEMALE
46% MALE

66% FEMALE
34% MALE

Participants were relatively evenly distributed between their class status (year in school; see Figure 3.5). In the sample, seniors had the largest representation, followed by juniors. Sophomores and freshmen were considerably less represented.

Figure 3.5. Participant Representation, By Year in School

Note. Percentages do not add to 100%. One school (1.66%) specified "Graduate/Masters" and was excluded from this figure.

Sixty-six percent of the students were involved in a cocurricular activity at their institution (defined as organizations, campus publications, student government, fraternity or sorority, intercollegiate or intramural sports, or academic groups or honor societies) and 45% considered themselves to be leaders in these activities. There was an interesting, but not unexpected, relationship between year in school and involvement or leadership. As shown in Figure 3.6, overall, freshmen reported the most involvement on campus, with sophomores, juniors, and seniors reporting incrementally less involvement each year. In contrast, as shown in Figure 3.7, fewer freshmen identified as leaders, and leadership tended to peak in the senior year. While these results are not surprising, they provide confirmation of what many student affairs practitioners assume happens regarding involvement during the college years.

Figure 3.6. Cocurricular Involvement, By Year in School

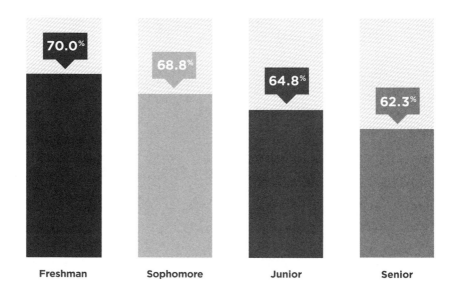

Figure 3.7. Cocurricular Leadership, By Year in School

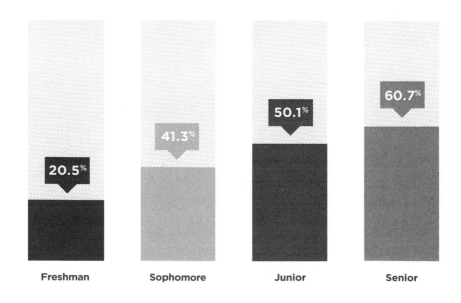

Findings

The findings from this research offer a unique view on the potential for a variety of college experiences to develop career-ready skills. What is most notable is that, according to their self-reports, students clearly do not agree with the belief among business leaders and the general public that they are not gaining the skills employers want. As shown in Figure 3.8, in almost every case, 90% to 99% of students indicated at least some level of skill in each area. The most notable exception appears to be selling and influencing, for which 22% of respondents indicated they had not gained this skill in college and an additional 11% indicated being at the beginner level for this skill. As this chapter will show, selling and influencing could be an area in which cocurricular experiences could make a considerable impact, as could quantitative analysis, career-specific knowledge, computer software skills, and writing and editing reports—other areas in which students report less skill.

Figure 3.8. Self-Reported Desirable Skills

The highest reports of being an Expert were for the skill of **Workflow Planning**.
The skill of **Selling and Influencing** had the highest percentage of Beginner responses
as well as the highest report of No Skill responses.

Question for further reflection: *At your institution, how do you think student perceptions of desirable skills compare to employer perceptions?*

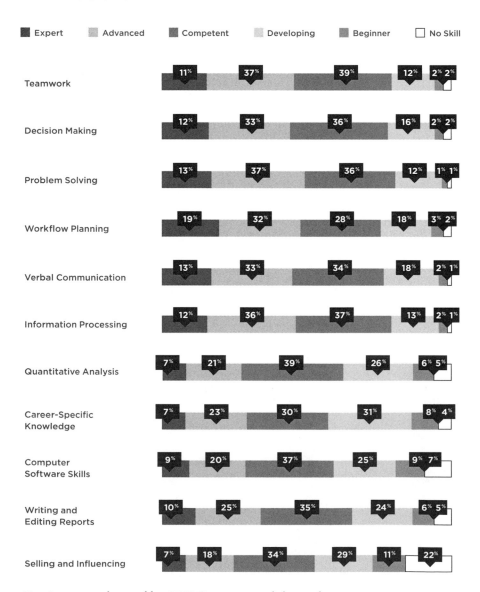

Note. Percentages do not add to 100%. Data were rounded up to the nearest percentage.

A myriad of experiences can develop the skills studied in Project CEO, as illustrated in Figure 3.9. It should be noted that in every case, students indicated that they gained the most from their classes. Taking classes is virtually the only experience that all students will have in common during their time at an institution. Additionally, internships appear to be a powerful source of learning with regard to career skills. This is also not surprising, since this is what internships are designed to accomplish. But not every student will have the opportunity to participate in an internship while in college. Similarly, not every student will have the time or inclination to seek involvement outside of the classroom. And although today's college students are working considerably more than previous generations, not every college student will have a job during their time in college (Carnevale, Smith, Melton, & Price, 2015). The sections that follow discuss the impact of a variety of experiences outside of the classroom on the development of employability skills.

Figure 3.9. Development of Skills through Experiences

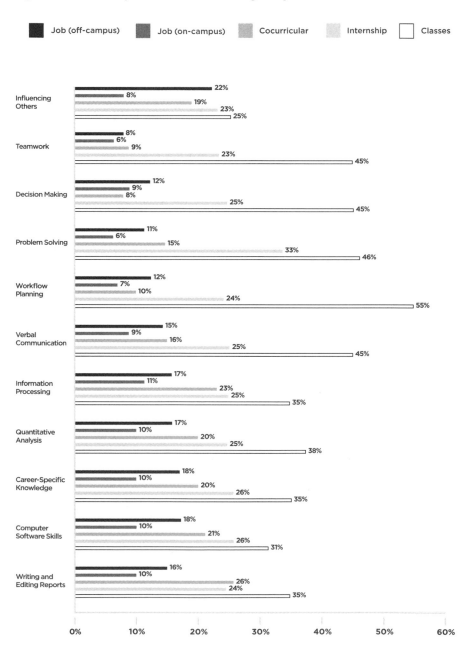

Note. Percentages do not add to 100%. Percentages were calculated based on responses collected vs. respondents.

Internships

Internships are usually regarded as the gold standard of job-related experiences. The data from Project CEO support the claim that internships are powerful learning opportunities. With regard to the different experiences outside of the classroom studied, students found internships to be most influential in teaching every skill studied, with the exception of teamwork.

Students also attributed considerable skill development to participating in internships. The mean for skill reports from students who participated in internships and practical experiences was higher than for those who did not participate in these experiences. For those who participated in internships and practical experiences, the skill with the highest average report was workflow planning; the skill with the lowest average report was selling and influencing.

While internships clearly are an important experience for developing jobs skills, securing one poses its own challenges. First, a true internship requires a supervising academic department that gives students credit for their participation. While many institutions offer scholarships to help pay for the credit, many do not. This essentially means that the student must pay to work. Unless their academic program requires an internship, students may find it more advantageous to consider more flexible options, such as job shadowing or another informal way of learning the ropes. Also, while many internships pay the students for their work, many do not. The complexities of ensuring compliance with the federal labor laws, which ensures protection of employees against abusive or predatory behavior by businesses, can be a deterrent to businesses. These hurdles explain why the potential of cocurricular involvement to develop employability skills is such an enticing idea.

Cocurricular Involvement

The term *cocurricular experiences* refers to meaningful experiences outside the classroom that contribute to a student's overall learning and development in college. The research presented in this chapter supports the philosophy that participation in cocurricular experiences is beneficial to students, especially by providing them with skills that employers desire.

No experience outside of the classroom appears to promote learning about teamwork more than cocurricular experiences. Cocurricular programs are also on par with internships in developing verbal communication skills. Even in other areas for which they had less impact, cocurricular experiences still made a considerable difference. In such areas as career-specific knowledge, writing and editing reports, information processing, workflow planning, problem solving, decision making, and the ability to sell to or influence others, students reported that cocurricular experiences were a rich area of learning related to these skills. This was particularly important for selling and influencing, a skill that students were most likely to say they were not gaining through coursework. An area like computer software skills also presented an opportunity. Nearly one fifth of the students who responded to the survey indicated that they had not developed computer skills from college classes. Finding ways to impart computer skills through cocurricular experiences could help institutions close this gap.

If cocurricular experiences contribute to the development of skills, one would expect that as students participate over time, their skills would likewise improve. The study tested this notion by asking students to rate themselves in each of the 11 skills. It then looked at what sorts of experiences students had participated in, and for how long. In the six skills most affected by cocurricular involvement, the self-rated mean score for each skill was higher for involved students than uninvolved students and higher among student leaders than those who were merely participating in cocurricular activities. In other words, the more deeply involved students were, the higher their self-reported mean score. The study also considered how students' degree of involvement influenced their perceptions of learning. Involved students were asked to select the category that best described them from the following choices:

- Somewhat involved in a single organization
- Somewhat involved in multiple organizations
- Very involved in a single organization
- Very involved in multiple organizations

For the six areas that cocurricular activities affected the most, the average response for students who were somewhat involved in one organization was the lowest; students who were somewhat involved in multiple organizations and students who were very involved in one organization tended to rate their learning similarly, with both jockeying for position in the middle; and the highest average response came from students who were very involved in multiple organizations. Responses are illustrated in Figures 3.10 and 3.11.

Figure 3.10. Average Self-Reported Ability, By Overall Involvement

Most students who said they were involved reported their involvement level as "Somewhat involved in multiple organizations." The average response of skill reporting was the highest for students who identified themselves as being "Very involved in multiple organizations."

Question for further reflection: How can your institution better integrate career competencies into involvement opportunities on campus?

Figure 3.11. Average Self-Reported Ability, By Overall Involvement

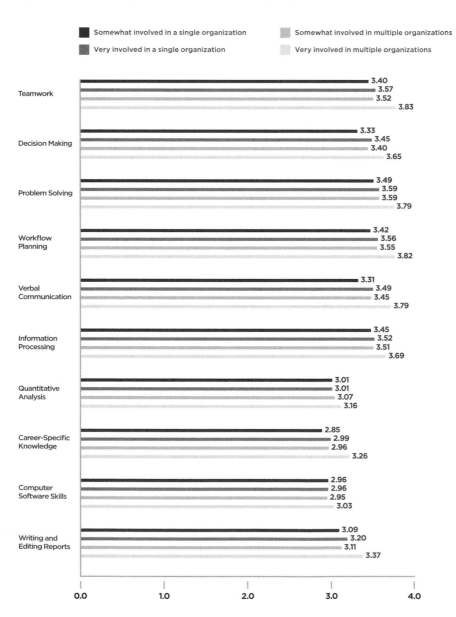

Note. Scores were measured on a 4-point scale.

It is important to note that there are many good reasons not to get overly involved in multiple organizations, so these findings are not a recommendation that every student take this approach. But the findings do suggest that while both breadth and depth of involvement matters, perhaps depth matters just a bit more. In most cases, the average self-rating of students who were somewhat involved in multiple organizations was similar to the average self-rating of those who identified as very involved in one. This suggests that the perceived development of skills is perhaps attributable not only to the quantity of experiences, but to the quality as well.

Work On and Off Campus

It is certainly intuitive to think that students develop work skills from jobs. What is surprising is that students tend to indicate less growth and development from these experiences than they do their cocurricular experiences, with a couple of notable exceptions. Students experienced greater gains in computer skills from both on-campus and off-campus jobs. And they perceived off-campus jobs as developing their skills of quantitative analysis more than cocurricular experiences.

An opportunity to enhance students' career readiness may be found in closing the gap between how much students are learning in their off-campus jobs compared with what they learn from their on-campus jobs. Given that on-campus jobs take place in an educational environment, it would seem reasonable to conclude that students would derive more impact from on-campus jobs. But this appears to not be the case. In fact, students indicate that they learn considerably less from on-campus jobs than on-campus ones. We can only speculate on why this might be. First, many jobs on campus require students to be eligible for the federal work-study program, which is based on financial need. It seems plausible that students who work on campus are more likely to come from families with lower household incomes and might also be more likely to be first-generation college students. As is discussed in the next section, first-generation college students tend to express less learning from these experiences overall. This factor could be influencing how aware these students are of what they are learning from their on-campus jobs.

Differences in expectation may be another potential explanation for this finding. There may be a tendency to view work–study primarily as a financial aid program and therefore expect very little of students. Businesses are expected to be profitable and generally prefer not to hire more people than they need. While a campus employer may be willing to let a student leave early to study for an exam, off-campus employers may be more likely to hold students accountable if they don't appropriately schedule their lives. It is possible that learning outcomes could be improved simply by requiring more of student employees and providing opportunities for them to reflect on what they are learning in ways that they are less likely to encounter in private businesses off campus. At the very least, the data from Project CEO provides a way for universities to benchmark their progress and determine whether they are improving the work–study experience.

First-generation college students are an increasingly significant, yet understudied, population for higher education. They are significant because they are a growing demographic in the general student body and they bring a cultural perspective different from that of the traditional 18-year-old, first-year student with parents and family members who have completed the 4-year college experience. They are understudied because there is no standard method to capture who a first-generation student is, much less an agreed-upon definition of *first-generation*. Simply defined, a first-generation student is one for whom neither parent (nor guardian) has a 4-year degree. Research about this group often points out specific demographic differences between them and their non-first-generation peers. Common characteristics attributed to first-generation students suggest they are typically older, belong to an ethnic minority group, are more likely to live at home or off campus, come from low-income households, and speak a first language other than English. Reports also suggest that first-generation students tend to work full time and enroll in either part-time or non-bachelor's programs at higher rates than their non-first-generation peers. In this survey, respondents were identified as first-generation based on their answers to two questions:

1. What was the highest level of education completed by your parent/mother/guardian?
2. What was the highest level of education completed by your parent/father/guardian?

Any student who answered "Did not complete high school," "High school," or "Unknown" for both questions was considered a first-generation student. Of all the respondents to our survey, 27% were identified as first-generation (see Figure 3.12). Included in the survey findings presented in Figure 3.13 is a comparison of responses from first-generation students to those of their non-first-generation peers. These data points represent the self-reported skill attainment from those who answered "Yes" to having participated in cocurricular activities, on-campus jobs, or off-campus jobs. A review of the data indicates clear patterns in how the first-generation group reported skill attainment.

Figure 3.12. **Percentage of First-Generation Students**

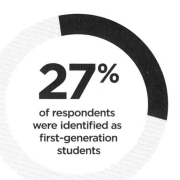

Figure 3.13. Skill Attainment, First-Generation vs. All Other Students

More first-generation students are reporting skill development through off-campus employment than all students combined. The highest-reported skill was **Selling and Influencing**. First-generation students also reported a lower incidence of skill development through cocurricular experiences compared to all other students combined.

Question for further reflection: *What does this mean for the ways we support first-generation students on campus?*

■ First-Generation Students   ▦ All Other Students

Classes

Cocurricular

Job (on-campus)

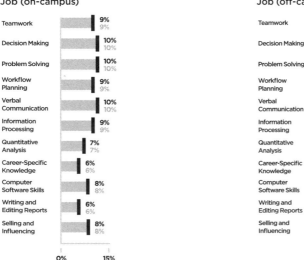

Job (off-campus)

Note. Percentages do not add to 100%. Percentages were calculated based on responses collected vs. respondents. Of the six categories, only four are represented in this figure.

Compared with the non-first-generation responses, data from the first-generation group indicate a lower perception of skill attainment for all 11 skills in both cocurricular experiences and on-campus jobs. Conversely, the first-generation group self-reported skill attainment from off-campus jobs at higher rates than their peers. Again, this was true for all 11 skills. These results generate more questions than answers—as is often the case when discussing first-generation students as a group—and create opportunities for further study. Questions for future research include the following:

- Did first-generation respondents report greater skills attainment from off-campus jobs versus other experiences outside the classroom because they work of campus at higher rates and therefore have more opportunities to gain skills in these settings? Or, are they participating in all three settings equally but gaining more skills from the off-campus jobs?
- If, as suggested by the data, first-generation students tend to work off campus more than on campus and are participating in fewer cocurricular activities, what is the reason?
- Is there opportunity to build on this momentum and help working students acquire even more skills?
- Do first-generation students actually participate in cocurricular opportunities at a lower frequency than the general population? If so, as is suggested by the data, why is this the case?
- If rich, frequent, cocurricular participation is most beneficial for skills attainment, how can institutions support first-generation and other students who work off campus and encourage them to participate in more cocurricular experiences?
- If first-generation students participate in cocurricular activities at the same rate but report less skills attainment from the experience, why is this?

The two final questions highlight the general approach to studying first-generation students: Is it appropriate to consider the impact of first-generation status with regard to developing career skills? Are we making too many assumptions? For example, while first-generation students often come from lower socioeconomic households, it is not true that they all do. In fact, financial status, not first-generation status, may dictate whether a student has an off-campus job. The patterns in the data are promising and suggest we are looking in the right places if we want to support student success in higher education, but we need to carefully consider our results and build on what we know.

CONCLUSION

It is clear that public trust in higher education among business leaders and the general public is deteriorating. And while these data can do much to change those opinions, some will dismiss the data because students are evaluating their own learning. But why is so much more trust placed in the opinions of business leaders? The students are being asked to describe their perception of their own learning experience; business leaders are often being asked to evaluate a large and sometimes nonspecific group of new hires. Could this line of reasoning not fall prey to the tendency to see today's college students as inferior when compared to students of yesteryear, a bias that is nearly as old as time itself?

More than 400 years before the dawn of the common era, Socrates was quoted by his student Plato as having said of the next generation, "They have bad manners, contempt for authority; they show disrespect for elders and love chatter in place of exercise. . . . They no longer rise when elders enter the room. They contradict their parents, chatter before company, gobble up dainties at the table, cross their legs, and tyrannize their teachers" (Patty & Johnson, 1953, p. 277). This means that for 2,500 years, the older generation has been saying that the younger generation will never live up to the standards of their predecessors. Perhaps this is why so many business owners, politicians, and even faculty and staff at institutions of higher education hold such a bleak view of how well students are being prepared for the challenges of work. But students themselves perceive gaining these skills from a variety of sources. Very few indicate that they are not gaining these skills in college.

As we look at the multitude of ways in which students can develop employability skills, cocurricular activities appear to show a lot of promise. First, many students are already participating in these activities. Second, there is no reason to believe that the institutions participating in the study were already consciously cultivating these skills through participating in their programs—except insomuch as the soft skills investigated in this study are closely aligned with or similar to learning outcomes that are typical in these programs. It is hoped that as institutions place more emphasis on the development of soft skills from cocurricular activities, these outcomes can be further improved.

Another exciting possibility is that student work on and off campus can be enhanced as a means of developing soft skills. Some very promising models for doing so are presented in many of the chapters that follow. The relationship between a student's need to work as a means of paying for school expenses and the number of hours he or she must work can be discouraging. However, if programs can be developed to help students develop the skills employers want, it could provide a much-needed advantage for otherwise disadvantaged students.

REFERENCES

Carnevale, A., Smith, N., Melton, M., & Price, E. (2015). *Learning while earning: The new normal*.
    Retrieved from https://cew.georgetown.edu/wp-content/uploads/Working-Learners-Report.pdf
National Association of Colleges and Employers. (2014). *Job outlook 2015*. Philadelphia, PA: Author.
Patty, W. L., & Johnson, L. S. (1953). *Personality and adjustment*. New York, NY: McGraw-Hill.

4

Providing Transformative Experiences for First-Generation Students

Steve Westbrook

The adjective *transformative* is defined as "causing or able to cause a change, especially causing someone's life to be different or better in some important way" (Merriam-Webster Learner's Dictionary, 2015). This is exactly what we as student affairs professionals hope happens for all the students we work with. The fact that students' lives are improved through their engagement with the programs and services we provide on our campuses might be the tagline we would wish to use to market our craft. While we strive to create transformative experiences for all of our students, these efforts may be even more important when they effect students who are the first in their family to seek a postsecondary education.

Why all the fuss about first-generation students? They are just students, right? And after all, we have spent years developing best practices that can be deployed to help students successfully transition from secondary into postsecondary education and persist until graduation. Why should we treat first-generation students differently than continuing-generation students? Why are transformative experiences more critical to this group? With limited resources, how can we afford to provide the focused attention these students need? The better question may be: Can we can afford not to focus on this cohort?

This chapter addresses these questions and reviews some of the challenges that threaten the success of first-generation college students upon entering higher education. It also discusses the importance of helping first-generation students to succeed. It then examines several ways that student affairs practitioners can influence the transformation of first-generation college students and reviews the reasons the transformation of these students can be so important.

WHY FIRST-GENERATION STUDENTS ARE SO IMPORTANT

Why is it so important to focus on first-generation students? The most concise answer to this question might simply be that the United States can't produce the needed number of career-ready college graduates without their success. Improving both access and completion for first-generation students is one of our most critical national issues. Because of the evolving global and technology-driven economy, up to 65% of available jobs in 2020 will require a postsecondary education. At the rate our institutions are now producing graduates with at least an associate degree, job demand will exceed the supply of qualified graduates by 5 million (Carnevale, Smith, & Strohl, 2013).

Superimposed on these sobering projections is the fact that fewer than 50% of all prospective first-generation students enroll in post-secondary education the year following high school, compared with more than 80% of their continuing-generation peers (Engle, Bermeo, & O'Brien, 2006). We can't be sure how many of those potential first-generation students considered furthering their education after high school but never successfully enrolled. There are no reliable statistics that can illuminate for us how many of these prospective students

simply give up before they start because of the maze of Byzantine processes they must negotiate to apply for college, access the financial aid
this group counts on to afford to enroll, and find affordable housing,
books, and supplies. The percentage of 2014 ACT-tested high school
graduates indicating their parents had no college degree reached 42%,
but when the number of students who did not respond to the question
was added, that percentage rose to 59% (ACT, 2014). While it is likely
a number of those high school students who tested never matriculated,
the size of the potential group is substantial.

Even with these obstacles to enrollment, the size of the first-generation cohort who successfully enroll remains large. According to
estimates, first-generation students comprise anywhere from 43% to
50% of overall enrollment in higher education. Regardless of where the
actual percentage falls, the number of students involved is significant.
The inclusion of so many first-generation students in higher education
is heartening. But even when a first-generation student does enroll in
higher education, he or she has difficulty persisting (Horn & Nunez,
2000; Nunez & Cuccaro-Alamin, 1998; Warburton, Bugarin, & Nunez,
2001). There is evidence that first-generation students leave college
before earning a degree at twice the rate of their continuing-generation
peers (Choy, 2001). The Pell Institute for the Study of Opportunity
in Higher Education (2008) reported that first-generation students,
especially those from low-income families, drop out at a rate almost
24 percentage points higher than their continuing-generation peers.
Within 8 years of enrolling, almost 70% of continuing-generation students will earn a degree while less than 30% of first-generation students
will do the same (Choy, 2001).

We must collectively address the success of the first-generation
student cohort because we cannot continue to see such a substantial
group of citizens fail to achieve the education needed to successfully access the job market. Even with the increasing cost of higher

education, earning a degree still ranks as one of the clearest paths to both economic independence and social mobility.

A more future-focused answer to why this group is so important relates to the long-term impact the success of these students will have on the success of their own families going forward. The Bureau of Labor Statistics has posited that students who graduate with a postsecondary degree can expect to earn up to 70% more than those with only a high school education. But maybe more importantly, the success of first-generation students breaks the generational cycle of educational underachievement and enables these new graduates to provide for their children the social and cultural capital that their parents were unable to provide for them. The bottom line is that the children of successful first-generation students will be more likely to seek higher education after high school—and will be better prepared to succeed when they enroll—because their parents, through their own personal success, were able to establish a new family standard.

UNIQUE CHARACTERISTICS OF FIRST-GENERATION STUDENTS

Over the past several decades, much has been studied and discussed regarding first-generation students. Although one can find several definitions for the term, a *first-generation student* is commonly defined as a student whose parents or guardians have no education beyond high school. This characteristic can mean that these students shoulder not only their own dreams and aspirations, but often those of their families as well. In the long run, their success can break the generational cycle of educational underachievement within families and enable these new graduates to provide the social and cultural capital for their children in the future that their parents may have been unable to provide for them.

By contrast, the first-generation student's peers who have had at least one parent or guardian matriculate in postsecondary education are known as *continuing-generation students*. Much of the literature related to first-generation students compares and contrasts the characteristics and outcomes of these two groups, and we should not be surprised to find that there are differences between them. Terenzini, Springer, Yaeger, Pascarella, and Nora (1996) examined both first-generation students and continuing-generation students on 37 precollege characteristics and found a significant difference between the groups on 14 of the 37. The areas in which these groups differed most were family income, with first-generation students more likely to come from a lower socioeconomic background; and race/ethnicity, with first-generation students more likely to be African American or Hispanic. These two characteristics are most likely to impact the two key areas that present the greatest challenge to first-generation students—the social and cultural capital that flows from parent to child.

SOCIAL AND CULTURAL CAPITAL

Why are we concerned with social and cultural capital? What do these terms actually describe, and how do they relate to career-readiness skills sought by employers? Bourdieu (1986) defined *social capital* as "the aggregate of the actual or potential resources which are linked to possession of a durable network of more or less institutionalized relationships of mutual acquaintance and recognition" (p. 248). Simply put, social capital is the name we give to the resources students can access based on their parents' membership in influential groups or the relationships and networks of influence and support enjoyed by their parents. Bourdieu went on to define *cultural capital* as the forms of knowledge, skills, education, and advantages that a person possesses.

He suggested that parents are able to provide their children with cultural capital by transmitting the attitudes and knowledge needed to succeed in postsecondary education. While we have to be careful about painting any group with too broad a brush, first-generation students are unlikely to come from families that are able to transfer social and cultural capital to them in the same quality and quantity as their continuing-generation peers receive from their families. The recognition and development of career-readiness skills may be more intuitive for students who can benefit from the capital they have been able to access through their parents, so we cannot ignore that the opposite may also be true.

CAREER-READINESS SKILLS

The National Association of Colleges and Employers (NACE; 2015) defined *career readiness* as "the attainment and demonstration of requisite competencies that broadly prepare college graduates for a successful transition into the workplace" (para. 3). After surveying more than 600 representatives of organizations that hire college graduates, NACE distilled the top 10 skills sought by employers for career readiness. (See Chapter 1 for a detailed discussion).

Generally, continuing-generation students enter college better equipped to more quickly and completely take advantage of the opportunities available to them to enhance these competencies. Many first-generation students sense an immediate difference between themselves and their continuing-generation peers in this regard. This is where institutions of higher education can make a strong impact on the future of first-generation students by implementing intentional programs and providing targeted services that assist them in discovering and learning to articulate the strengths they already have and help them connect to opportunities to enhance their existing skills and develop those they do not yet possess. We have to be informed about our approach, but we also have to be quick.

BEST PRACTICES

First-generation students arrive in college less prepared than their continuing-generation peers. Based on this realization, we should not be shocked to find that first-generation students are also less equipped to employ the active coping strategies we encourage new students to use when they encounter difficulties in college. Therefore, it is of little surprise to find that these students report lower social and academic satisfaction compared with their continuing-generation peers, and this dissatisfaction can manifest itself in the students leaving college. That is why transformative experiences early in a first-generation student's matriculation are critical for the successful development of career-readiness skills in this cohort. It is obvious that success requires persistence. It should be just as obvious that persistence requires support after access.

Within the first few weeks that new students start college, they will begin to develop a perception of their ability to control their own motivation, behavior, and social environment—a sense of their self-efficacy. Compared with their continuing-generation peers, first-generation students are less likely to begin college with a strong sense of self-efficacy. What naturally follows is a tendency for a first-generation student to hesitate to interact with faculty and peers during their early college careers because they arrive less prepared for these interactions and can harbor a sense of impostership, a feeling that they don't belong in higher education and could be discovered as unworthy if they bring attention to themselves. This desire to "fly under the radar" makes early engagement with first-generation students challenging—but critical.

The centrality of the classroom to the development of career-readiness skills is primary, and a positive relationship between students and faculty members is key to a first-generation student's persistence. But our task as student affairs practitioners is to create an environment to complement the classroom with cocurricular experiences that are transformative. After all, students spend more time outside class than they do in class, and we have always known that students learn from every experience they have in college.

The evidence of best practices for developing career-readiness skills in first-generation students in the cocurricular realm is increasing but still slim. There is a growing body of work that better informs our practice with this group, as well as promising examples of unique first-generation-focused student success programs. The most common issue seems to be finding ways to effectively scale these programs in a time of constrained resources. Due to this reality, it sometimes becomes necessary to adapt existing programs that are proven to work well with continuing-generation students to meet the special needs of our first-generation ones. We have to be careful. The ways in which first-generation students differ from continuing-generation students have a profound impact on the ways our interactions with them can help. While we think we have great programs and services to help all students develop, refine, and articulate career-readiness competencies, we have to think twice about one-size-fits-all approaches. Evidence shows that we cannot simply interact with first-generation students in the same way we interact with continuing-generation ones and expect the same results, especially during the first year (Pascarella, Pierson, Wolniak, & Terenzini, 2004). First-generation students react in different ways to many of the best practices that have been vetted in undergraduate education and advocated by faculty and student affairs professionals.

The following practices have been proven to be effective.

- **Early connection with other first-year, first-generation students.** When isolated, first-generation students often shy away from engagement and are left to contend with feelings of impostership alone. Creating opportunities for new first-generation students to meet one another and celebrate the important step they are taking together can be a powerful tool in helping first-generation students to succeed. Creating these connections before the start of class, or very early in the students' first term, can provide a sense of belonging and camaraderie that may ease engagement with this cohort.

  These connections might be informal, but the creation of an organization of students who identify as first-generation can be a powerful tool. Such a group could not only establish a peer group for the students to affiliate with, but also reach out to others on the fringe of involvement and create a welcoming and less threatening means of early engagement. When we think about it, a group of this type is no different than any other group of students with a common interest. The advantage for us can be the establishment of a vehicle by which we can more successfully channel critical support in a time-sensitive manner. The leaders of this group will enhance several career-readiness competencies, while the members of this group will benefit from a "home base" from which they can more safely approach the complexities of their new college life.

- **Early connection with successful first-generation upperclassmen.** Students can be more influenced by others with whom they share something in common. This phenomenon should be a guide for creating mentoring relationships between successful first-generation upperclassmen students and incoming first-generation students. These relationships can benefit both students involved. The first-year student mentees gain support from successful students who share a common identity with them, while the mentor students are able to enhance career-readiness competencies through their work.

Evidence suggests that facilitating the integration of first-year first-generation students with successful first-generation student mentors in both curricular and cocurricular activities may actually see the first-generation students flourish more than continuing-generation students would in similar settings. This occurs because the skills being developed by first-generation students are new and exciting for them. In comparison, continuing-generation students already have comparable skills in place when arriving at college as a result of the social and cultural capital they have been able to develop over a longer period of time in a different setting. This integration can be accomplished through paired courses that group first-generation students with each other and successful mentors. A real key to making these courses impactful to the development of career-readiness skills is the exposure to career development visioning early within the curriculum. This practice can help first-generation students better identify career paths they might not have explored previously. Investigation and preparation for professional internships during the first year can also help first-generation students make more informed course and major selection decisions.

- **Creation of high expectations paired with support, both academic and cocurricular.** Vincent Tinto (2012) emphasized through his work that "no one rises to low expectations" (p. 10). This may be especially true for first-generation students. While these students may come from backgrounds that increase the fragility of their persistence, to expect and require less of them because of this circumstance does this cohort of students a disservice. While academic expectations and support are often the purview of others on our campuses, the expectations and support student affairs practitioners create and provide in the cocurricular programs offered are as important. We should not expect less of first-generation students than we do of their continuing-generation peers, but we do have to recognize the social and cultural capital they may be lacking and support their growth in these areas.

- **Intentional and inescapable involvement.** How often have we heard of that percentage of students who actively resist engagement? Not only do we create programs that "lead a horse to water," sometimes we "take water to the horse." But hydration, in the end, is still up to the horse. Let's be careful about counting first-generation students in the "active resister" category. Their desire to not be discovered as "unworthy," hence their avoidance of involvement, can sometimes trump their desire to engage. It is important for us to employ intentional strategies that make the opportunities for engagement practically inescapable. Remember, in the end it is still up to the student. Our mission is to create an environment that makes it safe for students who are unsure of their place among their peers to take steps toward developing a stronger sense of self-efficacy.

FIRST-GENERATION STUDENTS ARRIVE WITH EMERGENT SKILLS

The experiences first-generation students encounter as they access higher education may create a foundation of career-readiness competencies, and student affairs professionals can help enhance these skills. An approach of identifying and accentuating these emerging skills could solidify a sense of self-efficacy for these students that will carry them through the critical transitional periods they will face.

Such a period of self-discovery can create the basis for the ongoing development of remaining competencies. Remember—there is no eventual success without initial persistence!

There are two competencies we can start with: decision making and problem solving, and leadership. Then there is an important area we can concentrate on to help first-generation students feel more in control of their futures: oral and written communication.

Decision Making and Problem Solving

First-generation students are influenced less by their parents than their continuing-generation counterparts primarily because they seek parental advice less (Westbrook & Scott, 2012). Thus, first-generation students may develop more self-reliance earlier in their college careers than continuing-generation students. Where this skill might evidence itself first is in the navigation of the sometimes bewildering college application and financial aid processes. While most continuing-generation students have the assistance of parents or guardians to guide them through the admission and financial aid maze, first-generation students have to solve many of these problems on their own. While an argument can be made that the necessity of this less-guided approach may cause the loss of otherwise qualified prospective students who simply give up when the confusion wins out, an equal argument can be made that those who successfully work their way through the ins and outs of these gateways have already demonstrated an ability to solve problems. Through the process of admission, first-generation students have learned to either find the information needed or seek the expert advice of those who can help inform their task. Our challenge may be to help first-generation students understand the significance of what they have accomplished, articulate the skills demonstrated, and translate that understanding into a building block of their self-efficacy.

Leadership

An attribute of leadership, as defined by NACE (2015), is the ability to assess and manage one's emotions to successfully navigate through a situation. Although a student's navigation of the college application maze without capitulation is one indication of this attribute, there are other and more impactful ways first-generation students demonstrate leadership. While transitioning into higher education, first-generation students may be dealing with a feeling of guilt for their success, or they may deal with families that resist their desire for education. Many also deal with being the higher education standard-bearer for their families.

It is not unusual for a first-generation student to suffer what Covarrubias and Fryberg (2014) have called "family achievement guilt" (p. 421). This conflicted feeling students may have when surpassing the achievements of others in their family creates a need for them to develop the ability to assess and manage their emotions in order to successfully navigate through this situation.

Some first-generation students may feel themselves punished by their families for what is seen as an act of betrayal by bettering themselves through higher education. Brookfield (2006) described this phenomenon as "cultural suicide" (p. 84), a situation in which students who persist in higher education regardless of the negative feedback received from family members in effect divorce themselves from familial connections.

Another issue for first-generation students may be that family members project onto them unmet educational aspirations. It is not an unusual circumstance for first-generation students to be proxies for their family members while seeking an education. This may manifest itself within the student as anxiety and fear of failure, since failure would be not only a personal defeat but also a defeat for the entire family.

Using the NACE definition of leadership, we can see how students experiencing either of these situations would demonstrate attributes of leadership.

Oral and Written Communication

First-generation students are generally underprepared to interact with faculty and others in positions of authority when they enter college (Padgett, Johnson, & Pascarella, 2012). These students express feelings of disconnection with faculty and administrators and perceive a lack of empathy from these authority figures. The time-honored "reach out for help" mantra that we often espouse in new-student orientations and freshman seminars can create anxiety in first-generation students that may lead to further withdrawal until it is past the point for any eventual assistance to matter. If we expect these students to be able to intuitively seek out communication with those who may be able to assist them the most during times of struggle, we might be mistaken.

This is an area in which the creation of a first-generation student organization can be helpful. The organization can provide a platform for developing strategies that students can use to practice engagement with authority figures in a nonthreatening setting. Seek the help of "student-friendly" faculty and administrators in combating this unease by having them role-play with those students who might find it difficult to reach out when help is most needed and would be most timely.

CONCLUSION

Without a doubt, first-generation students face significant obstacles that are not common among their continuing-generation peers. These obstacles don't disappear when the students enter college, and, in some cases, they may increase. Yet we have only recently begun to modify our student success initiatives to support these students. It can be a difficult challenge to reach students who often have limited time for cocurricular engagement sometimes coupled with a desire to remain anonymous. That we must also accomplish this at a time when resources, both human and financial, are stretched additionally complicates our task. We may find ourselves acknowledging the opportunity before us but avoiding addressing it directly because it is easier to fit the student to the model than it is to modify the model to fit the student. Even when we learn of or establish unique and effective programs that positively impact the success of our first-generation students, they are often difficult or expensive to scale, so we settle for small successes while the larger prize goes unclaimed.

Much can be learned from first-generation students. They step outside their comfort zones in search of transformation. Student affairs educators must do the same. To provide transformative experiences, we must learn to transform.

REFERENCES

ACT. (2014). *First-generation students: The condition of college and career readiness 2014*. Retrieved from http://www.act.org/newsroom/data/2014/states/pdf/FirstGeneration.pdf

Bourdieu, P. (1986). The forms of capital. In J. G. Richardson (Ed.), *Handbook for theory and research for the sociology of education* (pp. 241–258). Westport, CT: Greenwood Press.

Brookfield, S. (2006). *The skillful teacher*. San Francisco, CA: Jossey-Bass.

Carnevale, A. P., Smith, N., & Strohl, J. (2013). *Recovery: Job growth and education requirements through 2020*. Washington, DC: Georgetown Center on Education and the Workforce.

Choy, S. (2001). *Students whose parents did not go to college: Postsecondary access, persistence, and attainment* (National Center for Education Studies Report 2001-126). Retrieved from http://nces.ed.gov/pubs2001/2001126.pdf

Covarrubias, R., & Fryberg, S. (2014). Movin' on up (to college): First-generation college students' experiences with family achievement guilt. *Cultural Diversity and Ethnic Minority Psychology, 21*(3), 420–429. doi:10.1037/a0037844

Engle, J., Bermeo, A., & O'Brien, C. (2006). *Straight from the source: What works for first-generation college students*. (January Report). Washington, DC: The Pell Institute for the Study of Opportunity in Higher Education.

Horn, L., & Nunez, A. (2000). *Mapping the road to college: First-generation students' math track, planning strategies, and context of support* (National Center for Education Studies Report 2000-153). Retrieved from http://nces.ed.gov/pubs2000/2000153.pdf

National Association of Colleges and Employers. (2015). *Career readiness defined*. Retrieved from http://www.naceweb.org/knowledge/career-readiness-competencies.aspx

Nunez, A., & Cuccaro-Alamin, S. (1998). *First-generation students: Undergraduates whose parents never enrolled in postsecondary education*. Washington, DC: National Center for Education Statistics.

Padgett, R., Johnson, M., & Pascarella, E. T. (2012). First-generation undergraduate students and the impacts of the first year of college: Additional evidence. *Journal of College Student Development, 53*(2), 243–266.

Pascarella, E. T., Pierson, C. T., Wolniak, G. C., & Terenzini, P. T. (2004). First-generation college students: Additional evidence on college experiences and outcomes. *Journal of Higher Education, 75*, 249–284.

Pell Institute for the Study of Opportunity in Higher Education. (2008). *Moving beyond access: College success for low-income first-generation students*. Washington, DC: Author.

Terenzini, P. T., Springer, L., Yaeger, P. M., Pascarella, E. T., & Nora, A. (1996). First-generation college students: Characteristics, experiences, and cognitive development. *Research in Higher Education, 37*, 1–22.

Tinto, V. (2012). *Completing college: Rethinking institutional action*. Chicago, IL: University of Chicago Press.

Transformative. (2015). In *Merriam-Webster Learner's Dictionary*. Retrieved from http://www.learnersdictionary.com/definition/transformative

Warburton, E. C., Bugarin, R., & Nunez, A. (2001). *Bridging the gap: Academic preparation and postsecondary success of first-generation students* (National Center for Education Studies Report 2001-153). Retrieved from http://nces.ed.gov/pubs2001/2001153.pdf

Westbrook, S., & Scott, J. (2012). The influence of parents on the persistence decisions of first-generation college students. *Focus on Colleges, Universities, and Schools, 6*(1), 1–9.

5

Making Assessment
Relevant to Students

Darby Roberts

earning Reconsidered defined *learning* as "a complex, holistic, multi-centric activity that occurs throughout and across the college experience" (Keeling, 2004, p. 5). The definition recognizes that learning is not solely a classroom experience (nor is it only a cocurricular experience). Learning is not bound by time or place, and students are not unidimensional recipients of knowledge. In student affairs, we recognize that students learn, grow, and develop through the myriad of experiences they have. Ideally, a college education prepares students to continually learn throughout their life.

But, does higher education in its current state produce students who can think critically, solve important societal issues, and change the world? In *We're Losing Our Minds: Rethinking American Higher Education*, Keeling and Hersh (2011) criticized how we define the quality and value of a college education today:

> Learning is what matters in higher education; questions of cost, efficiency, completion, and access, important as they are, are relevant only if students learn. We want to shift the national conversation from a primary focus on the metrics that make up magazine rankings to a serious discussion about the effectiveness

of our colleges and universities in doing what they are there for: higher learning. (p. vii)

Student learning in college is a complex endeavor, but it is important that all higher education professionals continue to focus on key issues to prepare students for the future. Without that effort, we as student affairs professionals do a disservice to students who engage in higher education.

Employers want new college graduates to possess a variety of skills—communication skills, decision-making skills, and so forth—that are discussed throughout this book. A number of recent surveys indicate that employers are not convinced students are gaining those skills in college. And while it is possible that college students are not gaining these skills from their experiences either inside or outside the traditional classroom, it is at least as likely that they are gaining these skills but are not aware of this learning. The remainder of this chapter addresses making outcomes salient to students, engaging students in the learning process, measuring student learning, and communicating with stakeholders. The key is to include students and other stakeholders throughout the collegiate experience to ensure students are prepared to be competent and successful in their careers.

MAKING LEARNING OUTCOMES SALIENT

Much discussion is happening on the national level about learning outcomes and accountability, particularly for undergraduate students. In 2008, the Association of American Colleges and Universities proposed four overarching essential learning outcomes as part of the Liberal Education and America's Promise (LEAP) project: knowledge of human cultures and the physical and natural world, intellectual and practical skills, personal and social responsibility, and integrative learning. Each outcome was then further defined.

For example, the intellectual and practical skills outcome was described to include inquiry and analysis, critical and creative thinking, written and oral communication, quantitative literacy, information literacy, and teamwork and problem solving (Association of American Colleges and Universities, 2008).

The Lumina Foundation, through the Degree Qualifications Profile, proposed five learning categories for an associate, bachelor's, or master's degree: specialized knowledge, broad and integrative knowledge, applied and collaborative learning, civic and global learning, and intellectual skills (Adelman, Ewell, Gaston, & Geary Schneider, 2014). Intellectual skills specifically include analytic inquiry, use of information resources, engaging diverse perspectives, ethical reasoning, quantitative fluency, communicative fluency, and program-specific intellectual and practical skills (Adelman et al., 2014). While the framework does not address the field of study or the assessment methods, it does focus on what the student knows or is able to do in order to earn a degree. It also provides the flexibility for institutions to determine how the outcomes are implemented and assessed.

In its annual survey to determine the most desirable skills sought by employers, the National Association of Colleges and Employers (NACE; 2014) found the 10 abilities to be teamwork, decision making, problem solving, workflow planning, verbal communication, information processing, quantitative analysis, career-specific knowledge, computer software skills, writing and editing, and selling and influencing. There is no shortage of frameworks for learning outcomes to describe what graduates should know or be able to do following their college experiences.

In addition to the proposed national outcomes, most higher education institutions today have stated learning outcomes, learning domains, or goals for their graduates. If the institutions are public, their state may also have learning outcomes. If the institution is part of a larger system, that system may have learning outcomes. Within the institution, units may also have specific outcomes relevant to their area. For example, the State of Texas has the following learning outcomes: critical thinking, communication, empirical and quantitative skills, teamwork, social responsibility, and personal responsibility (Texas Higher Education Coordinating Board, n.d.). The Texas A&M University System (n.d.), composed of 11 institutions, has outcomes that address critical thinking and problem solving, communication, globalization and diversity, decision making and social responsibility, specific knowledge, and integration. Texas A&M University (n.d.) has outcomes that address the depth of knowledge for a degree, critical thinking, communication, personal and social responsibility, working collaboratively, preparing for lifelong learning, and social, cultural, and global knowledge. In addition, academic or student affairs units and programs may have specific learning outcomes based on their mission and purpose. While the outcomes are similar, they all have particular nuances.

Those are all important skills and abilities that institutions proclaim to provide and that employers are looking for. Although those stated outcomes are laudable, institutions may not thoroughly and consistently connect the student experience to the outcomes. Even before those outcomes are measured, they have to become ingrained in the institution itself and trickle down to students. Administrators, faculty, student affairs staff, alumni, and others should be talking about the outcomes with students. Even after the outcomes are established, they can be hard to measure in a meaningful way for both the individual student and the institution as a whole. If students do not take the assessment methods seriously, the stated proficiency level may be an inaccurate representation of student learning.

ENGAGING STUDENTS IN LEARNING

Students bring to college their previous knowledge, experiences, attitudes, and values, which impact their learning at higher education institutions. More than likely, students will meet people different from themselves, become proficient in a specific knowledge area, and be challenged in ways they might not have been previously. During their college careers, students will attend class (in person or online) and may have other learning experiences such as living on campus with a roommate, attending tutoring sessions, maintaining a part-time job, being held accountable for violating campus rules, leading a student organization, studying abroad, and more. All of these contexts provide learning opportunities that stretch a student's mind, body, and spirit. Students do not flip the learning switch when they walk out of the classroom. While some students see college as a holistic experience, others miss connecting curricular and cocurricular learning. Student affairs professionals serve a role in helping students make meaning across environments and experiences. They challenge students to synthesize learning in all areas of their lives through intentional conversations, crisis intervention, mentoring, supervision, advising, and more. In the student affairs environment, there is no grading system to determine if students have learned. Instead, we have previously relied on "I know it when I see it."

How do we prepare students for that multifaceted world? Of course, students learn foundational knowledge in their chosen major, but they will be most successful in their careers if they know how to learn and continue to seek out formal and informal development opportunities. Learning can be a complex web of analysis, synthesis, and evaluation of information and values.

Astin (1984) defined a highly involved student as someone who "devotes considerable energy to studying, spends much time on campus,

participates actively in student organizations and activities, and interacts often with faculty members and other students" (p. 297). Astin
recognized both the physical and psychological energy that students
commit to their experiences as necessary, but also finite, resources. As
student affairs professionals, we engage students and also challenge
them to make decisions about where they devote their resources, and
we also help them synthesize their learning across environments.

Ideally, students take an active role in their own learning, rather
than just being receptacles that get passively filled on a daily basis.
Although not all of their experiences are academic in nature, many
provide learning opportunities that can be translated into different
situations. Students can apply course content or the process of working
in groups to their student organizations or their employment. Many
students have internships, giving them the opportunity to apply their
course knowledge in a real-world setting. Student leaders get to hone
their communication, critical thinking, and conflict management skills
in a relatively safe environment. But in order to truly learn from the
experiences they are having, students need to be active participants in
the learning process, which typically includes some form of reflection
before, during, and after those learning experiences.

For learning to be most effective, students need to devote time for
reflection. Unfortunately, not all students know how to truly reflect,
and faculty and staff do not always teach students this skill. Student
affairs has begun to incorporate more intentional reflection into students' out-of-class experiences where staff can help students interpret
experiences into new insights. Students have a relatively easy time
describing the "what" in terms of what they saw and what they did, but
they sometimes struggle with what that means for their values, beliefs,
relationships, and future actions.

Reflection can take many forms, and it does not always need to be
complicated. It can be verbal, written, or even graphical using pictures

or drawings. It can be done in a group or individually, formally or informally. For example, students participating in a service–learning project may be asked about their preconceived notions about the social justice issue prior to the project. After the project, they might be asked to compare their prior beliefs with what they learned during the project and describe how they have changed their perspective, if at all. Students on a weeklong service project may be given a daily journal to note their feelings, insights, challenges, and so forth. Each evening the students could process the day's events as a group and learn from each other. The journal many or may not be turned in to the program coordinator for a summative assessment of students' reflections.

Another example could be an after action review after students implement a large-scale program or conference. The student leaders could reflect about what happened, what went well or could have gone better, and what changes could be made in the future. This could easily be described as "What? So what? Now what?" Ideally, these conclusions would be included in any transition documents for the next leadership team. As student affairs professionals, we can and should engage students in their active learning to make it relevant, meaningful, and transformative.

Student affairs professionals have a unique opportunity to be involved in students' learning and development. They may spend more individual and small group time with students than faculty, they may give frequent and ongoing feedback about performance, and they may be in positions to help students integrate their learning in a meaningful way. Students may rely on their organization advisors and supervisors for advice and counsel because students develop long-term mentor–mentee relationships with caring professionals. These relationships can also form with faculty, and student affairs staff should encourage students to bolster those relationships as well.

This places a great deal of responsibility on student affairs professionals. Not only do we need to understand student development theory, we need to understand student learning theory and assessment. We also need to be attuned to career development and higher education priorities. In addition, we need to know about what goes on in the classroom. As Dungy (2011) stated, "For those in student affairs, it's time to stop saying that our programs complement the teaching and learning that occurs in the classroom when at too many campuses student affairs has no relationship with the faculty and no idea about what the student's experience is in the classroom" (para. 11).

Just as learning does not stop at the classroom door, it does not stop when students receive their diplomas. As they move on to graduate school or the world of work, alumni continue to grow and develop. In this time of rapid societal, technical, and political change, jobs that did not exist before will be created potentially before students move through their undergraduate curriculum. Technology and globalization have had a tremendous impact on career preparation and progression. Technology has changed the way businesses operate and communicate, and they may be operating on an international level. To be successful in that environment, graduates must be technologically and culturally proficient. They may also change careers several times during their lives, which was uncommon a few decades ago.

While most institutions list their learning outcomes/objectives/domains on their websites, they may or may not overtly incorporate those into the lives of their students, faculty, and staff. How often do students hear about the outcomes? Only at freshmen or transfer orientation, or are they included in every syllabus, posted on office and residence hall walls, sent out in annual campus e-mails from the president, and appropriately assessed by academic level each year? Before we can expect students to perform the outcomes, we first need to tell them what they are, and then continue to remind them of the larger contextual outcomes throughout their experiences. Supervisors of student employees could revise their job descriptions based on the learning outcomes, and student organization advisors could mentor student leaders in developing relevant outcomes. Faculty may not have time to teach some of those soft skills in their courses, because they have so much content to teach in a relatively short period of time. Faculty may expect that students already possess those skills or will develop them on their own. As students complete their college experience, we have to connect those skills to their post-undergraduate experiences. Students need to be able to articulate those outcomes as well as perform them on the job. Through assessment, we can form a better understanding of what students know or are able to do at a certain point in time.

MEASURING COCURRICULAR LEARNING

One of the best places to start in determining what areas to measure in cocurricular learning is the curricular environment. What are the institution's learning goals and priorities? What does the institution say about its graduates? Other than mastering the content in a major, many of the additional outcomes and goals relate to the cocurricular environment: critical thinking, teamwork, ethical decision making, cultural competence, and so on. Student organization advisors, student employee supervisors, and other staff who interact with students on a regular basis can identify outcomes, make plans to develop those skills with the students, and implement assessment on a regular basis.

As Keeling and Hersh (2011) concluded, "Assessment should not be an afterthought or an add-on intended to satisfy some requirement; it is the only way to tell whether learning experiences of all kinds achieve their purposes" (p. 15). Regardless of whether learning takes place in the classroom or in a student organization, assessment needs to be incorporated into the experiences from the very beginning. Assessment should be used to improve student learning and programs, not just for accountability for external organizations.

The assessment of learning can also be aligned with initiatives in which the institution is already participating. This could be a national instrument, such as the National Survey of Student Engagement or the Student Experience in the Research University Survey. Many instruments will also include the option for locally developed questions. Depending on the questions, staff can analyze the data to further understand how student affairs impacts learning. Institutions may also use qualitative methods to assess learning through portfolios or by collecting essays from a sample of students to be analyzed with a rubric.

Faculty typically measure learning through tests, papers, projects, lab work, presentations, and portfolios that ultimately lead to a grade for a given course over a set period of time for a cohort of students. It is usually structured, time-bound, and built around an established curriculum. On the other hand, in student affairs, measuring learning can be more fluid, driven by the context and the individual experiences. Although not all curricular assessment is appropriate or possible in cocurricular activities, there are opportunities to apply those methods in an out-of-classroom experience.

Measuring learning in cocurricular activities can typically be described as direct or indirect. Direct measures include those that require students to actually demonstrate their ability to perform a skill, while indirect measures ask students to reflect on their ability to perform a particular skill. Direct measures could include observing students making a presentation and rating them on an oral communication rubric. Perhaps the observer does that several times over an academic year to provide the student feedback with an opportunity to improve. An indirect measure of oral communication could be asking students to rate their skills on a scale of 1 (*poor*) to 10 (*excellent*). Because student cocurricular experiences may not always lend themselves to direct evidence collection, it is important that staff collect multiple indirect measures to provide stronger evidence of outcome accomplishment.

Many methods can be used to assess student learning in cocurricular activities. They range from informal to formal, individual to program, formative to summative, and quantitative to qualitative. While an in-depth description of each area is beyond the scope of this text, there are a few examples that illustrate options in assessing student learning in cocurricular experiences.

Stevens and Levi (2012) described rubrics as tools to define learning outcomes and levels of performance on tasks. Students are used to being evaluated using rubrics, which are common in secondary and higher education in a curricular setting. They can be used to clarify the outcome, define specific sub-areas, and describe levels of performance. Rubrics can be useful in evaluating observations, written work, or portfolios.

The Association of American Colleges and Universities (n.d.) developed the VALUE Rubrics (Valid Assessment of Learning in Undergraduate Education) in 2007–2009 as part of the LEAP initiative. Faculty and other higher education administrators developed the rubrics based on the topic and the criteria commonly used to assess learning. The 16 rubrics can be adapted to individual circumstances, and they provide a foundation if staff have not developed rubrics previously. In addition, the rubrics aligned with the 10 NACE skills are included in the appendix of this book as an additional resource.

Using surveys may be appropriate for some experiences. In particular, the use of pre/post or post/then can provide evidence of learning over time. In the pre/post method, students are provided a test or survey before an experience (course, workshop, leadership experience, etc.). Following that experience, students are retested or resurveyed to see their gains in knowledge. One disadvantage of this method is that students don't know what they don't know, so they may overinflate their perceived ability. To counteract that bias, the post/then method could be used. Rather than assessing students before the experience, they are assessed only at the end, but are asked what they knew before the experience and what they learned. Ideally, students then have a more accurate perception of what they knew and did not know prior to the experience and an accurate perception of the learning that took place.

At the end of an experience—for example, a leadership position or a student worker position—having students partake in an exit interview provides an opportunity for them to reflect and articulate learning. It also provides valuable feedback to the staff member about how to improve student learning. Questions could be asked about what students learned (about themselves and useful skills), how they will apply what they learned, how they would describe their experience to an employer, and how they learned to work with those who are different from themselves. Section II of this book will provide multiple examples of how staff have developed learning outcomes, created learning opportunities, and assessed that learning.

The assessment of student learning needs to be an ongoing, systematic process rather than an episodic or random one. For many institutions, assessment in the spring may make sense because students are finishing their leadership experiences, preparing for graduation, and changing employment. But if an institution needs to know the change or improvement over time, then some assessment has to be implemented earlier. Just because assessment should be a continuous process does not mean that everything needs to be assessed all the time.

COMMUNICATING WITH STAKEHOLDERS

Not only do we need to assess student learning, we have a responsibility to share that learning competence with stakeholders. Stakeholders can include faculty, staff, administrators, students, the career center, legislators, parents, employers, and many others. Each group may have a different level of desired information, but they all have an interest in seeing that students are receiving a deep education to prepare them to be productive members in a diverse society. Faculty may want to know that students have learned to improve their teaching, parents want to know that learning was beneficial, and employers want to know that new employees can apply learning to a new environment. When we communicate with stakeholders, we need to determine what they need to know and how best to represent the information.

What do stakeholders care about in terms of learning? They want to know that students have had valuable experiences that exposed them to new ideas. They want to know that students have developed transferable skills (communication, ethical decision making, problem solving, etc.). Institutions need to be able to provide evidence that all students are graduating at an acceptable level of outcomes. Programs need to provide evidence that students in their program are learning what they are supposed to be learning. Students need to articulate to others what they know and are able to do as a result of their experiences. Not only do stakeholders care about learning outcomes, they also care about retention, persistence, timely graduation, and gainful employment. The more students are engaged in meaningful experiences, the more they are likely to experience those other outcomes as well.

In determining when to communicate with stakeholders, consider when they will be most interested in results and need the information to make decisions (resource allocation, recognition, program improvement, etc.). Summer may not be the ideal time to share assessment results and improvements with students, because students are not on campus. It may make more sense to share information in the beginning of the semester. If it is important to share the results with the students who participated in the assessment, it may be best to contact them when the results are analyzed and plans for improvement are made.

The audience impacts where results are shared. Staff may have the opportunity to present assessment information at an internal department at a staff meeting, at a university-sponsored symposium, or at a conference. Students may peruse the student newspaper, read campus e-mail, or look at bulletin boards in the residence halls, which can direct them to a department website. Social media plays an important part in sharing information and meeting stakeholders where they are. Results can be posted on Facebook, Twitter, Instagram, Yik Yak, and the next new creation. The career center and alumni association might be strategic places to share information. Important stakeholders then get access to information about the success of students as they enter the world of work. Other locations may also present prime opportunities to communicate with important stakeholders.

The information needs to be shared in a way that stakeholders can easily digest. Some stakeholders like the bottom line—numbers, comparisons, trends—while others like stories or pictures of individual experiences. A student testimonial can be a powerful statement, but so can a chart that shows a 15% increase in the retention rate over 2 years of first-generation, at-risk students who complete a transition program.

Sharing specific pieces of information about student learning can take many forms. It could be a multiple-page report that thoroughly discusses the data, or it could be a one-page handout highlighting the key points. It could be a colorful and catchy infographic or a PowerPoint presentation. The data can be presented graphically using bar charts, pie charts, line graphs, pictograms, tables, or figures. On the other hand, text could be used to tell a story or explain quantitative results. Technology can be useful in sharing results—think about the impact of a student video that describes learning that took place in a cocurricular experience and how that changed the student's perspective.

CONCLUSION

The current higher education and post-graduation employment environment is really a call to student affairs to be a partner in learning and assessment. Expectations have been raised about what students know and are able to do during and after college. While the curricular process has not significantly changed for decades (after finishing X number of credits, students receive a degree in a particular area), the cocurricular environment has been challenged to provide evidence of learning, value, and support of the curriculum. Student affairs needs to be included in the discussions of the future of higher education, which include access and equity, competency-based education, and the cost of higher education.

Students learn through all of their college experiences, both in the classroom and in cocurricular activities. Their environment is fluid and dynamic. In student affairs, we have an obligation to engage students in reflection about their experiences, to help them make connections and synthesize their learning; we need to make learning explicit and expected. Through student organization advising, supervision, meetings, and residence hall programs, student affairs practitioners sometimes have greater one-on-one interactions with students than faculty do. We need to incorporate learning into student experiences.

When we assess student learning, we need to be able to articulate the results from the institution, program, and individual levels. This requires the ability to implement assessment using multiple methodologies over a period of time. As a profession, we can no longer ignore the calls for assessment and evidence; we need to be proactive in the assessment process. That process includes being proficient in not only data collection and analysis, but also information sharing and using that information to make evidence-influenced decisions.

Subsequent chapters will provide specific examples of employer perspectives, student preparation and experiences, career services resources, and functional-area commitment to skill development and assessment. These examples provide a model for other campuses to adapt to make learning assessment relevant to students.

REFERENCES

Adelman, C., Ewell, P., Gaston, P., & Geary Schneider, C. (2014). *The degree qualifications profile: A learning-centered framework for what college graduates should know and be able to do to earn the associate, bachelor's or master's degree.* Indianapolis, IN: Lumina Foundation.

Association of American Colleges and Universities. (n.d.). *VALUE rubric development project.* Retrieved from http://www.aacu.org/value/rubrics

Association of American Colleges and Universities. (2008). *College learning for the new global century.* Washington, DC: Author.

Astin, A. (1984). Student involvement: A developmental theory for higher education. *Journal of College Student Personnel, 25,* 297–308.

Dungy, G. (2011). *Campus chasm.* Retrieved from https://www.insidehighered.com/views/2011/12/23/essay-lack-understanding-between-academic-and-student-affairs

Keeling, R. P. (Ed.). (2004). *Learning reconsidered: A campus-wide focus on the student experience.* Washington, DC: ACPA–College Student Educators International & NASPA–Student Affairs Administrators in Higher Education.

Keeling, R. P., & Hersh, R. H. (2011). *We're losing our minds: Rethinking American higher education.* New York, NY: Palgrave Macmillan.

National Association of Colleges and Employers. (2014). *Job outlook 2015.* Bethlehem, PA: Author.

Stevens, D. D., & Levi, A. J. (2012). *An introduction to rubrics: An assessment tool to save grading time, convey effective feedback, and promote student learning* (2nd ed.). Sterling, VA: Stylus.

Texas A&M University. (n.d.). *Undergraduate learning outcomes.* Retrieved from http://us.tamu.edu/Faculty-Administrators/Undergraduate-Learning-Outcomes

Texas A&M University System. (n.d.). *Student learning outcomes.* Retrieved from http://empoweru.tamus.edu/learning-outcomes/

Texas Higher Education Coordinating Board (n.d.). *Elements of the Texas core curriculum.* Retrieved from http://www.thecb.state.tx.us/index.cfm?objectid=427FDE26-AF5D-F1A1-E6FDB62091E2A507

6

New Models for Partnerships Between Cocurricular Programs and Career Services

Justin Lawhead, Jamie Bouldin, and Teresa E. Simpson

State legislatures, the federal government, the media, parents, students, and even alumni are putting pressure on colleges to invest more time and attention to help more students not just to run the academic gauntlet and reach graduation day, but to obtain gainful employment (Fischer, 2013; Philabaum, 2015; Postal, 2016). Conversations on higher education's purpose and return on investment are occurring nationwide (Miller & Grubb, 2014). In a recent study by *The Chronicle of Higher Education* and American Public Media's Marketplace, employers had trouble finding recent graduates qualified to fill positions at their companies or organizations (Fischer, 2013). Nearly a third gave colleges just fair to poor marks for producing successful employees, and they criticized bachelor's-degree holders for lacking basic workplace proficiencies, like adaptability, communication skills, and the ability to solve complex problems (Fischer, 2013). As a result, employers will continue to challenge higher education to produce candidates who are better prepared for the workforce (Hart Research Associates, 2015). Additionally, with the rising cost of higher education, students are also evaluating and choosing colleges and universities based on whether they have curricular and cocurricular programs focused on career development and employment preparation (Hullinger, 2015). As a result, student questions are changing from "Is there Greek life on campus?" to "When can I start an internship?" (Connor & Fringer, 2015). All these variables are creating a shift in how universities are engaging students and connecting them to career development and job placement.

This chapter reviews in greater detail why this shift is happening—and how institutions are responding. It includes a discussion of how career services offices are moving from a service orientation (workshops, individual advising) delivered by one office, to a connections model, where career guidance occurs within existing communities and networks and supporting students becomes an institutionwide effort. Further, the chapter examines how collaborations between career services and cocurricular programs yield new methods to help students successfully enter the world of work.

CHANGING EXPECTATIONS

College students and the institutions they attend are paying more attention to post-graduation employment as an expected outcome of completing a college degree. For instance, 87.9% of students attend college with the goal of getting a better job (Contomanolis, 2014). In several studies, students cited fulfilling career goals as a primary motivation for earning a degree (Astin, 1993; Boyer, 1990; Pascarella & Terenzini, 1991), and colleges face demands to be accountable for the educational and career outcomes of graduates (Baird, 1996). Freshmen often identify enhanced employment opportunities as an expected outcome of college, with a majority indicating that two "very important" reasons for attending college are "to be able to make more money" or "to get a better job" (Sax, Astin, Korn, & Mahoney, 1998).

Higher education institutions are focusing more on postgraduation employment; it is a stated student expectation, contributes to positive institutional image, and can provide accountability measures for departments and programs (National Association of College and University Business Officers, 1992). Because of increases in higher education costs and competition among institutions for enrollees, colleges are becoming more consumer-oriented and concerned with their students' satisfaction level. Institutions face elevated pressure to demonstrate the contribution and value of programs and services that are intended to meet those student needs (National Association of College and University Business Officers, 1992). This evaluation of education worth and contribution to career success is not only being done by students; employers, too, have expressed concerns about graduates' readiness for work.

Employers want evidence that graduates have career readiness skills such as problem solving, critical thinking, ability to work on a team, and strong oral and written communication (National Association of Colleges and Employers [NACE], 2015). Hullinger (2015) stated that in one national survey, 60% of employers complained that job applicants lack interpersonal and communication skills. Employers referred to students as being able to pass exams but unable to identify or solve problems on the job, or negotiate, or lead a meeting (Hullinger, 2015). Employers consider students' demonstrated attainment of those soft skills as an essential component of workforce readiness.

Higher education often addresses the employment needs of graduating seniors with programs and services to assist with job searches, interview preparation, résumé creation, and job fairs. However, students' readiness to implement job searches and career plans may be more critical to their success than the availability of services to assist them (Kanfer & Hulin, 1985). Students' readiness to attend to job search activities and their success in obtaining job offers may depend on each student's resolution of developmental issues related to identifying and implementing a career plan (Schwab, Rynes, & Aldag, 1987). The degree to which students engage in activities such as preparing a résumé, researching prospective employers, and networking with friends and family may reflect their internal readiness to make the transition from talking and thinking about career plans to actually implementing them (Kopelman, Rovenpor, & Milsap, 1992).

Employers endorse several emerging educational practices that 2- and 4-year colleges are implementing to ensure that students graduate with the knowledge and skills needed to succeed. They are most supportive of practices that demonstrate students': (a) depth of knowledge in their major as well as broad skills, (b) ability to apply their college learning in real-world settings, and (c) ability to conduct research and evidence-based analysis (Society for Human Resource Management & *The Wall Street Journal*/Career Journal, 2008). Employers also see potential in practices that require students to focus on ethical decision making and involve direct experience with methods of science to understand how scientific judgments are made (Society for Human Resource Management & *The Wall Street Journal*/Career Journal, 2008). Through extensive research between the private sector and higher education, Hart Research Associates (2010) discovered the following:

- Employers endorse learning outcomes for college graduates that are developed through a blend of liberal and applied learning.
- Employers believe that colleges can best prepare graduates for long-term career success by helping them develop *both* a broad range of skills and knowledge *and* in-depth skills and knowledge in a specific field or major. (pp. 1–2)

In order for career services professionals to successfully meet the needs of both employers and students, they will have to build meaningful connections through partnerships. They will need to develop career communities of learners and networkers that engage students and alumni for a lifetime (Dey & Cruzvergara, 2014). The shift must be from an office to a system, where career services is an institutional responsibility and student success is shared by the full university community (Dey & Cruzvergara, 2014). This will also involve working with a variety of student affairs areas to promote a community rich with connections and career development opportunities that are embedded within cocurricular experiences and supported through opportunities like student organizations, leadership training, and volunteer experiences. Student affairs professionals can support student career development by linking student involvement and corresponding outcomes to desired employment competencies.

Student affairs educators can more effectively support career development by finding ways to teach students to understand and articulate the skills they gain from student involvement that promote career preparation and readiness (Peck et al., 2015). In an audio podcast with *Radio Higher Ed*, Kevin Kruger (2014), president of NASPA–Student Affairs Administrators in Higher Education, said, "Faculty and student affairs all need to be more engaged here. . . . We need to look beyond the career center to a more holistic experience. . . . The notion of developing a meaningful career is something students should be engaged in throughout their entire academic experience."

COMMUNITY-FOCUSED CONNECTIONS

Dey and Cruzvergara (2014) attested that the mission of future career centers will be to build meaningful connections through partnerships and develop career communities of learners and networkers that engage students and alumni for a lifetime. Trends are pointing to a more integrated model of customized connections and communities—one that extends the responsibility of college employability beyond the walls of career centers (Dey & Cruzvergara, 2014). This shift creates an ecosystem that fully engages the entire university network of students, alumni, faculty, employers, families, and surrounding communities (Dey & Cruzvergara, 2014).

Contomanolis (2014) stated that institutions are shifting away from the philosophy that career services is one office's responsibility; instead, they are embracing the notion that successful career outcomes is everybody's business. Career preparation does not have to exist on separate turf; it can be done through academic departments, included in course instruction and assignments, and incorporated in existing advising procedures. Partnership building and collaboration are increasingly prevalent among the most effective career offices, and such partnerships are particularly vital to academics, alumni relations, and fundraising (Contomanolis, 2014).

As Chan & Derry (2013) noted in the paper "A Roadmap to Transforming the College-to-Career Experience," in order to provide students with intentional attention and access to key university resources, Michigan State University (MSU) developed "neighborhoods" in which MSU resources are brought to students where they live. According to the authors, first-year students live in one of the five neighborhoods where academic support, health and wellness, and intercultural and residential resources are provided in an effort to help students grow, discover themselves and the world around them, and develop long-lasting relationships. At the core of these neighborhoods are the Engagement Centers, which serve as the main access points to the resources offered (Chan & Derry, 2013). The Engagement Centers host workshops in all areas of college life—such as how to use the library effectively and how to manage personal finances—but they also host such career-related programs as résumé building and how to search for an internship, the authors noted. MSU students use Engagement Centers to prepare for college and for the future, connect to campus resources, achieve academic success, live healthy lifestyles, explore new cultures, and engage with the MSU community (Chan & Derry, 2013).

Chan & Derry (2013) also described a program implemented at the Hope College Career Development Center (CDC) to establish a common language and process for student self-exploration across campus. As the authors discussed, a major initiative has been to create a pilot program with the residence life staff to have first-year students in several residence halls take the Clifton Strengths Finder assessment. The CDC then connected with all First Year Seminar faculty advisors to incorporate the assessment in their fall First Year Seminar course, according to the authors. The program's intent is to have this tool play a significant role in the advising process as students and their academic advisors interpret the assessment results together and match a student's strengths to academic coursework (Chan & Derry, 2013).

At Stanford University (n.d.a), instead of waiting for students to come to the Career Development Center, career counselors go around campus and host meetups—informational chats in dining halls, in classrooms, and at student organization meetings, designed to engage students in conversations about careers. This effort is based on the career connections model, which focuses on developing clear bridges between all of the people, entities, and knowledge needed to form an opportunity ecosystem (Stanford University, n.d.b). Students can then tap into this web of career connections to achieve goals and find satisfying, meaningful work (Sullivan, 2013).

The intent of the Stanford program is to transform career services from a traditional transactional model, in which students make counseling appointments and attend lecture-style workshops and job fairs, to a career connections model, in which career centers reach out to students where they live and study on campus (Sullivan, 2013). This helps students explore their career interests and connects them with

mentoring and networking programs and experiential learning opportunities, such as off-campus "career treks" (Sullivan, 2013).

During a career trek, a group of up to 20 students spends approximately two hours at an alumni member's place of work (Stanford
University, n.d.a). Stanford Career Services found that students are eager
to learn about the organization as well as meet employees or Stanford
alumni and hear about their career paths (Stanford University, n.d.a).
Career treks also feature a hands-on component, such as participating
in a brainstorming session, observing research and development, or
taking part in a case study working session (Stanford University, n.d.b).

Queen's University (n.d.) has taken a proactive approach; it offers
students multiple resources for gaining employment-related experiences, including holding traditional informational interviews, meeting
with career student ambassadors, and talking with career advisors.
However, the Career Services department is also implementing a unique
program that entails identifying and matching cocurricular experiences
in order to support employee competencies acquisition and development, according to the university. The Cocurricular Opportunity
Directory provides position listings for students based on career interest, major, or learning opportunity development, the university noted.
Students can search for learning experiences that include, but are not
limited to, effective communication, intercultural competence, and
creativity and innovation (Queen's University, n.d.). Additionally, they
can find opportunities based on athletics and recreation, community
outreach and engagement, and politics and government (Queen's
University, n.d.).

Communitywide efforts provide students with an abundance of
resources and opportunities to find and build career competencies.
This movement is challenging the notion that one office is responsible for career development; instead, it uses a model of intercon-
nected institutionwide effort. Departments can also make a similar

impact via focused partnerships with career services, thus bridging student engagement experiences with career development exercises and preparation.

Cocurricular programs have long been a learning laboratory for students to acquire and develop career readiness skills. Student organizations and programming can offer the following types of instruction, among others: project and budget management, volunteer recruitment and selection, marketing, and effective conflict resolution. It is clear that these skills are applicable and relevant to future work experience. Those models and programs that best connect to career profiles, planning, and preparation will be the main focus of this chapter.

INTENTIONAL COCURRICULAR-FOCUSED PROGRAMS

Student leadership experiences allow students to attain initial career competencies—such as team building, collaboration, oral and written communication, critical thinking, and problem solving (NACE, 2015). However, Connor and Fringer (2015) found that career center directors encountered student leaders who were developing important skills but were not recognizing the skills' value and thus were not utilizing a process to capture them. One career center director explained the following:

> We find that students are really engaged and active on campus, involved with all kinds of experiential learning activities—internships, study abroad, student clubs and organizations. But when they come to us for help with their résumé and to prepare for the workforce, those things do not come to the surface. They go from activity to activity but are not understanding what they are getting out of it, and how it connects with life after college. (Connor & Fringer, 2015, p. 8)

The authors cited as examples resident assistants uncertain about how to discuss their experiences, student government leaders unable to relay accomplishments, and alternative spring break service trip coordinators unsure whether to list this experience on a graduate school application (Connor & Fringer, 2015).

Research by the Education Advisory Board (EAB; n.d.) shows that opportunities exist for institutions that wish to help students leverage campus involvement in order to achieve their postgraduate goals. This could be accomplished by changing perceptions about the value of cocurricular programming and providing guidance on how to articulate that value to prospective employers (EAB, n.d.). One method EAB (n.d.) proposed is for institutions to create a skill-seeker branding campaign linking various campus organizations and activities to the high-demand skills they provide. Departments would connect experiences to workplace competencies and promote them through such channels as orientation, social media, and posters (EAB, n.d.). The intent is to educate students about how cocurricular opportunities relate to career acquisition and development (EAB, n.d.).

Student leadership is one of the most common learning outcomes. Colleges and universities provide many curricular and cocurricular opportunities for students to develop leadership skills. In the curricular areas, students gain leadership experience through group projects, class presentations, and independent studies. Management, humanities, and military courses also teach leadership theory and practice. In the cocurricular areas, students gain leadership experience through involvement in athletics, Greek life, general clubs and organizations, and service and volunteer activities. Each of these activities provides students with ways to learn and develop specific leadership skills (Andersen, 2000).

Across the United States, campuses have created more than 100 formal leadership studies programs in the past 20 years. College and university officials have begun to adjust the mission statements of their institutions to emphasize student leadership development. Colleges offer students credit-bearing and cocurricular activities, sports, and service and volunteer activities that are dedicated to teaching leadership skills (Andersen, 2000). Institutions are also revising the curriculum to help students shape their employable skills development as part of program participation.

The University of St. Francis created mock hiring groups to give students strategies for improving their résumés, according to Connor & Fringer (2015). In small groups, student leaders were provided with blind résumés and job descriptions; they were to develop rubrics to assess them, rank them, and then present their findings to the larger group, the authors noted. The program provided students with new perspectives on high-demand skills, strategies for how to translate and more effectively articulate their skills, and résumé review and editing to immediately apply this new knowledge (Connor & Fringer, 2015).

The University of Dubuque (n.d.) has developed a cocurricular study guide. Its purpose, according to the university, is to help students develop a cocurricular plan that promotes participation in activities that complement their in-class academic experiences. The university's Office of Career Services identifies the guide as a tool to be used by students and by advisors as a way to encourage students to strengthen their educational skills, service, and knowledge (University of Dubuque, n.d.). The guide focuses on the following outcomes:

- Increase depth of knowledge.
- Write clearly, read with comprehension, and speak effectively.
- Understand the university's mission and vision.
- Gain hands-on experience.
- Develop awareness and respect for diversity.
- Value and recognize ethical perspectives and moral purpose.

- Actively participate in community service.
- Grow culturally, intellectually, and spiritually. (University of Dubuque, n.d.)

The guide also offers a variety of activities and learning experiences to support the intended outcomes; these experiences range from studying abroad to planning programs, to utilizing online tools provided by career services (University of Dubuque, n.d.).

The University of California, Santa Barbara (n.d.), created a program to build connections between student leadership experiences and career planning. According to the university, the student partnership program establishes relationships between members of student organizations and employers, graduate school representatives, and other professionals through a variety of programs. Student organization representatives apply to be student partners who can then receive personalized workshops, cosponsor events, and cohost employment-oriented panels, the university noted. The university's Office of Career Services offers the following opportunities to student partners and their organizations:

- sponsoring a career fair and gaining unique exposure to employers;
- attending student partner–only events;
- matching with employers, graduate school representatives, and other professional connections looking to serve as guest speakers;
- attending specialty career-related workshops for student organizations;
- receiving advance notice of events, workshops, and programming targeted to specific organizations; and
- linking to the Career Services website, which in turn promotes student organizations to employers seeking new hires and interns. (University of California, Santa Barbara, n.d.)

Additionally, the university noted, the Office of Career Services asks student organizations to market all the services it offers and to engage with the department via social media. Student partners also have opportunities to develop leadership and planning skills as they create programs to bridge experience with related career competencies (University of California, Santa Barbara, n.d.).

Wagner College (n.d.) offers an alternative program that focuses on developing competencies within cocurricular experiences aimed at supporting personal development and attaining career-related skills. The program uses professional coaching that focuses on exploring areas of significant personal interest, according to the college. Tactics include personal advice and group interaction along with portfolio use, written reflection, and oral presentations (Wagner College, n.d.). The program's intent is to help students stand out among other graduates when seeking employment (Wagner College, n.d.).

Wagner College (n.d.) noted that the program's competencies are identified as essential learning outcomes that were developed by higher education professionals and business leaders, and are intended to address the skills and knowledge needed for success in the 21st century. The Wagner College (n.d.) cocurricular competencies comprise the following:

- Aesthetic, creative, and intellectual expression
- Civic engagement
- Global stewardship
- Information and technological literacy
- Intercultural engagement
- Leadership
- Wellness

Students also participate in on- and off-campus activities, separate from coursework, and then assemble evidence of competency completion in an e-portfolio (Wagner College, n.d.). The e-portfolio is reviewed by an advisor, who guides the student composition of a five-page reflective essay titled "Citizenship Autobiography," and the essay and the e-portfolio are presented to a three-member panel that judges and approves the content, according to the college. Program coordinators cite benefits as connecting curricular and cocurricular experiences through written reflection to most effectively capture worth and enhancing verbal presentations that highlight each student's unique value proposition, the college noted.

These programs demonstrate how cocurricular activities contribute to attaining a wealth of important transferable employability skills. Institutions can bolster graduate employability by promoting and supporting cocurricular programs as skill development for future careers. Student affairs administrators can also support students by connecting them to networks of employers and alumni who can aid in transitioning these skill sets to the workplace.

Dey and Real (2010) stated that emerging technologies and social media advance a networking paradigm that focuses on a new level of connectedness for students and employers, as well as alumni, faculty, and families. This shift points to efforts that extend beyond the walls of an office to connected communities, where myriad strategies and resources are shared with future professionals (Dey & Cruzvergara, 2014). Two such efforts are programs and workshops that concentrate on how students can successfully transition into the workforce.

"Seahawks Taking Flight," the Senior Transition Workshop Series at the University of North Carolina Wilmington (UNCW; n.d.), is a cocurricular capstone program established in 2011. It begins with an inventory exercise in which students identify their college accomplishments and practice their 30-second elevator pitch, according to the university. Students who complete all four sessions (skill identification, financial planning, résumé and interview, and life after college) attend a certificate ceremony with local alumni, UNCW (n.d.) described. Student reflections indicated a new awareness regarding skills attained and a value for future employment, according to the university. A student testimonial stated the following regarding the value: "I found that the most helpful aspect of these workshops was the discussions with other students about reflections from time here at the university" (UNCW, n.d., para. 5).

The program is coordinated by career services but boasts partnerships throughout the division (UNCW, n.d.). The intent is for students to depart the institution with confidence in their personal accomplishments and with pride about their alma mater, UNCW (n.d.) indicated. Program coordinators stated that as a result of attending Taking Flight, more than 86% of students felt confident in their ability to connect specific skills gained at UNCW to potential jobs and careers (UNCW, n.d.).

The University of Memphis (n.d.) Personal Branding Conference is a one-day program focused on student transition to the workforce. Topics include, but are not limited to, preparation for interviews, social media strategy, elevator speeches, networking, community engagement, and developing your brand, according to the university. Students hear from community presenters who recruit and hire talent, local leaders who oversee workforce development, and young professionals who have successfully transitioned from higher education, the university noted. The conference is a partnership of Career Services, Student Leadership and Involvement, the Fogelman College of Business, and the Office of Multicultural Affairs (University of Memphis, n.d.).

Conference coordinators state that students have a personal brand they develop through cocurricular experiences (University of Memphis, n.d.). The conference then provides strategy sessions that focus on how students can identify and represent career competencies, which are part of that brand, according to the university. Conference

coordinators also recruit alumni who were actively engaged in cocurricular programs to participate in speed interviewing that concentrates
on effectively presenting how these student leadership experiences prepared them for the workforce, the university noted. The conference is
intended to empower students to know what they have to offer, what
they want, and how to ask for it (University of Memphis, n.d.).

CONCLUSION

Employers are seeking candidates who have and can articulate skills
necessary to transition into and operate effectively in the workplace.
Institutions of higher learning have candidates with these qualities,
but colleges and universities must be more intentional about creating programs that produce student awareness and demonstration of
these attributes. Universities should create divisional, university, and
community partnerships that provide reflection, employment connection, and application to current and future experiences (Walsh,
2015). For example, skill inventories can be incorporated into the
training curriculum for student workers and leaders. Applications
for leadership positions should require résumés and cover letters (K.
George, personal communication, July 16, 2015). Career services
should be leading these efforts and serving as knowledge centers for
best practices and innovation (Contomanolis, 2014).

The focus must shift from a standard one-office practice to an ecosystem (Dey & Cruzvergara, 2014). Career services should become a
presence that permeates the institutional culture and experience (Dey
& Cruzvergara, 2014). But for this type of ecosystem to be developed,
career professionals must recognize the opportunity to activate the
large and complex network that exists on a college campus in order
to connect key stakeholders (Dey & Cruzvergara, 2014). One of the
richest networks is the vibrant cocurricular programs that exist within

higher education today. Intentional partnerships can bridge learning and development with career competences being sought by employers, and subsequently enhance the experience and services provided by several different student affairs departments.

REFERENCES

Andersen, K. L. (2000, April 25). *Student leadership development: A closer look at student gains* (Master's thesis). Retrieved from https://theses.lib.vt.edu/theses/available/etd-04282000-14470036/unrestricted/AndersenK.pdf

Astin, A. W. (1993). *What matters in college? Four critical years revisited.* San Francisco, CA: Jossey-Bass.

Baird, L. L. (1996). Learning from research on student outcomes. In S. Komives, D. Woodard, & Associates (Eds.), *Student services: A handbook for the profession* (3rd ed., pp. 515–535). San Francisco, CA: Jossey-Bass.

Boyer, E. L. (1990). *College: The undergraduate experience in America.* Carnegie Foundation for the Advancement of Teaching. New York, NY: Harper and Row.

Chan, A., & Derry, T. (2013, May). *A roadmap for transforming the college-to-career experience.* Retrieved from http://rethinkingsuccess.wfu.edu/files/2013/05/A-Roadmap-for-Transforming-The-College-to-Career-Experience.pdf

Connor, M., & Fringer, T. (2015, July 8). *Re-thinking the co-curricular experience.* Retrieved from https://www.cmich.edu/ess/oss/Pages/ess-mini-conference.aspx

Contomanolis, M. (2014, October 16). *The new breed of career services professional: What is in the secret sauce of success?* [Blog post]. Retrieved from https://www.linkedin.com/pulse/20141016190028-2872947-the-new-breed-of-career-services-professional-what-s-in-the-secret-sauce-of-success?trk=prof-post

Dey, F., & Cruzvergara, C. (2014, July 15). *10 future trends in college career services.* [Blog post]. Retrieved from https://www.linkedin.com/pulse/20140715120812-11822737-10-future-trends-in-college-career-services

Dey, F., & Real, M. (2010, September). Emerging trends in university career services: Adaptation of Casella's career centers paradigm. *NACE Journal, 31*–35.

Education Advisory Board. (n.d.). *Preparing students for the workforce: Six co-curricular opportunities for experiential learning.* Retrieved from https://www.eab.com/research-and-insights/student-affairs-forum/infographics/preparing-students-for-the-workforce

Fischer, K. (2013). A college degree sorts job applicants, but employers wish it meant more. *The Chronicle of Higher Education.* Retrieved from http://chronicle.com/article/A-College-Degree-Sorts-Job/137625/#id=internships

Hart Research Associates. (2010). *Raising the bar: Employers' views on college learning in the wake of the economic downturn.* Retrieved from https://www.aacu.org/sites/default/files/files/LEAP/2009_EmployerSurvey.pdf

Hart Research Associates. (2015). *Falling short: College learning and career success.* Retrieved from https://www.aacu.org/sites/default/files/files/LEAP/2015employerstudentsurvey.pdf

Hullinger, J. (2015, May 18). *This is the future of college.* Retrieved from http://www.fastcompany.com/3046299/the-new-rules-of-work/this-is-the-future-of-college

Kanfer, R., & Hulin, C. L. (1985). Individual differences in successful job search following lay-off. *Personnel Psychology, 38,* 835–847.

Kopelman, R. E., Rovenpor, J. L., & Milsap, R. E. (1992). Rationale and construct validity evidence for the job search behavior index: Because intentions (and New Year's resolutions) often come to naught. *Journal of Vocational Behavior, 40*(3), 269–287.

Kruger, K. (2014, August 21). The expanding role of student affairs professionals in a changing higher education landscape (K. Dodge, interviewer) [Audio podcast]. *Radio higher ed*. Retrieved from http://radiohighered.com/2014/08/21/kevin-kruger-the-expanding-role-of-student-affairs-professionals-in-a-changing-higher-education-landscape

Miller, G., & Grubb, K. (2014, August 12). *10 ways you can be a change maker in career services*. Retrieved from https://www.linkedin.com/pulse/20140812142213-15676889-10-ways-you-can-be-a-change-maker-in-career-services#comments-7270190970954727285

National Association of College and University Business Officers. (1992). *College and university business administration*. Washington, DC: Author.

National Association of Colleges and Employers. (2015). *Career readiness defined*. Retrieved from http://www.naceweb.org/knowledge/career-readiness-competencies.aspx

Pascarella, E. T., & Terenzini, P. T. (1991). *How college affects students*. San Francisco, CA: Jossey-Bass.

Peck, A., Cramp, C., Croft, L., Cummings, T., Fehring, K., Hall, D., & Lawhead, J. (2015) *Considering the impact of participation and employment of students in campus activities and collegiate recreation on the development of the skills employers desire most*. Retrieved from http://nirsa.net/nirsa/wpcontent/uploads/NACA_NIRSA_White_Paper.pdf

Philabaum, D. (2015, January 1). *Talk is in the air—Career services must change!* Retrieved from http://careercenterstrategy.com/talk-is-in-the-air-career-services-must-change

Postal, L. (2016, January 31). Gov. Rick Scott challenges Florida universities to help graduates get jobs. *The Orlando Sentential*. Retrieved from http://www.orlandosentinel.com/features/education/os-rick-scott-universities-popular-majors-jobs-20160118-story.html

Queen's University. (n.d.). *Co-curricular opportunities*. Retrieved from http://careers.queensu.ca/students/want-build-experience/co-curricular-opportunities

Sax, L. J., Astin, A. W., Korn, W. S., & Mahoney, K. M. (1998). *The American freshman: National norms for fall 1988*. Los Angeles, CA: Higher Education Research Institute, University of California, Los Angeles.

Schwab, D. P., Rynes, S. L., & Aldag, R. J. (1987). Theories and research on job search and choice. *Research in Personnel and Human Resources Management, 5*(1), 129–166.

Society for Human Resource Management & *The Wall Street Journal*/Career Journal. (2008, June). *Critical skills needs and resources for the changing workforce: Keeping skills competitive*. Alexandria, VA: Author.

Stanford University. (n.d.a). *Invite your students to the workplace*. Retrieved from https:/beam.stanford.edu/alumni/invite-students-your-workplace

Stanford University. (n.d.b). *Stanford's career connections model*. Retrieved from https://beam.stanford.edu/about-us/stanfords-career-connections-model

Sullivan, K. J. (2013, July 8). Stanford's new career services director sets out to reinvent program. *Stanford News*. Retrieved from http://news.stanford.edu/news/2013/july/career-services-director-070813.html

University of California, Santa Barbara. (n.d.). *Student partnership program*. Retrieved from http://career.sa.ucsb.edu/students/student-partnership-program

University of Dubuque. (n.d.). *Co-curricular study guide*. Retrieved from https://www.dbq.edu/media/CampusLife/VPofStudentLife/CareerServices/Co-currricularStudyGuideFINAL.pdf

University of Memphis. (n.d.). *Personal branding conference*. Retrieved from http://www.memphis.edu/leadership/conferences/pbc.php

University of North Carolina Wilmington. (n.d.). *Taking flight*. Retrieved from http://uncw.edu/TakingFlight

Wagner College. (n.d.). *Co-curricular competency program*. Retrieved from http://wagner.edu/campus-life/cccp

Walsh, B. (2015, April 30). *That special something*. Retrieved from https://www.gse.harvard.edu/news/uk/15/04/special-something

II

IN PRACTICE
DEVELOPING EMPLOYABILITY SKILLS
THROUGH COCURRICULAR EXPERIENCES

The following chapters focus on the development of career-readiness skills in the context of a variety of cocurricular experiences. Participation in student organizations, campus activities, student government, collegiate recreation, service programs, leadership programs, and fraternities and sororities are discussed. These areas were selected as the focus of this book because they are largely student driven and because they represent experiences that are common on most college and university campuses and offer opportunities open to most. The authors include student affairs practitioners who are creating innovative models to address career readiness in their programs as well as leaders of professional associations who are working with their members to promote career readiness.

The chapters within this section may be helpful in a variety of ways. Each can be read as a stand-alone effort to understand the kinds of experiences that student affairs educators can use to build career-based learning into cocurricular experiences in specific areas. The chapters offer a starting point and a common language to articulate how students develop and grow. They could be assigned to students to help them make sense of their own career learning within a given experience. But even more, they offer the opportunity for readers to join in the conversation by focusing assessment activities and scholarship investigating the connection between participation in these activities and the development of career skills.

Taken together, the chapters in this section provide a holistic look at student learning through cocurricular experiences. The depth and breadth of opportunities for career-based learning as illustrated in these chapters demonstrates the relevance and importance of student affairs work in the 21st century. As one might imagine, there is considerable overlap between the programs featured in this section. Several strong themes develop that amplify the assertion that the deep and robust student learning taking place within cocurricular experiences plays a significant, and perhaps increased, role in preparing students for their careers.

7

Developing Employability Skills Through College Unions

John Taylor, Elizabeth Beltramini, and Crystal King

Recently, colleges and universities in the United States have seen an increase in student activism, much of it in response to issues about diversity and inclusion (Brown & Mangan, 2015). It is the role of colleges and universities to lead the country on challenging societal issues and, as the marketplace of ideas, to encourage free expression and participation in discussing controversial topics. The central location on a college campus for students to engage in such dialogue in a safe, inclusive, and welcoming environment is the college union (Barrett, 2014).

The college union serves as the meeting and gathering place for the campus community. It houses services to meet campus needs, such as restaurants, convenience stores, bookstores, and prayer and meditation spaces. Student organizations, campus departments, and external community groups hold their meetings, events, and conferences in the college union. Often the hub of activity, the college union serves as the community center for the college, where members of the campus join for celebrations, for special occasions, and to gain comfort during local and national tragedies. Game rooms and recreation centers allow campus community members to interact in social settings. Lectures, seminars, and programs facilitated by and held in the college union range from intellectual to experiential, with the collective goal of enhancing the academic success and personal development of college students. Additionally, gathering spaces and components such as music, art, and natural elements contribute passive learning opportunities. All of these pieces of the college union are intentionally arranged and work together to provide cocurricular education (Lane & Perozzi, 2014).

Unlike a mall off campus or an academic facility with retail outlets, the college union "serves as a learning laboratory for students through employment, engagement, and leadership opportunities" (DeSawal & Yakaboski, 2014, p. 1). It is a place where people of every major or position on campus, those living in residence halls or apartments, first-year students and alumni, might cross paths. In this way, it fosters cross-cultural understanding. Aspects of the building itself are arranged to further this education, such as historical artifacts memorializing traditions, symbolic artwork, sight lines that showcase involvement and programs, and the placement of services and offices (Gonzalez, 2014; Lazarus, 2012). Students who might have come to the union merely for lunch instead decide to stay and attend a program or seek out a volunteer opportunity (Pitts, 2016). As Doshi, Kuma, and Whitmer (2014) described, "Promoting activities that are unexpected provides opportunities for new relationships to develop, new happenings to take place, and unexpected encounters with peers, faculty, and artifacts within the building" (p. 13).

MORE THAN A BUILDING

Student involvement and leadership development experiences are also available in the college union through participation in volunteer roles, such as programming and advisory boards. Riepe's (2011) study of programming board officers revealed that students learn and develop skills in numerous areas including leadership, verbal communication, organization, and teamwork. Multiple studies have indicated that student involvement contributes to collegiate success (Astin, 1999; Bergen-Cico & Viscomi, 2013), and Gellin's (2003) meta-analysis of literature showed that student involvement has a positive impact on critical thinking—a necessary skill for graduates seeking employment. The Association of American Colleges and Universities' (2013) National Survey of Business and Nonprofit Leaders found nearly all employers surveyed (93%) thought "a candidate's demonstrated capacity to think critically . . . is more important than their undergraduate major" (p. 1). The same survey revealed that 95% also wanted candidates to demonstrate intercultural skills. The union offers an ideal environment to practice these competencies.

According to Magolda (1992), on-campus jobs help students learn how to work with different people and manage diverse situations. As part of a recent 10-year study, one alumna aptly described that employment in the union offers "the opportunity to work with colleagues and customers of many different races, genders, and cultures. [It] taught me how to keep an open mind and understand that not everyone learns the same way and not everyone has the same experiences. This experience is timeless and applies not only to my new work environment but also to my everyday life" (Towle & Olsen, 2015, p. 16).

Student employment and involvement in the college union provides the developmental benefits of being on campus along with real-life experiences similar to off-campus jobs (Devaney, 1997). Students might receive additional training and guidance in their union role but are often required to behave as professionals (Ducatt, 2015). In fact, nationally recognized restaurants that operate on and off campus have just as high expectations for quality and use just as demanding procedures in the union as in outlets outside the college setting. Similarly, college students working at local hotel and conference facilities use comparable skills to college union staff managing events and catering functions. A student building manager of a college union is responsible for the safety and operations of a large, high-capacity facility, analogous to anyone managing a large public facility in the community such as a movie theater, hotel, or performing arts venue. Recognizing that students who spend more time on campus are likely to be more successful (Astin, 1996), and that part-time campus jobs are associated with college satisfaction and completion (Furr & Elling, 2000), there is positive value to students staying and working on campus. As Ducatt (2015) said, "Hands-on daily experiences coupled with intentional staff development allow the union to provide a holistic learning experience" (p. 25).

In providing a well-rounded education, society expects that those who graduate from colleges and universities are prepared for the careers they choose. This chapter discusses the ways in which the college union contributes to the cocurricular experience and, ultimately, to developing career-ready students.

EMPLOYABILITY SKILLS DERIVED FROM STUDENT UNIONS

Verbal Communication

Student employees and student leaders serve as ambassadors for the campus, and as such must effectively communicate verbally with others who may be visiting or contacting the union, including other students, faculty, staff, alumni, and guests. This could mean providing a tour to a potential donor, speaking before a homecoming crowd, leading a programming board meeting, or soothing a frustrated visitor.

The college union information center, especially if it is also the primary campus resource for information, likely has the most interaction with customers, both in person and on the telephone. Negotiating this high customer service demand while achieving client satisfaction is a skill developed with practice. Besides providing accurate information, attendants are taught to respond in an articulate manner, to be aware of body language and nonverbal communication, and to clarify what is being said. Additionally, recognizing the diversity of a college campus, student employees are taught cross-cultural communication techniques. Such communication is intended to be respectful of differences and to convey friendly, welcoming, and inclusive messaging that exemplifies a college union.

Verbal communication that is not face-to-face is also common practice for college union student employees. It is not unusual for student employees to communicate via two-way radios. Recognizing that such communication is audible to the public, student employees must be cognizant of appropriate interaction on radios. In some instances, this may include using designated terms or codes in safety or security situations.

Policy enforcement is another common responsibility of student employees in a college union. Students are placed in an active position to educate and clearly explain policies, procedures, and practices that govern various building use. Student employees may be met with resistance because the rule they must communicate is preventing a building user from "having their way." These interactions empower students to implement creative solutions to issues while sharpening conflict management skills.

In other settings, verbal communication skills are developed through the daily encouragement of feedback from student leader to advisor, employee to manager, or more organized and formal means that align with employment beyond college. Many students themselves are supervisors of a union operation, managing groups of their peers. They are responsible for communicating clear goals and expectations to their staff members and holding peers accountable.

Mentorship opportunities are additional ways unions develop verbal communication skills in student employees. Because the ratio of student employees to full-time professional staff is often tilted in the students' favor, returning student leaders, even those without a supervisor designation, are relied on to provide guidance to new entry-level employees (Woods, 2016).

■ ■■ **COMMON EXPERIENCES**

Adam, a junior at the University of Michigan, was elected chairperson of the union's student governing board. Previously, student members of the board had presented plans for a renovated food court, as well as architects' potential designs, to various audiences. Now, Adam was serving as spokesperson for the board, making a speech at the ribbon-cutting ceremony. Afterward, he was interviewed by newspaper reporters at the event and quoted the next day as saying, "The combination of strong food operators and a newly renovated eating space will make the MUG area a great place for students to eat and hang out." As a communications major, Adam was able to enhance the verbal presentation skills he was learning in the classroom.

■ ■■

Workflow Planning

Many student employee and leadership roles within the college union require regularly planning, organizing, and prioritizing work. Time management in particular is a skill gained through involvement (Ducatt, 2015; Moderson & Woosley, 2014). This includes students ensuring they can manage their coursework, involvement, employment, and social commitments beyond immediate concerns. Demonstrated self-motivation and working on future or long-term projects during downtime are common learning outcomes that college union student employment programs track (Perozzi, 2009).

Students are called on to anticipate needs of peers and clients in planning events and programs. Student managers who oversee setup crews responsible for the room arrangements for meetings and events often meet weekly with their staff. They must schedule crew members at various times and according to when rooms need to be changed from one event to another. A single room may have three or four changes in one day, and one event may end at building closing with another starting the next morning at opening, each with a totally different set of meeting and room needs. The manager must not only schedule staff throughout the day and into the late evening, but also ensure the correct equipment is delivered and meeting details are provided.

Student leaders must also learn and develop project management techniques. Some college union program boards facilitate events comparable in scope and size to a professional concert production. For example, the program board that is part of the University of Texas at Austin's University Unions is the largest event-planning student organization on campus. Its annual Forty Acres Fest is a daylong carnival that includes student organization booths and performances, and culminates with a nighttime large-scale concert on the main mall. Such planning involves budgeting, contract review, advertising, ticket sales, event production, and coordinating artists' travel, lodging, and hospitality.

■ ■ ■ COMMON EXPERIENCES

As a student maintenance mechanic working in one of the largest and oldest college union facilities in the country, Sierra had a long list of preventative maintenance work planned during her shift. She had just started her rounds when the catering supervisor radioed that guests in the ballroom were complaining it was cold. She diverted from her rounds to stop by the ballroom. Sierra checked the temperature, closed the window that had been left open, and using her iPad she pulled up the digital controls for the building to slightly increase the heat in the room. Just then she received a radio call from the building manager that water was flowing from the second floor bathroom ceiling. She raced to the bathroom, isolated the cause of the leak, and shut off the water supply valve for the bathroom. She then called the maintenance director for authority to bring in a plumber to fix the pipe. At that point she knew the preventative maintenance work would need to happen on her next shift.

■ ■ ■

Teamwork

As noted by Kincaid and Gardner (1996), adults must be able to learn and work in teams to function in our society. For any organization to truly succeed, its participants must understand the roles of each team member and how that member's contributions positively enhance the larger team. A major challenge for executives managing union facilities is building a team that can maintain all of the responsibilities designated under the role, and building team cohesion from the multitude of staff representing a variety of life experiences and various stages of educational attainment. Further complicating this endeavor is the reality of a constantly changing workforce and constituency base.

Staff hires, retirements, interns, graduate assistants, and undergraduate student employees create a constant cycle of change, which has naturally motivated unions to design and maintain processes to quickly onboard staff and get them plugged into a culture of teamwork.

Developing respect for one another is an important characteristic of building a healthy team. As a form of continual engagement, training and team-building activities are often provided throughout the year for student leaders, employees, and departments. However, learning how to successfully develop teamwork skills often happens through practical application.

College unions are often large physical buildings, with multiple units needed on any given day to operate the facility. Students working in these areas learn to work as a team, as they see how each depends on the work of others (Empie, 2013). For example, the successful implementation of a wedding taking place in the building would involve the custodial, catering, and setup teams, all working in tandem. Custodial student staff may need to clean the ballroom where the wedding is to take place, followed by the setup crew to place and arrange tables, chairs, and audio/visual equipment. Last, the catering team is positioned to arrange the place settings and serve the meal. Following the event, all three teams must work together to clear tables, break down equipment, and clean the room.

It is through such coordinated efforts in a college union that students learn how to move seamlessly from a smaller unit working in a designated area, to a larger team accomplishing a greater goal. Working together, students develop a strong sense of trust and support for one another (Towle & Olsen, 2015). They don't want to let each other down, they cover for each other when needed, and they are committed to the college union as an organization. More experienced team members teach newer employees best practices. Group conflicts are usually resolved within the team rather than through professional staff involvement. These student employees are ultimately serving other students and the larger campus community, but it is the value they place in the college union team that maintains a strong sense of unity.

Students involved in cocurricular activities are 51% better at working in teams and at developing interpersonal relationships than their noninvolved counterparts (Moderson & Woosley, 2014). Student leaders and employees in the union appreciate that their roles offer the opportunity to get to know people who are different from them and who demonstrate a willingness to help or provide support when needed (Empie, 2013; Towle & Olsen, 2015). Many unions are even physically constructed with this idea in mind. A common trend is to collocate student organization offices, lounge space, and shared resources, prompting casual conversations and developing partnerships. Some take this a step further with advisory boards or coalitions that have representation from groups that seek to collaborate in new ways.

■ ■ ■ COMMON EXPERIENCES

Davidson College was one of four institutions featured in the PBS television program *Visionaries*, which produced a documentary about college unions. Davidson's Union Board election party was highlighted as an example of how unions foster teamwork by offering programs that bring together groups with differing views. The segment included interviews with the student presidents of the College Republicans and College Democrats. One participant, Rachael, commented about the value of working with others who are different: "I feel like I've had my views challenged and sometimes strengthened, but I love the dialogue we get to have together. . . . Some of the people I admire most on this campus are some of the people I disagree with most on this campus" (Mosher, 2014).   ■ ■ ■

Information Processing

Often, students engaging with programs and services in a college union are instinctively obtaining and processing information during their visit to the building. Pitts (2016) suggested that cultural awareness and understanding is frequently seen in the college union through intentional yet tacit ways: "The African American room displays information on the Negro Baseball Leagues and the Tuskegee Airmen. The Hispanic/Latino room has a display and information on the Treaty of Guadalupe Hidalgo and the Mexican-American war. The Native American room displays information on the different tribes in our state and copies of several treaties" (p. 13). Such intentional placement of displays allows students to obtain and process information through passive learning.

Additionally, multiple roles within a college union enhance development of this skill set, including information center employees, graphic designers, and program planners. An information desk attendant receives dozens of inquiries during a single shift and must be able to decipher what is being asked and then use the best resource to determine a correct or appropriate response. Although manuals may be available as a resource, or an Internet search engine just a click away, students are more importantly taught how to quickly clarify and process information that has been presented to them.

Student graphic designers who work in the college union are often given a concept or idea from a client, which they must process and expand on to create a visual piece that effectively communicates to a larger audience. The student may ask questions and provide draft concepts to allow the end product to be further transformed. Such an iterative process allows the student to obtain and process information as a method for refinement in developing a final graphic design (Rutherford, 2013).

When planning a program or event, a student needs to consider a variety of details and often work through a network of campus departments to secure funding, space, and approval. Specific information must be acquired from a bevy of sources. This could be something as simple as the correct pronunciation of someone's name or the forecasted weather, but typically also includes pricing for equipment rental, insurance required, egress needed for setup, and contractual obligations.

One consideration that will serve students well in a career setting is identifying and planning for potential risk mitigation, from physical risk assessment to assessing the potential risks to reputation (Gage, 2015). This type of information can be obtained and processed through any of the roles identified. The information desk attendant providing directions to an important alumnus recognizes the importance of having up-to-date maps available, the graphic designer understands how selected imagery influences how credible an initiative seems, and a program planner appreciates the importance of double-checking that all sponsors are included in a statement of thanks from the stage.

■ ■ ■ COMMON EXPERIENCES

In a planning meeting for the 50th anniversary of the student union at the University of Utah, it was clear to Jeff that tracking down alumni of the Union Board and Union Programming Council was an important step. Working with the campus development office, he and other students went through Union Board meeting minutes, yearbooks, and files to document individuals who had been involved in the union over the years. They entered this information into spreadsheets and coded it for import into the larger university database.

Next, they cross-referenced and removed duplicate information, merging contact records. Last, they scoured the Internet and alumni networks to find current contact information. From these efforts, more than 2,500 union alumni were invited to the anniversary celebration and a database of individuals is in place to serve future outreach initiatives. Now a lawyer in Salt Lake City, Jeff's experience working on this project helped him learn how to find and utilize archival information.

Decision Making and Problem Solving

While decision-making and problem-solving techniques are included in college union student employee training programs, they are also skills that become more refined through experience and increasingly responsible positions. Student managerial roles are often held by more tenured students, promoted from entry-level student positions within the college union. Professional staff teach applicable steps to identify a problem, analyze options, and develop solutions. However, the experiential component of responding to difficult situations greatly contributes to student learning and development in decision making and problem solving.

Often, this requires an understanding that there may be no perfect solution, and that even the best option might not work out as expected. Consider, for instance, an event held in the union. When hosting a program in the union, it can be difficult to predict the audience size. At times, a "good" turnout can create its own problems, necessitating that student leaders choose among designating a primary and overflow space or moving the entire event to alternative accommodations. Either way, participants may be frustrated. In this way, decision making also means tolerating ambiguity and being resilient (Towle & Olsen, 2015).

Although student leaders in the college union often strive for consensus, they also must determine how best to move forward when not everyone agrees. "According to ACUI/EBI [Association of College Unions International/Educational Benchmarking Incorporated] Student Leadership Assessment respondents, involvement in student organizations enhanced students' abilities to develop trust (58%), earn the respect of others (68%), manage conflict (60%), work effectively with others (72%), listen effectively (71%), and motivate others (65%)" (Moderson & Woosley, 2014, p. 17). When confronted with a problem, involved students learn how to consider perspectives and opinions and then make a decision. In leading a committee or program team, this can mean addressing a situation in which a colleague is not pulling his or her weight, reimagining a tired tradition, or charting a new direction when plans go awry.

In a student employment setting, individuals must make decisions about more immediate problems. Problem solving is how student audio/visual staff spend most of their day. Often under pressure to perform in the middle of an event or presentation, these individuals must be able to assess the issue in front of them and determine how best to solve it in an acceptable time frame for the client. As one student employee explained: "We are able to experience what it's like to have an upset customer or be working with somebody who you think maybe would cut you some slack because you're a student, but they don't. . . . I think that's very helpful when we talk about confidence, being able to manage different situations" (Ducatt, 2015, p. 25).

In many cases, students make up the majority of employees assigned to roles that operate a college union. In fact, during evenings and weekends, student building managers are typically responsible for the safety and overall operations of the college union as professional staff are not in the building. Students are frequently in the position of making decisions and solving problems, and they do so without hesitation or professional staff consultation. Beyond customer service, it is common for student employees in the union to gain annual training or certifications in CPR/ First Aid, using automated external defibrillators, fire, bomb threat, shelter in place, power failure, earthquake, unusual behavior or mental health emergencies, fights or physical altercations, and active shooter protocols. At times, student employees have had the unfortunate experience of having to rise to the occasion and lead the building through safety protocols when full-time staff is not present. These situations are never easy, but the outcome is direct skill development from real scenarios.

■ ■ ■COMMON EXPERIENCES

When Vivian arrived at 11:00 p.m. for her overnight shift at the union hotel, she learned that occupancy was at 90%. A short time later, a hotel guest came to the front desk indicating his room was very warm. Vivian went to the guest room and discovered that the room was in fact very warm. She examined the thermostat, which did not appear to be working. Vivian called the student maintenance mechanic to see if the thermostat could be repaired. At the same time, she checked the cleanliness of the few available rooms left in the hotel. When the student mechanic said he could not fix the heating problem, Vivian relocated the guest to another room. She apologized to the patron, and also gave him a breakfast voucher as a means of appeasement. Vivian was empowered to make decisions and solve problems, and in this case had to act quickly to maintain the satisfaction and trust of a patron.

Career-Specific Knowledge

Many of the skills learned through the college union are applicable to students' future careers. Front-line attendants in the college union use such customer service techniques as listening, empathy, and adaptability, which are critical for many professions. Student managers practice organizational and supervision skills. College union advisory board members develop political savvy, entrepreneurship, and strategic planning skills.

In some instances, academic programs are tied directly to identified roles. At campuses with hospitality, event planning, and restaurant management programs, college union positions in food service, catering, events, and hotel management allow students to apply what is learned in the classroom to the work setting. In addition to gaining needed practical experience, students in a marketing or graphic design curriculum are able to add the campaigns created for the college union to their professional portfolio. In addition, science-related programs are increasingly connected to learning opportunities in the union. Examples include bee farms, herb gardens, and green roofs, which agriculture students help manage; solar arrays and water conservation systems that are linked to a sustainability curriculum; and software programs and apps developed by information technology students.

While not connected to an academic major, other student leadership and employee positions in the college union can lead to the pursuit of a specific career. The proficiency gained by student managers of retail operations in the college union, such as a convenience store, enable them to consequently manage retail services in the public sector. In some instances, individuals invest in a franchise operation or start their own business. An example of a former student leader turned entrepreneur features an individual who saw the value of student involvement and subsequently founded a company to increase student engagement on college campuses. Similarly, a former student is using the organizational skills he learned as a college union governing board chair in his current role as chief of staff of a multibillion-dollar Internet company. Such examples suggest that the experience and skills learned through cocurricular involvement in the college union can contribute to a student's career path and future success.

■ ■ ■ COMMON EXPERIENCES

Alyssa was excited to join the marketing staff at Oregon State University's Memorial Union, knowing that 100% of graduates find professional positions in the field. Besides hours worked in the studio, she attended weekly learning sessions focused on design, media production, and marketing. Weekly lesson plans included comprehensive instruction on topics such as understanding a brand identity system, managing production costs, copyright and trademark laws, and inclusivity in marketing. Student learning outcomes were established at the start of the year, and in addition to working on marketing projects for campus clients, Alyssa was asked to reflect on her experience. Immediately following graduation, Alyssa received a job offer and was able to apply the real-life skills she gained from the training and work experience at the Memorial Union.

■ ■ ■

Quantitative Analysis

As the conversation about Big Data grows, the ability to analyze quantitative data is becoming relevant for most career pursuits. Student leaders and employees collect, examine, and interpret quantitative data to measure and improve college union programs and services. Daily building traffic, attendees at a program, and total sales of a retail operation are examples of typical data collected in a college union. Information center attendants maintain a record on the number and frequency of inquiries received. Student maintenance mechanics regularly monitor building temperatures and adjust mechanical systems as needed to maintain a comfortable environment for patrons. The convenience store student manager conducts inventory counts to determine how much product must be ordered, so that the store remains appropriately stocked for customer needs. Student leaders are commonly involved in budget management responsibilities and regularly review demographic data about program participation. Volunteer students who manage a food pantry initiative must analyze community needs to match services provided. A reservations assistant must track room occupancies, rental fees, and audio/visual inventory. A marketing intern frequently analyzes social media engagement indicators and adjusts campaign strategy as appropriate. Graduate assistants who work with student leaders in the union investigate learning outcomes data, norming rubrics, and rating scales to deliver better results. In these roles and more, students learn not only about methods to collect data, but also how to analyze data in relation to desired measurement purposes and goals.

■ ■■COMMON EXPERIENCES

As the lease for a printing services store in the union of a large public university was coming up for renewal, there was a general feeling that a convenience store would serve a better use of the space. Such a change would involve a significant financial investment to renovate the space, as well as a substantial commitment to self-operate a convenience store. While students on the advisory board were confident the change would resonate with the campus population and be financially successful, it was not prudent to act on anecdotal information. The board conducted a two-pronged approach to assessing options for the space. First, an e-mail survey was sent to a sample population of students. Second, student board members conducted intercept interviews in front of the copy store for an entire week. An analysis of the information they gathered indicated that there was strong desire and anticipated use for a convenience store. The college union invested more than $100,000 to renovate the space, and after hiring staff and stocking the shelves, opened the convenience store. The initial investment was repaid within 5 years, and the store continues to be successful and fill a campus need.

Selling and Influencing

The services and programs offered by a college union provide a great benefit to the campus community, and it is through the effort of students to sell and influence that they are successfully promoted. Involved student leaders are 40% better than their noninvolved peers at influencing others (Moderson & Woosley, 2014). The union governing board, which serves as the student voice on matters related to the college union, has a role to sell the value of the union to students at large. Student leaders on union boards serve as spokespersons, presenting at times to the student government or institutional leadership. Student managers and graphic designers market the programs, restaurants, and retail stores of a college union through various methods, ranging from advertising campaigns to social media engagement to in-store and point-of-sale promotions. Ticket office student employees sell tickets for university, community, and national entertainment. And students working in retail are trained in upselling strategies and customer service.

Additionally, many college unions house student organization offices, with allocation of such space typically recommended or decided by the union's student governing board. While it is important to note that allocation of such space must not be based on the purpose of the student organization (i.e., content neutrality), leaders of the organization still sell and influence in communicating their request. For example, at many campuses, the union advisory board holds interviews for student organization office spaces. Such interviews provide an opportunity beyond the standard application for students to persuade peers on the merits of their organization, how they will best use the assigned space, and how use of the space will enhance the effectiveness of the organization to contribute to the larger campus community.

■ ■ ■ COMMON EXPERIENCES

At California State University, Long Beach, students wanted to reduce the amount of material going to the landfill from the student union. They identified stakeholders and advocates, including a mix of student club members, student employees, faculty, and staff. They applied for and received a $5,000 grant to cover costs associated with the initiative. After conducting a waste audit on the union trash compactor, it was determined that 50% of the material was compostable. With this information, the students presented to the union advisory board a plan to contract with a new a service provider that could process the compostable material. Following the board's approval, a new retrieval process was implemented. However, the biggest obstacle was in changing the campus culture and educating students, faculty, and staff about what could be composted. The students created marketing materials, including posters, commercials, and releases on social media. A major success was their work in recruiting and training volunteer ambassadors who wore shirts with the campaign logo and educated diners about compostable items. They also set up information booths at the campus farmers market and other events to extend their message beyond the union. In its first year, the program diverted approximately 48,000 pounds of organic material from the landfill and reduced greenhouse gas emissions by approximately 11 tons.

Computer Software Skills

The experience of today's college students is heavily focused on technology, to the degree that it is critically important to their daily functioning (Martinez Alemán & Wartman, 2009). Most students have access to a computer, own a cell phone, and use social media sites (Lenhart, 2013). Even if they are less familiar with traditional computer applications like word processing and spreadsheet software, students are not afraid to be exposed to new forms of technology.

Most student positions within the college union use technology tools on a daily basis. Office attendants use basic word processing software, while marketing assistants use video, design, and illustration software. Reservation assistants and hotel employees manage room assignments through dedicated software, and information desk attendants communicate with some of their patrons online, via both e-mail and chat applications. A student event coordinator may input details and diagrams for a meeting into the college union scheduling system, which a setup crew member can later pull up on an iPad to correctly arrange the room. Those responsible for building operations must ensure Wi-Fi is stable and digital signage is accurate. Tech crew members spend much of their time ensuring presenters have their materials formatted to play appropriately. In addition, many student leaders use database programs to analyze statistics, manage budgets, or track inventory.

Students also often are responsible for training peers. It is not uncommon for college unions to house a computer lab, some of which remain open 24 hours a day. Such labs include a large number of computer stations, printers, scanners, and on-site technicians to assist patrons. The Student Center Campus Connection Lounge at Cleveland State University is staffed by a student to help others with Microsoft Office applications such as Word, Excel, and PowerPoint. Having such a resource in the union supports students' development of computer skills.

■ ■■ COMMON EXPERIENCES

Regina had been on the student Audio/Visual Tech Crew for 2 years when she was selected as the manager. She knew the importance of details when working with sound and technical equipment for meetings and events. Problems usually occurred because something simple was missed, like a cord not plugged in properly. She also knew that it had been difficult for her predecessor to adequately train new student employees in the fall, just when the demand for service increases most. She decided to create electronic training resources so that any employee could access them whenever needed. First she created a PowerPoint presentation with pictures of how to install and operate each audio/visual component used in the union. Next, she drafted a Word document of frequently asked questions and typical trouble-shooting instructions for tech equipment, including screengrabs of potential error messages. Last, she created a shared Google document for the staff to record any problems encountered or tricks learned with using the equipment. Regina thought the shared document would be an ongoing way for staff to teach each other. As a result of implementing these training materials, student workers consistently were able to reference the correct procedures, efficiency increased among new hires, and customer service ratings for events improved.

Writing and Editing Reports

An important set of skills for any job, writing and editing are used by college union student leaders and employees. A common area of responsibility that requires writing and editing is marketing the college union. Students are able to put their personal mark on updates and events in the college union. The messages created to communicate the services and programs have a strong impact on overall success. Recognizing this, a graphic design student will spend time to understand the desired end goal when working with the convenience store student manager on a promotion. Both students know that the message conveyed must be impactful in terms of content and visual representation, so the writing and editing process is extremely important to developing a final promotion. Such a piece also is likely only one component of a larger campaign for which students might be responsible. They must learn to write for various media, from a letter to the editor of the campus newspaper to a social media post, blog entry for the website, or printed brochure.

Writing is produced for both internal and external populations. Area and building manager logs are used in college unions to record what occurred on a given work shift. This is helpful to understand issues that may have arisen, or follow-up actions that may need to be carried out during the later shift. Additionally, the logs serve as an official record that could be used, for example, by police in conducting an investigation of a situation. They also can be used to influence future policy or procedural changes. In writing their shift log, building managers are cognizant of the multiple audiences that may view and use the document.

On a semiannual basis, student managers and leaders often have to document the performance of their peers. They learn how to draft comments that will be useful for an individual student's development as well as in advancing the organization as a whole.

Outside of designated positions in the college union, many facilities have components that promote written expression of ideas. For example, "democracy walls," made of glass or chalkboards, allow students to write opinions on the social and political issues of the day. These have been used to promote intercultural understanding through the written word.

■ ■ ■ COMMON EXPERIENCES

Each year, the Association of College Unions International sponsors an associationwide contest seeking the best marketing and promotion ideas; it receives more than 300 entries annually. Student talent is apparent in submissions ranging from brochures to multipage publications to posters. Professional-quality publications produced by students help promote the college union, with the end product often being more relevant to the student population because it is designed by peers. The "Be Your Best Self" promotion, created by Christina at the University of Maryland, Baltimore County, conveyed important messages about a designated driver program. A booklet on "Creating Trans-Inclusive Spaces," designed by Justice at Northwestern University, instructed faculty and event managers on how to more successfully welcome and serve transgender students. A gallery promotional pocket, created by William at California State University, Sacramento, served as a valuable resource to patrons viewing the union art gallery. The writing and editing skills students learn and use are evident in many of the entries.

■ ■ ■

ASSESSING EMPLOYABILITY SKILLS AS AN OUTCOME OF COLLEGE UNIONS

Student leadership and student employment roles in the college union are usually crafted to ensure specific learning outcomes. Additionally, many of the programmatic and physical facility components of the union are structured to promote learning and involvement (Lane & Perozzi, 2014). For professionals working in a college union, Student Learning is a core competency and Identifying Desired Outcomes and Assessing Outcomes are skills within that area (ACUI, 2012). Therefore, it is a central function to ensure students are gaining employability skills such as those described in this chapter. How such learning occurs is assessed using multiple methods.

External Review

Many college unions choose to garner an outside perspective on how well they are educating students. ACUI's College Union and Student Activities Evaluation Program uses peer consultants to assess a union's educational strategy, often using the Council for the Advancement of Standards in Higher Education's College Union Standard. Applying benchmarking data, reviewing existing assessment instruments, interviewing students, and reviewing reports are all part of the consultants' work to develop an accurate picture of the learning occurring with the union and potential opportunities for improvement.

Even resources available within a campus setting can provide an "external" viewpoint. Administrators, faculty, and outside staff can provide input on how well students demonstrate specific skills. Such data can be collected through comment cards, focus groups, and intercept interviews.

National Instruments and Frameworks

Whether seeking to assess students in identified roles or the general campus population, several national instruments are available to understand what students think they are learning through the union. For instance, the ACUI/EBI College Union Assessment, Student Activities Assessment, and ACUI/EBI Student Leadership Assessment provide rich comparative data across peer institutions (Rudisille & Hickey, 2011). Benchmarking one institution's results with the larger aggregate or a select institution type can enable a campus to better understand the successes and weaknesses of its current programs. In addition, companies such as Campus Labs, Compatibility, Skyfactor, and others apply data to help unions identify student personas and improve engagement factors associated with learning.

Unions seeking to assess learning on their own can still apply instruments used nationally, such as those from *Learning Reconsidered* (Keeling, 2004) and *Frameworks for Assessing Learning and Development* (Strayhorn, 2006). To ascertain learning resulting from the union environment itself, Padgett and Grady (2009) recommend applying Pascarella's (1985) framework for assessing the effects of differential environments on student learning and cognitive development.

Surveys

Perhaps the most common approach to assessing student learning is pretests and posttests or surveys (Bentrim, Sousa-People, Kachellek, & Powers, 2013). These are often distributed before and after a training opportunity but also may be used as a long-term approach, assessing student learning at the beginning of an employment or leadership role and iteratively thereafter. Data collected through surveys or evaluations can also be used to showcase the learning that occurs over time, as has been done at the University of Minnesota's Coffman Memorial Union as part of a 10-year assessment project (Towle & Olsen, 2015). As in an academic setting, surveys might be structured to ensure a student retains key concepts (e.g., written exams where students must select the correct procedure). Alternatively, they could be mapped to broader learning outcomes and ask students to discuss their competency in specific areas. Either way, such assessments are most productive when paired with feedback and an action plan to address shortcomings or desired goal attainment.

To help students realize their jobs as a next step in their career paths, supervisors should be sure to give critical feedback through evaluations. Evaluations of student employees should reflect the value of learning in the workplace, serving as formative and summative tools, and covering both job performance and learning. Again, job fit is important in this area: students should be selected for fit with their long-term career trajectory to the degree possible, and opportunities to grow and develop in ways that will benefit that trajectory should be explored (Watson, 2013).

Observation

Students in many roles may have their skills assessed through observation. For a retail worker, this might mean a "secret shopper" is used to evaluate the student's selling and influencing skills. A student board member might give a presentation and receive formal feedback on his or her verbal communication skills. A supervisor might review an information desk attendant's correspondence to assess the student's written communication skills. Such constructed observations yield strong examples that can help a student grow; however, even when not included in an assessment process, it is likely observation is used to some degree.

Simulation

For those skills that are not routinely used, a college union might assess student learning through simulations. Case studies and drills are common approaches to assessing a student's ability to obtain and process information and then make decisions and solve problems.

For example, in an active shooter drill, student employees would be assessed for their ability to gather the facts, communicate appropriately, and implement a plan. In a less dramatic scenario, audio/visual workers are trained to play "What If?": What if someone forgets an adaptor? What if the equipment is not set up as needed? What if the presenter's file won't open? These exercises enable students to test their competency and then address where they fall short. This approach is also critical in ensuring training information is retained (Grossman & Salas, 2012).

Reflective Assessment

One shortcoming of many assessment approaches is that there can be a discrepancy between what the union espouses it is teaching and what students are able to articulate they have learned (Lewis & Contreras, 2008). Several studies in the recent past have sought qualitative data from student employee alumni to better ascertain learning that students might not have elucidated as undergraduates. Essentially, with some distance from their student role, these alumni can describe how they have used skills developed from experiences in college unions as career professionals (Ducatt, 2015; Empie, 2013; Towle & Olsen, 2015). These findings have been garnered through interviews and reflective writings of former college union professionals. One alumna, who had been both a student employee and program board member, said:

> The most important thing I took away from my time working for Student Union and Activities was definitely a mixture of character and professional development skills. The student development outcomes have certainly come in very handy during interviews and often, in my experience, even impress employers. The outcomes also teach students a lot about themselves through resilience and self-awareness. . . . I've taken away friendships and a better understanding of my goals and strengths. (Towle & Olsen, 2015, p. 18)

Key Performance Indicators

As in an employment situation, student learning in the college union can also be evaluated in terms of business outcomes. A marketing student's ability to sell and influence may be determined by the results of a campaign. A convenience store manager's skills in analyzing quantitative data will be assessed by how well he or she predicts and accounts for inventory needs. A student leader's prowess at planning and organizing work is directly correlated to whether deadlines were met. Certainly in an educational setting, these are not the only metrics used, but they can be complementary to other measurements in assessing how students are applying knowledge to meet goals.

Mixed Methods

Most assessment in the college union will include several approaches to assessment. A common combination is a pre/post questionnaire, interviews with supervisors, peer evaluations, and self-evaluation (Lewis & Contreras, 2008; Towle & Olsen, 2015). These offer greater perspectives on how, for example, a student who thinks he or she demonstrates teamwork is perceived by colleagues and managers. "Before deciding on an approach to assessing students' learning and development, it is important to distinguish between performance evaluations and evaluation of learning and development as this can sometimes be seen as a potential barrier" (Hickmott, 2009, p. 230). When desiring to assess both performance and learning, Hickmott (2009) recommended a union determine multiple levels of achievement for each learning outcome, such as through triangulation or the use of rubrics that would limit the subjective nature of such assessments. Using multiple approaches to data collection and analysis can strengthen the assessment and provide a more robust picture of the skills students are gaining through the union.

CONCLUSION

College unions were founded on a philosophy of student participation. Therefore, student employees operate in a real-world work scenario where they often outnumber the full-time professionals. In some models, professionals even report to student leaders. In the college union, student employees and members of student organizations are expected to learn and practice skills that will serve them well after graduation. Some are general competencies needed in any professional role and others will benefit them in specific industries; however, regardless of career goals, their experience in the college union complements their academic coursework and makes for more well-rounded graduates.

As one student said, "I feel like working in the college union is the ultimate learning experience for college students. It meets your needs on so many different levels. It's an opportunity to make lifelong friends. It's an opportunity to grow skills that you may not realize that you needed. It's okay to say . . . 'I don't know how to transfer a call. I don't know—.' Those are things that you have the opportunity to learn in a safe environment working in the union" (Ducatt, 2015, p. 26).

REFERENCES

Association of American Colleges and Universities. (2013). *It takes more than a major: Employer priorities for college learning and student success.* Washington, DC: Hart Research Associates.

Association of College Unions International. (2012). *Core competencies and skill sets for the college union and student activities profession.* Bloomington, IN: Author.

Astin, A. W. (1996). Involvement in learning revisited: Lessons we have learned. *Journal of College Student Development, 37*(2), 123–134.

Astin, A. W. (1999). Student involvement: A developmental theory for higher education. *Journal of College Student Development, 40*(5), 518–529.

Barrett, L. (2014). Place matters, the college union matters: A quantitative study. *The Bulletin of the Association of College Unions International, 82*(6), 24–30.

Bentrim, E., Sousa-People, K., Kachellek, G., & Powers, W. (2013). Assessing learning outcomes: Student employees in student affairs. *About Campus, 18*(1), 29–32.

Bergen-Cico, D., & Viscomi, J. (2013). Exploring the association between campus co-curricular involvement and academic achievement. *Journal of College Student Retention: Research, Theory & Practice, 14*(3), 329–343.

Brown, S., & Mangan, K. (2015, November 24). Torn over tactics: Activists refine their demands as protests over racism spread. *The Chronicle of Higher Education.* Retrieved from http://www.chronicle.com/article/Torn-Over-Tactics-Activists/234328.

DeSawal, D. M., & Yakaboski, T. (Eds.). (2014). *The state of the college union: Contemporary issues and trends* (New Directions for Student Services, No. 145). San Francisco, CA: Jossey-Bass.

Devaney, A. (Ed.). (1997). *Developing leadership through student employment.* Bloomington, IN: Association of College Unions International.

Doshi, A., Kuma, S., & Whitmer, S. (2014). Does space matter? Assessing the undergraduate "lived experience" to enhance learning. *Planning for Higher Education Journal, 43*(1), 1–20.

Ducatt, M. (2015). Student employment in the college union: A source of student learning and self-efficacy development. *The Bulletin of the Association of College Unions International, 83*(4), 20–26.

Empie, M. (2013). Three practices to enhance on-campus student employee experiences. *The Bulletin of the Association of College Unions International, 81*(2), 16–22.

Furr, S. R., & Elling, T. W. (2000). The influence of work on college student development. *NASPA Journal, 37*(2), 454–470.

Gage, K. (2015). Events, risk to reputation, and the entry-level professional. *The Bulletin of the Association of College Unions International, 83*(2), 14–19.

Gellin, A. (2003). The effect of undergraduate student involvement on critical thinking: A meta-analysis of the literature 1991–2000. *Journal of College Student Development, 44*(6), 746–762.

Gonzalez, T. (2014). An inclusive union: Welcoming a diverse population. *The Bulletin of the Association of College Unions International, 81*(1), 32–37.

Grossman, R., & Salas, E. (2012). Helping trainees transfer skills in the workplace. *The Bulletin of the Association of College Unions International, 80*(3), 14–17.

Hickmott, J. (2009). Measuring student performance: Using appropriate evaluation tools. In B. Perozzi (Ed.), *Enhancing student learning through college employment* (pp. 221–238). Bloomington, IN: Association of College Unions International.

Keeling, R. P. (Ed.). (2004). *Learning reconsidered: A campus-wide focus on the student experience.* Washington, DC: ACPA–College Student Educators International & NASPA–Student Affairs Administrators in Higher Education.

Kincaid, R., & Gardner, J. (1996). *Student employment: Linking college and the workplace.* Columbia, SC: National Resource Center for the Freshman Year Experience & Students in Transition.

Lane, T., & Perozzi, B. (2014). Student engagement and college unions. In T. Yakaboski & D. M. DeSawal (Eds.), *The state of the college union: Contemporary issues and trends* (New Directions for Student Services, No. 145, pp. 27–38). San Francisco, CA: Jossey-Bass.

Lazarus, D. S. (2012). Re-visioning community. *The Bulletin of the Association of College Unions International, 80*(2), 12–17.

Lenhart, A. (2013). *How do they even do that? How today's technology is shaping tomorrow's students* [SlideShare slides]. Retrieved from http://www.pewinternet.org/2013/04/09/how-do-they-even-do-that-how-todays-technology-is-shaping-tomorrows-students

Lewis, J., & Contreras, S., Jr. (2008). Research and practice: Connecting student employment and learning. *The Bulletin of the Association of College Unions International, 76*(1), 30–38.

Magolda, M. B. (1992). Co-curricular influences on college students' intellectual development. *Journal of College Student Development, 33*(3), 203–213.

Martinez Alemán, A. M., & Wartman, K. L. (2009). *Online social networking on campus: Understanding what matters in student culture.* New York, NY: Routledge.

Moderson, K., & Woosley, S. (2014). Involvement, leadership, and learning: Using data stories to communicate value. *The Bulletin of the Association of College Unions International, 82*(3), 12–17.

Mosher, B. (Director). (2014, February 22). Building campus community – Episode 1901 [Television series episode]. In B. Mosher (Producer), *Visionaries.* Washington, DC: Corporation for Public Broadcasting.

Padgett, R., & Grady, D. (2009). Student development and personal growth in employment. In B. Perozzi (Ed.), *Enhancing student learning through college employment* (pp. 31–43). Bloomington, IN: Association of College Unions International.

Pascarella, E. T. (1985). College environmental influences on learning and cognitive development: A critical review and synthesis. In J. C. Smart (Ed.), *Higher education: Handbook of theory and research* (Vol. 1, pp. 1–61). New York, NY: Agathon.

Perozzi, B. (Ed.). (2009). *Enhancing learning through student employment.* Bloomington, IN: Association of College Unions International.

Pitts, B. (2016). Osmosis 101: Culture and the college union. *The Bulletin of the Association of College Unions International, 84*(3), 12–13.

Riepe, V. A. (2011). *What students learn as a result of being a chairperson and/or officer of a programming board* (Doctoral dissertation). Available from ProQuest Dissertations and Theses database. (UMI No. 3500076)

Rudisille, J., & Hickey. L. (2011). Identifying trends to improve practices in the college union. *The Bulletin of the Association of College Unions International, 79*(2), 16–24.

Rutherford. (2013). Why art, design, and communication are relevant for employment and citizenship. *Online Journal of Art and Design, 1*(3), 54–67.

Strayhorn, T. L. (2006). *Frameworks for assessing learning and development outcomes.* Washington, DC: Council for the Advancement of Standards in Higher Education.

Towle, M., & Olsen, D. (2015). Student employment matters: A decade of development outcomes analysis. *The Bulletin of the Association of College Unions International, 83*(4), 12–19.

Watson, S. T. (2013). *Student employment in student affairs units: Characteristics of educationally purposeful environments* (Doctoral dissertation). Available from ProQuest Dissertations and Theses database. (UMI No. 3568690)

Woods, A. (2016). Peer supervision effects on transferable skill development in on-campus employment. *The Bulletin of the Association of College Unions International, 84*(6), 18–25.

8

Developing Employability Skills Through Campus Activities

Adam Peck and Toby Cummings

The term *campus activities* may conjure a variety of vivid images—a group of students happily jumping on inflatable obstacle courses at an outdoor carnival, students flooding into a campus venue to see a concert produced by their fellow students, a coffeehouse program where students perform their own music and poetry, or a movie night to provide a break from studying. If there is one word that describes work in campus activities, it's fun!

But the concept of "fun" can be a double-edged sword. On one hand, fun is a secret weapon of the profession. Students find the challenge of putting on campus events to be both motivating and enjoyable. They often don't realize that what they are doing has significant learning benefits for them. If they do realize this, it's not necessarily why they are participating. They make friends, they provide service that others appreciate, and they often derive personal satisfaction from accomplishing the goals of the group.

On the other hand, the concept of fun can be very limiting to campus activities professionals. It implies that there isn't substance to this work. For campus leaders who must allocate increasingly scarce resources in higher education, campus activities may seem an easy area to cut. After all, the primary purpose of education is for students to learn. In difficult times, tending to students' entertainment may seem a luxury that the institution cannot afford.

The mission of campus activities is more than just providing entertainment to students who attend events; participating students have the opportunity to gain a variety of skills through both planning events and managing student organizations that plan events. In some ways, the events produced by the campus programming group are a by-product of the work of the group. They are like the steam that comes from the engine. They are necessary to create learning, but not really the product itself. The product of campus activities is the skill gained from participating.

This chapter explores how a variety of experiences in campus activities can provide students with the skills desired by employers. Skills that are common to students who are involved in these experiences as well as to students who are leading these experiences will both be considered. Suggestions for measuring learning along these dimensions will also be discussed.

UNIFYING LEARNING OUTCOMES
IN CAMPUS ACTIVITIES

Over the past 10 years, a reframing of teaching and learning has taken place in student affairs. A significant contribution to this movement was made by Keeling (2004, 2006) in the groundbreaking works *Learning Reconsidered* and *Learning Reconsidered 2*. In the first, he wrote, "Achieving the potential of [student affairs] requires that we broaden and diversify the understanding of learning now held by many faculty members and administrators—and some student affairs practitioners" (Keeling, 2004, p. 24). Many in student activities answered this call, and took it very seriously.

Campus activities professionals began to think of themselves as educators, and a serious effort to measure student learning began. In 2009, the National Association for Campus Activities (NACA) produced a document titled "Competency Guide for College Student Leaders" (Brill et al., 2009). This publication was an important first step in unifying learning outcomes occurring in campus activities programs. The document "serves as a learning map for student leaders as they grow and develop through participation in student organizations, community service, campus employment, grassroots activities, leadership positions, followership positions, mentoring relationships with campus activities advisors, etc." (p. 1). It focused on such areas as leadership development, assessment and evaluation, event management, meaningful interpersonal relationships, collaboration, social responsibility, effective communication, multicultural competency, intellectual growth, and clarified values. Additional areas including enhanced self-esteem, realistic self-appraisal, healthy behavior and satisfying lifestyles, interdependence, spiritual awareness, personal and educational goals, and career choices were also covered.

In 2016, NACA's Research and Scholarship Group released a new resource with a specific focus on career skills (Peck, Kane, & Davis, 2016). Called NACA NEXT (Navigating Employability eXperience Tool), the tool focuses on skills that match those identified by NACA as being most important to employers. This accomplishes at least two desired effects: (a) it helps students and advisors become more aware of how learning in campus activities helps students become career ready, and (b) it considerably narrows the quantity of learning outcomes. It is hoped that these effects may unify learning outcomes assessment in campus activities in ways that may make the impact of the profession as a whole more evident.

This project is also notable in another respect. The tool functions in an entirely electronic, online format. This makes it easier to determine how many institutions and individuals are using the tool and also allows for the collection of aggregate data about how advisors are rating students and how students are rating themselves. This provides a new source of robust, trustworthy data about what students are learning from their participation in campus activities. The guide is set up like a rubric on which student behavior can be scored by either advisors or the students themselves. When advisors evaluate students, it produces direct measures of learning that can be used by the individual advisor, the student, the institution, and NACA. When students use the tool as a self-assessment, they are provided with resources—including videos, articles, and NACA training and other resources—that are targeted toward and appropriate for their level of development. Advisors can see these resources as well, and can use them to create learning opportunities for their students. Suggestions for how this might be used to measure students' career readiness will be discussed later in this chapter.

The Project CEO benchmarking study discussed in Chapter 3 in this book and the data produced by NACA NEXT could produce a wealth of data about how students participating in campus activities develop and learn, especially with regard to those skills desired by employers. But perhaps even more exciting and impactful is how providing a turnkey assessment resource may encourage programs across the country to adopt common learning outcomes and definitions and, consequently, help to unify learning outcomes in campus activities. By providing to campus activities programs well-defined learning outcomes that can be independently measured across institutions and programs, educators in this area can articulate the role their experiences play in providing relevant skills to students. The sections that follow will discuss how each of these skills is being developed in campus activities and how they can be measured.

EMPLOYABILITY SKILLS DERIVED FROM CAMPUS ACTIVITIES

Verbal Communication

The field of campus activities runs on the power of ideas. For ideas to compete in this atmosphere, the proponent of these ideas must be able to explain them in a clear and compelling way. This is a rich atmosphere for developing communication skills. Students who are actively participating in their campus programming board or other organizations that plan events on campus will have the opportunity to propose events and explain the merits of these events to the group. Students leading these events will need to be prepared to give updates on the progress of an event, recruit members to volunteer for various aspects of the event, and lead brainstorming sessions to deal with issues as they arise.

One challenge that exists for any functional area is ensuring that all students have an equal opportunity to develop each of the desired skills. One way that Stephen F. Austin State University has addressed this challenge is by requiring each member of the campus programming board to propose and lead at least one event each year in order to maintain membership in the organization. This requires at least two presentations. The first is made to the officers of the organization, who may offer constructive feedback and refinements before the student is able to present to the entire programming board. This allows the students to refine their communication skills and also has the added benefit of providing a basis for assessment, which is discussed later in this section.

Students who move up the ranks of the organization get a few special opportunities to develop verbal communication skills. While fewer students will have these experiences, they are deeply impactful. For example, some students will have the chance to introduce a prominent entertainer, comedian, or speaker in front of an enthusiastic crowd.

Students can also gain verbal communication skills by presenting an educational session at a regional or national conference, either as a group or in tandem with their advisor. The process often involves submitting a written proposal that demonstrates that the students understand the subject matter on which they'll be presenting, but it also requires that they be able to put these abstract ideas into words. These presentations are often extemporaneous rather than scripted. While students work from notes, they still have to decide in the moment how they want to put this information into words.

■ ■■ COMMON EXPERIENCES

Avery serves as the chair of the concerts committee of the Student Activities Board on her campus. She was inspired to run for her position by her love of music and her interest in pursuing concert production as a career after college. She had given little thought to developing communication skills in this role. At the first event of the year, she was given the chance to introduce one of her favorite comedians when he performed on her campus. Before she went walked out on stage, the artist gave her a quick primer on how to make an introduction. He told her to wait until the lights came up to start talking, hold her note card so the crowd could see her face and added, "When you say my name, you'll get a big cheer—so save that for last." While she was really nervous before going on stage, it made her really proud afterward. She later told friends that she couldn't believe she had the opportunity to speak in front of such a large crowd. Years after graduation, she still uses the advice she learned from the comedian when she is called on to introduce others. She enjoys telling others how she learned this skill.

Workflow Planning

Student events are often complex. Imagine a student group that puts on the annual homecoming festivities, including a large outdoor concert, fireworks display, canned food drive, and daily activities to promote school spirit on campus. To be effective, leaders of each aspect of the overall initiative will need to work closely with the students who are assisting them in accomplishing their part of the homecoming experience. They'll also need to understand what is going on with the festivities overall. This will require the group to plan, organize, and prioritize the work. The officer in charge of marketing cannot complete marketing materials or write press releases until the full calendar of events has been designed and a theme has been chosen. Student leaders in charge of arranging for lights and sound for the concert will rely on those booking the artist, whose contract will specify what is needed. Even in this intentionally simplified scenario, the complexities quickly become overwhelming.

Unlike some other outcomes in campus activities where the link between what students do and what they learn may not be as intuitive, the skill of workflow planning is so inexorably linked with the work that student programming boards do that it is unlikely that any student who was engaged with the work of the group wouldn't learn something about it. A common technique for planning a major event is to make a detailed, minute-by-minute timeline of the event. In the case of very complex events, groups may create a timeline that details the months leading up to the event. Some of the learning that emerges in this sort of process involves considering the sequencing of key elements of the event—for example, in what order do major aspects of the event need to occur? Such questions require the group to walk through the abstractions of the event and make them concrete so issues can be anticipated.

Students in both formal and informal leadership positions within their groups, whether they are ongoing leadership roles like presidents and vice presidents of the student group or students tasked to lead major initiatives, will have the opportunity to do more than just observe the organization of major activities—they will need to develop the skills to carry them out. A frequent learning outcome from these kinds of leadership experiences is the ability to delegate. This involves assigning work to individuals whose abilities and interests suggest they'll be successful and following up with them to ensure that the work is successfully completed. This is a challenging and important learning activity for students. Some leaders may try to over-manage or micromanage, or the magnitude of the task may overwhelm them and, rather than depending on their fellow students for assistance, they shut down and work alone. The ability to delegate effectively is often a struggle for newer student leaders and some may complete their leadership experience without mastering this skill. But for those who do, they possess a skill that is highly coveted.

■ ■■ COMMON EXPERIENCES

Dan has been a member of his campus programming board for all 4 years that he has been at his institution. This year, he was selected to organize Music Fest. This is a major annual event on campus featuring a full day of music from a variety of acts. Additionally, there are vendors selling food and merchandise, prize giveaways, carnival rides, and games. Planning requires meticulous attention to detail.

Dan remembers his early days on the programming board and wonders how he was able to survive his first event. He was responsible for planning a community service project where his organization cleaned up a local park. He remembers with embarrassment how poorly the event went. He miscommunicated the start time and the community partner was left waiting for the group. He forgot the garbage bags in the office and had to go back to retrieve them. Finally, his failure to provide enough gloves for the whole group left many feeling frustrated. After the event, Dan set up a meeting with the group's advisor, who walked him through an event planning checklist that had been provided to him when he volunteered to coordinate the event. Dan admitted that he didn't think he needed the checklist since the event was relatively simple.

With each event Dan planned afterward, he got better at anticipating issues, clearly delegating to others, and tracking their progress. As he watched the last band perform at Music Fest, he was overwhelmed by a sense of pride at what he and his organization had accomplished and how far his organizational skills had advanced since his first year.

Teamwork

Campus activities work provides students with challenging and compelling experiences that require them to work together in order to accomplish meaningful goals. For many on the campus programming board, the first task of teamwork is likely learning how to serve as an effective member of the team. Teamwork involves discovering what skills and abilities the individual possesses and how they can be applied to the goals and objectives of the group. The popularity of programs such as Strengths Quest, an assessment to identify and harness one's talents, underscores the emphasis that educators have placed on understanding and maximizing students' personal strengths.

Leaders in campus activities are encouraged to identify strengths in others and leverage these to accomplish the group's goals. They must also assist the group in developing a compelling and shared vision, goals that lead to the accomplishment of that vision, and the strategies for accomplishing those goals.

For many groups, a concerted effort to develop the team takes place each year as new leaders assume their roles. At the beginning of a new year, student leaders and their advisors frequently hold retreats that address teamwork and the many allied skills that contribute to teamwork. Leading team-building activities is an expected competency of any skilled campus activities professional and many student leaders as well. These activities endeavor to teach skills that support the development of the team, such as listening, dealing with setbacks, harnessing creativity, solving problems, uniting visions, setting goals, and resolving conflicts, among many others.

■ ■■ COMMON EXPERIENCES

Devon and Kiesha recently broke up after dating for almost a year. They had become a couple after working closely together on the campus programming board. Since their breakup, it has become harder for them to work together effectively. This is especially troubling because both are currently serving as members of the executive board. Making matters worse, individual members of the programming board are starting to take sides. Alana, the president of the Student Programming Board, is troubled by what is happening. She asks Devon and Kiesha to stay after the weekly meeting to discuss the impact their breakup is having on the team. She helps them realize that for the group to function properly, they need to work to ensure that their personal issues don't divide the group. Each of the students involved learned how easily the chemistry of a group can be impacted by interpersonal issues.   ■ ■ ■

Information Processing

When one thinks about the ability to obtain and process information, the examples that come to mind likely involve experiences inside the classroom. Activities such as learning to use the library, researching papers, and critically evaluating the claims of others based on evidence can help to develop this skill. This kind of learning is often referred to as *information literacy* and the classroom can be an excellent arena to learn this skill. But a variety of experiences in campus activities can develop this capacity as well.

Students who participate in campus activities may research any number of issues related to event production. As many campus activities professionals can attest, work in this field can lead to some strange quests. A student leader may be tasked with finding a petting zoo for parents' weekend, finding a company that makes custom bobble-heads for the first basketball game, or finding the most cost-effective way to purchase glow sticks in bulk for a dance party. This requires not only web research skills but also the ability to critically evaluate what one is reading. Sourcing and evaluating vendors' marketing claims can provide the opportunity for students to develop the skill of obtaining and processing information.

A vivid example of the opportunity to obtain and evaluate information can be found at regional and national NACA conventions. These events can be powerful learning experiences for students who are selected by their institutions to attend. Attendees watch showcases of a variety of acts, including bands, comedians, and speakers, and participate in a Campus Activities Market Place that features products and events, like custom printed T-shirts or laser tag arenas, that appeal to college students.

These showcases provide a short sample of what the artist or agency is offering. The goal of a showcase is for participants to see performers at their very best. This means high-quality lights, staging, and sound.

A significant application of the skill of processing the information taken in at a showcase is to think about how a particular act would look in the performing environment of the student's own campus. While many campuses may have top-quality performance venues at their disposal, for those that do not, the students need to ask themselves, "Would this performer still be as impressive in a more stripped down environment?" They may also need to ask questions like, "Is this performer right for the particular event for which we are considering them?" or more directly, "Would students come to see an act like this?"

■ ■ ■ COMMON EXPERIENCES

Mike chairs the Coffeehouse Committee on his campus. A recent assessment showed that students were growing bored of the usual entertainment—acoustic singer/songwriters—provided at the monthly coffeehouse. As a result, Mark decides to peruse programs from previous NACA regional and national conferences to see what kind of entertainment might be available and how much it might cost. He finds a magician who is in his price range and, using the NACA website, looks up when the artist is scheduled to perform in his area, so he can save his group money when booking a performance. ■ ■ ■

Decision Making and Problem Solving

From selecting artists for performances to considering ways to manage risk in campus events, decision making is central to the work of a student programming board. The group has to choose among many options when making these decisions. While some decisions may have relatively low stakes, some have significant implications. Consider the programming board at a large university that is considering bringing a popular band to campus for a major outdoor concert and selling tickets to underwrite the costs of the event. It is not unusual for such an event to cost hundreds of thousands of dollars. If the group does not accurately forecast ticket sales, they may not only be bankrupted by the event but also not have sufficient funds to pay for other events, which could cause them to default on other contracts. While the details of such a decisions are dramatic when viewed through the lens of major events on large campuses, a microcosmic version could be just as devastating to a smaller school.

Within this scenario exist multiple levels of critical decisions. Should the event in question be undertaken at all? If so, what artist should be chosen in order to hit necessary targets in ticket sales? At what percentage of ticket sales should the budget be set? In other words, how many tickets does the group need to sell before it breaks even? What price should the ticket be (understanding that a higher ticket price helps the group break even more quickly, but may also mean that fewer students will want to buy tickets)? Certainly it is imperative that well-trained advisors assist students in these important decisions, especially to the extent that they are charged with managing financial risk on behalf of the institution, but students are critical decision makers in these situations as well.

Managing health and safety risks is also a key decision-making outcome for student leaders. Students have to determine how likely or severe certain risks are, then develop strategies to either eliminate or mitigate these risks. When individuals participate in activities, they assume that these events will be safe. The ability of students planning the event to think through risks that may be associated with a given activity is a common element of most events, and on many campus programming boards the process of foreseeing risks is crowdsourced to the largest number of people—the entire programming board.

The weather forecast for the day of the event also presents decision-making opportunities for student leaders. Making the call to postpone or cancel an event due to inclement weather is tricky, and there is no simple framework for making this kind of decision. It involves consulting with experts, determining the risks, and making the best decision possible under the circumstances. Experienced student affairs professionals frequently have stories about the times their determination to cancel an event or move it indoors due to weather went awry. Many will also be quick to point out that weather prediction is far from a certainty. Many different considerations are bundled into weather decisions. The safety of participants is key, but accidents that hurt students and visitors also bring negative press and damage the reputation of the institution and the student organization. Being involved in this kind of decision helps students develop decision-making skills.

■ ■■ COMMON EXPERIENCES

Sarah is the leader of the Film Committee, which is planning an outdoor showing of a movie. The movie is scheduled to start at 10 p.m. and end around 11:30 p.m. A few days before the event, the group begins to consult weather websites and determines that there is a 30% chance for rain. To make matters more complex, the movie company's contract stipulates that if the crew sets up the equipment, the institution will be liable for the full cost of the production. If it rains, the event will have to be stopped and the school's money will not be refunded. The group needs to make a decision 24 hours in advance to allow for any alternative plans. Sarah consults a meteorology professor, who tells her that while rain is likely during the day, it seems most likely to dissipate in the afternoon. But after 11 p.m., then the chance of rain will increase considerably. Based on Sarah's analysis of the situation, the group moves the event to 9 p.m. and is able to hold the event as scheduled.

Career-Specific Knowledge

In the Introduction to this book, Kruger and Peck discussed that impacting career readiness offers a number of benefits for student affairs in general. First and foremost, it benefits the students themselves. But helping students develop in their careers also helps a variety of higher education stakeholders understand the purpose of work in campus activities.

Experience in campus activities can help students prepare for a number of careers. Students frequently pursue careers in marketing, hospitality, entertainment, event planning, education, and many other fields. Students who participate on the student programming board have the opportunity to gain a variety of transferable skills that apply to any number of occupations. These skills include customer service, conflict management, professionalism, and personal and professional goal setting. Of course, the more intentionally these skills are developed, the more meaningful participation in campus activities will be for the students involved.

For students who become more deeply involved in these experiences, a new echelon of experience may open up to them. Students may pursue formal leadership experiences that help them develop the kinds of skills that lead to specific careers. For example, most programming boards have public relations and marketing officers, who inform and persuade their peers to participate in the group's programs and events, treasurers who track organizational expenses, and "member relations" or similar officers who may have elements of training and human resources in their job description.

When looking at whether students develop skills from the campus programming board that benefit them in their careers, there is little value in speculating whether students will find these skills useful. A far better way to approach this topic is to reach out to students who have been in the workforce for two or more years to learn whether they have had the chance to apply their skills. A qualitative approach could produce descriptive data that can help identify areas of student learning that can be assessed with current students. Student feedback can also provide guidance in creating learning activities that can help promote learning in the areas they identify. Some research questions might include the following:

1. What skills do these alumni attribute to their participation in the campus programming board?
2. What specific experiences within the programming board helped these alumni to develop these skills?
3. What training was helpful in developing these skills?
4. How useful have these skills been to these alumni in their current jobs?
5. What skills do alumni wish they had developed?
6. What can be done to help current students develop these skills more effectively?

These broad questions can guide a conversation that can lead to better understanding of how students are changed by these experiences, provide stories and descriptions that help campus activities professionals demonstrate that change to others, and help design new student learning.

■ ■■ COMMON EXPERIENCES

For some students, their roles do more than just give them transferable skills that could be used in their career; they directly prepare them for their career. Erin was an active participant in her campus activities board in college. While she liked many aspects of planning events, she found herself most drawn to the technical aspects of event production. Her favorite was figuring out what lights and sound were needed for musical acts. The more she did it, the more her expertise grew. Soon, she was an indispensable resource for her programming board. It was just presumed that she would handle any technical issues. Unbeknownst to Erin, the production company that was often hired by the university to produce these events had noticed her expertise as well. They began to hire her to work with their events outside the university and when she graduated, brought her on full time.

Quantitative Analysis

Twenty years ago, it might have been hard to imagine students gaining quantitative data skills from participating in campus activities. In the wake of the assessment era in student affairs, this connection becomes more relevant. Many institutions are involving student leaders in the collection and evaluation of assessment. This is a fruitful area for assisting students in developing quantitative literacy.

Campus programming boards and other groups that plan events on their campus could benefit from increases in quantitative skills in many ways. Student leaders who develop these skills will find that they are relatively rare among new college graduates, are in high demand, and make them very marketable. Additionally, by evaluating the success of previous events and initiatives, the quality of future events and initiatives will improve. Student leaders in campus activities can use these skills to assess the needs and wants of their campus, to evaluate the effectiveness of programs, and to predict and measure what their fellow students should learn from a variety of experiences.

General members of programming boards are more likely to gain quantitative reasoning skills as consumers of assessment than from developing or conducting assessments themselves. Of course, the more students are exposed to learning opportunities in this area, the more successful these sorts of initiatives will be. Quantitative reasoning skills develop as students seek to use data to make decisions. It is unknown how many programming boards use a consistent method of evaluating and assessing the success of their events or how many make the reporting of these data a regular agenda item in their meetings, but both would help students develop these skills.

As students' proficiency grows, they can start to assume more leadership for assessing events. Few boards have formal leadership positions dedicated to assessment. This is a missed opportunity. Such a position can help harness students' energy to accomplish necessary assessment, which can prove helpful for activities professionals who, like many others in student affairs, see their responsibilities grow while resources decline.

Gaining skills in quantitative reasoning is complex business. Unlike many other outcomes, the context for this kind of learning does not naturally occur in campus activities. Professionals will need to be very intentional in order to make it happen. There are common pitfalls regarding quantitative methods that must be overcome. For example, students often fail to consider whether a sample size is sufficient to draw meaningful conclusions about the subject of interest. Instead, they tend to be drawn to the percentage of responses. To illustrate this point, a survey of students may show that 85% of participants enjoyed the previous evening's event that more than 5,000 students attended. Students must be trained to ask how many individuals completed the survey in order to determine if the results are valid. The use of an online sample size calculator shows that if students are willing to accept a margin of error of 5%, a minimum sample of 357 would be necessary. Student surveys often have sample sizes that are much smaller than this. If they aren't trained to think about sample size, students are likely to base their decisions off highly dubious information.

Another common issue is that students will fail to ensure that their conclusions are supported by the data. For example, a student researching whether his or her peers would support an increase in the student activities fee might ask, "Do you think more money should be dedicated to student activities on campus?" Students, who generally like going to activities, might answer favorably, with 62% saying "yes" to this statement. Based on this information, the student reports that the vast majority of students are supportive of the new fee. While this might be true, because the student's question never mentioned a fee, it would not be accurate to draw this conclusion.

Another common issue is that of leading questions. Students often don't intend to ask leading questions, they just don't know how to recognize and limit their personal biases. Continuing with the example of the referendum to increase the activities fee, in an effort to gather students support, a survey is conducted. Higher levels of support would be helpful to the students, so instead of asking a question like "Would you support an increase in the student activities fee of 25 cents per credit hour?" they might ask the question in a way that is more likely to produce the desired result, such as, "Do you support increasing the student activities fee 25 cents per credit hour to put our school on an equal footing with other schools of our size?" An intentionally skewed survey is called a "push poll," and most consider it to be unethical. Teaching students about how to write questions in a neutral way is important.

Bad scales are also a common issue. Many graduate programs train students to ensure that scales are always "mutually exclusive" and "collectively exhaustive." That means that each answer is different from each other and together they represent all of the answers a person should want to give. The first issue often occurs when offering ranges. Overlapping categories is a common mistake. For example, in looking at ages, the following categories may be offered: "15–20 years old" and "20–25 years old." In this scenario, a student who is 20 wouldn't know which category to answer. The second issue can be addressed by providing students an opportunity to select "other" and give any reasons that may be unanticipated by the researcher.

A final issue is learning to ask if a sample is random. While there may be good reasons to look at what a select group thinks and draw a "purposeful" sample from those responses, a random sample is essential if you want to apply the results to the entire population. Looking at the example of the survey following the major event, even if the group could reach the 357 returned surveys needed to get a representative sample, what if the surveys were only given to students who stayed after the event to get the band's autograph? Would this not skew the results? Indeed, it would. The surveyors have to make sure that each person has an equal opportunity to be selected.

Identifying common pitfalls in assessment can help students become better collectors of quantitative data and better evaluators of these data as well. Certainly those wanting to go deeper can gain proficiency and skill in conducting valid research, but these considerations can establish a baseline of competency in this area. Advisors can train their students to ask these questions about quantitative research projects:

- Is the sample sufficient to draw meaningful conclusions?
- Are the conclusions supported by evidence?
- Are the questions leading or neutral?
- Are the scales "mutually exclusive" and "collectively exhaustive?"
- Is the sample random?

■ ■ ■ **COMMON EXPERIENCES**

Gloriana is a student majoring in marketing who is also involved in her campus programming board. In her classes, she learned how to evaluate the effectiveness of media campaigns. She decided to apply what she had learned to look at how her organization's events were being marketed to students. She determined that social media offered the greatest return on the group's investment of time and money—yet the group was not fully utilizing its social media presence. Her research helped improve attendance at events and also gave her a way to demonstrate her skills to potential employers.

Selling and Influencing

It is safe to say that most campuses have an area where students can gather and promote their events and initiatives. This area is often awash with activity. Students distribute handbills (small advertisements for upcoming events) and engage one on one with students they often don't know, to try to persuade them to attend events. Through this sort of experience, the most successful students learn how to craft a message that is specifically tailored to each person they encounter. This experience is so common that, at some point in their membership in the group, most students will participate in this kind of activity.

Some of the students who influence others in this environment are explicitly selling. They may be selling tickets to an event, baked goods for a fundraiser, or T-shirts promoting an organization or event. The process of convincing their fellow students to part with their money isn't an easy one. For those students not selling an actual product, they are still selling themselves. They seek out students they know and try to link their affinity for each other to a desire to support whatever cause they are advocating. For strangers, they try to make a personal connection that may cause the stranger to stop and hear more about what they are selling. Some settle for handing off a quick flyer to people who are busily scurrying past. For anyone who has ever had a job in sales, these experiences may sound very familiar.

Students who participate on programming boards also are frequently involved in marketing events. At a basic level, they may be hanging flyers and other promotional materials at various campus locations. Those who are approaching this job conspicuously are thinking about where they can place their marketing in a way that complies with the rules but maximizes visibility. Discussions in programming board meetings often center on how to reach desirable groups of students with marketing and personal appeals. Students gain the skill of crafting a message for a particular audience and bringing those marketing messages to life through their marketing and publicity experiences.

Most programming boards have formal leadership positions dedicated to marketing and public relations. Some have separate positions for both. Students who fill these roles have the opportunity to gain skills in leadership and influence in both respects discussed here. Like many leaders, they have to learn to practice influencing volunteers and other leaders to accomplish their goals—and they are influencing through sales and marketing.

Not to overstate the point, but those outside of the field of campus activities often do not think about the magnitude of sales for students and professionals in this field. It is very common for programs to support their event through ticket sales. Whether it's a very small school producing a dance that costs a few hundred dollars or a major university producing a concert with a six-figure budget, the consequences of failing to sell the number of tickets projected can have considerable impact. The fact that there are real consequences of failure in this context makes these experiences extremely compelling to students, essentially demanding that they persuade others or face serious consequences.

Influence can take many forms. It is related to leadership and has elements of persuasion and marketing. In his book *Developing the Leader Within You*, leadership expert John C. Maxwell (1993) wrote, "*Leadership is influence*. . . . Nothing more; nothing less" (p. 1). Many in the field of student activities see teaching leadership as among their primary responsibilities. Many good models for developing student leadership through cocurricular experiences already exist and quite a few are discussed in other chapters in this book. Additionally, as has been mentioned previously, the rubrics in the appendix can be applied to any number of artifacts of learning, such as students' writing about their ability to influence others, portfolios, and other projects in which students can demonstrate what they know about influencing others.

A more creative and unusual approach can be found in adapting the processes professional advertisers use to assess the success of their creative campaigns to assess both the effectiveness of marketing used to promote events and also the learning and development of those who design these campaigns.

Advertisers are interested in knowing how people learn about their product so they can focus their message in these media. One way this can be accomplished is by putting a different web address on different versions of the media message that offers some incentive for visiting the website. It could be a chance to win a private meet and greet with the artist, a discount on tickets, or another desirable prize. By doing this, the number of visits to the website can be tracked. If tickets to an event are being sold online, the number that click a link to purchase them can also be easily tracked.

Additionally, an easy way to direct students to these various websites is through quick response (QR) codes—barcodes that direct people to a designated website when scanned with a smartphone. Free QR code generators can easily be found online with a quick web search. When QR codes are embedded on posters, handbills, or even a Facebook page or website, they can track from what media students are most likely to have learned about a particular event.

■ ■■ COMMON EXPERIENCES

Kiet was interested in increasing school pride on campus. While researching some of the traditions of the school, he learned that, at one point, the school had kept a live version of its mascot, a bear, in a cage on campus. He knew that students and administrators alike wouldn't want an actual bear on campus, but he recognized that the story was unique and compelling. He rallied his fellow students to raise money to commission a sculpture commemorating the campus tradition, suggesting the placement in a large but underutilized plaza on campus. After the money had been raised and the statue completed, the location became a popular location for students to hang out and hold spirit-related events. His influence not only resulted in raising money for an initiative he cared about, but also influenced students' feelings of pride for decades of students to follow.

■ ■■

Computer Software Skills

It's clear that one area in which many presume today's college students have an advantage over their more experienced counterparts in the workforce is technology. However, though many can Skype, manage multiple social media accounts, and download music and movies without paying for them, can they use the kind of technology that matters to business leaders?

Educators can't simply define "computer skills" as any skill that relates to using computers. In the present age, this designation is simply too broad. The kinds of computer skills that employers are looking for are so much simpler that they could be easily taken for granted. On the basic end, do students know how to use word processing programs? Spreadsheets? Presentation software? Many might be surprised at the number of students who cannot use these basic programs.

On the more complex end, students who participate in campus activities have the opportunity to do more complex work with computers. Those who can make movies, use design software and web-based design tools, and manage social media will find these skills in demand. It's not hard to imagine how students who participate in campus activities might gain and benefit from these skills.

In recent years, a number of schools have begun to use organization management software for student leaders to communicate with those who participate in their organization, to advertise events and initiatives on the platform, and to provide paperless access to common paperwork provided by the university. At schools that use organization management software, members are often required to establish an account and manage their involvement with the organization. This at least provides a baseline of computer skill.

One way schools can enhance students' computer proficiency is to provide online training platforms with short educational videos that target specific skills students want to gain. For schools that want to do this, a good place to start is with a call to human resources to see if the institution already has established memberships in these kinds of programs and whether students have access. Schools that would like to accomplish these outcomes on a budget can use content available on video-sharing websites (such as YouTube, which students can access for free). Simply making a list of videos with common skills and providing it to students as a menu can prove very beneficial.

■ ■■ **COMMON EXPERIENCES**

Molly is a student who is responsible for tracking the number of volunteer hours in her organization. At first, she was using a tablet of paper to write down the hours, but when she was asked for reports, she had to make each one from scratch. Her advisor was surprised to learn that Molly had never used a spreadsheet and took a few minutes to teach her how to insert formulas. As the year progressed, Molly became increasingly proficient with the spreadsheet software. Now she uses it for all sorts of things and teaches other students how to use it.

■ ■ ■

Writing and Editing Reports

Learning to write is one of the most important outcomes of college and is central to students' academic experience. From introductory courses in rhetoric and composition to a myriad of research papers and other writing assignments, students will have the opportunity to develop writing skills from their classes. Many colleges and universities encourage "writing across the curriculum," where faculty are encouraged to require writing, even in those disciplines where it may not necessarily be expected. But what would writing across the cocurriculum look like? For educators who want to apply the structure of this project to campus activities, the prompts for writing are plentiful. Essentially, these projects can be developed by asking what skills we'd like students to be better able to articulate. The articulation of skills is a significant issue in the effort to make students more aware of what they are learning in cocurricular programs.

As this chapter demonstrates, students who participate in their campus programming boards have many experiences that can lead to gaining important and valuable skills. Writing about these skills can cause reflection that can help them understand what they are learning and also impact their ability to explain what they are learning to others. In this way, an emphasis on writing in student activities can have a positive impact on all the other outcomes as well. It also contributes to assessment of student learning in this area.

A concept that has become popular in recent years is called a "minute paper." This is a writing assignment for which students have to write for one minute. The time can be somewhat flexible, but the intention is to encourage students to get straight to the point and to put their effort into discovering insights rather than the quality of the writing itself. These papers can be great for tagging on to the end of a meeting, at the conclusion of a learning activity, or as an effective last-minute assessment. Some useful prompts might be questions like, "What have you learned about the role of influence in leadership?" or "How effectively do you manage your time? How have you improved? How would you like to improve further?" The answers can provide evidence of learning that can be measured with the rubrics provided in the appendix.

Another concept that can blend learning and assessment activities is the student leader performance review. These reviews can provide students feedback about how they are doing in a given role while simultaneously letting students learn how to diplomatically and clearly give feedback to others. This can go beyond just an evaluation of officers by the president of the organization. When this concept incorporates 360-degree feedback in which officers evaluate each other, students receive more feedback and more practice at providing feedback. Additionally, it can be an effective way for general members to provide feedback to the leaders of the organization.

Some would argue that the ability to write effectively is a relatively rare skill. Students who develop this skill in college will find that when they seek employment, this skill can differentiate them from even those with more experience in their career field. Campus activities professionals who make a conscientious effort to create opportunities for participants and leaders to develop this skill will be providing an advantage to involved students in gaining employment after college.

■ ■ ■ COMMON EXPERIENCES

Latoya was responsible for soliciting sponsors for the campus movie series. She began by visiting local businesses and explaining the benefits of advertising with the group. Many would ask her if she had any materials she could leave with them. Previous officers had not developed any, so Latoya created a simple one-sheet publication that explained the costs and benefits of advertising in the film series. She worked with her advisor to refine it, catch any spelling mistakes, and ensure that the wording was clear. Her efforts resulted in more advertising revenue than in previous years. ■ ■ ■

ASSESSING EMPLOYABILITY SKILLS AS AN OUTCOME OF CAMPUS ACTIVITIES

Hopefully, at this point in the chapter, a case has been successfully made that learning from participation in campus activities is abundant. The challenge lies in deciding what to measure and how to measure it. Clearly, the authors do not suggest that campus activities educators measure each of the 10 skills discussed in this chapter, but each is discussed as a guide for developing valid outcomes assessments for any outcomes educators may want to study.

Assessing Verbal Communication

There are many experiences in campus activities and event planning that can help students develop the skill of verbal communication. There are also assessment measures that can easily be implemented that not only provide evidence of student learning but also can help students improve. Direct assessment strategies work best because they seek to measure observable student behavior. An added advantage is that these strategies do not require advisors to set up artificial scenarios; advisors can simply observe students applying the skill and find ways to measure their abilities. When possible, it is very useful to compare previous examples so students can see how they are growing and developing.

An important first step in creating a direct assessment strategy is to establish a rubric. This book includes rubrics for each of the skills discussed. The process may sound complicated, but as with many skills, practitioners will also become more confident in their abilities as they become more experienced.

As previously discussed, Stephen F. Austin requires each member of its campus programming board to propose at least one event each year. This necessitates two presentations: one to the officers of the organization and a second to the membership as a whole. Students are coached by the officers on how they can improve their presentations. This may include notes on both the content of the proposal (ways to make the event better) and the delivery of the presentation. The presentation is also scored on a rubric designed for this purpose. For proposals that require significant refinement, another presentation to the officers may be necessary.

During the presentation to the membership, all members score the proposal on a rubric. This is used to determine if the event will be accepted and therefore produced by the group. It also provides a kind of pretest/posttest assessment of the students' improvements between the officer presentation and the presentations to the member-ship at large. This is an excellent example of an assessment activity that accomplishes three very important goals: It provides direct evidence of student learning in the area of verbal communication, it helps the student to improve, and it is embedded in the work of the group such that it does not require extra work from the advisor.

When articulating learning outcomes for campus activities, there is strong support for verbal communication as a learning outcome that should not be overlooked. It is imperative that campus activities profes-sionals develop strategies for measuring this skill in order to demon-strate the impact these experiences make on students.

Assessing Workflow Planning

Because events and activities are both the product and the context of student learning in this field, well-planned post-event analysis is imper-ative and a best practice of the best campus activities programs. But this analysis can prove challenging. In the fast-paced world of campus activ-ities, there may be a temptation to move on to the next event—giving the previous event a cursory 5-minute discussion before proceeding. But the potential for campus activities to develop the learning outcome of workflow planning will require a process that is given more value and which has been carefully designed for this purpose.

Post-event assessment works best when learning experiences and data collection are blended together. An example of this can be found at Bradley University, where student groups are provided with an electronic form that prompts them to evaluate their event. From the event-planning process, the timing of the event, the marketing of the event, and students' responses to the event, students can think about how their event can be improved in the future. This provides a valuable learning experience and naturally produces meaningful data that can be used to target training for student groups to improve in the future.

This process is intuitive, is not unduly onerous or time consuming, and helps students improve the next time they organize an event.

Programming groups on college campuses have to manage complex and challenging events. For those who want to improve the chances that students will develop these skills, providing some guidance for the planning and sequencing of events can be very effective. Ensuring meaningful discussion of the successes and failures of each event is also a valuable learning experience that should not be overlooked.

Assessing Teamwork

Considering the goals of the group, effectively measuring the goals will rely on some skill in developing them. A common framework called S.M.A.R.T. goals was developed by George Doran. In this framework, Doran (1981) suggested that goals must be "specific, measurable, attainable, relevant, and time-bound" (p. 36). If groups follow this guidance, by definition they should be able to determine if a goal was accomplished (specific) and be able to prove that the goal was met (measurable). Additionally, the group would only set goals that it means to accomplish (attainable) and that could be accomplished within the time frame in which the group was operating (time-bound). Finally, the group must be able to demonstrate that the goals were connected to the vision of the group (relevant).

So how can this be put into action? The group should develop a compelling vision statement that explains what the group could look like in one year; identify three to five goals that, if accomplished, would advance the group in the direction of the vision; and define a maximum of three strategies for each goal that represent practical steps to accomplish these goals. For example, members of the group may establish the vision that they want to become the first choice for entertainment among the students at the university. In pursuit of that vision, they may establish a goal such as "increase the total number of students who attend events from 16,000 students last year to 20,000 students in the current year." In support of that goal, they'd need to establish some strategies, such as "create a major event in the spring similar to homecoming that has a total attendance of at least 2,500 students" and "improve the marketing of the movie series in residence halls, resulting in a total increase of 1,500 students per year." Assuming these goals are attainable, it is clear that if they accomplished these two strategies, they would meet their goals. The strategies lead to the accomplishment of the goal and the goal leads to accomplishing the vision. At the end of the year, the group will be able to see how many of their goals were met. Likewise, they can see how many of the strategies were accomplished. This provides a quantifiable measure of success for the team and could be used to produce excellent direct assessment of student learning in the activities program.

It is the job of each individual on the programming board to find ways to use his or her strengths to accomplish the group's goals. It is the job of student leaders to help establish those goals and divide the task of accomplishing them among members. When this work is done effectively, the work is more meaningful to the students because it becomes more than just a loose collection of isolated learning experiences; it becomes a process for accomplishing significant and meaningful goals.

Assessing Obtaining and Processing Information

An important aspect of assessment is finding theory that explains student development within a given construct. In the area of information literacy, King and Kitchener (1994) advanced a model that can provide just such a structure. They refer to this concept as *reflective judgment*. This model is concerned with how students respond to "ill-structured problems," which are those problems that are not easily solved.

Much of what is done in campus activities presents ill-structured problems. Selecting a homecoming theme is an ill-structured problem, increasing awareness of and attendance at events is an ill-structured problem, and trying to coach improvement in members who are not upholding their responsibilities to the group is most certainly an ill-structured problem. Capitalizing on the opportunities that these problems present is the key. This likely requires a refocusing of how these kinds of issues are seen. Seeing them as learning opportunities rather than problems is an important start.

Assessing Making Decisions and Solving Problems

Because decision making is such an important learning outcome for students, it is critical that student affairs professionals find effective ways to measure it. Additionally, this outcome is not always salient to students. Assessment activity will be most effective when it helps students come to an awareness of what they are learning about decision making.

Adopting a framework for making decisions can help underscore considerations in making important decisions that the group might otherwise overlook. In the book *Decisions Matter: Using a Decision-Making Framework With Contemporary Student Affairs Case Studies*, Vaccaro, McCoy, Champagne, and Siegel (2013) discussed four stages for making important decisions: "identification of the problem, comprehensive scan of options, implementation [of solutions], and assessment [of the impact of solutions]" (p. 27). There are certainly other models for making decisions, but the strength of this approach is its simplicity. Students will become more and more comfortable if this framework is routinely applied to important decisions.

A simple way to see if student leaders have improved their decision-making ability would be to ask them to evaluate a case study prior to learning about the decision-making framework and a second case study at the end of the year, to see if they are better able to work through issues more effectively by using the decision-making framework. While every decision may not require such a methodical approach, for those that do, this resource can be very helpful.

While older, nontraditional students may have had a lot of life experience in making decisions, the opportunity for traditional-aged college students to make decisions that impact thousands of dollars and make life-or-death decisions affecting many others might not be present without cocurricular experiences. In campus activities, these sorts of learning experiences are abundant. Focusing on these experiences can help students develop a skill that is in high demand and will benefit them in any number of experiences beyond college.

According to King and Kitchener (1994), "Reflective judgments are made by examining and evaluating relevant information, opinion, and available explanations (the process of reflective thinking), then constructing a plausible solution for the problem at hand, acknowledging that the solution itself is open to further evaluation and scrutiny" (p. 18). Students vary in their ability to do this. The progression of ability is described in seven stages that are divided across three levels. The three levels are pre-reflective reasoning, quasi-reflective reasoning, and reflective thinking. In the pre-reflective reasoning stage, individuals see knowledge as certain and knowable and largely trust the opinion of experts in order to determine what to think or believe. In the quasi-reflective stage, individuals begin to reframe knowledge as more subjective and understand that they can be manipulated by others and also that they may construct their own understanding of the world in a way that favors what they already believe or what they want to believe. This may cause them to become skeptical of information, but they do not yet have the ability to manage that uncertainty to determine what they believe. At the reflective thinking stage, individuals are able to move beyond the paralysis associated with the uncertainty of knowing and can make their best decision based on available information.

They understand that there are degrees of certainty and are comfortable with this.

King and Kitchener's (1994) model provides a way of articulating student development in the area of evaluating information. In this way, it can be very useful for assessment. A resource for measuring student's competency is the Reasoning about Current Issues Questionnaire (RCI), which has been developed specifically for this purpose. The RCI asks students about a variety of current events and categorizes their responses as falling within a particular level within the model. This process uses trained evaluators. As you might imagine, this approach is designed to describe academic skills more so than those developed in cocurricular contexts, and there is also a cost associated with administering this assessment.

The rubric for obtaining and processing information (see appendix) is based on the work of King and Kitchener. This rubric works best when evaluating artifacts of learning such as reflective writing assignments. The book *A Day in the Life of a College Student Leader: Case Studies for Undergraduate Leaders* provides many useful prompts for writing about the challenges that leaders face (Marshall and Hornak, 2008). Students can be asked to write a short but specific response about how they would handle the cases presented in the book. The nature of the issues presented can provide ample context for seeing students' thought processes in action. Advisors can also write their own unique cases if they wish, perhaps even drawing on real examples from the work of the group. The rubric can then be applied, allowing the campus activities professional to categorize the level of reflective judgment the response represents.

Assessing Career-Specific Knowledge

As discussed earlier in this chapter, NACA has created a powerful resource to assist advisors at its member institutions in assessing to what extent students feel they are developing career-specific skills and how they rate themselves in each of these areas. NACA NEXT can be used by advisors to evaluate students (thus producing direct evidence of student learning) or allow the students to rate themselves. Advisors can also reevaluate the students later as a way of producing pretest/posttest assessment and demonstrate areas in which the student has improved.

For students who use the tool as a self-assessment, it offers feedback that is specifically targeted toward each student's level of competency as it is determined by the assessment. This resource was a project of the Research and Scholarship group with the support of the NACA Board of Directors. It represents a promising model for helping students understand and track their own development in this important area. It also provides a turnkey assessment method that can prompt discussion about career learning on campus.

In a time of diminishing resources, the field of student activities can prove its impact to stakeholders and to the students themselves by collecting data about this important learning outcome and by increasing awareness of the impact of student activities on career outcomes.

Assessing Analyzing Quantitative Data

A straightforward way to test students' ability to analyze quantitative data is to design assessments that suffer from common pitfalls and provide students with the opportunity to point out any issues they notice. This assessment should be given prior to training, then repeated after an educational intervention or even at the conclusion of the year. This sort of assessment activity will be most successful, of course, if the pitfalls that are used are routinely discussed as a way to evaluate quantitative research during regular activities of the group.

While quantitative reasoning may not necessarily be a common learning outcome in campus activities, it is an important one. Higher education as a whole needs to better prepare students in this area.

Curricular and cocurricular programs alike will need to provide opportunities for students to develop in this area.

Assessing Selling and Influencing

Assessments that measure students' ability to influence others can provide valuable information to those who plan events about how to market to others, but they can also be used to measure student learning. QR codes can direct students to web-based surveys about the effectiveness of the advertising. This can be used to measure how effectively those who designed the advertisement are influencing others. While surveys usually produce indirect evidence (the opinions of the individual about his or her own learning), this kind of survey allows the receivers of these marketing messages to evaluate the effectiveness of the message. This provides direct evidence of the ability of the designers of this marketing.

Many students pursue cocurricular involvement as a means of learning about the practice of leadership. Influence is a central quality of leadership. The impact of experiences within campus activities to develop and refine this quality deserves further attention as a means of demonstrating this impact to key stakeholders and, more importantly, to the students themselves. Models for measuring what students learn can be adapted from student leadership as well as from the world of professional advertising.

Assessing Computer Skills

There are a wide variety of commercially available training platforms to help students learn how to use common computer applications. Assessment is embedded within most of these training platforms. This makes it simple for the advisor, who can run reports that show what students learned from these trainings. These assessments are often derived from specific tests of skill and produce direct evidence of what students learn. For those taking the "homegrown" approach, assessment would be easy enough to design. After watching the video, make a list of take-aways and write questions that assess whether students learned them. A link to a short web address for an online survey can be included with the menu of videos. Students can be incentivized to complete the assessment by offering a certificate of completion for the course.

Computer skills may not be the first learning outcome that individuals think of when they think of participating in campus activities. But after a little thought, experiences to refine this skill are plentiful in campus activities. This is important because the national data reported in Project CEO indicate that this is an area of weakness for colleges and universities in general.

The multitude of experiences in campus activities that rely on computer skills and that could develop these skills raises an important question: Could the relatively low number of students who indicate they are gaining computer skills from cocurricular experiences simply be lacking awareness of what they are learning? If this is so, educators could impact this outcome simply by helping students become more cognizant of the computer skills they are gaining through their involvement in student activities.

Assessing Writing and Editing Reports

The skills of writing and editing have several major advantages in terms of assessment. First, assessing these skills is as intuitive as grading a paper. Even if professionals don't have a lot of experience in grading student work, all of them will have had the experience of receiving a graded paper back from a professor. It is not a foreign concept. Second, while a concerted effort may need to be made in other areas to produce "artifacts of learning" that can be assessed, if students are writing, then this writing becomes the evidence of skill. Assessing a student's competency in this area, therefore, can be done simply by applying the rubrics provided in the appendix of this book or those assessments provided through the VALUE Rubrics of the Association of American Colleges and Universities to the artifacts of learning described in this section.

For example, Stephen F. Austin uses this sort of technique for assessing the quality of its student newspaper. A simple rubric was developed that measures the quality of writing and the quality of information contained in news stories. For the advisor of the newspaper, who was trained as a journalism professor, this made assessment intuitive. Campus activities professionals can do the same thing with press releases, Facebook posts, or other writing that naturally occurs within the program.

CONCLUSION

Time and time again, we hear about employers in the global marketplace who are less than satisfied with their candidates' skill levels in areas instrumental to success at their company. Work in campus activities is undoubtedly fun. But it is more than just that. Campus activities offer compelling learning experiences for students who participate and who serve in leadership roles in these groups. While many learning outcomes can be fulfilled, campus activities professionals would be wise to consider those outlined here because they help demonstrate an impact that is valued by our institutions and their key stakeholders. Doing so would also help the entire field of student activities to better tell the story of how our programs and services benefit students as a whole. And when student participation in campus activities is linked to these desired outcomes, it illustrates the potential of higher education to prepare students for happy and successful lives through experiential learning.

REFERENCES

Brill, K., Croft, L., Ogle, J., Russell Holtz, S., Smedick, B., Hicks, M., & Coats, J. (2009, March). Competency guide for college student leaders—Newest project by the NACA education advisory group. Retrieved from http://www.sbctc.edu/resources/documents/colleges-staff/commissions-councils/cusp/naca_college_student_leader_competency_guide.pdf

Doran, G. T. (1981, November). There's a S.M.A.R.T. way to write management's goals and objectives. *Management Review, 70*(11), 35–36.

Keeling, R. P. (Ed.). (2004). *Learning reconsidered: A campus-wide focus on the student experience.* Washington, DC: ACPA–College Student Educators International & NASPA–Student Affairs Administrators in Higher Education.

Keeling, R. P. (Ed.). (2006). *Learning reconsidered 2: Implementing a campus-wide focus on the student experience.* Washington, DC: ACPA–College Student Educators International, Association of College and University Housing Officers–International, Association of College Unions International, National Academic Advising Association, National Association for Campus Activities, NASPA–Student Affairs Administrators in Higher Education, & National Intramural-Recreational Sports Association.

King, P. M., & Kitchener, K. S. (1994). *Developing reflective judgment: Understanding and promoting intellectual growth and critical thinking in adolescents and adults.* San Francisco, CA: Jossey-Bass.

Marshall, S. M., & Hornak, A. M. (2008). *A day in the life of a college student leader: Case studies for undergraduate leaders.* Sterling, VA: Stylus.

Maxwell, J. C. (1993). *Developing the leader within you.* Nashville, TN: Thomas Nelson.

Peck, A., Kane, C., & Davis, T. (2016, September). NACA NEXT: Assessing career skills developed through campus activities. *Campus Activities Programming, 49*(3), 34–37.

Vaccaro, A., McCoy, B., Champagne, D., & Siegel, M. (2013). *Decisions matter: Using a decision-making framework with contemporary student affairs case studies.* Washington, DC: NASPA–Student Affairs Administrators in Higher Education.

9

Developing Employability Skills Through Student Organizations

Becky Spurlock

Alyssa is a senior who is graduating from a liberal arts college with a degree in psychology. She is interested in a career in human resources (HR). Alyssa has lined up an interview with a company that has an entry-level opening in HR. As she prepares for her interview, the staff in the Office of Career Services suggests she prepare for behavioral interview–type questions that will require her to cite past examples of her experiences. Alyssa realizes that her summer internship will give her some examples, but it's her work with Alpha Phi Omega, a community service organization, that provides the most robust experiences to draw on. Alyssa notes several examples of her work on the worksheet provided to her:

- **Verbal communication:** Worked with 15 new members as well as the 45 current members on key events. Presented workshops on the history, values, and traditions of the organization. Met with local community service agencies to arrange volunteer events.
- **Teamwork:** Coordinated with the leadership team of Alpha Phi Omega to recruit and initiate new members. Worked

with new members to develop a sense of teamwork and commitment to the organization. Coordinated events with other campus groups, like Meals on Wheels, that share a passion for community service.

- **Decision making and problem solving:** Resolved travel problems related to transporting students from campus to a volunteer site. Figured out how to get all volunteers to complete background checks.

- **Workflow Planning:** Organized the new members in meeting their requirements, including significant service experiences, learning the history of the organization, and meeting the current members.

- **Information Processing:** Worked with the national organization to learn the requirements for membership and new member education program as well as develop the local chapter elements of the program, and then put it all together into a complete new member education plan for the chapter.

Francisco is a junior at a large public university and is studying engineering. He is nervous about getting a summer internship and has interviews with a few firms lined up. Francisco knows that his coursework thus far has prepared him for the work of these firms, but he is worried about how he keeps hearing that technical skills aren't enough, that employers want to hire people who also have interpersonal skills. Francisco spends a lot of his time in the lab and on his coursework. His advisor reminds him of his work with the Engineering Student Society. Francisco remembers how he started as a member and now serves as leader of the group. He recalls the time he negotiated a difficult situation on a site visit and how he made all the logistical arrangements not only with the site but also with the university in filing the necessary paperwork to get the trip approved. Further, the advisor reminds

Francisco how he handled the follow-up and then parlayed this experience into getting the members of his club to agree to a local mentoring program, so they could give back some of what they learned. Francisco realizes that his experience with the club is something he can talk about in an interview. He goes into the interviews with more confidence.

These are just two examples of how students have used their student organization experience in developing and communicating the skills employers are seeking. As the needs of employers evolve and as the demands for quantification of competencies students acquire in college increase, questions persist about the skills and competencies developed both in the curriculum and in cocurricular experiences on a college campus. How can we as student affairs professionals determine what skills or competencies students have acquired? How can students demonstrate that they have acquired these skills and can apply them in an employment setting? It is these persistent questions that this chapter undertakes to answer. But first, the student organization experience on campuses is discussed.

THE STUDENT ORGANIZATION EXPERIENCE

The development and growth of student organizations on college campuses has continued to thrive as students gather around a topic or issue, hobby, activity, or idea (Dunkel, Schuh, & Chrystal-Green, 2014). For some, the image of a student organization is a political group demonstrating or bringing speakers to campus. For others, student organizations represent the constant hum of activity going on around campus, from concerts and comedians to late-night dance parties or Frisbee golf on the quad. For many others, student organizations form around common identities or passions, like the Black Student Union or, at The University of the South, Pokémon. Student organizations are plentiful on campus, creating an entry point for leadership that is unparalleled in any other cocurricular offering on a campus. Small campuses like The University of the South (2016), with about 1,600 students, may have 100 registered organizations, while large institutions such as Texas A&M University (n.d.), with more than 59,000 students, has more than 1,000 organizations a student can join.

The earliest organizations tended to focus on governance, military, or religion but later expanded to include the plethora of organizations on campuses today (Dunkel et al., 2014). Generally speaking, organizations tend to fall into two types or statuses: university-sponsored organizations or registered/recognized student organizations. University-sponsored organizations contribute to the general goals of the university and serve large numbers of students. These organizations are typically required to have a faculty or staff advisor and are often assigned an advisor for whom advising the organization is a specific requirement of the job. These organizations often function like university departments. Registered student organizations are formed by and for students around a common special interest or to engage in social activities. These organizations often recruit their own advisors or, in some cases, might not be required to have an advisor (although advisors are encouraged). Organizations are often then broken into categories based on type; common groupings include academic, political, service, identity-based, sport clubs, general interest, honor, religious, military, spirit and traditions, and arts and culture. This chapter focuses on registered student organizations.

Most campuses run a process for new student organizations to form and another for organizations to annually re-register with the university. This annual registration process is important for maintaining a roster of organizations, as many tend to wax and wane with student interest. Having an accurate list allows universities to assist these organizations, helps students connect with their peers through participation in the organizations, and creates the foundation for several other processes at the university. These processes are part of coordinating the moving parts associated with organizations, including managing both legal and risk management issues, determining access to resources like student fee funds and meeting spaces, and archiving leadership and membership rosters for future use. As part of annual registration, universities often require both the completion of training as well as any new paperwork to verify members and communicate updates to campus policies or procedures. This process is also a connection point with students who may then spend the rest of the year largely disconnected from staff or advisory influence, save for requesting meeting space, funding, or policy clarifications.

Student organization involvement is about student development—the opportunity to learn critical interpersonal skills, among others, while interacting with peers, advisors, administration, alumni, and community members. The challenge and support model developed by Sanford (1967) proffered that student learning is at its most robust when students receive a balanced amount of challenge and support while moving through experiences. Too much challenge without support causes frustration, while too much support without challenge often stunts growth (Evans, Forney, Guido, Patton, & Renn, 2010). Student organizations often foster an environment that feeds off a challenge and support model powered by the student organization's infrastructure that includes policies, protocols, and advisors. The organizational experience is a learning lab opportunity for students to try on big and small leadership roles while they explore academic, career, and personal interests. For example, academic organizations and honor societies such as the Society for Women Engineers or the American Chemical Society can be an extension of the work of a particular department or major.

Students make connections through these groups that can translate to their professional development and experiences in a post-graduation world. This concept has been important for a long time. In the first edition of the book *Advising Student Groups and Organizations*, Dunkel and Schuh (1998) argued for advisors to help students start involvement logs to document their experiences. Today, this concept has evolved into more sophisticated engagement portals and cocurricular transcripts, replete with certificate programs in leadership and completion of graduation requirements for involvement, reflections, and portfolios. In fall 2015, the American Association of Collegiate Registrars and Admissions Officers and NASPA–Student Affairs Administrators in Higher Education announced a grant project funded through the Lumina Foundation to launch a pilot project to develop models for a more comprehensive student record as a means to evidence student learning outside the classroom. This partnership is also referenced in the introduction to this book. This project is a part of the quest to answer one of the persistent questions noted in the opening paragraphs: How can students demonstrate that they have acquired the skills employers desire?

Student organizations are rich learning labs where students can learn, lead, and fail. "Fail" is the key word here, as students need to experience failure to grow. Popular media are full of articles about students today being overly protected from failure by their parents and, thus, lacking resiliency. Put another way, there is concern that students today lack the ability to fail, learn, grow, and try again. Getting experience with failure and recovering from failure are important during these key developmental years, as the confidence that results can be an important driver in workplace success. Participation in student organizations offers a range of experiences and hierarchy to try on, from being a general member to the leader of an organization. This environment where students have the opportunity to try, fail, and try again is often missing from the curricular setting, where grades are the benchmark for learning. Unlike a classroom, the feedback that students receive in student organizations most likely comes from their peers. With peer feedback, whether through individual relationships or through attendance (or lack thereof) at an event, students have to face their successes and failures more publicly than in the classroom. The adage that students learn more outside the classroom than in it is often a nod to the learning lab environment of the cocurricular world, which is powered by student organization involvement.

Some people think of the time spent in organizations as frivolous or ancillary to the core learning enterprise of the university. At worst, it is seen as a distraction from curricular pursuits by faculty colleagues or even those stakeholders outside the collegiate environment who are attempting to streamline the college experience as a means to make college more affordable. Student organizations can be viewed as a nuisance as they pursue the ideas and events that matter to them. Whether it's scheduling a game of humans versus zombies or hosting an event for Holi, a Hindu festival that involves drawing and coloring paint on one another, sometimes the ideas organizations have for events can frustrate administrators charged with risk management or protection of campus grounds. With increased competition for resources within universities, including not just budget dollars but also space and student attention, it can be far too easy to deprioritize student organization needs or requests. Additionally, as competency-based education becomes a hot topic within academia, there is the possibility of focusing only on competencies developed in the classroom, to the detriment of students. Solving the challenge of how to document cocurricular experiences is a pressing need for the student affairs field that must be solved.

Put together, the landscape of student organizations, both the infrastructure and interactions from the university coupled with the learning lab environment, lead to a robust opportunity for the development of skills employers are seeking. This chapter explores the ways in which students can gain employability skills through participation in organizations. It begins with the areas that have the most promise for development in student organizations: verbal communication, teamwork and influencing others, decision making and problem solving, and workflow planning. The remaining employability skills are explored with less detail; although they are relevant, they do not offer the same potential for development in the student organization experience.

EMPLOYABILITY SKILLS DERIVED FROM STUDENT ORGANIZATIONS

Verbal Communication

Of all the employability skills identified by the National Association of Colleges and Employers (NACE; 2014), it is important to start with verbal communication, as it powers many of the remaining skills. Without the ability to communicate verbally, student organization leaders are likely to struggle with motivating others or working in teams. Employers have long demanded strong verbal communication skills from college graduates, in no small measure because this one skill can often make or break relationships. Student organizations offer many different experiences that can help students develop verbal communication skills. Regardless of the type of campus group (e.g., community service, departmental, or interest club), participation in a student organization demands good verbal communication from its members and even more so from its leaders. This section is organized around the experiences that give members or leaders the opportunity to practice or employ verbal skills, as well as the ability to sell to, achieve buy-in from, or influence others.

Presentations. Students who participate in student organizations often improve their verbal communication skills because they have to make presentations to their peers about their ideas or the committees they are leading. It's also common for student organization members to be tapped to serve on panels (e.g., for admissions days, orientation, or events for stakeholders like trustees, regents, or governmental leaders). Student organization members are often asked to introduce speakers during public forums or events. Each of these types of interactions provides an experience for practicing prepared presentations, an experience likely to be repeated in a work environment after graduation. Key skill development includes learning to speak clearly, to be heard, to offer coherent thoughts, and to connect with an audience to increase the success of the communication. Student organizations provide ample opportunities for presentation experiences.

Meetings. Student organization members get the chance to practice verbal communication on a regular basis, as many organizations meet weekly or biweekly. Leaders of organizations get to take these skills to the next level when they lead regular organizational meetings or facilitate conversations with their executive board or fellow members. In addition, organizational leaders often have to help work through conflict or discord in their group, which teaches them valuable facilitation skills. One student leader from Alfred University summed it up:

> If there was ever a time to learn how to run a meeting, it would be when you're running a meeting with the university president. Of course, other parts of developing communications skills have been important too, like sharing my opinion and dealing with conflict. I've had to learn how to effectively introduce everyone to each other to open a meeting, continue a conversation to keep things productive, and end with the recap and tangible goals. All of this in front of the most powerful person at the university.

Motivational Speeches. As the primary representative for the organization, organization leaders are often expected to make an annual request for funds to another group in order to gain funding for their events. Leaders of student organizations often champion causes or ideas to their fellow students, and to do that they may go into other organizational meetings to pitch an idea or get an organization on board with a shared project. This kind of persuasive communication is also important for student organization members when they are working a student organization fair or recruiting new members through other venues. Student organization members and leaders also need to motivate others with their verbal communications. This skill is used equally in group and individual settings. In group meetings, both members and leaders can use verbal skills to motivate members to move forward on a project. On an individual basis, this skill can be used to provide feedback to a fellow student on how to solve a problem, or to talk with a student who hasn't completed his or her responsibilities or commitments. While influence is an independent skill that is also discussed in this chapter, not all who possess the ability to influence others possess the skill to persuade others verbally.

Impromptu Speaking. Student organization leaders are regularly asked about their opinions on campus issues or are asked to provide feedback or input on campus projects, services, or events. Often these opportunities occur spontaneously, so leaders need to be prepared to state their opinion in a clear, concise, and coherent manner. This skill requires experience to develop, and student leaders are provided the context for that learning to take place.

Frequently, leaders are also asked to attend dinners with important campus guests, such as speakers, trustees, and community leaders. Learning how to engage in small talk, as well as to succinctly deliver a sound bite about who they are and what they do, is important for these events and can also benefit students in a variety of careers after college.

Learning how to speak out and represent an organization is one of the most important parts of leading an organization on a college campus. As organizational members or leaders grow their verbal communication skills, they will find their skills in teamwork and influencing others growing as well. Strong verbal communication both powers and supports skills development in other areas.

■ ■ ■ COMMON EXPERIENCES

Madeline is president of her student organization and must participate in the annual hearings in order to obtain the funds her organization needs for the academic year. The Funding Board is comprised of nine student leaders who are voting members, along with the nonvoting chair of the Student Government Association. Prior to her scheduled time in front of the Funding Board, Madeline developed a strategy for convincing her peers that her organization should receive the funding it needs. Madeline has just 10 minutes to present her case and answer the board's questions. This powerful experience taps into the presentation skills of making a pitch or request and responding to questions on an impromptu basis. Put together, this substantial experience helps Madeline gain and polish important verbal communication skills that she can document on her résumé, portfolio, or cocurricular transcript.

■ ■ ■

Teamwork

Teamwork is at the heart of the student organization experience. Campus groups are students who work together to achieve the goals of their organization. Put another way, most student organizations are largely self-directed. This is particularly true of registered organizations, which often begin and dissolve based on student demand, interest, and leadership. Although sponsored organizations are often more stable over the long run, in part because of the university investment in their success, they too rely on student commitment and teamwork to keep the organization afloat. Without teamwork, most organizational activity would come screeching to a halt.

Student organization members get experience and develop their teamwork skills in three primary ways: leading committees or teams, serving on committees and teams, and observing the organization in action. Remember, this is a learning lab environment! Organizational members are often tapped to lead committees or short-term projects, giving them an opportunity to step into a temporary leadership role. Also, on a regular basis, members get the chance to gain insight into the challenges or successes of their organizations through observations in meetings and other interactions.

Organizational leaders get to set the tone for teamwork by leading their members, their executive teams, and their partners. This often translates into project management skills—setting the goals for a committee or team, appointing the right leader to the role, setting parameters on the project including a timeline for achievement, and helping navigate the unexpected challenges that arise throughout the project. A sophomore student leader shared:

> I've learned that in order to make something big happen, it takes a team of devoted people working together efficiently and thoroughly. Being a leader does not always mean "to lead," but in fact it means much more. It means to teach . . . to plant a seed and let others become the destined leaders they are supposed to be. It means to expect the unexpected and go with what you can, never forgetting where you come from, and humility. It takes someone else to spark the leadership potential you have, and I would not be a leader if I were not a follower first.

Completion of a project presents an opportunity for recognition and thanks as well as the possibility of advancing a new project to build on the success achieved. Of course, like any team, sometimes one or more members do not fulfill their tasks and the leader has to consider how to help keep the group on track. When this happens, a leader taps into not only teamwork skills but also verbal communication skills, particularly in the area of motivational speaking.

In larger organizations, teamwork can manifest itself in terms of keeping the organization moving forward cohesively. But in small organizations, it's more likely to be a multitasking experience. A student leader of a small, cultural-based organization shared:

> Unlike holding a position in a larger club, leading a smaller club can require even more commitment. Part of my job is sparking students' interest in learning about a culture that seems very distant from our own. Since we are such a small group, I act as the president, the fundraising chair, and the treasurer.

Organizational leaders learn the important skill of motivation in leading their team. Students are busy individuals with a lot of pressing and time-sensitive demands. Motivating a team to completion of the task, program, or event is no small feat!

At their roots, student organizations are collections of students striving to meet similar goals. Whether those goals are developing service programs, putting on events, or raising awareness of a cause, motivating others is an essential skill for leaders of student groups. Students who can demonstrate this skill to potential employers will find themselves with a significant advantage in meeting their career goals.

■ ■ ■ COMMON EXPERIENCES

Miles is trying to figure out how to best build teams within an organization so members can achieve their ambitious goals for the year. He is convinced the best way forward is to work in teams. After having some personal experience taking Gallup's (n.d.) StrengthsQuest assessment through a workshop at the Career Services Office on his campus, he asks members of the executive leadership group of his organization to take the StrengthQuest self-assessment to identify their own strengths. Miles uses this information to create a Team Talent Map and to build committees and teams within his organization. By utilizing students' different strengths, Miles believes he has given organization members the best chance to achieve their goals.

Decision Making and Problem Solving

Leading an organization means constantly making decisions and solving problems. Most organizations have a budget—whether generated from student fees, dues, fundraising, or donations (or all four)—and student organization leaders typically have considerable discretion about how to spend their resources. They also have to decide on an agenda, program plan, or activities for the organization. When there is a lack of consensus, they have to decide for the group. Student organization leaders are master problem solvers because they have to be.

Because there is such a variety of organizations on a campus, there is a lot of variance in how much or how little an organization might try to accomplish in a given semester or year. There are nearly endless opportunities to make decisions and solve problems within student organizations because they are self-directed groups. Of course, organizations operate within the greater university structure, which means they have to negotiate the policies and procedures of a particular campus as well as adhere to any expectations by affiliations with any national organizations or structures. For example, the local chapter of Amnesty

International has to attend to the campus policies as well as those of the national headquarters. All of this provides a rich learning lab environment for making decisions and solving problems.

Members of student organizations can be very effective idea generators. The culture of most organizations is that the body of members makes the decisions after generating ideas that move the organization forward. The ideas of an organization often are generated by members as they are trying to solve problems, whether those of the group or of the greater campus. For example, a group of students at Bellarmine University in Louisville, Kentucky, created The Bellarmine Food Recovery Program to respond to the problem of food waste in the dining hall. After conducting extensive research, creating a network of partners, and working with the food services providers on campus, these students found ways to get unused food from the university to their community partners around Louisville.

To achieve the goal of reducing food waste, the students in the Bellarmine Food Recovery Program had to understand the scope of the problem. The students first learned about hunger, homelessness, and waste and began to identify assets and deficits that existed within their campus and surrounding community. The students decided to partner with the national organization of Food Recovery Network to make their plan work. In order to get Food Services on board, the students had to come up with solutions that would minimize the impact on capacity and resources of the university Food Services operation. The students had to solve the problem of keeping the food in safe temperature ranges during transport. Relying on their verbal communication skills, including the skill of influencing others, they recruited more than 20 weekly volunteers to pick up, package, and transport the leftover food to local agencies. They have recovered more than 5,000 pounds of food thus far and have helped decrease food insecurity in the community. In the spring 2015 semester, the students hosted a

Scrape the Plate event that helped raise awareness about food waste and challenged students, faculty, and staff to consider why they waste food. While this example certainly demonstrated careful planning and prioritizing of work (another employability skill), the dominant experience for the students was in solving complex problems and making decisions to achieve their goals.

Leaders also have to deal with failure on a regular basis—both their own failures and the failures of others. Each of these failures provides an opportunity to reformulate a plan—to solve problems and make decisions toward the goals of the organization. Learning this kind of resiliency and commitment in the face of transitions and change is skill development that will serve student leaders well on the job after graduation.

One of the most difficult issues student organization leaders face is dealing with unpopular decisions, including managing the social costs of their decisions. Fellow students will often look to their organizational leaders to negotiate policies and procedures, to respond when new policies or protocols are unpopular with students, or to push back on the university when a new student issue arises on campus. As a student shared:

> I developed a friendship with a fellow student in my group, but at the end of the semester, she had not met the minimum requirements to maintain her membership. In order to fulfill my responsibilities as the leader of this organization, I had to choose removing her at the risk of losing this friendship. This can make things quite uncomfortable and tense, especially in such a small school, but must be done to maintain the legitimacy of the organization.

Another example of this issue comes from Stanford University, where student leaders drafted and supported an inclusive membership policy change that created open membership with all student organizations. This protocol change was initially poorly received by the student body. The student leaders who supported the change when it was in development published editorials in the student newspaper to defend their decision to their peers. The student leaders found they lost social capital and connections during the process—they weren't invited to hang out with friends or were ignored when walking through campus. In this case, the student leaders' decision to stand up for what they believed in ultimately resulted in positive support for the change, but in the interim they felt more isolated as a result of their decision making. There were many lessons learned for these student leaders, particularly in thinking through how and when they offer support to an issue, how to negotiate conflict with fellow students, and how to respond when receiving negative feedback from peers.

■ ■■ COMMON EXPERIENCES

Colleen has discovered that a member of her organization has represented himself as its president while putting up controversial posters across campus. Colleen first learns of this via a letter from the Dean of Students Office that the organization has been suspended, pending an investigation. Colleen has to solve this problem as well as make a decision about what happens next. She works with her advisor and fellow organization leaders to gather information about what happened. They collectively decide to suspend the membership of the student who misrepresented his role in the organization, as well as publish an apology letter to the university for the content of the posters. The organization is reinstated by the university after these action.

Workflow Planning

So far this chapter has discussed organizations as being self-directed, meaning workflow planning often happens largely within the discretion of the organization. Combined with competing demands on student time, this creates an incredible learning opportunity to practice planning, organizing, and prioritizing work.

Time management is something all students need to learn in order to successfully manage the demands of the collegiate experience. Managing the time demands of courses alone is quite a feat, but most students also add in organizational involvement as well as fitting in employment and recreation time. Most students are involved in more than one organization at a time, and some choose to be involved three or more, with differing levels of participation, leadership, and overall demands. And just like a course syllabus, student organizations often have built-in requirements. Want to stay an active member of the Rugby Club Team? Well, members who miss more than three practices or games aren't allowed to stay on the roster. Every day, students are juggling different demands, including those of the organizations they choose to join.

Time management skill development for leaders of organizations is that much more intensified. Leading an organization comes with additional demands for time, including attending committee meetings and all organizational events, but those time demands can extend even further. At Belmont University, all student organization presidents are required to regularly attend the President's Council, a group comprised of all organization leaders. Regular attendance at this monthly meeting is required for an organization to remain eligible for student government funding.

In planning, organizing, and prioritizing work, organizational leaders have to consider when to abandon plans that are not working or when the conditions are right to push through—something more seasoned leaders even struggle to decide. Organization leaders also develop basic organization skills because their roles demand it—whether it's learning a new system of technology that helps them organize themselves or their groups, or following a system that has been prescribed to them by their advisor or their national office.

Collaboration is perhaps one of the key skills in this domain that student organization leaders have the chance to practice. While collaboration is a key element in the development of the ability to work in teams, which is discussed earlier, strategic collaboration falls more closely in line with planning, organizing, and prioritizing work. Most leaders learn quickly that the divide-and-conquer method of getting work done is limited in its utility. Strategic collaboration requires a shared commitment to the goals and ideas of the idea or event. The decision to collaborate often means adding to the time it takes to advance the work, because bringing along more people demands better communication and more time to build consensus.

Part of planning, organizing, and prioritizing work within student organizations should involve succession planning. Often, this important element of planning is overlooked. Successful organizations know that long-term sustainability lies in the ability to continually develop and invest in the future of the organization. Succession planning is a good example of one way students develop skills in this domain.

■ ■ ■ COMMON EXPERIENCES

Jeff is president of the Bellarmine Food Recovery Program and was one of its original founders. Jeff is graduating in a few months. Because this is a new organization and Jeff cares a great deal about the work continuing after he graduates, he spends his free time compiling key information in a notebook for the next leaders of the group. Jeff also leads an initiative to change the date of elections so that new leaders can be selected while the current leadership group is still on campus to ensure a smooth transition. By engaging in such careful succession planning, Jeff is helping this new group with workflow planning for the future.

Secondary Skills

The remaining employability skills developed within student organizations will be addressed in this section collectively. Because the student organization experience is so robust, opportunities to develop these skills do exist, but they are not as universal or likely to be developed across all organizations or experiences. Some helpful notes about each are included below.

Quantitative Analysis

Not all student organization experiences require students to regularly analyze quantitative data. But for students participating in leadership roles in more complex or larger organizations, this skill can be developed in three primary ways: creating and maintaining budgets, collecting and analyzing survey data, and writing proposals. Most student organizations seek funding from an outside source; to do this successfully, organization leaders will likely create a proposal. The strongest proposals include quantitative data that make the case for funding. Analyzing attendance data or cost per participant data is often a compelling way to demonstrate the cost efficiency or reach of a particular program or event.

Sometimes, student organization leaders are asked to write proposals outlining changes they wish to make to policies or procedures. These kinds of requests typically include benchmarking data from other campuses to support the case for change. Collecting and analyzing these data as well as writing the report provide a tremendous opportunity for student organization leaders to sharpen their analytical skills.

Career-Specific Knowledge

Many student organizations are developed around a shared passion or interest. In addition to the two clubs mentioned at the beginning of this chapter, other common examples include: student finance clubs, clubs based on a program of study (e.g., Psychology Club), and clubs based on interests and passions (e.g., Wellness Club). These organizational experiences can help students transform their interests and passions in formal and informal ways. Sometimes, an experience in a club or organization sparks a career interest that propels a student toward making a career choice.

Beyond this opportunity to develop interest in a career or content area, student organizations provide an opportunity to carry a wide scope of responsibility. Some student leaders have more budgetary responsibility or oversight of other leaders than they might in their first professional job! Because organizations are learning labs, students have the opportunity to try and fail and, as a result, engage in remarkable self-discovery that often leads them to figure out where they want to go next in terms of career development. With such an easy entry point into involvement, student organizations provide a low-risk opportunity to try something new. Students may quickly discover a passion for tutoring, public speaking, or organizing. Or, just as quickly, they may realize that although they possess the skills or talents for a task, they do not enjoy it, motivating them to pursue new skills.

Organizations are also great places to learn the important career skill of networking. Although some networking opportunities are limited to fellow students or campus leaders, they can extend to donors, alumni, and community leaders. Some organizations are local or unique to a particular campus, but others are part of a vast network of groups at various campuses united under a national office. Take, for example, the Society of Women Engineers. With more than 200 chapters at campuses across the nation, students have the opportunity to attend regional and national conferences and meet with other students as well as hiring managers and leaders in the field.

Computer Software Skills

It's hard to be successful in an organization without learning, using, and improving computer skills. Organizations often use common applications, like word processing and spreadsheets, to conduct their business. But sometimes students have an opportunity to gain unusual or advanced computer software skills. Many campuses employ websites or portals that allow students to conduct the work of their student organizations, which allows for students to build skills in both managing their organizational page and using a portal system. Student organization members and leaders have to be able to get their work done in an efficient manner. As a result, they are often the first to adopt and introduce new technology to help them work in group. Student organization leaders often turn to computer programs and services to help them manage regular tasks like collecting financial donations, due or managing fundraising. Other times it means using Google and other sharing programs to complete the work of their organization. Students also often learn how to use social media for organizational use, not just for personal use.

Scheduling is a major issue for most student organizations (and students in general), so they have pioneered the use of computers to make scheduling a little easier (OrgSync, n.d.). They now think about archiving documents for history or to help in succession planning. Often, student organization members have to learn to use publication software in order to produce marketing materials. This also can extend to using video editing and other computer programs to meet the needs of their organizations. Many organizations also manage their own web page, which means student leaders have to learn basic website management.

Writing and Editing Reports

Student organization members and leaders learn to write in a different form and format than they do within the classroom. Unlike writing papers, students in organizations tend to learn business communication skills. Student organization leaders also quickly learn how to write in order to reach a specific audience. Writing to fellow students, an advisor, other organizations, and campus leaders all require adopting different styles of writing, which is an important skill for communicating in the workplace.

Student organization members and leaders may have the opportunity to write articles or press releases for campus publications, or to submit small blurbs to the local newspaper or campus marketing and publications offices. And all organizations must maintain an updated version of their constitution or charter and by-laws. Most campuses require that students certify the organization's constitution and bylaws annually, which gives students in organizations regular opportunities to write and edit formal documents.

ASSESSING EMPLOYABILITY SKILLS AS AN OUTCOME OF STUDENT ORGANIZATIONS

Assessing student growth and development through participation in student organizations has some inherent challenges. Because the availability of student organizations on each campus is driven by student interest, there is a near-endless variety of student groups with distinct missions, values, and learning outcomes. This can make assessment challenging. Additionally, while many campuses have employees whose purpose it is to develop and promote involvement in student groups on campus, there are many campuses in which student organizations are more of a categorization of opportunities than a coherent program. Smaller institutions are less likely to have dedicated staff, and among the larger institutions that have these positions, the number of student organizations may make assessment complex and unwieldy.

Texas A&M University addressed this complex issue through its Student Leader Learning Outcomes project. This project "provides universal methods and tools for staff throughout Texas A&M University to use with student leaders in student organizations, programs, or activities to help in the assessment and documentation of enhanced learning in relation to the students' leadership experiences" (Student Leader Learning Outcomes, n.d., para. 3). A working group developed rubrics and training for student organization advisors and student leaders to collect and report valid, direct assessments of student learning from participation in cocurricular activities. This provides a novel approach to the dilemma of how to assess a vast number of student groups, especially at large institutions. The rubrics can be found on the website dedicated to the project (sllo.tamu.edu), and a fulsome discussion of the project can be found in the 2012 book *Learning Is Not a Sprint*, by Kathy Collins and Darby Roberts.

While the diversity of learning experiences inherent in student organizations can be daunting, a lot of commonality exists among student groups. Within this chapter, a strong argument has been made for the value of the skills identified by NACE. Institutions should strongly consider a focus on these skills for many reasons discussed throughout this book. For those seeking to measure these skills, this book provides two keys. First, rubrics for these skills are located in the appendix. These include detailed descriptions of behavior that is indicative of varying skill levels in each of these areas. The rubrics could be used to score students reflective writing such as journals, portfolios, or even applications for awards or participation in programs. Institutions could use this to create their own surveys that can be compared against the national averages—or could even use it to create a simplified way for student group advisors to rate their student leaders (producing direct evidence of student learning).

It is also quite possible that institutions are already collecting data that could be useful in assessing employability skill development in student organizations. Many institutions participate in the National Survey of Student Engagement (NSSE) from the Center for Postsecondary Research at Indiana University (2015). The questionnaire collects information in five categories and includes participation in educationally purposeful activities. Some of the questions cover the following topics:

- Leadership roles on campus
- Campus opportunities to be involved socially
- Measurement of house of participation in cocurricular activities
- Estimates of education and personal growth since starting college
- Contributions to knowledge such as speaking clearly and effectively
- Acquiring job or work-related knowledge and skills (career-specific skills)
- Working effectively with others (teamwork)
- Understanding of people of other backgrounds (teamwork)
- Solving complex, real-world problems (decision making and problem solving)

NSSE also offers the opportunity to add questions to the instrument, which would allow organizations to collect data more easily than a stand-alone assessment. Also, specific questions about the NACE skills could be added, which would provide the opportunity to cross-reference the data with items from NSSE.

Finally, while student organizations may be under-assessed, there are a variety of programs focused on career development that take place regularly and are more likely to be accessed. Some examples include résumé critique programs, career fairs, and workshops that focus on a variety of skills and topics. A wealth of data may be available simply by partnering with the career development office to ask that a question or two pertaining to student organization involvement be added to their existing instrument. Knowing whether students are actively participating in experiences outside of the classroom, to what extent they are participating, and what sorts of experiences they are engaging in can shine a light on how development differs for students who participate versus those who do not. This can help student affairs educators target areas that are potentially impacted by student organization participation and those that could be enhanced to improve results.

Assessment is most effective when it provides us with a glimpse of observable differences in what students know and are able to do as a result of participating in cocurricular programs. By using the tools provided in this book and by focusing specifically on the development of skills that can benefit students in their careers, we can help students meet their goals, and we can truly show that we are making a difference in their lives as well.

CONCLUSION

Student organization involvement is an important part of the collegiate experience for many students. Offering more training, resources, and support for both members and leaders of student organizations is a good way to help students develop key employability skills. A lot of good work is already happening in this arena, but more focused collaborations between career services and student activities professionals could allow for the creation of learning outcomes, better documentation of skill development, and stronger opportunities for students to express what they have learned through participation in student organizations.

REFERENCES

American Association of Collegiate Registrars and Admissions Officers & NASPA–Student Affairs Administrators in Higher Education. (2015). *AACRAO and NASPA name comprehensive student record implementation institutions: Two-day symposium kicks off* [Press release]. Retrieved from http://www.naspa.org/images/uploads/main/Lumina_Press_Release_Approved_10_20_2015.pdf

Center for Postsecondary Research, Indiana University. (2015). National Survey of Student Engagement. Retrieved from http://nsse.indiana.edu/html/annual_results.cfm

Collins, K. M., & Roberts, D. M. (2012). *Learning is not a sprint: Assessing and documenting student leader learning in cocurricular involvement.* Washington, DC: NASPA–Student Affairs Administrators in Higher Education.

Dunkel, N. W., & Schuh, J. H. (1998). *Advising student groups and organizations.* San Francisco, CA: Jossey-Bass.

Dunkel, N., Schuh, J., & Chrystal-Green, N. (2014). *Advising groups and organizations* (2nd ed.). San Francisco, CA: Josey-Bass.

Evans, N. J., Forney, D. S., Guido, F. M., Patton, L. D., & Renn, K. A. (2010). *Student development in college: Theory, research, and practice* (2nd ed.). San Francisco, CA: Jossey-Bass.

Gallup. (n.d.). StrengthsQuest. Retrieved from http://www.strengthsquest.com/home.aspx

National Association of Colleges and Employers. (2014). *Job outlook 2015.* Bethlehem, PA: Author.

OrgSync. (n.d.). Company overview. Retrieved from http://www.orgsync.com/company

Sanford, N. (1967). *Education for individual development.* Retrieved from http://files.eric.ed.gov/fulltext/ED013353.pdf

Student Leader Learning Outcomes. (n.d.). Student leader learning outcomes project. Retrieved from http://sllo.tamu.edu

Texas A&M University. (n.d.). Student life: Student clubs and organizations. Retrieved from http://www.tamu.edu/student-life/index.html#clubs-organizations-recreation

The University of the South. (2016). *College of Arts and Sciences enrollment: Advent 2016.* Retrieved from http://registrar.sewanee.edu/downloads/enrollment-reports/U_of_South_Enrollment_Report,_Advent_2016.pdf

10

Developing Employability Skills Through Fraternity and Sorority Life

Daniel A. Bureau and Mark Koepsell

For more than 200 years, fraternities have been part of the fabric of American higher education (Gregory, 2003). Always controversial in the context of whether they contribute to or detract from the objectives of higher education, fraternities and sororities are indeed complex organizations (Asel, Seifert, & Pascarella, 2009). For one thing, institutions typically do not have influence over which students become members of these organizations. Fraternities and sororities on most campuses will select members using a predetermined recruitment or intake process. Such a process typically culminates with an orientation period during which members learn key skills to becoming successful members. Some of these skills may also translate beyond just being a good member into demonstrating excellence as a student, an involved campus leader, and a member of a diverse local and international community.

When electing to become a member of a fraternity or sorority, a student joins a chapter (likely a franchise of a regional or [inter]national organization, although the group could be unique to that campus). The chapters are governed on campus by a council (typically clustered by primary or like functions or types of organizations), within what is typically called the "Greek System" or "Fraternity and Sorority Community." Therefore, one student joins a collection of other students (organization or chapter), within a collection of chapters (council), within a collection of councils (larger "Greek System" or "Fraternity and Sorority Community"), within a college or university campus. Even within the same chapter, members may have very different experiences from their peers depending on their dispositions and willingness to align individual actions with explicitly and implicitly articulated organizational goals and values (Clegg, 2010; Reuter, Baker, Hernandez, & Bureau, 2013. Finally, if the organization is found on other campuses, the students also have the experience of being a member of something that even transcends what they have come to know as college in their context. Such an experience brings forth layers of possibility for how one might have a fraternity or sorority experience (Barber, Espino, & Bureau, 2015; Matthews et al., 2009).

How this community engages with and contributes to a campus is influenced by many factors including the extent to which alumni and administrators provide guidance and support for the chapter's operations in many areas including academic, leadership, service and philanthropic, and social development programs (Council for the Advancement of Standards in Higher Education [CAS], 2015; Jelke & Kuh, 2003; Mauk, 2006). Administrators working with these organizations are often engaged in advising councils and chapters about appropriate membership selection and educational practices, including ensuring chapters provide opportunities for members to develop skills that are vital for the global workforce. The achievement of widely held outcomes for these organizations, such as the standards articulated by CAS, depends on the support and resources chapters receive from all of these stakeholders. Employment outcomes, such as those recognized by the National Association of Colleges and Employers (NACE), may be developed within the context of members' fraternity or sorority experience, but also through ways they engage as general students within the campus and local community.

This chapter focuses on how fraternities and sororities aid in the development of members' employability skills. It begins with an overview of how these organizations may help develop such vital competencies; using existing literature and the observations of the authors' close to 50 collective years of personal and professional experience with these organizations. Additionally, ideas about how student affairs educators can develop and assess programs, resources, and services to facilitate learning and development outcomes in fraternities and sororities is provided. Because these organizations often exist beyond a singular campus, the chapter includes examples of not only how a fraternity and sorority life office might enhance these outcomes, but also how (inter)national headquarters staff can engage with stakeholders in these goals as well. The chapter ultimately addresses each employability skill and concludes with some ideas for how these skills may be enhanced and assessed through the context of fraternity and sorority life.

CONTEXTUALIZING THE FUNCTIONAL AREA OF FRATERNITY AND SORORITY LIFE

For as long as there have been fraternities and sororities, there have been concerns about how they exist in the context of higher education as well as advocates who believe these organizations provide distinctive opportunities that can provide a well-rounded college experience (Bureau, Ryan, Ahren, Shoup, & Torres, 2011; Hevel, Martin, & Pascarella, 2014). Many who advocate for fraternities and sororities, such as the authors of this chapter, also recognize the challenges and are committed to working with stakeholders to address the problems that come with young adults managing these organizations.

Challenges for administrators include the misuse and abuse of alcohol, hazing, sexual misconduct, and intolerance directed toward other cultures by chapter members (Biddix, Matney, Norman, & Martin, 2013; Kimbrough, 2003; Mitchell, Weathers, & Jones, 2013; Ryan, 2009). Consider the instances in which a fraternity is found in violation of policies due to provision of alcohol at a social function. This infraction can set off a chain reaction, leading to a series of events that undermine the credibility of fraternity and sorority life. A student drinks too much and goes to the hospital; a guest drinks too much at a party and becomes the victim of sexual assault; a new member is forced to drink as part of a hazing activity. Those kinds of instances happen all too often; there has been at least one hazing death as a result of fraternity membership reported annually since 1969 (Nuwer, 2015). While using alcohol is one example, some of the other ills of the interfraternal movement must also be countered, such as hazing in fraternities and sororities that are focused on specific cultural groups such as African American and Latino students (Kimbrough, 2003; Mitchell et al., 2013).

Administrators who see value in a fraternity and sorority experience likely advocate for an experience that is focused on leadership development, community and campus service and philanthropic activity, engagement in campus life, and connecting alumni and graduate members through a range of activities (Gregory, 2003; Hevel & Bureau, 2014). In addition to the evidence that these organizations pose great challenges to higher education, there is also evidence that members develop leadership skills (Kelley, 2008; Taylor, 2011), enhance dispositions toward community service and philanthropic pursuits (Martin, Hevel, & Pascarella, 2012), and may even develop skills with regard to interacting with diverse others (Martin, Parker, Pascarella, & Blechschmidt, 2015). For those who see value in these organizations, there is opportunity to educate young adults as they navigate managing a dynamic organization. Such tasks bring forth challenges that, with sufficient support and guidance, these students can overcome and, as a result, may develop skills that will help them in college and for a lifetime (Barnhardt, 2014; Kelley, 2008).

The perceptions on both sides of the aisle are not completely unfounded; some chapters within the larger fraternity and sorority community on a campus may be less inclined to positively contribute to the campus community. Through all of these complexities, a goal of those involved in the administration of these organizations (such as staff, faculty, alumni, and national organization representatives) is to help members positively contribute to their chapter, their campus and fraternity and sorority community, and global society (CAS, 2015). Additionally, it has become increasingly important to document how the key learning outcomes widely valued by higher education can be enhanced from membership in fraternities and sororities (CAS, 2015; Gallup, 2014; Strayhorn & Colvin, 2006). With these opportunities and challenges in mind, we now turn to the potential outcomes of membership, specifically those vital to employers, and how these outcomes have been achieved and can be strengthened through membership in fraternity and sorority life.

EMPLOYABILITY SKILLS DERIVED FROM FRATERNITY AND SORORITY LIFE

Verbal Communication

Through membership in a fraternity or sorority, students interact with a range of individuals. Interactions arise from both the activities a chapter organizes and those in which they participate. Individuals in fraternities and sororities are also likely to be engaged in other aspects of campus life; therefore, they interact with a number of students both in and out of the Fraternity and Sorority Community. Such interactions often require a student to speak with others, sometimes needing to explain their experience or provide insight into how they or their chapter can be involved in addressing complex problems. Through these interactions, students will be given opportunities to develop and strengthen such skills as their verbal communication capabilities.

Some organizations will feature education programs in which chapters articulate the importance of the skills they want each member to possess. While not totally synonymous, the skills students use to participate in social interactions influence their verbal communication skills. Gerhardt and Moderson (2014) explained that over 10 years of implementing the AFA/EBI benchmarking instrument (produced by the Association of Fraternity Advisors and Educational Benchmarking International) to assess outcomes of membership in a fraternity or sorority, members overwhelmingly identified the ability to transfer social skills to other settings as an outcome of membership: In 2003, about 68% of participants reported that their experience enhanced their ability to transfer social skills to other settings; in 2013, that number increased to about 80%. Long (2010) explained that about 86% of students who participated in the same national instrument during 2010 ($n = 9,462$) indicated the fraternity/sorority experience enhanced their oral communication skills to a more than moderate extent.

Not only do verbal communication skills become enhanced as a result of membership, but some have tied one's ability to tell a passionate story or to garner support through powerful oration to effective leadership in fraternity and sorority life (Harms, Woods, Roberts, Bureau, & Green, 2006). It has been clear over the years to us as authors that sometimes those who speak the best may not necessarily lead more effectively, but they do invoke a sense of excitement about a cause. These dynamics play out in fraternity/sorority life and are also vital skills students will need when they enter the workforce.

■ ■■ COMMON EXPERIENCES

Monica, a sophomore engineering major, has joined her sorority after completing the intake process. Coming into the organization with eight other women, Monica has expressed an interest in holding a leadership position in the chapter. Curious about how she might go about getting people to back her candidacy, she asks Alissa, a senior who previously served as president, about what she must do to be seen as a viable candidate for vice president. "You need to speak up Monica," Alissa says. "You're a behind-the-scenes kind of leader, but our chapter expects our leaders to be able to give direction and have a commanding presence. If you want to lead the chapter, then you'll need to find ways to develop the skills to verbally lead us. When you do so, people will see you emerge as someone who can effectively convey who we are and what we want to do for and with the campus community, key administrators, and the national organization. It might be best for you to begin in a committee role and try to get elected after you've established yourself as a vocal leader. Those kinds of positions will be good to help you learn those skills."

■ ■■

Teamwork

As in other student organizations and initiatives, participating students and those leading these organizations are charged with motivating their fellow students to set and accomplish shared goals. Most fraternities and sororities are affiliated with a national philanthropy. These are charitable projects for which students dedicate their time and energy. Through planning fundraisers and coordinating volunteer events, students learn to work in concert with others in the organization.

Additionally, fraternities and sororities are often actively engaged in all sorts of on-campus initiatives. From planning recruitment activities to participating in intramural sports or engaging in friendly competition with other organizations during times such as a campus Greek Week, teamwork is fundamental to student learning for the students who participate. It has been well documented that membership in a fraternity or sorority can bring forth positive gains developing teamwork skills, particularly in the first year of membership, though over time such skills tend to be less attributed to membership in a fraternity or sorority (Hevel et al., 2014). Long (2010) reported findings about members' perceptions of collaboration and teamwork from his study of almost 10,000 members using the AFA/EBI instrument. He found that 85% of respondents reported that their perception that the membership experience influenced their ability to work with others fell somewhere between good, excellent, and superior. Teamwork is also explained by other terms in the leadership literature such as collaboration, working together, developing a shared vision, and so forth. Findings from studies by Atkinson, Dean, and Espino (2010); Biddix and Underwood (2010); Dugan (2008); Kimbrough and Hutcheson (1998); and Taylor (2011) also indicate that increasing one's ability to work with a team is a primary outcome across all segments of fraternity and sorority membership. It is evident that members develop approaches to teamwork that help them relate to others in their chapters, the Fraternity and Sorority Community, the campus, and society.

■ ■ ■ COMMON EXPERIENCES

Antonio has recently been elected as the community service and philanthropy chair of his fraternity chapter. As both a freshman and first-semester sophomore, Antonio was a passionate supporter of his chapter's community service work—providing mentorship, tutoring, and positive interactions for disadvantaged youth at a local youth center. The challenge he is facing since his election is that of actually getting members to participate and share his passion for this service work. He asks Phillip, the previous chair, what his secret to success was. Phillip responds, "It's because you are trying to make people go and you are dictating their involvement. I found that if I got a core contingency of the membership excited about it, and engaged them in helping me recruit participation, together we accomplished so much more than I could on my own. That playground we built? Can you imagine if we didn't have a majority of the chapter involved in that project? Wow! But look at the impact we made working together as a team! Our legacy will live on at the youth center for so many years to come as a result!"

Decision Making and Problem Solving

There is certainly no lack of evidence that some large-scale problems in need of attention exist within fraternities and sororities. As previously mentioned, issues of alcohol misuse, hazing, sexual assault, and acts of intolerance occur more frequently in fraternities and sororities than in other aspects of student life (Sanders, 2012). Students in these organizations may be better known for causing problems, but less discussed is the powerful opportunity students have to engage their fellow students, as well as chapter and community leaders, in a governance model that forces them to reflect on the decisions they make and determine the approaches they take to problem solving. In fact, research indicates fraternity and sorority membership teaches students approaches to problem solving (Hevel, Martin, Weeden, & Pascarella, 2015). However, the same study examined critical thinking—an essential aspect of good problem solving—and the research determined that members who entered college with high levels

of critical thinking skills may retain those attributes; but for those entering college in the lower two thirds of the distribution of precollege critical
thinking skills, fraternity/sorority affiliation was linked to a statistically significant disadvantage in critical thinking skills by the fourth year of college.
Focusing on decision making and problem solving within the context of
fraternity and sorority involvement presents many advantages. Namely, the
problems that need to be addressed—such as countering alcohol misuse
and abuse, challenging students to get out of their comfort zone and interact with people from different backgrounds, standing up to inappropriate
behavior, and holding members accountable for academic performance—
are vital for the successful continuation of fraternities and sororities and
provide an excellent context for gaining this skill, which can differentiate
them from their fellow students as they seek employment after college.

As with many studies about fraternity and sorority membership,
researchers often do not ask, or fail to provide, analysis of how different
types of chapters within the fraternity and sorority community experience the development of these skills. Examining how these differences,
such as organizations/chapters with a social focus versus those with a professional, cultural, or academic focus, influence how students make decisions and solve problems in a team that may be more or less homogenous
could be important (Shalka & Jones, 2010). This information would help
fraternities and sororities explain how they prepare students for entrance
into a global society likely much more diverse than their chapter.

■ ■ ■ COMMON EXPERIENCES

As a junior, Tyler is serving in his second semester as the vice
president of risk management for his chapter. It is homecoming

weekend and a group of young alumni have come back to the chapter house looking for some connection to those days they now miss greatly. However, today's rules have changed, and some of the actions and behaviors acceptable 10 years ago are no longer tolerated. These alumni have set up a Slip 'N Slide in the backyard, dumped beer on it, and are encouraging the members and their guests to run and slide down it with the goal of not spilling liquid from their cup. Tyler is watching when a young member flies off the end and hits his head hard on a fence post, cracking his forehead open and likely needing stitches. Tyler now has to not only stop the games but also disperse the large crowd that had gathered to participate and watch. He first focuses on getting the member to medical treatment safely with two sober brothers. He then quickly rallies brothers he knows he can count on to help. He stops the game, assigns some members to disperse the crowd, and grabs the chapter president to go with him to have a serious talk with the alumni. Thinking on his feet to quickly solve the problem demonstrates how he is able to stop the activity and focus on getting the member help.

Workflow Planning

Involvement in fraternities and sororities often requires a significant investment of time. With a myriad of responsibilities, fraternity and sorority members must manage time and energy to ensure the many demands placed on them are met. Such demands include their academic requirements, chapter expectations such as fulfilling positions of leadership in the chapter or general community, and programmatic and educational mandates given by the fraternity and sorority life office (Atkinson et al., 2010; Bureau et al., 2011). Developing skills to manage time and properly plan, organize, and prioritize work can be an outcome of fraternity/sorority membership.

In this day and age, people must manage many tasks, with a range of information sources telling them how to do their work. College students and those in fraternities and sororities are learning to prioritize. They are struggling to consider how life as a young adult is throwing new challenges at them. Those challenges come in the form of coursework, but members of a demanding organization such as a fraternity or sorority must also be prepared to look ahead at all their responsibilities and plan accordingly for the ebbs and flows of what is likely a busy semester and academic year. Students engaged in fraternity and sorority life, who are seizing the opportunities to participate in a range of activities and roles while maintaining their academic pursuits, are likely practicing tactics to help them figure out their priorities; such tactics will be applicable for their future work, volunteer, and personal responsibilities.

COMMON EXPERIENCES

Joanna sits down at her desk on Sunday night to look at the week ahead. The sorority has scheduled a meeting on Monday night and a spaghetti dinner for the chapter philanthropy on Wednesday at which she has signed up to volunteer. She works 4:00 p.m. to 8:00 p.m. on Tuesday and Thursday and has a test on Thursday. She wants to attend a social event at her friend's fraternity on Friday and needs to drive 2 hours north to her parents on Saturday for her grandmother's 80th birthday. Finally, her role in student government requires her to attend a campus lecture on Monday as well—immediately following the chapter meeting.

Joanna has to examine the range of priorities and expectations placed on her for the upcoming week. Her sorority obligations are numerous, let alone working, studying, and attending other cocurricular and family obligations. How will she plan for the week? The sorority obligations certainly make her examine responsibilities differently than she did when she was not a member. Not only does the sorority have attendance expectations for meetings and philanthropy events, but the chapter is ranked number two across all chapters for its grade performance. This semester, the chapter set a goal of becoming number one. Joanna knows that her performance on the test will influence her final grade in her chemistry class and that she's somewhere between a B- and an A-, depending on how the test goes. She has to plan well enough to meet not only her own priorities but also those of the collective chapter. Each of the responsibilities also brings some level of work that she must perform: She must volunteer at the philanthropy project. She must work at her job. She must complete schoolwork. She must fulfill her student government obligations. All of these experiences, which tie back to her sorority experience, require her to plan, organize, and perform work.

Information Processing

As noted in Chapter 3 of this book, *information processing* is defined as "knowing where to find information and to apply critical thinking skills to evaluate this information in order to determine its credibility" (see p. 41). Encouraging critical thinking within fraternities and sororities is vital (Hevel et al., 2015). Take, for example, hazing issues: It is easy to explain that hazing is against the law (in most states) or against school policy; however, it is more difficult for those who work with fraternity and sorority members to help these students analyze and explain why hazing should not be practiced. This requires more than the application of a rule—it requires students to carefully explore their own values and to apply what they discover to their decision-making processes. They must obtain the information about the practices, reflect on how that information relates to their own values, and critically examine the data in order to justify their perspective or create new meaning.

Pike (2000) used the National Study of Student Learning data from one institution to identify whether differences in reported cognitive development were a direct result of fraternity/sorority membership, an indirect result of involvement, or a result of differences in the students' background (see Chapter 2 for further discussion). Fraternity/sorority members scored lower, although not significantly, on such cognitive development–related variables as library use but higher on areas in integrating new knowledge or gaining specific skills such as critical thinking. Turk (2012) examined how members of one fraternity across multiple campuses developed critical thinking skills and the factors that influenced higher levels of critical thinking. His findings revealed a strong correlation between critical thinking and higher academic performance. Academic performance is in part related to how one is able to find and process information; therefore, a practice for those working with these students would be to target chapters with lower or unacceptable academic performance and enact programs that would increase attention to academic priorities.

Students will have a range of opportunities to consider the rights and wrongs of information as well as determine how it can be appropriately applied. Common experiences across members include planning and executing events that are largely influenced by institutional or national organization policies such as social events or intake and recruitment practices. Additional experiences may be those that teach members about the values and norms of the chapter they are joining: new member education experiences, chapter educational workshops, and other learning experiences hosted by the chapter, the fraternity/sorority community, and the Office of Fraternity and Sorority Life.

■ ■■COMMON EXPERIENCES

Take the example of Tyler, the risk management chair, from earlier in this chapter. In addition to simply solving the problem that was laid out in front of him, he was put in a position to critically think about what was happening, how to care for the injured member, what the additional consequences of the event could be (safety, accountability, etc.), what the reactions of the participants might be and how to navigate them, how to effectively disperse the crowd, who could be trusted to engage in helping him, and so forth. As a result of this position, he was forced to critically examine how the events his fraternity organizes impact members and guests and to develop approaches to managing and solving the problems that accompany these events. ■ ■■

Quantitative Analysis

Fraternities and sororities are very much like small businesses that must make revenue and expenses align: Members pay fees to receive the determined benefits of the organization. Specific members are tasked with managing that revenue (i.e., the treasurer and his or her committee). In addition, for those with facilities, members may be involved in the volunteer board that oversees the house operations. Such individuals must create and balance a budget based on overall membership, facility occupancy, and costs of facility living expenses. Financial data is one type of quantitative data that members will have access to during their experience in a fraternity or sorority.

Outside of managing a facility and money, members are tasked with justifying decisions all of the time. Some members will take the opportunity to analyze data (e.g., voting on the budget, determining practices to reverse trends in membership decline). However, analyzing numbers and making sense of statistics and budgets are not necessarily occurrences that members will experience all too often. So, what operations of a fraternity or sorority might be enhanced in order to help more members practice and develop such skills?

Because numbers indicate some level of success on a desired outcome (e.g., a score on a test, the perception of people who use a service, the views people have about a topic), fraternities and sororities could enact more opportunities to collect needed data. For example, when evaluating a recruitment/intake initiative, could members be tasked with reviewing the number of potential members and those who accept invitations to join over time? What trends do they see? What might those trends mean? Could a philanthropy/community service committee be able to track participation in key events? How much money is raised? How happy were members with the activities in which they participated? Collecting information and determining ways to use it to improve the collective member experience is beneficial in that it improves the quality of the chapter, but it can also give members an opportunity to develop an essential skill that employers want from their employees. Because most fraternity and sorority communities have assessment, accreditation, or awards processes that are typically managed by chapter leaders, it could be beneficial to engage more members in helping with collecting and analyzing data for these processes.

▪ ▪ ▪▪ COMMON EXPERIENCES

Andrea is a junior business major who was recently elected treasurer of her sorority. The first time she examined the books, she was amazed at how much responsibility the job was going to require. In addition to simply managing the data entry of the accounting transactions, the position required developing a working budget, invoicing more than 150 members, collecting dues, tracking all of the bills that came in and paying them in a timely manner, regular communicating with her alumni advisory team and the headquarters, and even initiating a payment plan for members to follow. Additionally, because of her classroom knowledge, she realized she could collect multiple bids for services rendered and negotiate contracts. That was on top of using some skill to analyze numbers so she could effectively manage cash flow and determine dues amounts for the forthcoming budget. Andrea realized she was in fact running the same-scale financial operation as a small business.

Career-Specific Knowledge

Any number of publications that promote the value of fraternity and sorority life will espouse the value these organizations can have in helping students get ready for the "real world," most notably their future place of employment (Barber et al., 2015). While those skills may include abilities such as relating across differences, critical thinking, and teamwork (as already explained previously in this chapter), students must also have a forum in which they can rehearse skills they are learning in their courses that tie directly to working in their desired field (Long, 2010). For example, finance majors need to be able to practice managing money. Someone who wants to be a social worker needs to practice in a safe space.

Members of fraternities and sororities can help one another become effective in their chosen fields of study. For example, members who are pursuing the same career can identify gaps in each other's skill sets and discuss strategies for gaining needed experiences. Through these interactions, students' expectations about future work can be normalized.

Unlike many other student organizations, fraternities and sororities are intergenerational, and college students interact with fellow students at different times in college as well as with alumni at different points in their lives. As a result, it is likely that members will interact with others who have similar career goals, particularly those who have already taken the courses, had work experiences, and learned the lessons needed to be effective in a field. To enhance these employability skills, it is vital to connect college students to alumni in ways that attend to mentoring for developing career skills.

Professionals who work with fraternities and sororities should look beyond the undergraduate members to help facilitate this employability skill as an outcome of membership. Creating a database of fraternity and sorority alumni within the local community might help to bring forth professionals, possibly experts, who can mentor and guide members. These professionals can work with alumni associations to develop such networks for fraternity and sorority members. Students learn through seeing others who have succeeded and failed; fraternities and sororities, due to their infrastructure and intergenerational membership, provide a forum in which members can connect widely within a desired field of work.

■ ■■COMMON EXPERIENCES

Sierra is a sophomore pre-medical student who joined a sorority during the spring of her sophomore year. She might interact with other students in her chapter who are pre-med, possibly even nursing or biology, who can give insight into what approaches to taking classes, studying, and securing practical experience have been most effective for them. Sierra also may have the opportunity to secure internships or practical experiences in the medical field because of a connection she develops through an alumna member. The alumna member may also provide career counseling to members through a mentoring program or just as a result of attending the chapter's meetings and events.

Computer Software Skills

College students today are used to living life online. Many of them have been raised on computers. They may use technology for connecting with others, writing papers, and playing games. However, the global workforce demands more than just knowing how to type and search the Internet. Databases track membership and clients. Software is created to communicate with millions of customers. The responsibility to develop the skills needed to work well with computers (and technology in general) extends well beyond fraternities and sororities. However, professionals who work with fraternity and sorority members, at the headquarters and campus levels, should be concerned about members entering a workforce without this important skill, even if it does not seem like a subject that is naturally integrated into the cocurriculum.

Professionals working with fraternities and sororities can enact three simple tactics that may help members enhance their computer skills. First, create processes for submitting information that require the use of certain programs. For example, as chapters must report membership, providing them with a format using tables in a Word or Excel document may be a good lesson in using Microsoft Office. Another example would be to require chapters to develop a PowerPoint presentation of their annual awards packet.

Second, e-mail communication is important in the workforce.

Although college students may be well versed in social media, messages to the president of the company should not be sent in 140 characters with intermittent capitalization and no punctuation. Fraternity and sorority life professionals should maintain high expectations of students in this regard, asking students to write e-mails as if they were being sent to an employer or supervisor. Professionals should deliver messages in a manner that reflects what the student would be expected to provide in a professional setting.

Third, computers are forums for learning. Pedagogical approaches to workshop facilitation might change so that students attending workshops can engage with each other and the presenter, but there is also some expectation of submitting information. For example, at a meeting for community service chairs, the campus professional might spend the first half hour going through the process of service learning and how to integrate it into chapter events, and in the second half hour require attendees to surf the web to find five local agencies to support (developing browsing skills), create an Excel document that lists those five agencies with contact information (developing a spreadsheet), and draft an e-mail to the agency contact to request more information for the student's chapter to participate in volunteer or fundraising activities (drafting a professional e-mail). Reviewing each student's work can serve as a form of assessment of how the student approached communication with these important agencies and developed good computer skills.

■ ■ ■ COMMON EXPERIENCES

In his role as the recording secretary of his chapter, Ari is responsible for reporting to the headquarters membership data (including demographics and bio-connected information), chapter fundraising, chapter programming, recruitment statistics, any conduct reports, and overall highlights of chapter progress and well-being. As a fairly young, multicultural-focused organization, the headquarters just recently launched a chapter management system that tracks all of this information in one organized and centrally located online collection portal. Ari spent the better part of one day at national organization leadership training learning the ins and outs of the platform. Some of it was as easy as answering questions in a form. However, in some cases, it required uploading ready-made Excel templates and even some coding that needed to be integrated into the local chapter website. These skills are extremely similar to those required of so many companies and corporations today. The information technology department does not necessarily manage these tasks anymore; every employee needs to be able to navigate these systems. Ari now has a leg up in navigating and understanding how these management platforms operate, making it all that much easier for him to learn the next one.

Writing and Editing Reports

Writing and editing skills can make or break one's employment opportunities regardless of the profession. Graduates' ability to write may form the first impression they make on a potential employer. From the development of a résumé, to creating a cover letter, to drafting the thank you note or e-mail, learning to write and edit well are essential skills that must be refined in the college environment.

There is actually a surprising amount of writing going on in fraternities and sororities. From managing social media accounts to writing copy for marketing materials and press releases about important events, to submitting written reports to governing bodies and the national headquarters, student leaders with an interest in improving their writing skills can find more than adequate context to do so within these organizations.

What is often lacking is the opportunity to address writing with general members of this group. While many organizations would not identify helping their members learn to write and edit well as a responsibility of the organization (at the national or local level), those who administer these organizations would be wise to integrate opportunities for practicing these skills into educational processes. Such a responsibility can be integrated into the chapter's or Office of Fraternity and Sorority Life's academic programs. Some research on fraternity and sorority academic engagement indicates members in fraternities and sororities, due to either dispositions and/or organizational requirements, typically perform at or above levels of non-members after the new member intake process is complete (Bureau et al., 2011; Hevel et al., 2015). Focusing on writing and editing during the education program is an opportunity to not only practice these skills but also help members tell the story about the value of the fraternity/sorority experience. For example, as the close of new member education approaches, asking members to write an essay about the values of the organization and how those values play out in their daily lives may be an exercise that helps the students align more with the organization's purpose while giving them a chance to develop their writing skills. Potentially, chapter advisors might review the essays, offer feedback, and suggest edits. This process of writing/feedback/writing and editing/feedback can be reflective for the students as well as give them an opportunity to rehearse these important skills. Such a process also provides an opportunity for administrators to collect evidence about the academic performance and dispositions of the students. Such evidence can aid in dispelling perceptions of the fraternity/sorority experience as being only social in nature.

■ ■■COMMON EXPERIENCES

Maggie serves as the public relations and communications chair of her governing council. In this role, she oversees a team of member volunteers who create content for the council website, compiles and writes stories for the fraternity and sorority e-newsletter, manages the content delivery of the council's recruitment booklet, and writes press releases for both campus and community news outlets. This content is seen by thousands of individuals. It must be professional, concise, engaging, and effectively tell a story. The content must be free of basic spelling and punctuation errors, and it must be grammatically correct. ■ □ ■ ■

Selling and Influencing

For many, the fraternity/sorority experience has been a venue in which they have developed key leadership skills. Biddix and Underwood (2010) explained how one fraternity's national leadership program helped members to "influence change." Harms et al. (2006) found that members with the strongest voices and most seniority were most motivational and influential in a chapter, even more so than positional leaders. Through all of the literature on fraternity and sorority life and leadership, it has become evident that the ability to influence and motivate others is perceived as an important outcome of membership.

Opportunities to develop this skill abound. From the students who lead these organizations using their influence to encourage their groups to accomplish goals, to actually selling tickets to an event or encouraging donations to the group's philanthropy, students participating in fraternity and sorority life at all levels can learn to both influence and sell.

It is important that student affairs educators resist the temptation to study and develop this skill only among leaders within these groups. Much has been written about how leadership may differ for those in positions of leadership versus those who do not hold such roles (see Dugan, 2008). There is a view that leadership happens from anyone, from anywhere, at any time. For fraternity and sorority professionals, it is important to help ALL members, regardless of positional leadership, to find their voice and demonstrate leadership in the way they know best. Opportunities to lead in the global workforce may pop up at any time; therefore, creating opportunities for only leaders in a fraternity and sorority community to develop such skills may result in a diminished return on investment for others. Simply stated, if leadership is supposed to be an outcome for ALL members, then all members should be engaged in opportunities for leadership education.

To create such opportunities, it might be important to assess the extent to which students in fraternities and sororities need leadership education developed for them, or if they may have such dispositions and will find their own areas in which to enhance such skills. Using the Multi-Institutional Study of Leadership (MSL) annually for new members of fraternities and sororities may be a way to identify what dispositions students bring with them into membership (see, e.g., Dugan, 2008). Providing voluntary opportunities for any member to participate in fraternity- or sorority-specific leadership training during the first year of membership is a way to send a message that leading and influencing others in positive ways is a key skill needed as a member of the chapter, of the campus community, and of society. Participants in these voluntary opportunities may participate in another administration of the MSL to gather whether such interventions (as well as their collective experience) have informed or changed their approach to leadership. Results could be seen as an indicator of the quality of the students' experience, and professionals might work with chapter stakeholders to maintain and enhance the experience in such a way that ensures such skills are nurtured.

■ ■■ COMMON EXPERIENCES

Tyrone is a newly initiated member of his chapter. During the intake process, he participated with his fellow new member class in a guided hike over some tough mountainous terrain that ended at a high ropes course. Throughout the experience, Damion was struggling. He didn't find value in the activities, didn't understand why they had to "waste their day with this," and would rather have been on a sofa in the residence hall watching a football game. Tyrone made it his quest to get Damion "on board." He challenged him, he encouraged him, he joked with him, and in general just partnered with him on every challenging task. He never allowed Damion's attitude and would simply reframe every negative statement. By the end of the day, Damion commented on how much he gained from the experience. He felt he grew individually, and also both knew and trusted the new member class at a higher level. In fact, he joked with Tyrone about pushing him and being "a bully," and then smiled and simply said, "Thanks!"

■ ■■

ASSESSING EMPLOYABILITY SKILLS AS AN OUTCOME OF FRATERNITY/SORORITY MEMBERSHIP

It is difficult to isolate students' college experiences. Isolating the experiences within fraternity and sorority life is no different. However, the time spent on chapter projects and activities can be significant when compared with other types of involvement, particularly during the intake/recruitment/new member education period as well as when students hold leadership positions within the chapter and/ or the fraternity and sorority community. Fraternity and sorority professionals have a responsibility to assess the extent to which key learning outcomes occur as a result of participation in these organizations (CAS, 2015). Focusing on employability skills can be a way those tasked with administering these programs can provide evidence of the value these organizations bring to college and university campuses and to students' lives. A few potential assessment approaches include surveys, open-ended approaches, and direct measures.

Surveys

A common data-gathering source, surveys collect information from students at distinct points in their collegiate experience. For example, the National Survey of Student Engagement is administered to first-year students and seniors each spring. To assess employability skills outcomes, educators may focus on a specific point in time at which they want to use indirect methods such as surveys. The key is to determine what is important for one to know as a student affairs educator working with fraternities and sororities—is it how disposed these students are to developing the skills through membership? How well the students perceive that they have developed skills through involvement in their chapters? The answer will influence the timing of the survey and population assessed. For example, upon joining a fraternity or sorority, students could be invited to participate in a survey that asks them to explain their sense of achievement with each employability skill and how they may have gone about developing them. The assessment might be repeated the next year, after what could be considered a significant period of membership, to see if the students feel their membership has influenced the enhancement of such skills as well as what they have done as members to develop and enhance the skills.

Open-Ended Approaches

Students can explain their experiences better than anyone. Using open-ended approaches to collect information about perceptions of employability skill enhancement is important so that professionals can support survey data, collect information they can use in real time and that is tied back to students' key educational experiences, and tell a story to stakeholders about the value students receive from membership. Examples of each may be a focus group in which participants are asked to explain their leadership experiences or how they have developed teamwork competence. Fraternity and sorority professionals might use advising sessions or other meetings with students to ask questions and learn about the skills they are developing that will help them with their potential careers. For example, a campus professional might meet with 50 chapter and council officers over the course of a semester. Asking the officers at distinct points how they are developing such important skills as verbal communication, planning and organizing work, and analyzing quantitative data could be a great way to collect information in real time. The campus professional could then use such information to inform workshops and educational opportunities.

As students mature in their organizations and develop a range of skills, campus professionals may find opportunities to engage these students in activities that can help to determine the key skills they have developed as a result of their fraternity/sorority involvement. For example, as chapter presidents depart their position, there may be an opportunity to task each of them with writing four to six bullets about key skills they have learned and how they learned them. The campus professional can study the responses of all presidents and quantify the most common learning outcomes from serving in that role. Such information, while obtained through an indirect method, may help professionals to capture the most important skills to attend to when planning educational experiences. Such an activity may also help students articulate on a résumé what it is they took from their roles and prepare them to tell the story of the value of the experience as they enter the workforce.

Direct Measures

Direct measures are means to "test" students by giving them an opportunity to prove how they know something. For example, Tyler, as risk management chair of his chapter, could attend a workshop at which he learns appropriate event and social management skills (gaining the skill of workflow planning). At the workshop, he is tasked with taking a quiz that outlines steps needed to organize well-run events. He can be assigned a grade and given real-time feedback. The grade can be tied to such consequences as requiring him and possibly other chapter members to pass the quiz to have social privileges. Campus professionals could then say that some percentage of chapter members passed a test in which they documented their awareness of, understanding of, and ability to apply risk management procedures.

CONCLUSION

While fraternities and sororities have loud critics, they also have passionate advocates. These organizations contribute to campus life in many ways and context matters: Chapters on one campus may contribute more favorably to the campus environment than the same chapters on another campus. Members do not have a monolithic experience, although the groups do share common rites of passage that help the students to develop skills and foster a connection to the organization and alma mater.

Employability skills are of particular interest in this book, and fraternities and sororities certainly can provide opportunities to enhance these skills or develop new ones. College and university administrators and other stakeholders who seek to help these organizations must be intentional in creating educational opportunities for members to develop such skills. It is then essential to assess the impact of these learning experiences on students' skill development.

REFERENCES

Asel, A. M., Seifert, T. A., & Pascarella, E. T. (2009). The effects of fraternity/sorority membership on college experiences and outcomes: A portrait of complexity. *Oracle: The Research Journal of the Association of Fraternity/Sorority Advisors, 4*(2), 56–70.

Atkinson, E., Dean, L. A., & Espino, M. M. (2010). Leadership outcomes based on membership in Multicultural Greek Council (MGC) organizations. *Oracle: The Research Journal of the Association of Fraternity/Sorority Advisors, 4*(2), 34–48.

Barber, J. P., Espino, M. M., & Bureau, D. A. (2015). Fraternities and sororities: Developing a compelling case for relevance in higher education. In P. Sasso and J. DeVitis (Eds.), *Today's college student* (pp. 241–255). New York, NY: Peter Lang Press.

Barnhardt, C. L. (2014). Fraternities and sororities shaping the campus climate of personal and social responsibility. *Journal of Student Affairs Research and Practice, 51*(2), 128–142.

Biddix, J. P., Matney, M., Norman, E., & Martin, G. (2013). *The influence of fraternity and sorority involvement: A critical analysis of research (1996–2013)* (ASHE Higher Education Report). San Francisco, CA: Jossey-Bass.

Biddix, J. P., & Underwood, R. (2010). A ten-year study of individual outcomes from a fraternity central office leadership program. *Oracle: The Research Journal of the Association of Fraternity/Sorority Advisors, 5*(2), 1–21.

Bureau, D., Ryan, H. G., Ahren, C., Shoup, R., & Torres, V. (2011). Student learning in fraternities and sororities: Using NSSE data to describe members' participation in educationally meaningful activities in college. *Oracle: The Research Journal of the Association of Fraternity/Sorority Advisors, 6*(1), 1–22.

Clegg, K. S. (2010). *In search of belongingness: Perceptions, expectations, and values congruence within sorority new members* (Master's thesis). Oregon State University, Corvallis, OR.

Council for the Advancement of Standards in Higher Education. (2015). *CAS professional standards for higher education* (9th ed.). Washington, DC: Author.

Dugan, J. P. (2008). Exploring relationships between fraternity and sorority membership and socially responsible leadership. *Oracle: The Research Journal of the Association of Fraternity Advisors, 3*(2), 16–25.

Gallup. (2014). *Fraternities and sororities: Understanding life outcomes.* Retrieved from http://products.gallup.com/170687/fraternities-sororities-understanding-life- outcomes.aspx

Gerhardt, C., & Moderson, K. (2014). *Past, present and future. What have we learned about the fraternity/sorority experience?* Retrieved from http://afabackup.com/ProgramsEvents/AdvanceU/ThePastPresentandFuture.aspx

Gregory, D. E. (Ed.). (2003). *The administration of fraternal organizations on North American campuses: A pattern for the new millennium.* Asheville, NC: College Administration Publications, Inc.

Harms, P. D., Woods, D., Roberts, B., Bureau, D., & Green, A. M. (2006). Perceptions of leadership in undergraduate fraternal organizations. *Oracle: The Research Journal of the Association of Fraternity Advisors, 2*(2), 81–94.

Hevel, M. S., & Bureau, D. (2014). Research-driven practice in fraternity and sorority life. In G. L. Martin & M. S. Hevel (Eds.), *Special issue: Research-driven practice in student affairs: Implications from the Wabash National Study of Liberal Arts Education* (New Directions for Student Services, No. 147, pp. 23–36). San Francisco, CA: Jossey-Bass.

Hevel, M. S., Martin, G. L., & Pascarella, E. T. (2014). Do fraternities and sororities still enhance socially responsible leadership? Evidence from the fourth year of college. *Journal of Student Affairs Research and Practice, 51*(3), 233–245.

Hevel, M. S., Martin, G. L., Weeden, D. D., & Pascarella, E. T. (2015). The effects of fraternity and sorority membership in the fourth year of college: A detrimental or value-added component of undergraduate education? *Journal of College Student Development, 56*(5), 456–470.

Jelke, T., & Kuh, G. D. (2003). High performing fraternities and sororities. In D. E. Gregory (Ed.), *The administration of fraternal organizations on North American campuses* (pp. 273–298). Asheville, NC: College Administration Publications, Inc.

Kelley, D. R. (2008). Leadership development through the fraternity experience and the relationship to career success after graduation. *Oracle: The Research Journal of the Association of Fraternity Advisors, 3*(1), 1–12.

Kimbrough, W. M. (2003). *Black Greek 101: The culture, customs, and challenges of black fraternities and sororities.* Madison, NJ: Fairleigh Dickinson University Press.

Kimbrough, W. M., & Hutcheson, P. A. (1998). The impact of membership in black Greek-letter organizations on black students' involvement in collegiate activities and their development of leadership skills. *Journal of Negro Education, 67*(2), 96–105.

Long, L. (2010). *AFA/EBI fraternity/sorority assessment: Summary report 2010.* Retrieved from http://works.bepress.com/cgi/viewcontent.cgi?article=1059&context=ldlong

Martin, G. L., Hevel, M. S., & Pascarella, E. T. (2012). Do fraternities and sororities enhance socially responsible leadership? *Journal of Student Affairs Research and Practice, 49*(3), 267–284.

Martin, G. L., Parker, E., Pascarella, E. T., & Blechschmidt, S. (2015). Do fraternities and sororities inhibit intercultural competence? Findings from a four-year longitudinal study. *Journal of College Student Development, 56*(1), 66–72.

Matthews, H., Featherstone, L., Bluder, L., Gerling, A. J., Loge, S., & Messenger, R. B. (2009). Living in your letters: Assessing congruence between espoused and enacted values of one fraternity/sorority community. *Oracle: The Research Journal of the Association of Fraternity/Sorority Advisors, 4*(1), 29–41.

Mauk, A. J. (2006). Students in Greek-letter organizations. In L. A. Gohn & G. R. Albin (Eds.), *Understanding college student subpopulations: A guide for student affairs professionals* (pp. 239–261). Washington, DC: NASPA–Student Affairs Administrators in Higher Education.

Mitchell, D., Jr., Weathers, J. D., & Jones, M. A. (2013). *A 20-year history of black Greek-letter organization research and scholarship.* Retrieved from http://works.bepress.com/cgi/viewcontent.cgi?article=1051&context=donaldmitchelljr

Nuwer, H. (2015). *Hazing deaths.* Retrieved from http://www.hanknuwer.com/articles/hazing-deaths

Pike, G. (2000). The influence of fraternity or sorority membership on students' college experiences and cognitive development. *Research in Higher Education, 41*, 117–139.

Reuter, T. H., Baker, E. L., Hernandez, M., & Bureau, D. A. (2013). A values-based learning model to impact maturational change: The college fraternity as developmental crucible. *Oracle: The Research Journal of the Association of Fraternity/Sorority Advisors, 7*(2), 19–36.

Ryan, H. G. (2009). *Class matters: The experience of female college students in a Greek-letter organization* (Unpublished doctoral dissertation). Indiana University, Bloomington, IN.

Sanders, J. B. (2012). *Conduct issues with fraternities and sororities: University processes evaluated at four-year universities* (Unpublished doctoral dissertation, Middle Tennessee State University). Retrieved from http://etd.lsu.edu/docs/available/etd-11132012-111019

Shalka, T. R., & Jones, S. R. (2010). Difference in self-awareness related measures among culturally based fraternity, social fraternity, and non-affiliated college men. *Oracle: The Research Journal of the Association of Fraternity/Sorority Advisors, 5*(1), 1–11.

Strayhorn, T. L., & Colvin, A. J. (2006). Assessing student learning and development in fraternity and sorority affairs. *Oracle: The Research Journal of the Association of Fraternity Advisors, 2*(2), 95–107.

Taylor, G. E. (2011). An analysis of leadership programming sponsored by member organizations of the National Panhellenic Conference. *Oracle: The Research Journal of the Association of Fraternity/Sorority Advisors, 5*(2), 22–33.

Turk, J. M. (2012). *Explaining critical thinking skills, leadership skills, and openness to diversity in fraternity members: A quantitative analysis* (Unpublished doctoral dissertation, St. Peter's University). Retrieved from https://www.researchgate.net/publication/302507345_Fraternity_at_the_Crossroads

11

Developing Employability Skills Through Student Government Associations

Michael Preston and Adam Peck

As long as universities and colleges have existed, there has been a need for student governance (Miller & Nadler, 2006). The formation of student governing bodies, tasked with being the voice of their peers, began in the 1300s when European schools such as the University of Bologna established student guilds to look after the affairs of their fellow students (Cobban, 1975). These guilds played an important role for students, who were often from far-off cities and villages, helping them secure room, board, and work to support their education. However, despite the long history of student governance, its perceived importance, and the fact that the vast majority of colleges and universities have some sort of student government (Hu, Henderson, & Iacino, 2012) research about the impact of participation in student government on students is sparse and disconnected (McFarland & Starmanns, 2009).

Student government associations (SGAs) are often seen as the recognized voice of the student body on many contemporary college campuses (Hu et al., 2009). According to Laosebikan-Buggs (2009), the typical student government serves four distinct purposes:

249

1. The SGA serves as the officially recognized representative of the students at the university.
2. The SGA gives students an official voice in the university decision-making process by either recognized access to university administration or, in many cases, a vote on the college governing board.
3. The SGA is likely a recognized advocate for student clubs and organizations.
4. The SGA plays some role in developing campus finances, usually in the role of disseminating student fees.

There are more than 4,700 universities and colleges in the United States (Snyder and Dillow, 2012). These institutions of higher learning vary in size, mission, and educational program. Just as there are a variety of structures for colleges and universities, there are also many variations of governing bodies that represent students and their needs (Hu, Henderson, & Iacino, 2012). These groups can be called by a variety of names and they vary on how they are selected and the amount of influence and authority delegated to them by their university. Perhaps this variance contributes to a lack of understanding about the purpose of these groups.

In spring 2015, the University of Central Florida (UCF) surveyed more than 1,100 students on their impressions of their SGA. While more than 80% of the students surveyed replied that the SGA "utilizes my student fees for programs and services I find useful," less than 50% of respondents knew that SGA existed and 70% could not name a single program that SGA provided (UCF Student Government Association, 2015). Ironically, all students were surveyed while standing in line for an SGA-sponsored event on campus. Therein lies a key issue: Student government may be one of the more nebulous involvement opportunities on the average American college campus.

For example, more than 60% of students in the UCF survey responded mistakenly that SGA members had the power to make and enforce university policy, and more than 50% said that the SGA could hire and fire full-time employees (UCF Student Government Association, 2015). It appears likely that if students assume that the SGA has broad authority, then this misconception could fuel dissatisfaction with the effectiveness of the organization. After all, if students assume that the SGA has considerable power, it would be easy to assert that any inability to address whatever issue is a priority for students would stem from incompetence, inattention, or even corruption rather than the realities of the group's level of responsibilities within the framework of shared governance.

THE PURPOSE OF SGAS

So what do SGAs really do? While advocating on behalf of students is the overarching goal, how they do this is often a mystery. SGAs propose both binding legislation (often called bills) and nonbinding recommendations (often called resolutions). They host public forums on important issues and take the pulse of students through surveys and focus groups. To do this, they must research important issues on campus and develop potential solutions in consultation with other student leaders, faculty, staff, and administration.

While institutions benefit from student participation in shared governance, SGAs can also offer a valuable opportunity for students to develop their personal skills (Miles, Miller, & Nadler, 2008). Based on surveys and interviews with more than 200 student government members, Kuh and Lund (1994) outlined 13 skills that students reported were influenced by their participation in an SGA:

1. Self-awareness
2. Autonomy

3. Confidence
4. Altruism
5. Reflective thought
6. Social competence
7. Practical competence
8. Knowledge acquisition
9. Academic skills
10. Application of classroom knowledge
11. Aesthetic appreciation
12. Vocal competence
13. Sense of purpose

Kuh and Lund (1994) made the case that many of these skills result from the collaborative effect of the SGA experience. Study participants pointed to the SGA as an important place to hone and practice their academic skills as well. Numerous studies have also connected student government participation to students' development of civic engagement including an increased awareness of current topics and ideas related to government, an increased interest in participation in civic opportunities beyond graduation, and a better sense of their personal civic perspective (Kuh & Lund, 1994; Laosebikan-Buggs, 2006; Miller & Nadler, 2006; Terrell & Cuyjet, 1994).

There is a tremendous opportunity for student affairs practitioners to utilize the student government experience to develop many of the skills outlined within this book. For educators and advisors tasked with developing learning outcomes for SGA members, the clear connection of these skills with the skill set necessary to be a successful SGA leader can help the advisor write learning outcomes, develop assessment tools, and guide student reflection. This chapter explores how the experience of being a member of a student government can assist in the development of skills and abilities that can be transferred to the workplace and other aspects of professional life. In addition, this chapter illustrates how these skills can be useful for all students, regardless of major.

To better understand this process, this chapter follows a fictional student government member named Rosa. Rosa is a junior senator for her SGA on a large, urban campus. This is her second year of involvement, and she is considering running for student body president for her senior year. Rosa serves on a number of SGA committees, including the student fee allocation committee, the parking violations appeals committee, and the vice president for student affairs' Student Advisory Council. As the chapter progresses, it chronicles the experiences that help Rosa develop employability skills.

EMPLOYABILITY SKILLS DERIVED FROM STUDENT GOVERNMENT ASSOCIATIONS

Verbal Communication

Few cocurricular experiences offer so many opportunities to practice and refine the skill of verbal communication as participation in student governance. From the outset, many students must make campaign speeches in their run for office, or perhaps they must complete an interview with student leaders in the organization to fill a vacant spot. Students are often called on to read proposed legislation before the group and to speak in support of or in opposition to proposed legislation. They also must frequently respond spontaneously to questions posed by others. Active SGA participants would find it hard to avoid speaking in public.

As students gain rhetorical skill from their participation, they also learn how to structure and present their arguments. As one student senator at a large, southern university noted, "When I started in the senate, I did not know how to put together a good argument, but by the time I graduated, I got really good at knowing what the questions would be . . . answering them before they were even asked." This skill requires practical experience in order to develop. In many experiential learning environments, the fact that activities such as student government are enjoyable has the advantage of making students want to learn more in ways that classroom learning does not always inspire. But student government has an additional advantage: The students are often in a situation in which failing to adequately perform could cause them to lose face. The sometimes competitive environment of questions and answers as well as proponent/opponent speeches following the presentation of legislation are excellent arenas to observe this effect.

Like many other cocurricular experiences, the quality of learning activities in student government can be enhanced by advisors who develop ways to coach students and provide feedback based on the information presented, speaking style, and mannerisms. Creating clear channels for communicating feedback to all members can provide an excellent way to enhance learning in this area. This feedback can also provide a basis for valuable assessment data, which will be discussed later in this chapter.

Students can also develop verbal skills through committee membership. Committee membership provides a good way for students to learn how to verbally communicate in a small group. An example for how students can develop skills through committee activity can be found at the University of Florida (University of Florida Student Government Association, 2016). The university has six standing committees focused on the business of the senate and it routinely forms committees to address temporary issues or special projects. For example, a student who sits on the parking appeals committee may hear student testimony on why he or she should not receive a parking ticket. Using the testimony and evidence, committee members have a verbal exchange to determine, via consensus, the best course of action to take.

■ ■■COMMON EXPERIENCES

Rosa is preparing for the speech of a lifetime. Ever since she ran for the SGA, she has promised her student constituents that she will address the issue of providing dedicated parking for the many students who use scooters to travel to and from class. Currently, there is no place to park these vehicles on campus and many students are receiving improper parking violations for parking their scooters in the spots dedicated for motorcycles. After consideration in her committee, the time has come for Rosa to present her legislation, A Bill to Create Dedicated Parking Spaces for Motorized Pedestrian Vehicles (referred to as the Scooter Bill for short). This presentation will require her to utilize her verbal communication skills, including completing a 10-minute formal presentation on the bill, followed by a question-and-answer period, and ending with a meeting with the local student newspaper and a local television news station.

The process of developing verbal skills through student government participation began for Rosa before she was even elected to the student senate. She was elected through a process where she had to make a number of formal campaign speeches to interested students in an effort to convince them to vote for her. In addition, she had a number of informal conversations, many of which were one-on-one, to further convince her fellow students that she had the experience and vision needed to represent them in the student senate. ■ ■■

Teamwork

A unique challenge of working with SGAs is that each member is considered a leader. For students who take an authoritative approach to leadership, the potential for growth from participating may be inhibited. But for those whose definition of leadership includes getting the most out of a team, an SGA can provide many opportunities and resources for learning about teamwork.

For students participating in the Associated Students of the University of California, Davis (2016), senators are split into 11 permanent committees and a number of special interest and temporary standing committees, to focus on projects from their very first day in office. These committees have names like the Bylaw Review Committee, the Scholarship Committee, and the Student/Police Relations Committee. The Associated Students are also tasked with serving on dozens of campuswide committees ranging from conduct boards to athletic committees, each with its own agenda and outcomes. Most effective student governments require participation in similar experiences. These groups help student leaders focus on improving specific processes and outcomes that are important to their organizations and the institutions they serve. By narrowing the scope of responsibilities and encouraging students to focus their efforts within well-defined parameters, students can gain perspective on institutional governance and how various efforts can align for student success.

One advantage of experiential education is that it offers opportunities for students to learn from both success and failure. A student whose personality conflict with another leader derailed an important piece of legislation or a student who did not consult an important stakeholder group before proceeding can take these lessons with them to their careers after college.

Experiences alone cannot teach. It is important that student government programs plan learning around the important topic of teamwork. Florida Atlantic University (FAU; 2012) has developed a series of workshops and retreats that focuses on teamwork on multiple levels. These workshops and retreats are advised by student affairs professionals but are coordinated and executed by SGA leadership at FAU. These workshops, called "team builders," have an array of themes, such as anti-bias awareness, media relations, and ethical decision making. FAU students get to learn about these topics through working as a team and testing their teamwork skills (Florida Atlantic University, 2016). Because SGA members are trusted by their institutions to represent and address student perspectives, the ability to work together on behalf of students is important.

■ ■■ **COMMON EXPERIENCES**

Rosa is continuing to work on her bill to provide designated parking for scooters, but she will not be able to fulfill her vision without teamwork. To complete the bill, Rosa will need to work with scooter owners who have been ticketed to better understand the issue, university administrators to better understand their viewpoint and processes, and other SGA members to write and secure support for her bill. She will then need to enlist others to help her move her bill through the legislative process.

Rosa will also have to deal with some conflict. For example, she experienced an impasse during a committee meeting when a student senator challenged her definition of what constituted a scooter because it did not include mopeds or motorized bicycles. This conflict in definitions delayed the bill for one meeting as members worked together to investigate how other schools were addressing this issue. An SGA advisor assisted the committee by arranging for members to meet with the local department of motor vehicles representative and the director of parking to better understand the legal definition of a scooter. Rosa's bill was improved by the contributions of various members of the team. ■ ■ ■

Decision Making and Problem Solving

Laosebikan-Buggs (2009) suggested that the primary hallmark of a student government is to "give students an official voice in the university decision-making process" (p. 31). Student members of an SGA are faced with internal and external issues where they are called on to possibly render opinions, cast votes, or advocate for student interests. Without a keen ability to make decisions and solve problems, an SGA cannot be effective.

One way that SGA members make decisions in a student government is by voting. Most of the decisions made in an SGA are subject to a vote, so students must be prepared to vote through a decision-making process aimed at capturing the best interests of the students they represent. To do so, SGA members need to learn to recognize how their personal biases may shape their view of the decision. This can be a challenging, but very worthwhile, task. *Robert's Rules of Order*, used by the vast majority of effective SGAs, can provide guidance in making fair decisions. Groups that knowledgeably use *Robert's Rules* are able to ensure that decisions are made with sufficient representation and that the decision-making rules are fair and consistent for everyone. Also, because *Robert's Rules* is most often used by boards of directors or others at the highest level of organizations, few new college graduates are expected to know it. The deep knowledge that SGA members can develop from *Robert's Rules* can be both impressive and rare for recent college graduates.

Adding accountability measures can also help students learn how to make decisions more effectively. In some cases, the decision-making process for student government leaders is required to mimic that of any elected official. To maintain an environment of open decision making, SGAs at public institutions in a number of states including Florida, Alabama, Kentucky, and Oklahoma have to be aware of and follow all applicable open records or "sunshine" laws (Online Sunshine, 2016). In the state of Florida, student government committees at public universities are required to post meeting times, allow time for presentations by students, and offer equal time for opposing views (Bondi, 2016). While these laws are not decision-making teaching techniques in and of themselves, professional advising staff can use them to set the tone for why good decision making is an important skill to develop.

Institutions that wish to provide quality training for student leaders on this topic have quite a few to choose from. The American Student Government Association, National Association for Campus Activities, and the Conference on Student Government Association at Texas A&M University frequently offer tracks and educational sessions on decision making. These opportunities can take students away from campus to learn more about decision making through practice. Decision making in an SGA is important for both ethical and practical reasons. However, the practical reason may actually be more powerful. SGAs are often judged on whether students, faculty, and staff can trust their decisions and that these decisions were made utilizing as much information as they could consider and are free of process errors and unintended consequences.

■ ■ ■ COMMON EXPERIENCES

Once Rosa had a firm understanding of the issue, she was ready to pose potential solutions. She needed to decide whether to pursue a policy change to allow scooters to be classified as motorcycles, to designate specialized parking zones for scooters, or to simply make no changes and just work to better inform scooter owners about current options. Each option had implications in terms of cost, policy development, and even student perception that the issue was even resolved. Rosa was well aware that her decision would influence the potential for any bill presented to be implemented on campus.

In Rosa's case, each of the three possible options had pluses and minuses. Classifying scooters as motorcycles would crowd out motorcycles in designated parking, leading to more ticketing issues for a totally new population, not to mention that scooters outnumbered motorcycles 3 to 1 on campus. While specialized parking zones had the most student support, university administrators stressed concerns that there might not be adequate space and the locations proposed could block foot traffic, not to mention the expense of signage and paint. Finally, to do nothing except launch an informational campaign was shot down in committee for not doing enough to resolve the issue, so that option was unlikely to pass the senate.

Rosa decided to hold an open forum to discuss her three options and had a panel of university officials there to answer logistical questions. In accordance with her university's open meeting policy, she issued a formal meeting announcement in the student paper and invited local press to cover the session. The open forum worked. The decision was made to pursue a bill that expanded the classification of motorcycles to include scooters, but with the compromise to add additional spaces to the parking zone currently reserved for motorcycles. This decision was met with some resistance, since the trade-off was that scooters would now be subject to the same $50 annual parking pass required for motorcycles. However, considering that a parking ticket costs more than $150, many scooter owners present felt $50 was an acceptable fee for access to safe and dedicated parking. University administrators confirmed at the meeting that if passed by the student senate, the spots could be changed by the next academic term. This compromise was the lead story in the student paper and was highlighted at the university's board meeting as an example of good teamwork and problem solving.

Workflow Planning

Many student leaders struggle with time management. This can be an especially daunting task for leaders in student government. Consider, for instance, the SGA president (although other officers in these organizations may face similar challenges). Few students will have the opportunity to serve in this prestigious role. The learning benefits for the students who do, however, are exceptionally robust. Among the many challenges students in this position face is keeping their role as SGA president in balance with the rest of their life, not the least of which includes their role as a student.

In addition to attending weekly meetings of the whole organization, keeping regular office hours, attending committee meetings, and going to any events or forums sponsored by student government, the SGA president is often among the first students thought of by faculty and administrators in seeking student input. By policy or statute, the SGA president may be required to serve as a voting or ex officio member of a variety of campus boards or committees and convene such important processes as fee allocation proceedings.

Students who are effective at prioritizing and planning their work can make reasoned decisions about which projects they can take on and which projects they should decline. However, it is often the case that student leaders have a difficult time recognizing which committees and commitments should take priority and which ones can be delegated or turned down. Advisors can assist in this process by helping SGA leaders see the larger context of their leadership experience and by encouraging student leaders to delegate.

Often, delegation does not come naturally to these students, especially considering that they often feel responsible for ensuring that initiatives are pursued and goals are met. They may feel especially culpable if they made ambitious campaign promises with the full intention of keeping them, but struggle to balance the many demands of college. Most seasoned student affairs professionals have a well-worn speech, honed through years of repetition, just for this occasion.

Student governments as organizations must also plan, organize, and prioritize work if they are to be effective. This work may take the form of strategic planning sessions, which look sometimes years into the future, or legislative agendas that guide SGA senators in developing and sequencing future legislation. This can be a significant challenge, especially among organizations that are exceptionally prolific.

■ ■■ COMMON EXPERIENCES

To accomplish her goals, Rosa would need an effective plan for presenting, passing, and implementing her scooter bill. The long list of steps and deadlines was stressful for her, because she was also planning her SGA presidential campaign, had her normal committee duties to fulfill, and had to study for her midterm exams, which were right around the corner. She needed a plan and other students' help to get all of the work done.

Rosa sat down with her advisor, who gave her a worksheet on setting priorities called the "Eisenhower Matrix" (Baer, 2014). Rosa plotted her competing priorities on a matrix with two headings. The first heading was based on how "important" the task was, the second indicated how "urgent" the task was (Baer, 2014). She was encouraged to prioritize issues that were both important and urgent, to consider eliminating items that were neither important nor urgent, and to delegate items that were urgent but not important. Based on the conversation, Rosa had a better idea of how to sequence the priorities in her life.

Quantitative Analysis

Applying the skill of analyzing quantitative data in student government can be easily overlooked. Perhaps this is because the kinds of experiences that develop this skill often happen behind the scenes. For example, the treasurer crunches numbers to prepare the budget for presentation at a public meeting or a student reviews survey data to support a piece of proposed legislation. The work is not glamorous, but it is very important.

It may also be easier to picture those in leadership positions developing this skill as opposed to the rank-and-file members. But there are many opportunities for all participants in student government to learn about quantitative literacy. Student government is often called on to routinely discuss and vote on its own budget, make allocations to student groups requesting funds, or critically evaluate a variety of data presented to support legislation. Opportunities to gain quantitative literacy can be developed for both those presenting data and those interpreting it.

In particular, hearing appeals for financial support is an area that can provide tremendous learning about quantitative reasoning. In many cases, students participating in student government listen to proposals from student groups for either annual funding or funding for specific initiatives. They must then take a critical approach to what they hear, determining if these requests have merit as well as whom and how many students these programs will benefit. For example, Wichita State University in Kansas has a process where student organizations can apply for funding for events, trips, and other expenses (Wichita State University Student Government Association, 2015). These bills and their corresponding costs are charted and tracked by student government members to ensure they follow the guidelines of the SGA and their respective universities. SGA members must learn to evaluate what they are hearing, asking questions like, "What is the estimated attendance for this event and what will the cost per participant be?" or, "Why are you requesting this money from us versus making other fundraising efforts?" or even, "How did you spend the money we allocated to you previously?" These kinds of questions ensure that SGA members are not only upholding their responsibilities to students to ensure that money is fairly and equitably spent, but also gaining quantitative skills in the process.

This skill is highly desirable to employers, perhaps because so few employees can demonstrate their effectiveness in this area. This gives student leaders a decided advantage. One former SGA comptroller reminisced on his tenure as the organization's chief financial officer, saying: "I can honestly say that while my accounting classes helped to make me proficient in my role as comptroller, I got my job with the Florida Turnpike based on my work with SGA. They kept telling me how impressed they were that I managed a $19 million budget as an undergrad" (UCF Student Government Association, 2015, p. 20). If advisors were to carefully consider the learning outcomes that are possible for the SGA, they would be wise to place a high priority on the ability to analyze quantitative data. One reason is that those presenting budgets or communicating about data are often just learning about how to do these things and their work will often reflect that. If students are to be full participants in the shared governance of the university, they must demonstrate that they take seriously their role in institutional decision making.

■ ■ ■ **COMMON EXPERIENCES**

Once it became clear to Rosa that she was on the right track with her scooter plan, she realized the plan needed to include a number of situations where she would be challenged to inter-pret quantitative data. This included a student survey where students selected the motorcycle locations they wanted to expand to meet their needs, a census of current scooter own-ership on campus, a forecast for scooter ownership for the next 10 years, and a budget analysis on whether the $50 fee would cover the costs of these changes. All of this information would prove powerful and important both for developing the bill and for a question-and-answer session during debate.

After SGA members conducted the scooter survey, they noticed that the 3 to 1 ratio of scooters to motorcycles was actually closer to 2 to 1 and that not as much space would need to be designated. This lowered previous budget estimates, so university officials were able to lower the cost of scooter reg-istration to $40. This change was met with positive responses from students.

■ ■ ■

Information Processing

One of the core competencies for any decision maker is the ability to obtain and process information. SGA membership is uniquely suited for this skill. Because many SGAs have a bill or resolution process, there are ample opportunities for students to hone the skills of finding supporting information and critically evaluating that information. As one SGA senator explained: "When I began in my current job, I quickly realized how SGA helped in my ability to gather evidence. At my job you just can't get approval because you have a great idea, you have to have evidence to show why this will work including market analysis, customer requests, and other information. SGA helped me prepare for that" (UCF Student Government Association, 2014, p. 4).

Students may encounter obstacles to developing these skills. Among these are that it takes hard work to find credible information on a given topic. With many competing demands, students may not take the time to collect information or ensure that the information is trustworthy. Another barrier is that, without much experience in research, students may only seek out information that confirms what they believe. This may cause them to present information from sources that have a clear bias or that offer no credible support for their assertions (King & Kitchener, 1994). In the absence of a structured program to help students develop critical thinking skills (either inside or outside the classroom), students may not be able to distinguish between high- and low-quality information (King & Kitchener, 1994).

To teach SGA students how to obtain and process information for legislative purposes, students should be provided with a framework for critically evaluating information they receive. These guides are framed by the questions that students who are proposing legislation are generally asked, such as:

- What is the purpose of this legislation?
- With whom should I speak to better understand the issue that this legislation addresses?
- What resources or changes will need to be made to implement this legislation?
- What evidence exists that this legislation is necessary?
- How would the author of the bill or resolution know that it was successful in accomplishing the goals of the legislation?
- What questions should the author of the legislation anticipate from the senate on this legislation?

If these questions are answered satisfactorily, then the legislation can likely proceed and its chance for success improves. By obtaining and processing information through the SGA, students learn that there are more places than the library to learn these skills. This helps the students become more flexible in their information-gathering solutions, which in the future can lead them to make a better case in the board room.

■ ■ ■ COMMON EXPERIENCES

The example of Rosa that has carried through this chapter effectively illustrates the importance of students being able to obtain and process information. Before she could conduct the survey of student needs, before she could perform a census of scooters on campus for the project, before she could develop a budget, Rosa needed to have the necessary skills to know where to go and obtain and then process information. Using the Internet, Rosa was able to locate several institutions that had designated parking permits for scooters. She found the e-mail addresses for personnel in the parking offices at these institutions and inquired about how much they charged for scooter parking permits, how many were registered on their campuses, and whether a change in revenue had occurred from adding designated parking for scooters. She also found a web page dedicated to promoting scooter ridership that offered a projection that the number of scooters on the road was expected to dramatically increase in coming years, but she was ultimately unable to see how the group supported its conclusions so she did not use that data. Rosa was able to apply critical-thinking skills she gained from her previous experiences in SGA to ensure that she only used high-quality information.

Rosa had developed this skill through her experience in the SGA. In the previous year, Rosa proposed a bill to add a Korean BBQ stand in the university quad area without doing any research. To her embarrassment, if she had just consulted with others she would have learned that area of campus was not zoned for a food establishment and the university had plans for a Korean BBQ in the university commons just 100 yards away. A fellow senator pointed out this fact during debate and the legislation failed. One of the senators who spoke against the bill was on the university food services committee and offered that next time she should consult him on such matters. Rosa vowed to always do her research for any future legislation she would write.

Career-Specific Knowledge

One of the advantages of being a member of student government is the array of opportunities available for just about any student to develop career-specific knowledge. While the first thought may be that most students who participate in an SGA are pre-law, government, and public service majors, the types of students and their career aspirations can be as varied as the universities they represent. Many SGAs are structured to have representatives from each college or major academic unit. This ensures that the participating students will be mindful of the diverse needs of the institution, and it also means that career development can take many different forms for these students.

While tasks such as writing and presenting legislation may come to mind first when thinking of SGAs, the broad missions of these groups often present many other opportunities for students to develop and hone skills that could benefit them in their careers. Leaders are needed to create and maintain websites, write press releases, plan events, field inquiries from outside groups, track budgets, keep office hours, answer phones, or oversee major initiatives. The list of opportunities abounds.

Of course, SGA membership presents tremendous benefits for students who are interested in a career in public service, law, or politics. Participants in student government can experience what it may be like to be in a real situation where representative decisions are being made. Many SGAs in the United States tend to model some version of the U.S. system of government, so there can be a direct link to the practical application of the skills needed in public policy or legal work. For example, students often get asked to serve on committees where they get to review and suggest changes to institutional policy, adjudicate parking tickets, work with university police on campus safety initiatives, or serve on grade appeal or academic dishonesty committees. Students get to influence budgets, pass bills and resolutions, and make recommendations on many student-focused decisions.

It should also be noted that not all of the experiences that these students have are limited to their role on their campus. Student governments, especially those at public universities, may have the opportunity to meet with real law and policy makers to express their opinions on pending legislation or to communicate their priorities. This is especially true at large institutions. All of these opportunities can lead to a skill set any budding lawyer or public affairs student would find a useful addition to their résumé.

Student leaders can also assist their fellow students by mentoring newer members on how the organization works and the expectations therein. The UCF Student Government Association (2015) sponsors a mentorship program that pairs students who are looking for certain career-focused experiences with members currently serving in the executive cabinet. A communication or marketing student is paired with the director of public affairs or an accounting student is paired with the comptroller. In many cases, the participating students receive course credit for their involvement through the university's co-op program. This mentorship program ensures that future generations of SGA members are properly trained, and it also allows these students to learn these skills early on with a form of career exploration.

SGA alumni are often asked to conduct reflection interviews in which they are asked what the SGA taught them, how they were influenced, and how they use their SGA skills in the workplace. As one former student senator replied: "SGA helped me understand not only how government works but also gave me a chance to experience government in a real setting. I was able to travel to Tallahassee and watch the Florida Senate meet, and I met the senator I am interning for now at an SGA reception. So I would say what I got out of it [student government] was twofold."

■ ■■ COMMON EXPERIENCES

Before joining SGA, Rosa met with her advisor in the School of Business. She was intending to major in marketing with a minor in public planning. Eventually she wanted to work for an economic development corporation, chamber of commerce, or municipal government to help them develop plans to attract new business and tourists to economically struggling cities. Rosa had grown up in a large Midwestern town that was struggling. After graduating, her goal was to return to assist with the recovery. Her advisor suggested she participate in the SGA because it would offer an opportunity to develop many of the skills she would need to take on that role once she graduated, including all of the skills outlined in this chapter. In addition, her SGA experience would assist her in understanding how decision-making bodies like a city council might work, which could also help her gain insight into her real career interests.

■ ■■

Computer Software Skills

Technology is abundant on modern college and university campuses. Laptops, smartphones, and tablets are almost as common as textbooks and notepads. However, there is a difference between the use of technology and the computer skills necessary to navigate the modern workplace. Basic computer skills tend to be the ones that most (if not all) computer-literate people possess—the ability to use the Internet, word processing software, and e-mail. Going beyond the basics requires a higher level of understanding of technology and their uses (King, 2012). These skills include database management, working over shared networks, navigating social media, using presentation software, and understanding cloud computing (King, 2012). Four of these skills are discussed here.

Database management. Like many organizations, student government associations deal with a lot of data. Proficiency with database programs can help students access, process, and present these data. How many students have attended SGA events this year? Can we run a report on the number of sophomores who are currently participating in student organizations? These sorts of questions require an understanding of how to use (and sometimes build) databases.

Shared networks. Computer-mediated collaboration is a reality of the modern age. Students participating in student government can gain this skill by leveraging shared networks to work on joint projects online. Students may use shared networks to author or edit a piece of legislation, to let committees mark up a bill, or even to write and edit proposed content for a newsletter or press release. Many students will not have the opportunity to refine this skill until they enter the working world.

Social media. Most people tend to think of students as being well versed with social media simply because social media are deeply ingrained in students' lives. But the ability to use social media is not the same as managing social media. When used thoughtfully, social media can be powerful tools for communicating with constituent groups. When used carelessly, social media may cause the same kinds of scandals seen with elected officials who do not exercise good judgment either in what they post themselves or in whom they trust to manage their social media presence. In November 2015, the SGA president at the University of Missouri had to walk back a message he tweeted about Ku Klux Klan members being confirmed on campus (Chasmar, 2015). Students and staff expressed regret that he did not fact-check before sending the tweet, causing panic and alarm. In February 2015, an officer in the George Mason University SGA was removed after political tweets angered students (Fourth Estate, n.d.). The dichotomy between the way student leaders see their peers interact on social media and the expectations inherent to being a student leader can be problematic. Failing to recognize these differences can bring serious reputational damage to the students themselves and the institutions they serve.

Presentation software. Student government members make many presentations. They are often called on to convey complex information in a clear and understandable fashion. Mastery of presentation software can be a significant tool in communicating this information effectively. This involves creating presentations that are uncluttered and that can be easily read from the distance at which others will be viewing it. Students may also learn how to incorporate such media as videos or music that can help keep viewers' attention. While students may take a public speaking class or be asked to make presentations in other classes, speeches in student government are often about issues about which students are passionate and have the power to make changes that they care about. This creates an incentive to ensure that the speech reflects positively on both the individual and the organization.

The present generation may be more connected to technology than ever before, but this does not necessarily translate directly to the kinds of computer skills that employers are looking for. Fortunately, students have ample opportunity to develop these skills through participation in SGAs. These opportunities can be enhanced significantly through training and support provided by those advising these groups.

■ ■ ■■ **COMMON EXPERIENCES**

In her efforts to develop her legislation, Rosa had to utilize a number of new applications to which she had recently been introduced. To survey the students about their impressions and recommendations for the bill, she used a survey tool developed by her business school. She was also granted access to the university's budgeting template through the shared network so she could arrange budget proposals based on a number of scenarios. Both tools helped her develop skills that expanded beyond the computer skills she used every day in her college work.

Rosa used a number of these presentation tools in her many public presentations on the Scooter Bill. She used a live survey tool where participants could respond to a poll question via text message, developed a Prezi presentation in which she embedded a variety of visual and audio components to help communicate her talking points, and routinely hosted an online chat where students could ask questions about the bill. She even had her counterpart at another university, whom she had consulted in the legislation development process, join the committee meeting via video to add his experience to the conversation. Rosa's use of technology helped her to be very effective in her role with SGA and also provided her with skills that would impress potential employers. ■ ■ ■■

Writing and Editing Reports

Being a member of a student government organization gives students the opportunity to practice their writing and editing outside the classroom. Opportunities to write as a member of an SGA can be extensive and include writing legislation, assisting in the crafting of policy statements, and developing brochures on SGA programs and services, to name just a few. From technical documents to opinion pieces for the student newspaper, the types of writing opportunities can mimic a modern office environment.

A common type of writing and editing a student in an SGA is most likely to do is craft and develop legislation for the organization, including resolutions, recommendations for policy changes, spending bills, and other formal documents. Because the documents produced by SGAs at public institutions are often public records, and SGAs at many private institutions publish legislation on their websites or forward them to upper administration, they are usually expected to be free of errors so that they reflect positively on the organization and the institution. If the legislation contains poor grammar, confusing wording, or technical errors, these mistakes can alter the meaning of the bill and interfere with future organizational efforts. This helps students understand how failure to catch errors can affect how others evaluate the quality of their insights.

Advisors can utilize many resources to teach and assist students with their writing and editing skills. Sometimes, it can be as simple as enlisting the university writing center to assist with editing and advice, but some SGAs take a more proactive approach to writing legislation. Johns Hopkins University (Palmer, 2015) offers a workshop to assist students in developing, editing, and presenting effective legislation, and the American Student Government Association (n.d.) provides online modules to help students improve their writing skills.

■ ■ ■COMMON EXPERIENCES

When Rosa began in her role with the SGA, she did not consider herself to be a strong writer. Even now, it is not uncommon to find her at her university's Writing Center getting advice and editing her papers and other writing assignments. As she approached the writing stage of the Scooter Bill, she remembered some earlier legislation that she had submitted with careless mistakes that had hurt the chances that her legislation would be passed. So, Rosa worked with her SGA advisor, utilizing a writing template developed by the organization to make sure all of the required elements of the bill were present. She then asked the SGA secretary (an English major) to edit the bill for grammar and stylistic mistakes. This helped her bill look clean and professional.

Selling and Influencing

During the 2014–2015 academic year, the Student Senate at North Carolina State University (n.d.) had 94 pieces of legislation come to the floor, of which about two thirds (62 of 94) passed. Each one of these pieces of legislation had to be vetted, reviewed, and debated a minimum of three times according to organizational documents. So, in essence, students engage in the art of achieving buy-in about 300 times a year before they even get to outside committee appointments, working with administration, and speaking to students. This organizational expectation allows students to practice the art of persuasive influence.

The act of achieving buy-in is not limited to just inside the senate chamber. Student government members expend energy in achieving buy-in from students through conducting elections and holding information sessions. In addition, students are able to practice the art of achieving buy-in through negotiating and working with university administrators to move forward with student initiatives. This type of negotiating takes a different set of skills, since often the administrator has the ultimate authority to make the decision. But the opportunity to advocate for broad initiatives that could impact the operation of an entire institution is rare for students at such an early stage of their lives. This is one of the great potentials of student government participation.

■ ■■ COMMON EXPERIENCES

Finally, the day had come for Rosa to present the Scooter Bill to the student senate. After all of her planning, decision making, writing, thinking, and coalition building, her bill was up for final approval. As she approached the lectern, she knew she was ready. She had done her homework, had created a well-crafted bill, was prepared for just about any question she could get, understood the process, and had even invited the director of parking services to attend the meeting. Now, it was time to sell her idea to the senate.

Rosa's bill passed unanimously. Her hard work paid off with a new university policy on scooters on campus, and, the following summer, the first parking spaces were designated. The Parking Appeals Committee reported an 85% drop in scooter violations and Rosa won her election to become the student body president.

ASSESSING EMPLOYABILITY SKILLS AS AN OUTCOME OF STUDENT GOVERNMENT ASSOCIATIONS

The point that direct assessment of student learning is the gold standard in cocurricular programs has been made frequently within this book and is commonly understood among student affairs administrators with assessment responsibilities. Since direct assessment is predicated on measurable changes in behavior or attitude, it's imperative that educators find ways to discern this change. This change is often observable in something referred to as artifacts of learning. A good artifact of learning makes student learning visible. This section will identify some of the artifacts of learning that SGA membership can produce as a means of discussing how this learning might be measured.

Turning qualitative experiences into data often involves rubrics. There are many great sources of rubrics. This book includes rubrics on each of the skills discussed in this chapter. Other great sources are the VALUE Rubrics (Valid Assessment of Learning in Undergraduate Education) designed by the Association of American Colleges and Universities (AAC&U; n.d.) and the Texas A&M University Student Leader Learning Outcomes (SLLO; n.d.) rubrics. Each of these rubrics can be instrumental in providing a means to measure observable change from experiences in cocurricular areas.

Legislation

Writing and presenting legislation is the cornerstone of SGA participation. Most participants will draft some legislation during their service. Some SGAs require that students author at least one piece of legislation per year. This makes legislation an excellent artifact because it is central to the purpose of the organization and because several important skills are observable within legislation. For example, effective bills and resolutions benefit from strong research. Does the legislation reflect an accurate understanding of the issue to be addressed? Did the student speak to individuals on campus who understand this issue best? Did the student see how other schools are addressing similar issues? The VALUE Rubrics can help SGA advisors evaluate the quality of information literacy, which they define as "the ability to know when there is a need for information, to be able to identify, locate, evaluate and effectively and responsibly use and share that information for the problem at hand" (AAC&U, n.d., p. 12). This rubric describes varying levels of competency within this skill, from a low level in which the member "accesses information randomly, retrieves information that lacks relevance and quality" to a member who "accesses information using effective, well-designed search strategies and most appropriate information sources" (AAC&U, n.d., p. 12). The clear and intuitive connection between these descriptions of behavior and the learning that is observable in legislation makes this a very effective assessment strategy.

Another goal of legislation is to propose solutions to issues. This positions legislation as an ideal way to observe how well students make decisions and solve problems. Again, the VALUE Rubrics can be effective here—specifically, the rubric on problem solving (AAC&U, n.d.). This rubric evaluates the student's ability to "define the problem, identify strategies and propose solutions" (AAC&U, n.d., p. 24). This has an intuitive link to legislation.

The writing of bills and resolutions is inherently persuasive. The student is attempting to convince those listening to agree with and adopt his or her solution. The ability to influence others is an important leadership skill that is highly prized by employers. The lack of well-tested rubrics could present a problem for assessing this skill. However, included within this book is a rubric for the skill of influence. Another important indication of whether the bill is persuasive to those hearing it is whether those present voted in favor of the bill. But this alone is not a sufficient indicator of success. Some SGAs may be prone to vote for almost everything that comes their way, or some may vote against a proposal for strategic reasons not related to the persuasiveness of the bill. This is where a survey methodology could prove useful—asking SGA members why they voted for or against legislation could give insight into their thought process.

While student government may not be the first experience that one thinks of when considering the development of the ability to create and edit written reports, quite a bit of writing takes place within these groups. Often, legislation must be reviewed and passed by a committee before coming to the floor for a vote. Marked-up versions of the bill, which contain the feedback and editing from committee members, could be a valuable source of information about the author's ability to write and edit. In organizations where this is not the case, it's not unusual for legislation to come to a vote of the full organization with typographical, formatting, spelling, and grammatical errors. The number or type of errors that students make can be scored on a rubric. In some cases, it could be as simple as counting and reporting the number of technical errors, perhaps before and after training intended to reduce these errors. Of course, more specific rubrics are available to provide an in-depth analysis of a student's ability to write and edit, including those in the appendix of this book.

Public Speaking and Proponent/Opponent Speeches

Not only do student governments do a lot of writing, they also do a lot of speaking. This includes speeches given by candidates running for elected positions and students speaking in favor of legislation they wrote or in opposition or support of the legislation proposed by others. Strategies for assessing verbal communication do not differ much from those intended to assess written communication except that they tend to work best when assessed in real time. VALUE Rubrics, SLLO, and this book all contain rubrics to assess verbal communication. While ink-and-paper rubrics can be useful, a number of high-quality tools for creating and using electronic rubrics can be found online. This makes the collection of data from the experience of speaking in public simple, intuitive, and intrinsically connected to the day-to-day work of the student government advisor.

Verbal communication is not the only skill that can be developed through speaking in public. The quality of research, organization, or persuasion is often evident when students give speeches. Students may also use presentation software that can provide a glimpse at how effectively they use technology. Many of the same resources that have been recommended to assess written communication can also apply here.

Surveys and Budgets

While not every student will have the opportunity to administer a survey or prepare a budget, those who do will have a valuable and arguably unique learning experience. The availability of free, web-based survey technology has made the mechanics of surveying significantly easier than it has been in the past. But this amplifies the need for teaching the skill of quantitative reasoning. Surveys with low numbers of respondents or sloppy sampling procedures are not uncommon, and are sadly not necessarily limited to student researchers. A benefit of focusing on this skill is that students often lack even the most basic knowledge about conducting effective assessment or research. Even short-term educational programs can produce dramatic results that could be illustrated with a simple pretest/posttest methodology that is based on the specific information students are being taught. Finding trainers shouldn't be that hard. Faculty and staff who are considerably well versed on this topic can usually be found on most campuses. Due to the growth in student affairs assessment in recent years, practitioners may not need to look beyond their own division.

Preparing budgets is a significant responsibility that is often invested in certain officers within the organization. While treasurers certainly participate in this process, interpreting and scrutinizing these budgets is the job of any conscientious member of the organization. Many SGAs also allocate funds to student groups that request them. The submission of a budget is often an expected part of this process. This can prompt many questions. Is the amount being requested reasonable considering the number of students who will be served? Are the estimated costs accurate? Did the group use last year's funds for the purpose for which they were intended? When designing assessment for this learning, both this book and AAC&U have rubrics to assess quantitative literacy, and Texas A&M has a rubric focused on fiscal responsibility.

Assessment should not be thought of as an additional responsibility that is separate from daily student affairs work. By focusing on generating artifacts of learning that are embedded within the normal activities of a student government participant, we as student affairs educators can produce assessments that are relevant and intuitive and, most important, that help students to improve.

CONCLUSION

For many, the significant role that student government participants play in representing their fellow students regarding important institutional decisions may obscure the many benefits of participation in these groups. It is important to remember that students are both leading and learning. Students who participate in student government are given the opportunity to develop skill sets that span all 10 of the skills identified by the National Association of Colleges and Employers (2015). While more research investigating this link is needed, the research presented in this book offers a promising start. By adopting these skills as learning outcomes for student government, student affairs professionals can achieve a variety of positive outcomes for our profession. First, it can show how participating in student government can provide students with skills that employers want. Second, by sharing a common definition of these terms, student affairs professionals can align learning outcomes across many institutions in order to demonstrate the broad impact of student participation in a variety of contexts and structures.

REFERENCES

Associated Students, University of California, Davis. (2016, January). Permanent committees. Retrieved from https://asucd.ucdavis.edu/government/legislative/permanent-committees

Association of American Colleges and Universities. (n.d.). *VALUE rubric development project.* Retrieved from https://www.aacu.org/value/rubrics

Baer, D. (2014). Dwight Eisenhower nailed a major insight about productivity. *Business Insider.* Retrieved from http://www.businessinsider.com/dwight-eisenhower-nailed-a-major-insight-about-productivity-2014-4

Bondi, P. (2016, January). *Florida attorney general—The "Sunshine" Law.* Retrieved from http://myfloridalegal.com/pages.nsf/Main/DC0B20B7DC22B7418525791B006A54E4

Chasmar, J. (2015). *University of Missouri student body president apologizes for spreading false KKK threat.* Retrieved from http://www.washingtontimes.com/news/2015/nov/12/payton-head-mizzou-student-body-president-apologiz

Cobban, A. B. (1975). *The medieval universities: Their development and organization.* London, England: Methuen.

Florida Atlantic University. (2012, August 26). Student government association. Retrieved from https://fau.edu/sg/leadership.php

Fourth Estate. (n.d.). *Student government removes undersecretary of dining over tweets.* Retrieved from http://gmufourthestate.com/2015/02/23/student-government-removes-undersecretary-of-dining-over-tweets

Hu, S., Henderson, C. E., & Iacino, J. (2012). Student governance and involvement in institutional leadership. In P. J. Schloss & K. M. Cragg (Eds.), *Organization and administration in higher education* (pp. 66–79). New York, NY: Routledge.

King, J. B., Jr. (2012, February 6). *On board online.* Retrieved from http://www.NYSSBA.org

King, P. M., & Kitchener, K. S. (1994). *Developing reflective judgment: Understanding and promoting intellectual growth and critical thinking in adolescents and adults.* San Francisco, CA: Jossey-Bass.

Kuh, G. D., & Lund, J. P. (1994). What students gain from participating in student government. *New Directions for Student Services, 66,* 5–17. doi:10.1002/ss.37119946603

Laosebikan-Buggs, M. O. (2006). The role of student government: Perceptions and expectations. In Miller and Nadler (Eds.), *Student governance and institutional policy: Formation and implementation* (pp. 1–8). Greenwich, CT: Information Age Publishing.

Laosebikan-Buggs, M. (2009, December 20). *An investigation of the impact of student government involvement at one public historically black university on the career choice of African American student participants.* Retrieved from http://scholarworks.uno.edu/cgi/viewcontent. cgi?article=2083&context=td

McFarland, D., & Starmanns, C. E. (2009). Inside student government: The variable quality of high school student councils. *Teachers College Record, 111*(1), 27–54.

Miles, J. M., Miller, M. T., & Nadler, D. P. (2008). Student governance: Toward effectiveness and the ideal. *College Student Journal, 42*(4), 1061–1069.

Miller, M. T., & Nadler, D. P. (2006). *Student governance and institutional policy: Formation and implementation.* Greenwich, CT: Information Age Publishing.

National Association of Colleges and Employers. (2015, November 18). *Job outlook 2016: The attributes employers want to see on new college graduates' resumes.* Retrieved from http://www.naceweb.org/s11182015/employers-look-for-in-new-hires.aspx

North Carolina State University. (n.d.). Student government: Legislation. Retrieved from https://sg.students.ncsu.edu/legislative/legislation

Online Sunshine. (2016, February 28). *The 2016 Florida statutes.* Retrieved from http://www.leg. state.fl.us/Statutes/index.cfm?App_mode=Display_Statute&Search_String=&URL=0200-0299%2F0286%2FSections%2F0286.011.html

Palmer, C. (2015). SGA meeting features bill writing workshop. *The Johns Hopkins News-Letter.* Retrieved from https://nlonthedl.wordpress.com/2015/09/10/sga-meeting-features-bill-writing-workshop

Snyder, T. D., & Dillow, S. A. (2012). *Digest of educational statistics: 2011.* Retrieved from http://nces.ed.gov/pubs2012/2012001.pdf

Terrell, M. C., & Cuyjet, M. J. (1994). *Developing student government leadership.* San Francisco, CA: Jossey-Bass.

Texas A&M University Student Leader Learning Outcomes. (n.d.). *Rubrics.* Retrieved from http://sllo.tamu.edu/rubrics

University of Central Florida Student Government Association. (2014). *SGA career survey.* Unpublished. University of Central Florida.

University of Central Florida Student Government Association. (2015). *Spring SGA student survey.* Unpublished. University of Central Florida.

University of Florida Student Government Association. (2016, January). *Standing committees.* Retrieved from http://www.sg.ufl.edu/GovernmentBranches/Legislative/StandingCommittees

Wichita State University Student Government Association. (2015, August 22). Organization funding. Retrieved from http://webs.wichita.edu/?u=sga&p=%2Forganizational_funding%2F

12

Developing Employability Skills Through Collegiate Recreation

David Hall and Pamela Watts

Collegiate recreation has grown tremendously over the past 30 years. Collegiate recreation programs and facilities around the country see some of the highest numbers of student participants coming through their doors on a daily basis. According to Forrester (2014), 75% of students use on-campus recreation center facilities, programs, and services, 80% of whom participate at least weekly. While early programs were designed for social and physical health benefits, recent decades have demonstrated that vibrant recreation programs contribute to the educational mission of the institution. The idea that collegiate recreation is an ancillary or optional activity, lacking critical or intentional elements of student development and the overall educational experience, is a perception of the past.

Collegiate recreation programs offer a variety of inclusive programs and services with the intent of developing lifelong healthy habits, including, but not limited to, physical exercise. The physical health benefits of exercise and sport are well understood. What is also now known are the positive effects of exercise on brain function. In *Spark*, author Dr. John J. Ratey (2008) explained "how exercise improves learning on three levels: first it optimizes your mind-set to improve alertness, attention and motivation; second, it prepares and encourages nerve cells to bind to one another, which is the cellular basis for logging in new information; and third, it spurs the development of new nerve cells from stem cells in the hippocampus" (p. 53). Simply put, exercise improves learning.

On college campuses, physical and mental health benefits are not the only goals for sport and recreation; rather, sport and recreation are also an effective platform for student learning and student development. Participation in programs and services, as well as student employment in collegiate recreation, are designed to achieve student learning outcomes and contribute to the overall educational mission of the institution. Collegiate recreation provides opportunities for students to apply classroom learning to real-world situations, which is critical for developing the skills employers want.

Research demonstrates that recreation programs are achieving these aims. Students are developing skills—including effective time management, increased self-esteem, technology proficiency, conflict resolution, verbal and written communication, and leadership—that are transferable to the work world and the world outside collegiate recreation programs. Forrester (2014) found that collegiate recreation is critical for effective recruitment and retention of students. Leadership skills developed through intramurals and sport club programs have also been documented (Dugan, Torrez, & Turman, 2014). Ratey (2008) found that students' access to and participation in recreation and sport supports optimized brain chemistry for learning. Students are not only experiencing the positive effects of physical activity during college, but are taking that learning into their leadership roles and decision making after graduation.

In addition to the benefits of engaging physically through collegiate recreation programs, it is evident that participation and employment within collegiate recreation allows for student growth and development in many tangible ways. This includes the acquisition and development of employable skills, essentially lifelong skills that shape students into becoming better citizens and employees. This chapter focuses on the intentional ways best practice collegiate recreation programs enhance a student's collegiate experience in and out of the collegiate recreation center.

EMPLOYABILITY SKILLS DERIVED FROM COLLEGIATE RECREATION

Verbal Communication

Teaching and facilitating verbal communication among student employees, student leaders, and participants is essential to the success of collegiate recreation departments. This skill is intentionally fostered within programs using evidence-based practices. In intramurals, participants self-govern to create game plans, practice schedules, and team-building activities, as well as exchange and practice verbal communication through discussion and interpretation of rules and regulations. Sport club captains learn how to communicate policy, facilitate team meetings, and act as liaisons between their teams and faculty and staff. Membership on a recreational sports advisory board facilitates problem-solving activities and reflection, as well as civil resolution of conflicts or disagreements. By necessity, members learn to effectively communicate their wants and opinions to administrative staff to create change.

While many other experiential programs are primarily focused on volunteer student leaders, collegiate recreation also focuses on student employees. Fostering positive student learning outcomes (SLOs) is intentional in best practice programs; verbal communication exercises via staff training are incorporated into programs on an ongoing basis. Collegiate recreation professionals understand that how they and their students communicate—with each other, with participants, and with all internal and external customers—is probably the single most important factor in their success. It is evident that most collegiate recreation departments devote resources to teaching this skill and providing intentional structure that leads to its development through student employment and leadership/participatory opportunities.

◼ ◻ ◼ ◼ COMMON EXPERIENCES

Jason, a senior at the University of West Florida, began his employment at the recreation center with little experience in customer service. He initially struggled with verbally communicating to patrons why certain rules, such as those regulating dress code or proper footwear, needed to be followed. He found it stressful to have to approach students who might have gotten into an argument during a heated game on the court. However, 3 years later, his outlook and confidence has evolved. Jason stated, "We've always emphasized conflict resolution and how to de-escalate situations and communicate with students. We've also always role played in customer service settings while speaking to patrons." Other common experiences include phone etiquette training, selling memberships and services, CPR/First Aid certification processes, and student supervisor–led policy and procedures trainings and question and answer sessions.

The University of West Florida also intentionally incorporates assessments and verbal communication exercises with conflict resolution into its annual all-student staff training. An associate director at the University of West Florida noted that "we write SLOs for most of our training topics. For example, we train all student employees in a standardized method of conflict resolution, which we developed in partnership with a communication professor. We also test our conflict resolution training during the year by having each employee articulate an example of a conflict they've faced in the workplace and how they resolved it. Then we assess whether their solution used each of our three steps."

PLANNING, ORGANIZING, AND PRIORITIZING WORK

A common theme found in collegiate recreation research and benchmark studies is that students who participate or work in collegiate recreation almost universally report improving their ability to organize and plan their work and improve their time management skills (Forrester, 2014; Hall, 2005; Kerr & Downs Research, 2002). This happens organically in many collegiate recreation programs. The planning, scheduling, and operational pieces crucial to event and program management lend themselves to students having to adapt, adjust, and utilize their time by setting priorities.

Student participants on all levels leverage this skill. Those who attend a group exercise class, play an intramural sport, play on a sport club team, or take an instructional class all have to identify time to do so, prioritize their daily schedule, and determine priorities of classwork, employment, and leisure time. They experience balancing the demands of those pieces of their life with social, academic, work, wellness, and even family demands. Those shared experiences teach them to plan ahead.

Student employees and leaders in collegiate recreation plan multiple activities and events, create complex schedules for employment shift coverage and intramural leagues, and develop in-depth plans for outdoor trips that include complex logistics. This is just a sample of what students experience, and this breadth of activities helps them develop their own style and process to plan out their responsibilities.

The more they engage in these experiences, the more adept they become. Developing instructional program plans, group exercise routines, or cocurricular learning plans enhances planning, organizing, and prioritizing one's work.

■ ■ ■COMMON EXPERIENCES

Tammy is a sophomore at Cornell University and works in collegiate recreation as a student facility supervisor. She shared how her work has helped her learn how to prioritize: "Unfortunately, first you kind of need things to become chaotic before you can truly understand that as a single person, you can't do everything that you want. When things truly get crazy, that's when you really understand what's most important and how to prioritize those things. Working at campus rec has taught me how to help balance prioritizing both at work and in school."

■ ■ ■

Teamwork

The concept of teamwork is embedded in all of collegiate recreation. Intramural teams, competitive sport club teams, and extramural teams exist and must function well as a unit to succeed. Every day, collegiate recreation leaders must work as teams to succeed. For example, intramural officiating crews must work as teams to be successful, outdoor facilitators must establish a collective rapport before they can effectively lead a group, and student staff lifeguards must work together to ensure the safety of participants. In turn, professionals in collegiate recreation incorporate being able to work as a team into their everyday work and interactions with student employees and participants.

Those leading in collegiate recreation programs can serve as part of a team of employees or in a team leadership position, such as sport club president or intramural team captain. Programs are often large, so a variety of leaders work within the collegiate recreation team structure. Employees in leadership positions have some intentional common experiences, including recruiting and selecting fellow team members; facilitating activities or skill acquisition exercises for fellow team members; teaching skills to other team members; responding to and engaging team members in crisis response or incidents; and communicating the goals of the team or department.

The development of teamwork is crucial to the very essence of recreational programs and activities. A student participant at Stony Brook University noted:

> Teamwork is clearly on display during intramural and sport club competition. Off the fields, the teamwork and communication that occurs behind the scenes is critical to a team's success. Intramural sport teams, for example, use teamwork when deciding which sports to play, names to use, and, most importantly, communicating schedule conflicts. Teamwork in this instance allows the team to participate on days/times which work for the majority of the team to avoid the dreaded forfeit.

■ ■■ COMMON EXPERIENCES

Samantha, a sophomore at Stony Brook University, participates in collegiate recreation and works as an intramural supervisor. Her experience as an employee and participant is an example of how working as a team in collegiate recreation is part and parcel of any best practice collegiate recreation program. Reflecting on her team captain, Samantha noted that he "always encourages us to be the best 'team' on the field. We spend 6–12 hours in fall training plus 2–4 hours in sport-specific training. Those hours plus the time we spend working together and attending meetings really promote teamwork so we are able to be the best team on the field."

Obtaining and Processing Information

Obtaining, understanding, and processing information is another everyday aspect of collegiate recreation programs and services. Student leaders constantly seek and interpret best practices to apply to challenging situations and formative decisions. For example, when intramural supervisors plan a training for flag football officials, they often refer to an official manual, such as the *NIRSA Flag & Touch Football Rules Book & Officials' Manual*, and watch instructional videos to see examples of when and how those rules are enforced. This training also includes the visuals of learning proper hand signals. Officials must use the resources afforded to them to obtain and process this information before incorporating it into a plan to teach or instruct others. Good training programs teach students how to obtain this information, how to process the information by providing written and oral communication, and how to best respond or act on information they receive, as needed.

Both student leaders and participants have many opportunities to obtain and process information. Intramural and sport club participants obtain and process information about the rules and policies of sports. Participants in personal training or group exercise programs obtain instructions and information, which they process and implement in order to effectively perform exercises beneficial to their physical health. Personal trainers and outdoor leaders gather important background information on clients and utilize that information to engage with them through intentional, customized programs. Student sport club leaders or recreation advisory board members obtain information from professional organizations, benchmarking data, and annual reports, which they synthesize into recommendations to collegiate recreation professionals. Student officials obtain information through formal trainings, evaluations, and written rule books, then process and apply that information during the games they officiate.

Collegiate recreation's robust risk management protocols are also a key example of an activity that provides meaningful opportunity for students to obtain and process information, as well as to incorporate prior learnings. Student employees are trained through policy manuals and formal trainings, then they are required to process that information and apply the learning to real-world incidents. An important part of the learning process is the practice of intentional reflection following a major incident. Student participants and leaders engage with faculty and staff to conduct in-house evaluations (via reports or meetings), where they gather and record information and consider how to improve future responses.

Collecting information, analyzing it, and producing data that can be utilized to improve programs and services is now part of best practice programs within collegiate recreation. Collegiate recreation programs rely on student employees and leaders in particular to be the first responders in obtaining and processing this information before passing it on. Even without intentionally seeking to develop this skill, student participants and leaders inherently obtain and process information, which allows them to participate in and enjoy the cocurricular experience in a collegiate recreation program.

■ ■ ■ COMMON EXPERIENCES

Megan and Heather are graduate associates at Springfield College. They obtained instructor certification in CPR/First Aid and took responsibility for training and scheduling all student employees who were required to receive CPR/First Aid certification. They felt the certification course had a real impact because all student employees had to obtain the necessary information to pass the course, work together or independently to process and/or discuss it, and demonstrate their understanding by passing both written and oral exams.

Decision Making and Problem Solving

The nature of collegiate recreation requires students to manage facilities, oversee programs, and assess the inherent risks of physical activity, which occur only within our programs (intercollegiate athletics being the only exception). Recreation facilities are often open at least 16 hours per day. Programs often run from early morning until after 11:00 p.m. Given this reality, students must be able to make decisions and solve problems without guidance for collegiate recreation to be successful as a whole. As such, intentional training, learning outcomes, and hands-on experiences are essential for collegiate recreation professionals to teach students.

Students share many experiences through participation in collegiate recreation programs that allow them to develop problem-solving and decision-making skills. Students and officers within sport club programs must assess the skill levels of fellow students, decide on playing times, develop strategies for game plans, interpret rules, and make and implement quick decisions under pressure. Further, students who participate on a collegiate recreation advisory board or sport club council interpret financial procedures, learn fee structures, make decisions on budget allocations, solve policy and procedure issues with professional staff, and make decisions on short- and long-term planning.

Many common experiences exist for student leaders and employees as they manage programs, services, and operations, often without guidance. Collegiate recreation professionals devote large amounts of time, effort, and resources to teaching decision-making and problem-solving skills through a variety of opportunities. These experiences include, but are not limited to, resolving conflict between members or fellow students about policy interpretation or guidelines; recognizing and managing risk in a variety of settings; implementing emergency action plans in case of evacuations, fire alarms, injury, or accidents; identifying and performing basic facility maintenance; scheduling or rescheduling contests based on a variety of factors (e.g., weather or officials' availability); and handling the discipline of fellow students by interpreting policies and deciding on appropriate action.

Many of these skills-based learning approaches by collegiate recreation professionals are intended to produce outcomes where students make sound decisions and eventually develop the ability to solve problems on their own. Student officiating is a quintessential example of a collegiate recreation activity that forces a student to act and think like a leader in the workplace. On the field, student officials apply their training, past experiences, and reasoning skills to make split-second decisions with limited information. The ability to communicate verbally, the ability to work in a team setting, and the ability to obtain and process information are all skills necessary to making sound decisions and solving problems. It is an overarching goal of collegiate recreation professionals to provide students with experience and training they can use to solve problems and make decisions in the absence of professional staff.

■ ■ ■ **COMMON EXPERIENCES**

John, a student at Springfield College, is the coordinator of intramural sports and a certified basketball official. While officiating, his knowledge of rules must be strong, but quick decision-making ability is just as important to make a call, explain it if necessary, and stand by it. John is then held accountable for that decision and is required to logically defend it to participants, coaches, and peers. John practices and perfects this leadership development process over and over throughout a game and during a season, which gives ample opportunity to evaluate and improve on his decisions. By participating in this process, he is ultimately practicing the everyday work he may one day experience as a department head, an association leader, or an executive. John is one of an estimated 60,000 officials who live this experience on campus every year.

■ ■ ■

Career-Specific Knowledge

Participation and leadership in collegiate recreation fosters career-specific skills development for many groups of students in a variety of settings. Most obviously, the plethora of employment opportunities in recreation facilities and programs provide learning environments where students experience day-to-day elements of a workplace, often for the first time. These basic career skills include timeliness, learning to work with a supervisor, supervising and training one's peers, adopting or implementing a dress code, understanding company culture and policies, and making decisions with autonomy. These paid opportunities develop both students who intend to join the collegiate recreation profession and those that pair their passion for recreation and sports with other career paths. Volunteer participants and leadership positions, in programs like intramural and sport clubs, also provide similar opportunities for students to develop these skill sets. As both a participant and now a leader in collegiate recreation, a graduate assistant noted that "I've learned more as an undergraduate and graduate in the recreation setting than the academic setting."

Student participants in collegiate recreation have a variety of observational and hands-on opportunities to gain and develop career-specific skills. For example, student employees in a recreational facility or program work closely with faculty, staff, and student leaders to learn and apply practical skills, such as the everyday monitoring of facilities (e.g., chemical levels in a pool or care of appropriate equipment). Intramural athletes develop teamwork, conflict resolution, and management skills while working as a team to select players, manage schedules, work within policies, and self-coach the team. Participants in group exercise classes, a ropes course, or a climbing wall observe and experience group facilitation and group management skills.

Collegiate recreation leadership roles give students ample opportunity to gain and use career-specific skills, such as human resources management, marketing, and budgeting. Sport club officers are often charged with interviewing, hiring, and managing their own officials for the duration of their season. Officers also lead processes for recruiting and selecting new participants. Simultaneously, many clubs begin the season with a small budget (or no budget at all) from their school, which leaders supplement with revenue generated through promotion and marketing activities, and subsequently plan, prioritize, and implement with the help of their team.

While leadership in collegiate recreation programs and activities arguably prepares students best for careers in recreational facilities or sports management, collegiate recreation participants at all levels gain invaluable career-specific skills that can be applied far beyond the recreation center. Through practical experience, participants and leaders have opportunities to engage in event management, complex logistics planning, risk assessment, and marketing and promotion on and off campus. Leadership and training in these skill areas are most often at the initiative and the responsibility of student leaders, who then transfer that leadership off the field. In this way, collegiate recreation offers sport and play as a medium for bigger picture student development and equips students with skills that can be applied to a variety of careers across disciplines.

■ ■ ■ COMMON EXPERIENCES

While studying fisheries and wildlife management at Oregon State University, Jake joined the soccer club as a participant. After playing for a season, he stepped into a leadership role as an officer, in which capacity he managed the team's finances. Although moving into an officer position meant juggling school, soccer, and work, the experience challenged him to better prioritize and he discovered that "when I was busier, I was more effective."

The following season, Jake took on even more responsibility as soccer club president, and as such he encountered many real-world situations that challenged him to exercise career-specific skills, such as real-time problem solving, complex logistics planning, risk assessment, and managing people and events. On one occasion, Jake had the opportunity to lead his team in planning a national soccer tournament on Oregon State University's campus. When six teams dropped out of the tournament at the last minute, Jake leveraged his event management skills to quickly assess his options. Since the tournament had been popular from the start, the organizers had decided to create a waiting list, from which Jake worked to persuade additional teams to attend on short notice. With a full roster, the tournament could proceed. Jake noted, "These events help you realize and plan for the worst case scenario and give students a good look at real-world experiences." Since graduating from Oregon State and becoming a young professional, Jake now serves as a volunteer soccer coach for the Oregon State soccer team.

Quantitative Analysis

Collegiate recreation offers participants and leaders practical, hands-on opportunities to gather and analyze data. Student participants and leaders engage in activities that help them better understand how to analyze and interpret data and subsequently present and communicate their findings in a meaningful way.

Student participants have opportunities to work with quantitative data on both individual and group levels, both in and out of the recreational facility. On a technical level, student employees in recreational facilities are exposed to and often help collect large amounts of data as part of their daily job duties. These activities can range from collecting demographics of general facility usage or class participants, to collecting the specifications of equipment or buildings and playing fields. Participants realize the benefit of this data collection (e.g., which fitness machines are most often being used) when they observe that the data are then used to positively guide the operation of facilities and programs (e.g., professional staff budget for more treadmills). Groups of participants also have opportunities to collect, review, and analyze demographic data. For example, sport clubs that host a tournament gather and analyze participation statistics, allowing group members to collectively make decisions about their immediate activities and operations, as well as engage in long-term planning for future tournaments, travel, and events.

Student leaders in collegiate recreation have the opportunity to not only participate in the collection of data, but analyze and guide what types of data provide the most value. Student leaders have robust opportunities to analyze quantitative data by monitoring and analyzing financial data through creating, implementing, and tracking budgets. For example, many sport club leaders plan, track, and evaluate their income and expenses sources for the club. Student employees plan, track, and evaluate both ongoing program budgets and special event budgets. Student supervisors use program data and budget guidelines to create staffing schedules. Additionally, student leaders on recreational sports advisory boards learn how to interpret and measure data to shape the decisions of a comprehensive collegiate recreation program.

Collegiate recreation offers student participants and leaders daily interaction with quantitative analysis. While program participants and student employees regularly give and collect data as part of their activities and duties, leaders have the opportunity to dive even further by identifying the best data to collect, using their analysis to improve systems, and presenting their findings to stakeholders. These daily interactions give students insight into and experience with the practical ways that data are used in the workplace to constantly monitor and improve services and programs.

■ ■ ■COMMON EXPERIENCES

Rebecca began her career as a student employee in collegiate recreation as a freshman at James Madison University, where she became an informal recreation assistant. As part of her daily duties, Rebecca was responsible for tabulating participation demographics, such as the number of male and female participants on the basketball courts or on each racquetball court. In this capacity, Rebecca experienced some of her first encounters with real data collection.

As Rebecca's skills developed, she took on more responsibility and with it encountered more and more opportunities to further develop her quantitative skills. Rebecca was promoted to operations supervisor and in this capacity she was then responsible for managing the student employees charged with collecting demographic data. Now, as a graduate assistant in facilities and fitness at the University of Southern Mississippi, she analyzes data collected by student employees to identify trends that affect the facility and programs, such as an increase or decrease in participation. Rebecca's data analysis is crucial for providing the most valuable programs and services for students and has a direct impact on the University of Southern Mississippi's collegiate recreation facilities.

Selling and Influencing

Participation and leadership in collegiate recreation give students inherent opportunities to develop and fine-tune the skills of achieving buy-in from, selling to, or influencing others, regardless of the level of their prior experience or expertise. Participants and leaders are responsible for the development and implementation of a variety of these activities, such as member recruitment and selection, securing a budget, and collaborating with external partners for service projects or fundraising, all of which are integral to the success of collegiate recreation programs as a whole.

As a member of a sport club, participants are an integral part of selling the team to stakeholders. Recruiting new members and fundraising gives participants opportunities to influence peers, family members, alumni, other student organizations, and the university in pursuit of a common goal (e.g., purchasing equipment, hiring a coach or official, traveling to a tournament). Participants may even identify and engage external stakeholders, such as the owner of a local pizza chain or yogurt shop, as partners in the fundraising pursuits. Season to season, participants are responsible for maintaining these positive and fruitful relationships with alumni and past sponsors.

Leaders play a crucial role in helping participants develop these skill sets, and leaders continue to advance their own skills in the process. In many critical activities, leaders act as spokespersons and brand managers for the team or groups of students. This type of leadership role is often given structure through formal councils and advisory boards. The Campus Recreation and Unions Department at the University of California, Davis, has a long-standing and well-established model of advisory councils that inform different areas of collegiate recreation, including sport clubs, intramurals, and the umbrella Campus Recreation Advisory Council. On these councils, groups of volunteer students review student appeals, raise issues of concern to professional staff and university stakeholders, and are asked to give advice and buy-in to major department decisions and policy changes before they go into effect. According to a collegiate recreation professional who works with these groups, students on these councils become empowered "to make transparent and defensible decisions" as a group, as well as develop their own voices and influence as they better "understand the complexity behind decision making that may seem simple at first glance."

By the nature of its activities, collegiate recreation requires all those involved in it to exercise buy-in and influence. As volunteers balancing school, work, and collegiate recreation, a student leader and fitness class instructor noted the "passionate force" that drives her fellow instructors to be so committed and devoted to sharing their craft with others. This passionate force is inevitably the necessary ingredient behind collegiate recreation participants' and leaders' persuasive power over their peers to leverage student fees to build new facilities, advocate for new programs, or raise and grow their own team operating budgets season after season.

■ ■■ COMMON EXPERIENCES

At the University of Oregon, a string of referenda votes was held to leverage student fees for the construction of new recreational facilities and a student union. The referenda process brought together student organizations, student leaders, and individual advocates from all across campus to bring the project to fruition. After the issue was raised with the student government, the all-student Student Affairs Facility Advisory Committee was formed. As more groups sought to be represented on the committee, a senior administrator observed that other student organizations and students on campus wanted to be a part of student leadership organizations that have influence.

Student advocates for the referenda took on a hard task. By nature of the length and time of the project, the same senior administrator reflected on the advocates' challenge of selling an initiative when the currently enrolled students who vote on the referendum will pay the per-term fee, but graduate before the facility opens and never get to use it. To leverage buy-in, student leaders instead considered how to frame the issue in a way that influenced their peers to understand that this is legacy leadership. Students leveraged social media campaigns, staffed tables in the recreation center with visuals highlighting design concepts, hosted town halls, and sought endorsements from key stakeholders, including the Intra-Fraternity Council, the Student Union Board, and Student Recreation Center Advisory Board. After many months of collaborative educational and advocacy campaigns, the referenda successfully passed. ■ ■■

Computer Software Skills

With the pervasiveness of modern technology in and out of the classroom, most students have the advantage of being well-versed in basic computer skills even before becoming participants or leaders in collegiate recreation. Collegiate recreation students leverage basic skills, like word processing and using spreadsheet databases, to acquire, analyze, and distribute information vital to the day-to-day operations of all cocurricular activities. Collegiate recreation, however, also offers unique ways for participants and leaders alike to continue to acquire and develop advanced employable computer skills.

Beyond the basics, collegiate recreation participants use computers and specific software as a medium to learn about and participate in a variety of activities. At the group level, many intramural and sport clubs use league scheduling software to create online platforms for participants to gather information about eligibility processes and subsequently sign up to participate in a team or league. On an individual level, many participants use fitness wearables or smartphone or web applications to track their personal progress and achievements. Student employees are often trained on collaborative scheduling software to track their work schedule and hours, file- and drive-sharing applications, and online survey tools.

As collegiate recreation participants rely on computers and software to facilitate participation, collegiate recreation leaders rely on technology to successfully create, implement, and evaluate the variety of programs and activities they offer participants.

Student leaders are responsible for maintaining scheduling databases and quantitative databases of facility and program statistics; they leverage presentation software to facilitate trainings and effectively communicate about their programs to external stakeholders. Leaders use design software to create digital and print marketing and promotional materials; capture, edit, and distribute videos and images of activities; and host and update websites, which participants rely on to access information and sign up for activities. Additionally, many volunteer sports and intramural club leaders use application and field-specific software (e.g., event planning and risk management software packages) alongside university faculty and staff.

Both basic and advanced computer skills are critical for collegiate recreation participants and leaders to engage in and successfully implement programs and activities. Through this engagement, participants and leaders use and develop computer skills through practical application, which is crucial to workplace success. Development of these skills is often tangential to classroom learning, but students may not even realize the impact and value of the development until they enter the workplace equipped with the competence and knowledge employers seek.

■ ■ ■ COMMON EXPERIENCES

Rebecca has held various student employee positions in collegiate recreation and is now a graduate assistant. In all these positions, developing her computer proficiency skills has played a crucial role in her ability to effectively communicate and collaborate with the collegiate recreation team, allowing the team to deliver the best programs and services to students. As part of a team, Rebecca uses student staff scheduling software, such as WhenToWork, to be able to easily and effectively coordinate her schedule with her teammates, track her own hours and those of the student employees she oversees, and ensure the different areas of the facility are safely covered at all times. Rebecca's team also uses drive- and file-sharing software, such as GoogleDocs, so everyone can be on the same page and communicate more effectively. Rebecca has learned to use data collecting and analytics software, such as Fusion, which allows her to better analyze facility access, track equipment, and identify trends in participation and demographics, all in a common tool and language that the team can use to make important decisions about what kinds of programs and services to offer. Having access to common software tools and the opportunity to develop the ways she uses these tools to communicate allows Rebecca to continually strengthen the technical skills necessary to do her job effectively.

Writing and Editing Reports

Collegiate recreation is often overlooked as an environment for fostering writing and editing skills. However, collegiate recreation programs have infrastructure that allows students the opportunity to write and edit in certain program elements. Approaches differ in intentionally teaching writing and editing to student leaders and employees versus the student participant.

Student participants have a variety of opportunities to exercise their writing and editing skills. Primarily, student participants learn how to present written information in concise ways that are understandable to a variety of audiences. Completing documents for informational purposes such as intramural entry forms, personal training Physical Activity Readiness Questionnaires, and membership or guest forms are examples of common writing experiences by participants. Participants also have the opportunity to collaborate with collegiate recreation professionals, who provide guidance in the editing process.

Beyond participation, collegiate recreation programs have opportunities built into employment and leadership experiences for student writing and editing. Personal trainers write exercise prescription plans; facility supervisors write reports regarding injuries, accidents, and incidents; intramural and sport club employees write contest reports and evaluations of officials and many help write and edit policy and procedure manuals. Sport club and advisory board members also write and edit budget proposals and requests for facilities and equipment, and assist in writing and editing policy. Student employees often have the opportunity to collaborate with professional staff and constantly improve their writing through staff feedback channels. Many collegiate recreation professionals help students seeking careers in the field write and edit their résumés.

Many of the skills learned in a best practice collegiate recreation program are intertwined. Writing and editing are often part of larger discussions and plans regarding overall communication. Professionals in the recreation field understand how all communication is critical to the success of the field. Collegiate recreation professionals consider the ability to write clearly and concisely a highly desired skill in their staff, and they strive to provide student participants, employees, and leaders with opportunities to develop this skill before entering the workplace in and out of collegiate recreation.

COMMON EXPERIENCES

Lee is an alumnus of the University of North Carolina, where he was vice president of the golf club. Each year, Lee joined the club president and other officers in submitting proposals to the sport club director for resources, trips, and budget dollars. The sport club director would sit with them and review edits, best ways to present information, and suggestions on presentations. Lee recalls that "we worked on our writing skills and learned how to be clear and concise given this type of process. Editing was also important since we learned to help edit each other before we submitted proposals after the first year we did this."

ASSESSING EMPLOYABILITY SKILLS AS AN OUTCOME OF COLLEGIATE RECREATION

Collegiate recreation engages a majority of the student body through participation and employment. Students who participate and or are employed in collegiate recreation departments gain critical skills that have been identified as important to employers in the 21st century economy, where the needs of the workforce have changed dramatically from yesteryear. The use of student learning outcomes (SLOs) is a well-established practice in collegiate recreation. They often measure the acquisition or improved proficiency of such skills as verbal communication; obtaining and processing information; planning, organizing and prioritizing work; teamwork; and other necessary skills desired by employers and discussed in detail in this chapter. This intentional process provides students with a gauge of their learning and allows departments to improve their training methods and program offerings.

To ensure students apply their cocurricular experience to real-world situations intentionally and effectively, training and development for student staff in the areas of customer service, supervision, risk management, and communication (verbal and nonverbal) should be designed to include assessment based on predefined SLOs. This allows for direct assessment to be embedded in all training programs that directly and indirectly measure the aforementioned skills employers seek—all while improving the students' performance as collegiate recreation employees. Some ways in which those skills are measured are through accurately completing written exams for risk management procedures and demonstrating skills such as setting up equipment, performing hand signals correctly for officiating, communicating during building evacuation drills, and passing a sport-specific written rules exam. Similarly, when assessment is an intentional part of a best practice collegiate recreation program, student leaders on advisory boards and sport club councils receive experiences and feedback on such skills as writing and editing, oral communication, working collaboratively as a team, technology proficiency, and influencing others. These trainings and experiences allow safe and constructive environments in which participants can evaluate their decision-making and problem-solving skills. These opportunities are ideal for pretest/posttest methodologies.

Although measuring the impact of collegiate recreation experiences to effectively develop employability skills can be challenging, a number of methods are used to evaluate development and growth. Quantitative methods like external and self-assessment and evaluation tools are used to indicate success, as is benchmarking. Additionally, qualitative methods like observation of competence, growth, or participation are crucial in measuring the impact of collegiate recreation experiences on employability skills development. Some of these common methods are discussed here.

Self-Reported Assessment and Evaluation Tools

A number of self-reporting assessment and evaluation activities are leveraged to help students identify their comfort and competence level with different skills. Students often self-report through assessment the skills they learn in a collegiate recreation program, such as becoming more prepared to handle conflict, work in a diverse environment, prioritize work, and communicate with others. Springfield College recently assessed student employment experiences in student affairs through focus groups (21 students participated). When responding to their direct work experience, one student stated "as an intramural official, I feel we learn to communicate better than most student employees because we have to explain our decisions and establish a relationship with the players or other students."

External Assessment

Alternatively, many collegiate recreation departments leverage many forms of external feedback, including staff-evaluation and participant feedback. Leaders and groups of participants who host tournaments and events on and off campus receive immediate feedback on the success of their work from participants, faculty, and staff through participant surveys. Many departments formally evaluate officials through tools that consider how they process and communicate information nonverbally (e.g., through hand signals).

Benchmarking

The development of employability skills has also been measured on a larger, aggregated scale through a number of large benchmarking studies. In his 2014 study, Forrester found that students involved in recreation programs reported significant increases in group cooperation and teamwork skills as well as communication skills. Kerr & Downs Research (2002) also found that students reported an increased ability to function as part of a team. The ability to make decisions and solve problems is also measured through national benchmarking tools, such as the *Quality and Importance of Recreational Services: Technical Manual and Survey* (Center for Assessment Research and Development, 1997).

Observed Competence

Perhaps the most commonly used technique for measuring the development of employment and other soft skills is the observation of a demonstrated application, in which professional staff or experts in the field see direct evidence of student learning. For example, students show evidence of their acquisition of computer skills through demonstrated growth in email etiquette and professional communications; advanced and innovative applications of basic programs, such as Microsoft Word, Excel, PowerPoint, and Publisher; and eventual competence as users and even trainers of career-specific software and databases. Development of skills like teamwork and communication can be evidenced by the success of sport clubs and intramural teams through sportsmanship ratings and win/loss records of club teams. Accurate membership applications and data collection records, as well as effectively communicated written and oral reports by sport club councils or recreation advisory boards, all indicate levels of proficiency by student leaders and employees. The training and communication used in assessing nonemployees like sport club leaders and advisory board members often mirror the structure that employees in program or operations areas receive within a collegiate recreation program. Although sometimes intangible, competence in some of these areas can be seen by comparing best practice examples to student output while incorporating training and development to bridge that gap until final products are delivered and observed by professional staff. Students can be observed putting these enhanced skills into practice through a budget submission for sport club, a fee proposal and justification document by an advisory board, or simple feedback by professional staff after observing customer service/phone etiquette and oral communication with stakeholders.

For example, a longtime collegiate recreation sport club professional marked success of the development of career-specific skills among the participants in leaders in her department when a local business continually called to ask for more graduates to be sent their way, because of their noted ability to plan events and work with customers.

Demonstrated Growth Over Time

Beyond observing skill development statically, the lasting impact of these experiences beyond the scope of college recreation is often self-realized by students, and employers, over time. During his tenure as soccer club president and now as a coach, Jake from Oregon State University observed participants begin to gain confidence, learn to use their voice, and develop into leaders. Watching participants first experience these eye-opening moments and start self-realizing these skills, the leader reflected that "they really don't know what they are gaining" when they first join as a participant.

Similarly, developing a skill set to create influence can primarily be measured by increased success of the campaigns and activities themselves over time (e.g., increase in funding or retention of sponsors). For example, the more often a group of participants is able to pitch their program to a university or external stakeholder and receive more funding, or a leader is able to influence a team to cohesively adopt and implement a plan, the more evident the impact.

Retention or Increased Participation

Retention of student participants and student employees is a mark of the successful impact of many collegiate recreation experiences. An increase in participation, or growth in the kinds of roles and responsibilities a student participant takes on, is an even better indicator of skills development. The University of California, Davis, Advisory Council model measures success by the active participation of the members. Of these programs, a collegiate recreation professional noted that both staff and students are responsible for "inviting a culture of inclusivity" where council members are trained and encouraged to engage fellow peers and participants to leverage the council's help, and professional staff ad hoc council members are ready and willing to listen to the voices the council raises. Impact from this process can then easily be measured by the number of student participants who feel empowered to bring an idea or concern to the council and trust the department to take appropriate action.

CONCLUSION

It is difficult to capture the variety of skills students gain from their involvement in a collegiate recreation program, due to the depth and breadth of program offerings and involvement opportunities. In addition to the physical and mental health benefits of sport and recreation, participants and leaders are given myriad options to learn and grow consistent with the educational mission of institutions of higher education. Collegiate recreation leverages sports and physical activity as a platform for student learning and development. It is an intentional process grounded in student development theories and supported by a growing body of evidence of the positive impact on students.

As the field has evolved, collegiate recreation has demonstrated a crucial role in recruiting and retaining students, helping them persist and succeed academically as well as develop a sense of community and affinity for the institution. To support the rapid expansion of programs and services, student employment has grown exponentially, creating valuable, real-world work experiences and employable skills that prepare students to succeed in the workplace after graduation.

At a time when higher education is increasingly scrutinized for the cost of an education and whether collegiate recreation impacts employability, professionals in this field will continue to be leaders in helping students develop the soft skills necessary to succeed after college. Observed positive student experience and a growing body of research demonstrate the value collegiate recreation has played in preparing students for real-world experiences since its inception. Now as collegiate recreation develops the next generation of leaders and young professionals, it is more pertinent than ever for members of this field to tell their story.

REFERENCES

Center for Assessment Research and Development. (1997). *Quality and importance of recreational services: Technical manual and survey.* Corvallis, OR: NIRSA: Leaders in Collegiate Recreation.

Dugan, J. P., Torrez, M. A., & Turman, N. T. (2014). *Leadership in intramural sports and club sports: Examining influences to enhance educational impact.* Corvallis, OR: NIRSA: Leaders in Collegiate Recreation.

Forrester, S. (2014). *The benefits of campus recreation.* Corvallis, OR: NIRSA: Leaders in Collegiate Recreation.

Hall, D. (2005). *A comparison of participants and non-participants in a campus recreation program* (Unpublished doctoral dissertation). University of the Pacific, Stockton, CA.

Kerr & Downs Research. (2002). *Value of recreational sports on college campuses.* Corvallis, OR: NIRSA: Leaders in Collegiate Recreation.

Ratey, J. (2008). *Spark: The revolutionary new science of exercise and the brain.* New York, NY: Little, Brown.

13

Developing Employability Skills Through Identity Development and Engagement Programs

Terrence L. Frazier and Alex C. Lange

Where do I go for help when the majority of the
faculty and staff don't look like me?
No one at this university understands my experience.

The sentiments above reflect those of minoritized college students, from students of color in the mid-1900s to today. A need became evident for colleges and universities to provide some form of support to these historically underrepresented students. Offices and departments emerged whose focus was to serve historically underrepresented students as they gained greater access to higher education (Shuford, 2011). (The first section of Stewart's [2011] book offers a good discussion of the development of multicultural student services.) As the visibility and needs of different marginalized identities became more prominent on college campuses, different offices and centers were established to meet the needs of these students (e.g., women's centers, gender and sexuality resource centers, offices for students with disabilities) (Kupo, 2011). Over time, the purpose of identity development and engagement programs (IDEPs) became twofold as they relate to this chapter: provide direct services for and support the retention and success of a given marginalized population, and provide education and programs about the given identity category for all students (e.g., safe space training, racial justice training). These services and programs are aimed at helping students acquire skills and competencies to navigate an increasingly diverse and global world.

While helping students navigate their campus environments, identity development and engagement educators are helping to create developmentally supportive spaces for students using a variety of lenses. For some students, the identity development and engagement office is viewed as the only safe space on campus. The goal of these offices is to ensure that all students have equitable educational experiences. Some see identity development services as targeted only toward members of minoritized and marginalized student populations; however, many IDEPs take a both/and approach—programs are created both for specific populations and individual identities, making identity development and engagement services accessible to everyone, not just those who hold a particular identity (Marine & Nicolazzo, 2014).

In forwarding a both/and model of practice, IDEPs help students develop an array of skills. This chapter discusses five of the top 10 skills identified by the National Association of Colleges and Employers (2014) that students learn in depth through identity development and engagement programs:

- Verbal communication
- Teamwork
- Workflow planning
- Information processing
- Selling and influencing

The other five skills—decision making and problem solving, career-specific knowledge, quantitative analysis, computer software, and writing and editing reports—will also be discussed. Finally, different methods to assess these particular skills will be expanded on.

In this chapter, the phrase "identity development and engagement programs" is used as a catchall for the offices, centers, and individuals that provide services and programs for students with minoritized identities and help individuals understand different social groups. This comes from a recognition that while there are professionals who focus on this work full-time, different functional areas promote development and engagement around identities through other programs and services, often depending on institution type as well as where different units are housed within the organizational structure.

THE ROLE OF IDENTITY DEVELOPMENT AND ENGAGEMENT EDUCATORS

Before examining the specific skills students gain through IDEPs, it is important to contextualize the ongoing unrest that has become more visible in recent years on college and university campuses. In 2015, high-profile incidents involving race at the University of Missouri, Yale University, and other institutions perpetuated the notion that college and university campuses (re)produce hostile climates for students of color among a host of other marginalized identities. These types of incidents are not new; they are, however, more visible due to increased student activism and social media (Harper & Hurtado, 2007; Hurtado, Milem, Clayton-Pedersen, & Allen, 1999; Linder, 2015).

In an era in which students demand accountability and redress for these types of environments, IDEP practitioners occupy an important role for institutions, being well-versed in the issues students describe from numerous reports and studies while also facilitating dialogues and mending segregated relations on campus. It would behoove all campus administrators and IDEP educators to work alongside students in addressing these campus climate issues. Not only can these efforts help students gain the skills described in this chapter, but they can also help to create more just, caring, and thriving campus communities with equitable educational experiences and outcomes.

EMPLOYABILITY SKILLS DERIVED FROM IDENTITY DEVELOPMENT AND ENGAGEMENT PROGRAMS

Verbal Communication

On many college campuses, programs that seek to facilitate dialogue across different identities aim to bring together people to discuss diversity, inclusion, equality, and equity, seeking to build relationships between and among people of similar and differing communities. While the aim of these programs is often to address and discuss these inclusion concerns on college and university campuses, dialogue programs help students gain and develop necessary verbal communication skills. It is one thing for students to be able to think creatively and construct complex notions through their internal thought processes; however, it is another for students to be able to clearly communicate these ideas to others.

One of the most famous examples of an IDEP that promotes verbal communication skills is intergroup dialogue (IGD). IGD seeks to bring people together in dialogue around contentious issues while emphasizing a strong learning community and taking action to address the inequities discussed (Zúñiga, Nagda, Chesler, & Cytron-Walker, 2007). IGD focuses on a small number of students at a time (12–18), bringing together people from two or more identity groups. Cofacilitators who reflect the identities being discussed and represented in each of the groups guide meetings. Knowledge and meaning are co-constructed by participants (Zúñiga et al., 2007). At the core of its philosophy, IGD is about building a relationship between participants that engages both the heart and the head; it is not about debate or convincing someone else they are right.

Above all, dialogue programs like IGD are about intentional communication and "voicing" (Hopkins & Domingue, 2015). Voicing is a particular skill that "captures how participants think about what they are going to say, when and how they will speak, and how asking questions is crucial for increasing their understanding of others" (Hopkins & Domingue 2015, p. 397). These skills in voicing are crucial for effective verbal communication.

■ ■■ **COMMON EXPERIENCES**

The Michigan State University Intercultural Aide program is comprised of an integrated, intercultural framework that seeks to educate students using a globally integrated curriculum and facilitate a campus climate where intercultural engagement is valued (Gazel, 2007; Gazel, Lange, & Brown, 2015). Part of the engaged learning opportunity framework of the program is weekly round table discussions (RTDs), facilitated by intercultural aides, which focus on controversial issues. The program has grown to include hundreds of participants representing diverse backgrounds coming together to discuss these issues. Common ground rules are developed and discussions take place in four locations on campus each week. The RTDs are committed to increasing knowledge of social issues and building genuine relationships among participants.

Elliot is a White transgender student leader in the Intercultural Aide program. Before the start of each weekly RTD, Elliot explains the program's goals to participants, saying, "This is a place for dialogue, not decision making." In a particular week, the program focuses on the experiences of transgender people and their experiences of violence. While much of the conversation will focus on gender, Elliot and the cofacilitator will continue to push participants to think about their multiple identities and how to effectively communicate with one another. One of the key components of communication and dialogue through this program is active listening. Active listening is the other side of the coin that is effective verbal communication (Hopkins & Domingue, 2015). When conveying ideas, it is important to use the language others have used to make a point. Elliot often uses the language the group has been using to help participants navigate some of the tougher parts of the dialogue. It is important to do this to show that Elliot is both paying attention and seeking to help others understand. Elliot also helps the group learn more about one another by using questions rather than making declarative statements. These questions were not random; they were intentional and thought out before they were voiced to the group, created using a method of questioning Elliot learned to help others learn through repeated practice of weekly RTDs in training.

Teamwork

As Thomas Friedman (2006) wrote in *The World Is Flat: A Brief History of the 21ˢᵗ Century*, people must learn to work with others and view the world in global ways. To do that, people must first gain an understanding of others. Students who are involved with IDEPs gain skills to open their mind and learn to appreciate how different cultures—and those who identify with those cultures—complement one another, including in team and group settings.

Students gain many opportunities to learn how to work on a team by being involved with IDEPs. One of the greatest skills students learn is how to accept other people and build on their strengths. Once students possess that skill, they can transition to work on many different types of teams. They then have the ability to listen to others' viewpoints to make a team stronger. IDEPs host such experiences as IGDs, which promote social justice by bringing together differing social groups to engage in communication that creates bridges across social differences, which in turn fosters stronger teams (Hopkins & Domingue, 2015). Being part of IDEPs improves students' ability to work across differences and work toward social change.

■ ■ ■ COMMON EXPERIENCES

DuJuan is a member of Emory University's Issues Troupe, a group that uses theater as a tool to explore the issues that deeply affect college students. Issues Troupe is composed of students who write and perform short vignettes, skits, and plays that seek to increase awareness of such social justice issues as identity, stereotypes, cultural differences, and privilege. The group co-constructs these performances, pulling from previous resources or writings while also combining their writing with their own experiences and campus contexts to create shows that are relevant to Emory's campus student population.

Alongside his fellow team members, DuJuan develops topics to address through theater performance. The group has been invited to kick off the first-year relationship violence and sexual misconduct training for new and transfer students. To prepare for this training, DuJuan and his team must work together to accomplish their goal—to increase awareness of issues related to relationship violence and sexual misconduct, including skits and vignettes around consent, healthy sexual boundaries, and more. DuJuan and another member of the team have background knowledge about sexual assault issues on campus that they gained from the campus's Title IX office, which provides information to students through a series of educational programs. However, other members of DuJuan's team have not gone through those educational programs. Thus, it is important for DuJuan to share knowledge with the group while capitalizing on the others' strengths to make the piece come to life. For instance, while DuJuan has background information, he knows other members of the team are better at writing. Thus, through knowledge sharing, the team together plans what the piece will say and how it will be presented before the training. ■ ■ ■

Workflow Planning

Planning, organizing, and prioritizing are necessary skills for students across all identities, cultures, and organizations. Through IDEPs, students learn to create and organize programs and services that are intentional and seek to address specific goals and outcomes. Almost any program or meeting that an identity-based organization or function hosts must be thought out, and several angles and perspectives must be considered. To achieve certain priority objectives, students involved in identity-based, activism-focused organizations must carefully plan negotiations and discussions with campus administrators, elected officials, and other authority units.

In addition, programs that seek to bring people together to discuss or work across differences require an incredible level of intention and organization. Without common goals and set priorities, students may believe they are achieving certain ends when in fact they are not moving any closer to their desired outcomes. Students learn that planning, organization, and prioritization are not natural occurrences; they require attention.

■ ■ ■ COMMON EXPERIENCES

Kiara has been elected to serve as the conference chair for the annual meeting of the Midwest Bisexual, Lesbian, Gay, Transgender, Ally College Conference (MBLGTACC), one of the largest college conferences in the world. The conference brings together more than 1,000 students and their advisors and is planned and organized entirely by a student board from the host institution. While Kiara's institution is the host site of the conference, she and the conference advisor help to lead and guide a team of 10 conference subchairs, each charged with different tasks and aspect of the conference. Kiara has 2 years to prepare before the conference comes to campus.

During the application process, Kiara and her team composed a comprehensive bid that was presented to the voters from each state represented at the conference. The bid included letters of support from university administration, plans to secure funds and donors for the event, and selection of a theme.

After Kiara and her team won the bid to host the conference, they held weekly meetings to discuss the conference, creating a timeline and plan to achieve their necessary goals. While this conference team wanted to break previous records of conference attendance, they understood the first priority was for the conference to pay for itself. Thus, the team had to identify and solidify sources of funding within their first year of planning to better determine the cost of registration for attendees. The group also wanted participants to walk away from the conference with a plan to achieve social change at their home institutions, especially around gender marker information. Because attendees come from both across and outside the region, lodging and food became part of the planning. The conference team was also responsible for securing keynote speakers, developing entertainment for the evenings, determining how programs and curriculum would be developed, and more. Planning such a large-scale event as MBLGTACC helped Kiara and her team set goals, create time frames, and determine factors for what would be an would not be priorities for the team.

Information Processing

In the age of Google, gathering and obtaining information has never been easier, especially for college students. Students have access to incredible amounts of data, facts, figures, and information related to their major and interests. In IDEPs, students obtain and process information from more than just a textbook or traditional method of data collection and production. Those with marginalized identities have often found storytelling and lived experiences as sources of knowledge and information production (Delgado & Stefancic, 2001). With so much information being easily obtained, there is a greater need to help people process all of that information. Thus, the challenge for students in an open-access-information world is to discern which information is credible, trustworthy, and valid.

As previously discussed, students who desire to influence others must be able to understand people's particular motivations. For instance, campus administrators, especially in an age of accountability, are motivated by data about process and outcomes assessment as well as campus climate information (Thelin & Gasman, 2011). Students have access to a great deal of information about their institutions, particularly at public institutions. They have access to campus climate studies, localized reports from national studies like the National Study of Student Engagement, and annual reports from their institutions and a variety of offices. In addition, they have access to information through social media, which are focused on providing each individual user with content that is curated toward his or her desires and wants. However, due to its own design, social media oftentimes show users information that supports their existing beliefs rather than challenging them (Owad, 2006). Websites, such as Snopes.com, illustrate the vast amount of misinformation that can be consumed on the Internet each and every day. Students must learn how to discriminate between the accurate versus the inaccurate in the information they obtain, while simultaneously dealing with such large amounts of data, once they have collected it.

■ ■ ■COMMON EXPERIENCES

Tyler is a first-year student who comes from a rural part of Michigan. He doesn't know much about sexuality or gender beyond his own small-town experience. He wants to learn more about those in the LGBTQ community to better connect with others at his institution. Tyler had not had previous access to this information and was fearful of searching the Internet for answers, worried that he would not know which information was accurate without some baseline of information. Tyler, who now attends Michigan State University, remembered that the institution had a Lesbian, Bisexual, Gay, and Transgender (LBGT) Resource Center and e-mailed its coordinator of education to learn more about the options available to him.

Michigan State University's LBGT Resource Center facilitates a program called QuILL (Queer Inclusive Learning and Leadership). Formerly known as Safe Zone Training, QuILL is a two-part course designed to help educate students, faculty, staff, and community members on the foundations of sex, gender, and sexuality while also helping attendees to discuss practical strategies to put their learning into action. The first part of the course is presented online and is entirely dedicated to concepts, terminology, and helping participants develop frameworks for processing information, rather than just being able to reiterate terminology lists. The second part of the course is an in-person workshop designed to address gaps of understanding in the online course; it utilizes the frameworks taught in the first part to process how one interacts with and creates policies and systems inclusive of individuals who identify as LGBTQ.

Tyler, after learning about QuILL, signed up for the program. He found that the material was developmentally sequenced so he could learn about sex, gender, and sexuality. Tyler learned about various understandings of those identities as well as how to better comprehend new terminology he encountered based on its prefix or suffix, for instance. After completing the online course, Tyler found that the in-person workshop strengthened his ability to process his learning by applying it to a variety of case studies to determine good outcomes. After completing both parts of QuILL, Tyler found that he was better able to understand and empathize with people who identify as LGBTQ.

Selling and Influencing

It is always important to seek to understand first and then be understood; this is the core of influencing others (Covey, 2013). IDEPs help to develop skills to better understand oneself as well as others. One must know themself before they can lead. As one begins to understand others and their unique histories, backgrounds, and identities, it is easier to tune into their individual motivations. It is not enough to just make assumptions about someone to influence them; one must get to know others further to persuade and lead them in several types of environments.

Students who participate in IDEPs gain experience in influencing others. Many offices and centers host such events as cultural and history months, power and pride rallies, speakers bureaus, and town halls and discussion meetings. These programs both promote community development among marginalized students and also educate members of dominant groups about a given culture or identity. The latter aim of these programs is often to influence how one thinks about another culture or community of people. The student leaders who often organize these events learn valuable leadership skills and how to motivate others around a common cause or social issue (Haber-Curran, Allen, & Shankman, 2015).

One program in particular that has had an effect on influencing others is one many LGBTQ resource centers utilize: speakers bureaus. Also known as panel programs, these programs teach students how to share their stories of coming out and being marginalized by their sexuality or gender identity (Woodford, Kolb, Durocher-Radeka, & Javier, 2014). These panels are often presented as programs sponsored by a particular office or as part of coursework or class sessions in particular disciplines (e.g., sociology, social work, education). Giving students real-life examples of the privilege and oppression their peers face helps to promote learning gains and influence the thoughts and opinions of others (Garriott, Reiter, & Brownfield, 2015). Through storytelling and connecting with others, students can learn to influence others around them throughout their careers.

■ ■■ COMMON EXPERIENCES

Ezell is a Black cisgender male student who is majoring in engineering, preparing to return to school for his final year. Throughout the summer, he has been immersed in images of unarmed Black men being killed by law enforcement. He is in disbelief at the pattern and repeated images on the news.

Once Ezell returns to school, he speaks with the Office of Multicultural Affairs about hosting a town hall meeting about the recent public killings of unarmed Black men in the United States. Ezell previously worked with the office as a member of and leader in the Black Student Alliance, participating in ongoing leadership training with his advisor. Ezell and staff agree that the program should focus on not only bringing the community together but also explaining to others how these murders continue to be a part of a system that fails people of color in the United States.

At the event, Ezell speaks to the crowd about his thoughts and feelings on the continued violence against men of color in the United States. Rather than citing endless facts and statistics, Ezell begins the event with a story, recognizing that others develop empathy and learn on deeper levels when an emotional or personal connection is present (Haber-Curran et al., 2015). After opening the event with his connection to this systemic violence, he invites people in the crowd to speak to understand their perspectives. After each person speaks, Ezell checks for understanding and thanks the person for sharing (Egan, 2007). Ezell finds that others are more inclined to continue listening and taking in what he was saying when he both repeats and affirms their contributions.

By the end of the event, Ezell is able to challenge and affirm others' placement of values on Black lives. Ezell is also asked to write a weekly column for the campus newspaper, where he continues to develop his skills of influence through his written communication skills.

OTHER NACE EMPLOYABILITY SKILLS

While the five skills above are heavily evident in IDEP programs and services, they are by no means the only skills students gain.

Decision Making and Problem Solving

For student advocates and activists, decisions often must be made about who, what, when, and where to advocate for the student body. For instance, students wishing to advocate for the elimination of racism on campus may debate between marching toward the center of campus or marching to the president's office. For activists, both involve calculated choices. Marching to the center of campus will cause traffic backups and ensure that more of the campus community sees the students' activism taking place, likely guaranteeing their message is seen and heard. However, marching to the president's office will send an explicit message to campus administrators that racism will no longer be tolerated on campus. Student activists must weigh these options and decide which solution will ultimately lead to the accomplishment of their goal: the eradication of racism on campus. Decisions about how to achieve that goal are usually generated through dialogue programs that focus on helping students visualize the cause and effect of their decisions. These programs can take the form of weekly student leader roundtables where advisors help students debate various decisions, or they can be part of a greater leadership retreat where different organizations that support minoritized students come together to discuss action planning for a particular semester or school year.

Career-Specific Knowledge

Helping students develop knowledge related to their future careers is not only about helping them gain certain sets of competencies but also helping them identify gaps in their skill sets and creating strategies to address these needed experiences. For students who are interested in becoming community organizers or social workers, a great deal of career-related knowledge can be obtained from IDEPs. Students can gain hands-on experience supporting marginalized populations and communities, learning the unique needs of different groups while understanding the health disparities for those who engage in identity-related work. For students trying to address gaps in their skill sets, working with and alongside practitioners who are well connected on campus and may be understaffed themselves can be extremely beneficial. For instance, if a student is interested in gaining event-planning experience, practitioners can have the student help plan an annual cultural festival that takes place on campus to give that particular student experience in program planning in a low-risk environment.

Quantitative Analysis

Understanding the meaning of numbers in a variety of contexts is important for students who seek to create and sustain institutional change, such as those who work with practitioners in IDEPs. Students often use data to back claims of discrimination and institutional inaction as it relates to their negative experiences on campus. For instance, students at a particular university may cite a lack of faculty diversity along the lines of race and gender as the institution lacking care or concern for diversity or inclusion, even though one or both of those may be core values of the institution. Rather than relying on anecdotal evidence to make that claim, students have learned through peer leader learning or student leader retreat experiences how to use data to back their claims to university administration. In addition to analyzing quantitative data at an institutional level, students also learn how to evaluate data they collect from their own program assessment. After attending a workshop on assessing programs, students learn how to collect and analyze data in meaningful ways to improve their programs in the future.

Computer Software Skills

As social media technologies increase in size and scope, marginalized students learn how to use these platforms at rates greater than their peers, as these social media outlets give them a voice in ways they did not have access to before. In addition, in an effort to advertise their own programs, students learn how to use programs like the Microsoft Office suite as well as components of the Adobe suite, such as Photoshop. Under the guidance of practitioners, students come together under the guidance of 101 workshops and informal teaching programs to learn more about how to use certain technologies. For instance, through partnerships with other offices, IDEP educators help educate minoritized students on software like Microsoft Excel and Word and Adobe Photoshop, because of historical barriers to learning about these programs. Rather than sitting through a class or lecture, students learn side-by-side with their peers, which allows them to ask questions live and gaining immediate feedback. Practitioners can also give students different projects to allow them to explore and develop multimedia competencies. For instance, in advertising the upcoming drag show, students can rent equipment from a source on campus, most often the library or multimedia center, to draft scripts, record and edit video, and develop a promotional message to be shared via social media prior to the event. This allows students to develop promotions for their own events while also learning a given skill related to video development.

Writing and Editing Reports

While some institutions require students to take writing courses during their undergraduate experience, it is important that students are given opportunities in their cocurricular contexts to practice their writing. Practitioners can utilize reflection prompts and 5-minute essays to help students work on their writing skills. For instance, in reflecting on their learning in the QuILL web course and workshop, participants are asked for their top three takeaways from the session. Specifically, they are asked, "What are the three most important learnings you are taking away from this training? Why those three? How can you use this information in different contexts?" Presenting these questions at the end of the training session gives students a great way to reflect on their experience with the program while also encouraging them to explain their learning in a written form that others will be able to read and understand.

ASSESSING EMPLOYABILITY SKILLS AS AN OUTCOME OF IDENTITY DEVELOPMENT AND ENGAGEMENT PROGRAMS

The particular skill(s) practitioners seek to assess and evaluate will change the particular measure or method. Practitioners seeking to cultivate these skills in students must do so with a specific learning outcome design and intervention method in mind to achieve skill development (Barham & Scott, 2006). Once programmatic interventions are delivered, it is time to assess learning and make recommendations for future interventions. Assessing the learning and skill development of students who participate in IDEPs can be undertaken using both direct and indirect measures of learning utilizing quantitative or qualitative assessment tools (Keeling, Wall, Underhile, & Dungy, 2008; Upcraft & Schuh, 1996).

Rubrics are one method of assessing student skill development. Skills such as influencing others and verbal communication are not easily assessed through self-reported, indirect learning measures. To this end, practitioners can use rubrics to meet student learning and assessment needs. Rubrics can be either developed locally based on the individual programmatic interventions IDEP practitioners create or standardized nationally. For instance, the Association of American Colleges and Universities (AAC&U) launched the Liberal Education and America's Promise (LEAP) initiative in 2005. LEAP sought to promote the value of a liberal education and identify essential learning outcomes that all college students should achieve as preparation for successful participation in civic life and the global economy. To better assess learning for the AAC&U LEAP outcomes, the VALUE Rubrics (Valid Assessment of Learning in Undergraduate Education) were developed. These rubrics, developed by faculty members, academic staff, and student affairs staff across the country, sought to evaluate learning in several of the LEAP Essential Learning Outcomes. Presently, there are free, accessible rubrics for the following outcomes that overlap with the skills this chapter seeks to assess: critical thinking, oral communication, foundations and skills for lifelong learning, inquiry and analysis, and quantitative literacy. These rubrics can be used by practitioners to assess some of the skills discussed above. The rubrics are easy to use and avoid discipline-based jargon.

Allowing students to self-report their learning through indirect measures may also be helpful to assess learning. While indirect measures of learning are not as valid and trustworthy as direct measures (Keeling et al., 2008), there is merit in having students assess their own learning. Even though some research indicates that students may not always be best at assessing their own learning, students who had a strong sense of progress in their development were accurate about their new learnings (Bowman & Seifert, 2011). At the end of their involvement with a particular program or project, students can use self-assessment sheets, such as those provided by the Jossey-Bass Student Leadership Competencies Database, to assess their learning. The Competencies Database seeks to provide a concise way to evaluate each of the 60 dimensions of a particular competency, including knowledge, value, ability, and behavior (Seemiller, 2014). Competencies related to the skills discussed in this chapter include, but are not limited to, "Advocating for a Point of View," "Verbal Communication," and "Group Development." These self-reported measures can be coupled with one-on-one conversations with advisors and mentors to allow the student a chance to reflect on their self-reports while also receiving feedback from practitioners.

Finally, for programs like QuILL, learning can be directly measured using quantitative measures. For instance, the QuILL web course utilizes both formative and summative assessment tools to measure if and how students are learning the content. There are questions between the different content modules within the QuILL web course, helping to assess whether students understood the material in a particular section of a module. The end-of-course text requires participants to receive a 90-percentile score or greater to "pass" the web course and qualify for an in-person workshop.

CONCLUSION

IDEPs seek to educate the entire campus community about different identities, communities, and cultures, while also helping students discover and amplify their voice. Many may see the work of IDEPs as being just about advocacy and social change. The work of these programs goes beyond that. The services that these offices and centers offer students greatly enhances their skill development. It is important for practitioners to help students understand how their activism and engagement experiences connect to their résumés and job interviews. Students in IDEPs gain the same skills as those students who participate in functional areas like service–learning or community engagement; student affairs practitioners can help students make those connections and teach them to discuss these experiences post-college. The best leaders and employees are those who understand who they are in relation to others.

REFERENCES

Barham, J. D., & Scott, J. H. (2006). Increasing accountability in student affairs through a new comprehensive assessment model. *College Student Affairs Journal, 25*(2), 209–219.

Bowman, N. A., & Seifert, T. A. (2011). Can college students accurately assess what affects their learning and development? *Journal of College Student Development, 52*(3), 270–290. doi: 10.1353/csd.2011.0042

Covey, S. R. (2013). *The 7 habits of highly effective people: Powerful lessons in personal change.* New York, NY: Simon & Schuster.

Delgado, R., & Stefancic, J. (2001). *Critical race theory: An introduction.* New York, NY: New York University Press.

Egan, G. (2007). *The skilled helper: A problem-management and opportunity-development approach to helping* (8th ed.). Pacific Grove, CA: Brooks/Cole.

Friedman, T. L. (2006). *The world is flat: A brief history of the twenty-first century.* New York, NY: Farrar, Straus and Giroux.

Garriott, P. O., Reiter, S., & Brownfield, J. (2015, July 13). Testing the efficacy of brief multicultural education interventions in White college students. *Journal of Diversity in Higher Education.* Advance online publication. doi: 10.1037/a0039547

Gazel, J. (2007). Walking the talk: Multiracial discourse, realities, and pedagogy. *American Behavioral Scientist, 51*(4), 532–550. doi: 10.1177/0002764207307741

Gazel, J., Lange, A. C., & Brown, P. G. (2015, October). *Holistic intercultural engagement: Advancing a both/and model of practice.* Presentation for the Michigan College Personnel Association Annual Conference in East Lansing, MI.

Haber-Curran, P., Allen, S. J., & Shankman, M. L. (2015). Valuing human significance: Connecting leadership development to personal competence, social competence, and caring. In J. E. Owen (Ed.), *Innovative learning for leadership development* (New Directions for Student Leadership, No. 145, pp. 59–69). San Francisco, CA: Jossey-Bass.

Harper, S. R., & Hurtado, S. (2007). Nine themes in campus racial climates and implications for institutional transformation. In S. R. Harper & L. D. Patton (Eds.), *Responding to the realities of race on campus* (New Directions for Student Services, No. 120, pp. 7–24). San Francisco, CA: Jossey-Bass.

Hopkins, L. E., & Domingue, A. D. (2015). From awareness to action: College students' skill development in intergroup dialogue. *Equity & Excellence in Education, 48*(3), 392–402. doi: 10.1080/10665684.2015.1057446

Hurtado, S., Milem, J., Clayton-Pedersen, A., & Allen, W. (1999). Enacting diverse learning environments: Improving the climate for racial/ethnic diversity in higher education. *ASHE-ERIC Higher Education Report, 26*(8), 1–140.

Keeling, R. P., Wall, A. F., Underhile, R., & Dungy, G. J. (2008). *Assessment reconsidered: Institutional effectiveness for student success.* Washington, DC: International Center for Student Success and Institutional Accountability.

Kupo, V. L. (2011). Remembering our past to shape our future. In D. L. Stewart (Ed.), *Multicultural student services on campus: Building bridges, re-visioning community* (pp. 13–28). Sterling, VA: Stylus.

Linder, C. (2015, November). *An intersectional approach to selectively supporting student activists.* Paper presented at the annual meeting of the Association for the Student of Higher Education in Denver, CO.

Marine, S. B., & Nicolazzo, Z. (2014, November 3). Names that matter: Exploring the tensions of campus LGBTQ centers and trans* inclusion. *Journal of Diversity in Higher Education.* Advance online publication. doi: 10.1037/a0037990

National Association of Colleges and Employers. (2014). *Job outlook 2015.* Bethlehem, PA: Author.

Owad, T. (2006). Confirmation bias: A ubiquitous phenomenon in many guises. *Review of General Psychology, 2*(2), 175–220.

Seemiller, C. (2014). *The student leadership competencies guidebook: Developing intentional leadership learning and development*. San Francisco, CA: Jossey-Bass.

Shuford, B. C. (2011). Historical and philosophical development of multicultural student services. In D. L. Stewart (Ed.), *Multicultural student services on campus: Building bridges, re-visioning community* (pp. 29–37). Sterling, VA: Stylus.

Stewart, D. L. (Ed.). (2011). *Multicultural student services on campus: Building bridges, re-visioning community*. Sterling, VA: Stylus.

Thelin, J. R., & Gasman, M. (2011). Historical overview of American education. In J. H. Schuh, S. R. Jones, & S. R. Harper (Eds.), *Student services: A handbook for the profession* (5th ed., pp. 3–23). San Francisco, CA: Jossey-Bass.

Upcraft, M. L., & Schuh, J. H. (1996). *Assessment in student affairs: A guide for practitioners*. San Francisco, CA: Jossey-Bass.

Woodford, M. R., Kolb, C. L., Durocher-Radeka, G., & Javier, G. (2014). Lesbian, gay, bisexual, and transgender ally training programs on campus: Current variations and future directions. *Journal of College Student Development, 55*(3), 317–322. doi: 10.1353/csd.2014.0022

Zúñiga, X., Nagda, B. A., Chesler, M., & Cytron-Walker, A. (2007). Intergroup dialogue in higher education: Meaningful learning about social justice. *ASHE Higher Education Report, 32*(4), 1–128.

14

Developing Employability Skills Through Leadership Development Programs

Gayle Spencer and Adam Peck

The landscape of higher education dramatically changed in the 1960s and 1970s. One of the major reasons was the Higher Education Act of 1965, which, for the first time, extended need-based financial assistance to the general population. At the same time, the civil rights movement allowed for the challenging of laws and practices that excluded minorities from attending some colleges and universities (Brock, 2010). Add to the mix the social activism occurring on campuses, particularly protesting against the Vietnam War. In 1972, the Watergate Scandal slowly began to unfold (Bernstein & Woodward, 1974). As a result, Richard Nixon resigned as president on August 8, 1974 (Kilpatrick, 1974). The effects of Watergate were immediate and long lasting. It reinforced the growing disillusionment and lack of faith in the government, particularly among the baby boomers who were attending college.

It is in this context that the teaching of leadership as a discipline began in the 1970s (Council for the Advancement of Standards in Higher Education [CAS], 2015). During a time of such distrust of politicians and those who ran the government, coupled with students' demand for more of a role in the governance of colleges and universities, it would

337

make sense that the discussion and teaching of leadership would be of growing interest on college campuses.

THE LEADERSHIP EDUCATION AGENDA

The leadership education agenda in higher education began in mid-1980. By the end of that decade, an estimated 600 colleges were teaching leadership courses (CAS, 2015). Today, many colleges and universities have comprehensive leadership programs. This effort is often campuswide, and programs often occur through student affairs units as well as separately through academic colleges and other departments on campus.

Because leadership education is relatively new and the body of knowledge is limited, skepticism has been raised about the validity of leadership as a discipline. As a result, in 2013, Andenoro et al. developed the document *National Leadership Education Research Agenda 2013–2018* to address the areas of research that student affairs professionals should focus on in the next 5 years. One of the biggest challenges in identifying the agenda is the interdisciplinary nature of leadership. The diversity of perspectives owing to the number of fields in which leadership is taught (e.g., colleges of business, agriculture, or engineering; student affairs departments) makes it difficult to find a common definition of leadership education as a discipline. In the context of this report, *leadership education* is defined as "the pedagogical practice of facilitating leadership learning in an effort to build human capacity and is informed by leadership research and theory. It values and is inclusive of both curricular and co-curricular educational contexts" (Andenoro et al., 2013, p. 3).

In addition to the discussion of the relevancy of leadership education as a discipline are the challenges associated with these leadership education initiatives. Those challenges include instructional and curricular design, consistency, and assessment (Andenoro et al., 2013).

When discussing teaching, learning, and curriculum development, Andenoro et al. (2013) examined four areas, which must be explored:

- **Develop transdisciplinary perspectives for leadership education.** Educators must intentionally develop interdisciplinary connections to disciplines such as instructional and curricular design, program assessment, student development, and training and development to inform our work and how we view teaching and learning associated with leadership education.
- **Explore the capacity and competency development process for the leadership education learner.** By developing a deepened understanding of innovative and effective teaching and learning, leadership educators can identify emerging techniques and innovative teaching approaches.
- **Explore the role of the individual learner in leadership education.** Factors such as developmental readiness, leadership self-efficacy, motivation to learn, and leadership experience all impact how we develop curriculum and instruction, as well as affect the learners themselves.
- **Explore curriculum development frameworks to enhance the leadership education transfer of learning.** When developing curriculum, various designs must be considered. Learning environments must be learner, knowledge, assessment, and community centered.

THEORETICAL FRAMEWORKS AND LEADERSHIP DEVELOPMENT PROGRAMS

One great strength of leadership development programs is that they can be tailored to fit the needs of each individual institution. Sowcik, Lindsey, and Rosch (2013) suggested that any leadership program should be grounded in a theoretical framework that is consistent within the context of its college or university; this will allow each program to have creativity and autonomy in its offerings while avoiding excessive standardization of programs. This also challenges the discipline in demonstrating its overall impact on students as there is no universal curriculum.

Another important consideration that affects the quality of leadership programs offered is the professional qualifications of those administering these programs. How were they educated and trained? What theoretical frameworks are being used to design the programs? Is there consistency in the programs offered from university to university? The answers to these questions affect how the leadership discipline is perceived and received in academia.

The following are some of the most salient results from *Findings from the Multi-Institutional Study of Leadership – Institutional Survey: A National Report* (Owen, 2012), an assessment of collegiate programs that included a sample size of 89 institutions:

- Most campuses identified themselves as being at the early stages of building critical mass (48%), or as working to enhance the quality (35%) of their leadership development programs.

- Most programs claimed to be grounded in theoretical approaches to leadership, yet 64% often relied on personality assessments, heuristics, and other nontheoretical approaches to program applications.

- The preparedness of leadership educators varied greatly. Most reported little to no coursework in leadership studies (52%).

- While many leadership educators claim to engage in regular assessment of student learning (79%), program evaluation, and use of national standards (45%), many do not make full use of those data.

- Few leadership programs (14%) engage in regular strategic planning, which in turn does not allow for the closing of the assessment loop by connecting planning and results.

As the field of leadership education advances, it will be imperative to ground programs in theory, to ensure that educators receive formal training, and to make strategic planning and assessment a regular occurrence.

There seems to be agreement that leadership programs should be based in a theoretical framework. Many of the theories used in leadership education programs are competency based. Some of the more frequently used theories are the social change model (Astin & Astin, 2000); *The Leadership Challenge* (Kouzes & Posner, 2012); *The Student Leadership Competencies Guidebook* (Seemiller, 2014); and *Emotionally Intelligent Leadership* (Shankman, Allen, & Haber-Curran, 2015).

"Competencies are knowledge values, abilities and behaviors that help an individual contribute to or successfully engage in a role or task" (Seemiller, 2014, p. xv). Competencies are important and tie leadership and career together because they help provide a framework to design experiences for students, which help to link their leadership competencies to their chosen career field. As the use of competencies is commonplace in many professional organizations and about 75% of businesses (Seemiller, 2014), it would make sense to develop a leadership program tied to competencies. A program should identify the competencies it would like to have students develop as a result of participation in the program, create curriculum around these competencies, and then measure student development and learning around them.

LEADERSHIP DEVELOPMENT PROGRAMS AND CAREER READINESS

All of the top 10 National Association of Colleges and Employers (NACE; 2015b) employability skills, if they are not already, can and should be included in leadership program curriculum. In addition to making these skills part of a leadership program, another consideration is how leadership educators can help students articulate the skills they have developed because of their leadership experiences. Students should be able to give employers salient examples from their leadership experiences that relate to their future employment. The term for this is now called *career readiness* or "the attainment and demonstration of requisite competencies that broadly prepare college graduate for a successful transition into the workplace" (NACE, 2015a, para. 3).

Students should consider activities that will aid in their development of competencies. The concept of career readiness should help draw students to leadership programs as they make the connection that career readiness begins the minute they step on a college campus. It is in a student's best interest to plan a college journey that will enable him or her to gain these employability skills while having rich and meaningful leadership experiences, both in the curricular and cocurricular setting.

This chapter discusses each of the 10 skills (NACE, 2015b) with examples of how they can be integrated into leadership programs. By incorporating these skills into program curricula, the purpose of leadership programs can be reframed for a number of key stakeholders. This focus can help students see leadership programs as not only an opportunity to gain a variety of esoteric and disconnected skills but also the means to develop skills that will have practical usefulness throughout their lives. Faculty should see leadership programs as contributing to students' preparation for their career in ways that the classroom cannot always address. These programs should demonstrate to business leaders that students are receiving the training and education they need to perform at the highest level from their first day of work.

EMPLOYABILITY SKILLS DERIVED FROM LEADERSHIP DEVELOPMENT PROGRAMS

Verbal Communication

There is a natural connection between learning outcomes in leadership programs and the development of verbal communication skills. Whether they are holding small group discussions on leadership topics, teaching leadership concepts to others at a conference or retreat, or even reporting to the group at the conclusion of a learning activity—having students share what they learn with others can test their comprehension of the topic, help them make sense of what they are learning, and promote their verbal skills. As the French essayist Joseph Joubert wrote, "To teach is to learn twice" (Price, 2005, p. 244).

At the Illinois Leadership Center at the University of Illinois at Urbana–Champaign, leadership student employees are trained to make presentations about the Leadership Center to students in classrooms, at student organization meetings, and at informational booths and fairs on campus. They are required to develop a presentation that is comfortable for them and that uses their own words to explain their topic. To ensure that the presentation runs smoothly and covers all the necessary material, students present with a partner. Each presentation the students give differs based on the group and the number of participants. Altering the program's content allows students to practice flexibility and adaptability as a presenter.

Another program in which interested and qualified student staff present to student groups is the Leadership Development Workshop program. Students are trained on material that has been developed for specific leadership topics, such as communication and team building, then they present the content to student organizations. These presentations are overseen by an undergraduate student employee who is responsible for coordinating the program and scheduling the group presentations. This experience can develop other skills beyond verbal communication such as planning, organizing, and prioritizing work.

Students also can develop their verbal communication skills by presenting a capstone experience from a leadership endeavor. For example, students in an emerging leaders program can give an end-of-year presentation about what they learned, students who have completed a leadership portfolio can share their work with others at a completion ceremony prior to receiving a leadership certificate, or students who have participated in a community service project can make a presentation to the community partner they volunteered with.

■ ■ ■ COMMON EXPERIENCES

Neil, a senior and leadership student employee at the Illinois Leadership Center, had this to say when asked about a skill that has improved because of his experiences:

> After my first semester at the Illinois Leadership Center, I can say that my ability to effectively and efficiently communicate verbally has increased significantly. Whether it be a formal presentation or speaking to a friend or classmate, the variety of outreach presentations and pitches I have done for the ILC have provided me plenty of opportunities to practice and improve my ability to communicate.

■ ■ ■ ■

Teamwork

One of the most sought after skills by employers is the ability to work in a team structure. Particularly when asked about working on group or team projects in class, students often indicate that the experience is not positive. One would like to believe that students who participate in academic programs or courses that require teamwork are being assisted by faculty to develop teams that work well together as they attempt to complete a group project. That is often not the case, as faculty do not spend time on helping students consider how to work effectively in their groups or teams. Yet participation in the cocurriculum offers a multitude of opportunities for teamwork that are compelling and fun for students. For institutions looking to promote learning about working in teams, cocurricular experiences may have many significant advantages for developing this skill.

One of the ways that leadership programs can help students acquire the ability to develop and function effectively in teams is by modeling activities that provide the hands-on experience of working in and managing teams. This should go beyond just doing icebreakers, instead encouraging students to think in terms of long-term group development, such as that described in the *Five Dysfunctions of a Team: A Leadership Fable* by Lencioni (2002). In his model, Lencioni contended that groups are dysfunctional due to absence of trust, fear of conflict, lack of commitment, avoidance of accountability, and inattention to results. Lencioni recommended that people need to spend more time building relationships in their teams, making it safe for people to say what they truly think, thus helping the group to really discuss items and make good decisions. As this trust and honesty builds, team members will hold each other more accountable for their work and stay focused on the end-result or goal of the team.

Student facilitation models. It is not uncommon for universities to have programs where experienced student leaders serve as consultants for other student leaders and student organizations. These experienced leaders offer a variety of services, such as consulting with a student group, identifying needs, and helping develop a program for that group. It is also common for these leaders to present sessions on a variety of leadership topics. Examples of these types of programs are the Bowling Green State University Center for Leadership Student Leadership Assistants, the Bradley University LINCS program, and the Intersect i-Program at the University of Illinois at Urbana–Champaign.

- *Bowling Green State University.* The Bowling Green State University Student Leadership Assistants are peer educators who assist the Center for Leadership in researching, developing, administering, and assessing an array of student leadership development and recognition programs. The Student Leadership Assistants provide leadership program development, outreach to and consultation with other student organizations and university departments, and event planning committee work. They present at retreats, workshops, and sessions. They have more than 40 prepared programs they can present, or they can tailor a presentation to meet the needs of the group (Bowling Green State University Center for Leadership, n.d.).

- *Bradley University.* The Bradley University Leaders Instilling kNowledge through Cooperative Service (LINCS) Program is a capstone program for seniors who have an interest in leadership and community involvement. The goal of the program is to provide students with additional leadership opportunities through mentoring, facilitating the Bradley University Elite Leadership Retreat, serving as a resource for other student organizations, and conducting high school outreach. LINCS members facilitate workshops for Bradley student organizations, EHS 120 classes, and community organizations on such topics as leadership in college, teamwork, time management, communication, values and ethics, and other topics as requested (Bradley University Lewis J. Burger Center for Student Leadership and Public Service, n.d.).

- *University of Illinois.* At the University of Illinois, the Intersect i-Program is an 8-hour leadership program that focuses on learning skills in relationship building and team development. One of the unique parts of this program is that the small group facilitators are undergraduate students who are trained to facilitate the small group activities and discussions, which occur throughout the program. The small group facilitator role is a highly sought after experience for students (University of Illinois at Urbana–Champaign Illinois Leadership Center, n.d.).

In leadership programs, verbal communication is both a means and an end. It is a means in that it is a significant way in which students develop leadership skills—through conversations with each other and through teaching important concepts to others. It is also an end because, as students practice the skill of speaking and listening to each other, they develop a rare and desirable skill set and an essential leadership skill (University of Illinois at Urbana–Champaign Illinois Leadership Center, n.d).

■ ■■COMMON EXPERIENCES

Rachel, a senior who works as a student employee at the Illinois Leadership Center, reflected on her ability to work in teams, saying:

> Through working at the Illinois Leadership Center, my ability to work in teams has tremendously improved. I have learned the importance of relationship building within your team, in that it encourages trust, healthy conflict, and team cohesiveness. Furthermore, I have learned the skill of task delegation as well as how to work with and communicate with people that are different than yourself. ■ ■■

Decision Making and Problem Solving

Leadership and problem solving are inherently connected. The practice of leadership is not about identifying problems for others to solve, but leveraging the abilities of the group to solve them. Problem solving cannot be taught through lecture; it requires hands-on experiences that let students apply what they have learned. Many prepackaged training resources are available to assist in developing this skill. One example of such a program is the group activity "Win as Much as You Can" (Gellerman, 1970), which is "a very competitive activity that shows the impact of various win-lose situations on groups where they need to make decisions to compete with other groups and on other instances cooperate with other rival groups to win as much as possible" (Training Course Materials, n.d., para. 1). Students have to work in small groups and make decisions that affect their small group as well as the larger group of which they are a part. This activity provides lessons on many levels, from trusting others to understanding how decisions sometimes need to be made for the greater good, not just for the advancement of one's own small group.

Another example is a "desert survival" scenario in which students are placed in teams and told they have been in a plane crash and they are the only survivors (Lafferty, n.d.). They are asked to rank 15 items salvaged from the crash site, in order of their relative importance to their survival based on the situation described by the simulation. First, the students rank the 15 items individually and then they meet with their team to decide how to rank the items as a group. More often than not, students fare better in this scenario when they collaborate with others than when they rank the items individually. The activity helps to reinforce the notion that people make better decisions and are more effective when they work together than separately (Lafferty, n.d.).

Another way to have students work together to make decisions and solve problems is through outdoor adventure training. High and low ropes courses are very popular and the experiential learning components of these activities allow for powerful learning experiences, particularly with existing or new teams that are trying to improve interpersonal and team relationships. An interesting concept that is part of these training experiences is "challenge by choice" (Neill, 2008). This concept is simple in principle, but complex in practice and reality. Participants are invited to voluntarily participate in each of the various activities and challenges. A participant may choose to sit out an activity and this right is to be respected by others in the group and instructors. This helps to create a group culture that genuinely respects the individual's right to choose his or her degree of participation in any activity. It also helps to reinforce that an individual is to take personal responsibility in choosing his or her behaviors and actions. In addition, the principle recognizes that individuals may learn and grow more by refusing to participate occasionally than in unthinkingly or resentfully always participating.

It is not just the content of leadership programs that can teach the skill of problem solving but also the act of putting this skill into practice through actual programs and events. Students who lead these programs can gain this skill through working with a team or organization to schedule meetings for their group, managing registrations for a program that the organization is sponsoring, or planning a leadership retreat for their student organization.

◼ ◼ ◼COMMON EXPERIENCES

Sangita, a junior at the University of Illinois at Urbana-Champaign, reflects on her experiences as president of her sorority:

As president of my sorority, there were many times I needed to make decisions and solve problems. Through my experiences, there were three concepts I learned. The first is that problems will always arise and it is important to take them as they come—there is no reason to panic or worry, simply move forward with what you can do rather than worrying about what is going wrong or what could have been done. I have also learned that the most important thing to maintain while problem solving and making decisions is to remain calm. It is important to listen to all sides of the story without bias, asking for advice from supervisors and taking that into consideration if necessary, and then making a decision that will benefit all involved parties. In this way all followers feel understood and taken care of and the problem has been effectively solved. The final concept is that the skill of problem solving and decision making is often closely related to being able to adapt your leadership style to the situation and the people involved. Different people react differently and as a leader one must be able to tailor their reaction to the individual to move forward in an effective way. For example, some people react better to private conversations and gentle suggestions, whereas some prefer public recognition for a job well done.

Workflow Planning

Setting priorities is a constant challenge for student leaders. In the Project CEO benchmarking study referenced in Chapter 3, it was reported that 23% of the students completing the survey described themselves as "very involved in multiple organizations." While this may indicate a lack of ability to plan and organize one's life, it also speaks to the opportunity to further develop these skills.

Student leadership programs can be a useful resource for preparing students to meet the challenges of being a student leader, such as serving as an officer for a student organization. Many of the tasks that student organizations pursue require advanced leadership skills. Setting and tracking goals, delegating tasks, planning major initiatives and events, or even working toward the solution for societal problems requires careful planning and execution. Although many leadership programs teach these kinds of skills, students' realization that these skills could assist them in their future careers may be a bit rarer. Leadership educators need to help students make this connection, helping them to realize that leadership is not just a disconnected set of skills but qualities that can be applied to various situations to help a group meet its goals.

While teaching leadership courses at Kansas State University, an author of this chapter frequently assigned papers exploring the link between students' own leadership experiences and the course materials. Students often wrote about their experience serving as Homecoming chair for their fraternity or sorority. This is an excellent example of an experience that created an opportunity to learn about planning, organizing, and prioritizing work. The biggest challenge these leaders often faced was delegating tasks to other members of the group, as they were not confident in their peers' ability to complete work. The stakes were high—winning Homecoming Week was important to the fraternities and sororities. Leaders wanted to present their organizations well during the week of events and were afraid to let others take on the work in case it was not done correctly. Because of this, the leaders preferred to plan and organize work themselves to ensure completion rather than delegate tasks, which if done poorly might require the leader and group to do the work over. This is an excellent example to contrast the typical view of delegation (e.g., giving work to others) against what leadership expert and author Steven Covey (2004) called "gofer delegation" and "stewardship" (p. 173). If leaders simply practice gofer delegation (go for this, go for that), they do not invest the team in the process. By practicing stewardship delegation, leaders provide clear guidance on what is expected and let the team members determine how to accomplish the goals. Understanding the difference can be a powerful learning outcome for students.

One of the most difficult tasks for student leaders to perform is succession planning. This includes developing a plan for other students to know how to ascend into leadership positions and holding transition meetings or workshops for old and new leaders. The succession planning includes having checklists, calendars, and protocols available for the next leaders to use in their leadership role. An important element to assisting other leaders in meeting their goals is appropriate assessment of the program, including the events and activities that the organization puts on. This will also help the organization to be able to sustain itself over time. A student leader's ability to conclude his or her time in such a way that future leadership is prepared to be successful is an important indicator of one's ability in the area of planning, organizing, and prioritizing work.

■ ■ ■ COMMON EXPERIENCES

Andy, a recent graduate from the University of Illinois at Urbana-Champaign, had this to say as he reflected on what he learned and was able to apply based on his collegiate leadership experiences:

> Throughout my college experiences, I had many opportunities to work in a group setting, each time a little different from the next. As I started my college career, it was hard to work with other students because of varying opinions and stubbornness. As I got more

involved in leadership activities on campus (e.g., seminars, workshops, and trainings), I developed patience and awareness. By graduation, I had positively transformed my group skills. I was able to take charge when necessary, prioritize, and communicate to set realistic goals. These skills that I have sharpened through my experiences in college have helped me transition to the workplace smoothly.

In my line of work, I must coordinate with members of a project group spread all across the world. Establishing priorities can be difficult because of group member preferences, cultural differences, and time. It is important for all members of the group to take into consideration everyone else's opinions and concerns within the group. Once a mutual understanding of the group's dynamics has been reached, realistic goals can be set.

Maintaining group engagement and delegating responsibilities have helped lead to success. The critical factor leading toward achieving goals in a group setting boils down to one thing: communication.

Information Processing

When thinking about student leadership, one may tend to think of the leadership that occurs within the confines of the campus itself. Few may realize the extent to which students are using their leadership skills and abilities to tackle significant global problems. In *Leadership for a Better World: Understanding the Social Change Model of Leadership Development*, Komives and Wagner (2009) wrote, "College students across the country are finding many ways to make a positive difference on their campuses, in their communities, and even the world" (p. 7). The ability to do so effectively will require students to learn to obtain and process information, applying critical thinking skills to help determine what they believe.

Today's college students must try to make sense of a massive amount of easily available but often conflicting information. This has created what Peck (2014) called "The Digital Dilemma," noting that "while this vast quantity of often conflicting information should make students less confident in what they know and believe, it seems too often to have the opposite effect. Highly dubious information passes as truth based only on the credibility of being found on the Internet. In many cases, students lack the skills to evaluate the claims of various sources" (para. 3). Traditional approaches to leadership are often overly reliant on skill building and may neglect the cognitive processes that support leadership ability.

Modern leadership programs would be wise to consider focusing not just on helping students determine what they believe, but also on why they believe it. This focus relies on an understanding of one's "personal epistemology" (Hofer & Pintrich, 2002, p. 3), which involves how leadership educators come to understand what we believe, what gets to count for knowledge in our estimation, and how we evaluate the "knowledge claims" of others (Hofer & Pintrich, 2002, p. 3). This requires higher order thinking skills. Bloom (1956) developed what he called the "Taxonomy of Educational Objectives" in a book of the same name. He made a distinction between lower order learning outcomes, such as "knowledge" and "comprehension," and higher order outcomes, such as "application," "analysis," "synthesis," and "evaluation." The taxonomy was revised in 2001 by Anderson and Krathwohl, who positioned "creating" at the top of the list of higher order skills.

For many students, there may not be an intuitive link between the development of higher order thinking skills and participation in developmental leadership programs. In the report *High-Impact Educational Practices: What They Are, Who Has Access to Them, and Why They Matter*, Kuh (2008) listed leadership programs among "high impact practices," which are "learning practices that have been widely tested and have been shown to be beneficial for college students from many backgrounds" (p. 9). These practices have been demonstrated to assist students in the development of higher order thinking skills.

Kuh (2008) identified specific conditions that must be met for high-impact learning to occur. These practices "typically demand that students devote considerable time and effort to purposeful tasks," and place "students in circumstances that essentially demand they interact with faculty and peers about substantive matters" (Kuh, 2008, p. 14). Further, "These experiences often challenge students to develop new ways of thinking about and responding immediately to novel circumstances as they work side by side with peers on intellectual and practical tasks, inside and outside the classroom, on and off campus" (Kuh, 2008, p. 15). They also promote situations where "participating in one or more of these activities increases the likelihood that students will experience diversity through contact with people who are different from themselves" (Kuh, 2008, p. 15). It is not difficult to imagine how we can design leadership programs that meet these conditions.

At Stephen F. Austin State University, the Freshman Leadership Academy engages between 80 and 100 first-year students in a semester-long leadership course and cocurricular leadership program. Students work in teams on a variety of high-impact projects related to the program's work with nonprofit organizations around the world. Students have tackled such significant issues as human trafficking, after-school programs in developing countries, and the plight of institutionalized children in Eastern Europe. Students propose strategies for addressing these issues and work collaboratively with their peers to carry them out. At the conclusion of the program, students are selected to receive scholarships (some of which cover all expenses) for international travel to the locations with which they have been working. This program was selected for a NASPA Excellence Award (bronze) in the category of Student

Union, Student Activities, Greek Life, Leadership, and Related in 2015. This kind of model demonstrates how high-impact elements can seamlessly integrate with leadership curriculum as a way of helping students go beyond developing leadership skills, to developing higher order thinking skills as well.

■ ■ ■ COMMON EXPERIENCES

Kent, a recent graduate from the University of Illinois at Urbana–Champaign, reflected on how he learned to obtain and process information:

> At the university, I was able to improve myself in many facets. Credibility was a key component to the research I did for individual and group assignments. Many people believe anything they read or hear on the Internet, on TV, in a book, or in person. In some cases, the information could be correct, but there are gaps in how the information was reported. Through my experience leading group projects in undergrad, I started to realize that not everything I read or heard was correct. In some instances, I would find that portions of information were fabricated or not fully explained, deeming them unusable. Instead of using random sources on the Internet, I turned to peer-reviewed scientific and educational publications to back my work. Though I cannot prove that all of the information in these publications is factual, the credibility is much greater than random Internet findings.

Quantitative Analysis

Student leaders can develop quantitative reasoning skills in many ways. They may balance budgets, calculate service hours, estimate expenses, or even conduct assessments of the effectiveness of their programs or the skills students are learning from these experiences. Likewise, there are often positions within student organizations and other cocurricular experiences that are dedicated to these tasks. Providing training to these students can be an excellent way for student leadership development programs to affect these skills.

While leadership educators have become increasingly proficient at the various methods for conducting valid assessments of student learning in their programs, there is room to grow in teaching students who lead these experiences how to collect and interpret assessment results. Peck (2010) wrote, "Many of us settle for the baseline outcome that students know they are learning something from their co-curricular experiences, without stopping to consider the kinds of dynamic opportunities that may exist when we invite students to track their own process along the dimensions of learning that we endeavor to measure" (para. 3). Leadership programs could be developed to help students become active participants in measuring and tracking their own progress in ways that could increase students' commitment to learning and help them to develop some useful quantitative skills as well.

■ ■ ■ COMMON EXPERIENCES

Thomas, a sophomore at the University of Illinois at Urbana–Champaign, reflected on his experience in a leadership research lab:

> As a student of the university, I found opportunities as a sophomore to develop my quantitative data analysis skills. Specifically, I joined a Leadership Research Lab as an undergrad assistant. This lab uses quantitative data

to analyze the effectiveness of programs offered on campus. As an assistant, I enter data into programs, and then help the lab interpret the data. Along with providing me experience in academic research, I also developed greater quantitative reasoning abilities. Statistics are important, but they can also be manipulated to fit certain needs. That's why gaining quantitative analysis experience has been an important part of my undergraduate experience.

Career-Specific Knowledge

While it is not uncommon for leadership programs to be nested and focused on the context of leadership within specific academic units such as business or, more recently, STEM (science, technology, engineering, and mathematics), the focus on transferable skills proposed by this book offers a way to merge traditional leadership education with career-focused education in a way that makes intuitive sense to students and educators alike. Models are still emerging, but the authors of this chapter have both found ways to apply what they have learned about this topic to leadership programs on their own campuses. The two programs that follow illustrate different approaches to merging leadership and career education.

The Certified Student Leader Program at Stephen F. Austin State University. This program is built around five competencies that are informed by the NACE employability skills. The program labels them: communication, teamwork, influence, organization, and decision making. Leadership training has been restructured to focus on these skills. The fall leadership conference, the freshman leadership academy, and even training for student employees on campus feature these skills.

Although students are encouraged to engage with these programs, they are not required to do so. The key element of the program is the process of applying for certification in each skill. When students feel they have achieved mastery in one of the skills, they submit a special cover letter and résumé along with two references. One reference must be from a fellow student. The information is then reviewed by an expert content reviewer and either the certification is confirmed or feedback on how to improve is given. Once students are certified in all five areas, they receive Certified Student Leader status. This program bridges the need for leadership training with the need for students to learn how to articulate what they are learning.

Career Development Program at the University of Illinois at Urbana–Champaign. This program is designed to help students develop leadership skills that will help them become career ready as they develop through college and transition into work life after graduation. The professional staff looked at research and best practices of student employment, reviewed the existing student positions within the Illinois Leadership Center, and considered how these positions can develop competencies within the Illinois leadership model. Students will be organized into teams that are led by graduate students and undergraduate students who participate in the prestigious Graf Intern program. In total, about 20 leadership student employees will be divided among the following five teams: Customer Service Representatives, Marketing and Branding Specialists, Leadership Programming Specialists, Leadership Education Specialists, and Leadership Research and Assessment Specialists. Learning outcomes are embedded in the position descriptions and regular reflective activities are conducted with these students, including midyear and final evaluations, weekly team meetings with reflection components, career readiness training, and a capstone team presentation on what was learned and accomplished. This program should provide a compelling model for providing hands-on learning about leadership connected to student employment, but within the context of a student leadership development program.

Regardless of the student's career path, organizations need leaders. Combining leadership education with career preparation can help prepare our students not for just a job, but a rewarding career. It can also help us demonstrate our commitment to employers and other stakeholders to provide educational programs that help students graduate from college career ready and prepared to tackle the many challenges of their first post-college job.

Computer Software Skills

There are many connections between computer skills and leadership skills. At a basic level, most people (leaders included) need to know how to use technology to be successful in their personal and professional lives. Also, technological knowledge is powerful currency. Research conducted by French and Raven (1959) provided a foundation for how people conceptualize power, an important consideration in leadership, and found that expertise is an important consideration. In a world increasingly ruled by technology, expertise in this area carries additional weight.

Additionally, new technologies are being released every day that can make the job of a leader easier. From social media platforms that allow easy communication within a group to goal-setting apps that can be used to track progress on personal and professional goals, many technologies can assist students in being effective leaders.

Those who use these technologies effectively can influence many of the other skills addressed here. For example, using a reminder app may help students plan, organize, and prioritize work. Effective use of word processing software should help students improve in the area of writing and editing, as can websites that analyze writing and provide a readability score, show students words that they overuse, and provide reports on such concepts as words per sentence or sentences per paragraph. There is also a clear connection between computer proficiency and the ability to obtain and process information. At libraries across the country and around the world, the space once occupied by books is increasingly being replaced with digital collections. This stands as a testament to the increasing digitization of information.

Contemporary student leaders will need to leverage technology thoughtfully in order to maximize its potential to help those they lead to meet their goals. Leadership skills have remained consistent over the years, but the means of applying the skills of leadership continue to evolve. How technology can impact leadership is an interesting and evolving field of study.

■ ■■ COMMON EXPERIENCES

Veena, a second year Master's in Business Administration (MBA) student, reflected on the use of computers for students today:

> Computers have drastically changed how students and, more generally, people manage, share, and consume information. While organizing events as vice president for the Society of Women in Business, I constantly had to think about the most efficient way to reach my student audience, manage organizational duties, and communicate with speakers and professors who actively participated in our events. Though e-mail is a preferred medium to convey information, we got a better response and engagement from members when we shared information about the organization's activities through our Facebook page. This also helped us stay connected with our alumni base of women MBAs who we frequently invite

for conferences and Registered Student Organization events. One of our biggest fundraising events—the Annual Silent Auction—was a grand success because we made use of online auctioning tools. This helped alumni participate virtually in the event even if they could not join in person. Gauging success and collecting feedback about our events also became simpler with online tools such as SurveyMonkey. This helped us collect feedback anonymously and identify areas for improvement. With the limited time available to us as student leaders, we were able to do a lot more with the help of such web applications and social media tools.

Writing and Editing Reports

In their book *Academically Adrift*, Richard Arum and Josipa Roksa (2011) painted a bleak picture of student learning across the board. Speaking specifically of student writing, the authors expressed little hope for the future, noting, "In the most optimistic scenario, students will continue their meager progress, leading to less than impressive gains over the course of their enrollment in higher education" (p. 37). What is more, as Walvoord (2014) pointed out, "Writing is not a separable quality of student work; rather, it is enmeshed with critical thinking, information literacy, problem solving, quantitative reasoning, and other skills" (p. 1); the only known antidote to bad writing is for students to "write frequently [and] receive feedback" (p. 6).

There are surprising numbers of opportunities for students to write in leadership programs. Educators in these programs would be wise to take advantage of these opportunities to the fullest extent possible. Not only do these exercises present opportunities to improve student writing, but they also produce opportunities for reflection. Boud and

Keogh (1985) suggested that structured reflection is foundational to learning from experience. Reflection, however, can often be neglected. While reflective writing is often considered in terms of its potential to be used for assessment, it is also useful in helping students make sense of what they are learning.

Reflective writing can take many forms. A popular one is called a "minute paper" (Angelo & Cross, 1993, p. 29). Using this technique, students are provided a prompt and are asked to write for approximately one minute about what they have learned. This approach can be both quick and effective. Angelo and Cross (1993) estimated that it should take no more than 2 minutes per response to analyze what students have learned. While this information can certainly be useful in assessment, it may also provide a way to give prompt feedback like the kind suggested by Kuh (2008) to meet the conditions of high-impact experiences. More important, it makes students think about what they are learning in ways that can make learning more noticeable to them.

One approach to reflective writing across a longer period of time can be found in leadership portfolios, which can be developed in electronic or traditional ink-and-paper formats. The University of Illinois at Urbana–Champaign offers the Leadership Certificate Program. This program is centered on the completion of a portfolio, which is intended to allow students to display their leadership-related skills and experiences in a portfolio that contains evidence, data, and examples of a student's participation in the certificate program (Illinois Leadership Center, 2016). Students include many elements that require them to write and describe their personal leadership development, such as reflective essays, a personal statement, and an explanation of their personal development plan (Illinois Leadership Center, 2016).

Developing writing skills is a desirable goal in its own right, but is also closely entwined with the development of cognitive skills as well. Perhaps more important, when students write they must make sense of how these experiences are working together to help them develop and grow. While many programs are likely doing this very well, as we scan the landscape of leadership education it also appears to be an approach that deserves more broad application.

■ ■■COMMON EXPERIENCES

Nicole, a senior at the University of Illinois at Urbana–Champaign who completed the Illinois Leadership Certificate Program, reflected on the writing requirements for the certificate:

> It seems that it is a common belief among college students that they are too busy to participate in reflective writing. Having reflective writing as a requirement for completing the Leadership Certificate Program allowed me to critically look back on my experiences and dissect what were the most important aspects of leadership development that I gained from these various programs. The reflections have a word limit—which made me edit my writing to be as concise as possible. Not only did the certificate program advance my strategic thinking and develop my teamwork and communication skills, it also helped me become a better writer by providing me opportunities to acknowledge and reflect on my leadership experiences.

Selling and Influencing

Dwight D. Eisenhower defined leadership as "the art of getting someone else to do something that you want done because he wants to do it, not because your position of power can compel him to do it, or your position of authority" (The American Presidency Project, n.d., para. 15). This involves the ability to influence others. While the inclusion of the concept of sales may initially throw off some leadership educators, with further thought, the connection between influence and sales makes intuitive sense. Helping students make this connection may help them see how leadership programs provide them with a skill that is in demand by employers.

One popular way of teaching this skill is through the inclusion of an "elevator pitch," which is "so named because it should last no longer than the average elevator ride" (Pincus, 2007, para. 2). These can be very useful in leadership programs. Letting students practice developing and presenting an elevator pitch can help them in many ways. They may practice selling the benefits of their student organization to others in a format like an involvement fair, or they may practice explaining the skills they have gained as a student leader to potential employers.

At the Ignite Leadership i-Program at the University of Illinois at Urbana–Champaign, students work on an area of change they would like to implement. As part of this experience, they make 90-second pitches to a peer to work on how they articulate what it is they are trying to accomplish. The peer who is listening gives feedback for 90 seconds and then the process is reversed for the other student to give their pitch and receive feedback. This is done for five rounds to let students see how they can hone their verbal communication skills to make a pitch that is clearer, more succinct, and easier for their peers to understand (University of Illinois at Urbana–Champaign Illinois Leadership Center, n.d.).

In the Freshman Leadership Academy at Stephen F. Austin State University, students participate in an activity called Join Me, which allows them to apply this skill. While many students may do something similar, this activity was developed just for this group to practice the skill of influence. Students are placed in one of four groups. Two groups are defined as "recruiters" and the other two are called "independents." The recruiter groups brainstorm ways to attract new members from the independent groups, each of whom can make their own decision about what groups meet their needs. Then each of the recruiting groups makes an elevator pitch for independents to join their group. The groups are free to develop whatever mission or purpose they wish for their hypothetical group. Because this is an introductory course on leadership, the students are often not well versed in this kind of leadership challenge. Coaching points often revolve around encouraging the groups to focus on how the independents could benefit from participation, rather than just explaining the purpose of the group or why the group would like the independents to choose them. Seldom have groups used any of their prep time to visit with any independents to ask them what they want from the experience, failing to ask even the simple question, "What sort of leadership experience are you looking for?" The exercise often drives home the importance of learning to see leadership challenges from the perspective of those one hopes to lead.

Leadership and influence are closely aligned. When designing a cocurriculum geared toward helping students develop the skills identified by NACE (2015b), there would seem to be few experiences that are as well poised to help students develop the skills of achieving buy in, selling, and influencing. Perhaps the best way to enhance the effectiveness of these programs is not to require new content but to simply help students understand how the skill of influence could benefit them—not just in the context of their student leadership, but in their careers as well.

■ ■ ■ COMMON EXPERIENCES

Mandy, who was a senior at the University of Illinois at Urbana–Champaign when she served as vice president of public relations on the Panhellenic Council, described what she learned about achieving buy-in from, selling to, or influencing others:

> I worked to promote events to the community through social media, advertising, and word of mouth. Most often, college students do not have the time to pay attention to every event that is happening on our campus, which inspired me to think more creatively on ways to publicize. I designed eye-catching graphics and posted photos of members of the community at our events. Throughout the year, I learned how to influence an audience by noticing what types of social media posts received the most attention and which events were more highly attended. Instead of saying, "This is the event. Please come," I changed my language to talk about how their attendance at the service-based event directly helps people in our community or how the hour they listen to a stress management speaker can teach them better ways to juggle their commitments. The skills I learned in this leadership position have stuck with me and I have used them in job interviews, recruitment, and anytime I share my opinion with others. It has strengthened my ability to persuade and influence the people around me to listen to what I have to say and take action.

ASSESSING EMPLOYABILITY SKILLS AS AN OUTCOME OF LEADERSHIP PROGRAMS

There is little consensus in the leadership education discipline regarding overall assessment of programs. Without this, many believe there will be a lack of program accountability and direction (Andenoro et al., 2013). A common approach to assessing these programs is to provide assessments such as surveys that are administered at the conclusion of a particular event or program. This is often referred to as *summative assessment*, which was defined by Maki (2010) as capturing "students achievement at the end of their program" (p. 8). Although this kind of assessment can be useful to educators, it underscores the unfortunate viewpoint of assessment as primarily useful for external accountability (Kuh, 2015). With no longitudinal assessment of growth by students, it is difficult to know the true impact of the program, and growth can be challenging for the student to perceive as well.

What we need is a more *formative assessment*, defined by Maki (2010) as "assessment (that) captures students' progress toward institution- or program-level outcomes . . . as significant milestones in their learning journey" (p. 8). Well-designed formative assessment helps students perceive learning while it is occurring. This provides experiences that not only allow good assessment but also connect this assessment to learning. It also complements the intention of high-impact experiences to provide frequent feedback to students as a way of improving their performance (Kuh, 2008).

An excellent resource for conducting formative assessment is NACA NEXT (Navigating Employability eXperience Tool; see Chapter 8 for further discussion). This resource is available to member campuses of the National Association for Campus Activities and can be used either by students as a self-assessment or by advisors to evaluate their students. Users complete an evaluative questionnaire based on the skills identified by NACE and the scores are compared to the mean scores of other students who have completed the assessment. Resources for further development of each skill are then suggested based on the level of skill as determined by the assessment. This can be used for pretest/posttest assessment or as a periodic assessment for students involved in long-term programs.

If designed effectively, writing assignments can be very impactful formative assessments because the process of writing is inherently reflective and can often lead the student to insights they might not have otherwise considered without the opportunity to stop and take meaning from the experience. Applying rubrics such as those included in this book can help measure the student's level of proficiency in each of these skills.

Assessment should not be viewed as something that occurs exclusively at the end of a given learning experience, neither should it be viewed as separate from a given learning experience. A focus on formative assessment in leadership programs can prompt educators to look for ways for students to perceive what they are learning over time and to play an active role in their own learning and development in the leadership program.

CONCLUSION

Career readiness is a growing topic of discussion for employers, higher education professionals, and the public. The connection between what employers want and the skills and competencies taught routinely in developmental leadership programs are strikingly similar. Creating leadership experiences in curricular and cocurricular environments is instrumental to students' development throughout their college career. Students can develop their leadership experiences in the classroom, the lab, and their careers. It will also be critical for those involved in leadership education programs to be able to assess and measure how students specifically grow and develop their self-efficacy because of their participation in these programs.

REFERENCES

The American Presidency Project. (n.d.). *Remarks at the Annual Conference of the Society for Personnel Administration.* Retrieved from http://www.presidency.ucsb.edu/ws/?pid=9884

Andenoro, A. C., Allen, S. J., Haber-Curran, P., Jenkins, D. M., Sowcik, M., Dugan, J. P., & Osteen, L. (2013). *National leadership education research agenda 2013–2018: Providing strategic direction for the field of leadership education.* Retrieved from http://leadershipeducators.org/ResearchAgenda

Anderson, L. W., & Krathwohl, D. R. (2001). *A taxonomy for learning, teaching, and assessing: A revision of Bloom's taxonomy of educational objectives.* New York, NY: Longman.

Angelo, T. A., & Cross, K. P. (1993). *Classroom assessment techniques: A handbook for college teachers.* San Francisco, CA: Jossey-Bass.

Arum, R., & Roksa, J. (2011). *Academically adrift: Limited learning on college campuses.* Chicago, IL: University of Chicago Press.

Astin, H., & Astin, A. (Eds.). (2000). *Leadership reconsidered: Engaging higher education in social change.* Battle Creek, MI: W. K. Kellogg Foundation.

Bernstein, C., & Woodward, B. (1974). *All the president's men.* New York, NY: Simon and Schuster.

Bloom, B. S. (1956). *Taxonomy of educational objectives: The classification of educational goals.* New York, NY: Longmans, Green.

Boud, D., & Keogh, R. (1985). *Reflection, turning experience into learning.* London, England: Kogan Page.

Bowling Green State University Center for Leadership. (n.d.). Student leadership assistants. Retrieved from https://www.bgsu.edu/center-for-leadership/student-leadership-assistant.html

Bradley University Lewis J. Burger Center for Student Leadership and Public Service. (n.d.). LINCS. Retrieved from http://www.bradley.edu/campuslife/studentleadership/leadership/lincs/index.dot

Brock, T. (2010). Young adults and higher education: Barriers and breakthroughs to success. *The Future of Children: Transition to Adulthood, 20,* 109–132.

Council for the Advancement of Standards in Higher Education. (2015). *CAS professional standards for higher education* (9th ed.). Washington, DC: Author.

Covey, S. R. (2004). *The 7 habits of highly effective people: Restoring the character ethic.* New York, NY: Free Press.

French, J., & Raven, B. (1959). The bases of social power. In D. Cartwright & A. Zander (Eds.), *Group dynamics, research and theory.* London, England: Tavistock Press.

Gellerman, W. (1970). Win as much as you can. In J. W. Pfeiffer & J. E. Jones (Eds.), *A handbook of structured experiences for human relations training* (Vol. 2, pp. 62–66). San Francisco, CA: Pfeiffer.

Hofer, B. K., & Pintrich, P. R. (2002). *Personal epistemology: The psychology of beliefs about knowledge and knowing.* Mahwah, NJ: L. Erlbaum Associates.

Illinois Leadership Center. (2016). *Illinois leadership certificate program participant manual.* Retrieved from http://illinois.edu/cms/5816/participant_manual_july_2016.pdf

Kilpatrick, C. (1974, August 9). Nixon resigns. *The Washington Post,* p. A01.

Komives, S. R., & Wagner, W. (2009). *Leadership for a better world: Understanding the social change model of leadership development.* San Francisco, CA: John Wiley and Sons.

Kouzes, J. M., & Posner, B. Z. (2012). *The leadership challenge: How to make extraordinary things happen in organizations* (5th ed.). San Francisco, CA: Jossey-Bass.

Kuh, G. (2008). *High impact educational practices: What they are, who has access to them, and why they matter.* Washington, DC: Association of American Colleges and Universities.

Kuh, G. D. (2015). *Using evidence of student learning to improve higher education.* San Francisco, CA: Jossey-Bass.

Lafferty, J. C. (n.d.). *Desert survival situation.* Retrieved from http://www.humansynergistics.com/Products/TeamBuildingSimulations/SurvivalSeries/DesertSurvivalSituation

Lencioni, P. (2002). *The five dysfunctions of a team: A leadership fable*. San Francisco, CA: Jossey-Bass.

Maki, P. (2010). *Assessing for learning: Building a sustainable commitment across the institution*. Sterling, VA: Stylus.

National Association of Colleges and Employers. (2015a). *Career readiness defined*. Retrieved from http://www.naceweb.org/knowledge/career-readiness-competencies.aspx

National Association of Colleges and Employers. (2015b). *Job outlook 2016*. Bethlehem, PA: Author.

Neill, J. (2008). Challenge by choice. Retrieved from http://wilderdom.com/ABC/ChallengeByChoice.html#SchoelMaizell2002

Owen, J. E. (2012). *Findings from the multi-institutional study of leadership institutional survey: A national report*. College Park, MD: National Clearinghouse for Leadership Programs.

Peck, A. (2010). Putting the student back in student learning. *NetResults*. Retrieved from http://www.naspa.org

Peck, A. (2014, Summer). Overcoming the digital dilemma: Developing and measuring critical thinking gained through cocurricular experiences in a time of information overload. *The Journal of Technology in Student Affairs*. Retrieved from http://www.studentaffairs.com/ejournal/Summer_2014/OvercomingTheDigitalDilemma

Pincus, A. (2007, June 18). *The perfect (elevator) pitch*. Retrieved from http://www.bloomberg.com/bw/stories/2007-06-18/the-perfect-elevator-pitchbusinessweek-business-news-stock-market-and-financial-advice

Price, S. D. (2005). *1001 smartest things ever said*. Guilford, CT: Lyons Press.

Seemiller, C. (2014). *The student leadership competencies guidebook: Designing intentional leadership learning and development*. San Francisco, CA: Jossey-Bass.

Shankman, M. L., Allen, S. J., & Haber-Curran, P. (2015). *Emotionally intelligent leadership*. San Francisco, CA: Jossey-Bass.

Sowcik, M., Lindsey, J. L., & Rosch, D. M. (2013). A collective effort to understand formalized review. *Journal of Leadership Studies, 6*(3), 67–72.

Training Course Materials. (n.d.). Activity–negotiation–win as much as you can. Retrieved from http://www.trainingcoursematerial.com/free-games-activities/conflict-resolution-influencing-and-negotiation-activities/win-as-much-as-you-can

University of Illinois at Urbana–Champaign Illinois Leadership Center. (n.d.). i-Programs. Retrieved from http://leadership.illinois.edu/programs-services/i-programs

Walvoord, B. E. (2014). *Assessing and improving student writing in college: A guide for institutions, general education, departments, and classrooms*. San Francisco, CA: Jossey-Bass.

15

Developing Employability Skills Through Service and Community Engagement Programs

Jon Dooley, Robert Frigo, and Mary Morrison

When Harvard College was founded in 1636, the United States was forever changed. The country now had a formal academy to prepare leaders and citizens to actively participate in the democratic experiment that would become the United States of America. Harvard was essential in readying not only an enlightened clergy but "leaders disciplined by knowledge and learning" along with "followers disciplined by leaders" (Rudolph, 1962, p. 7). More than three centuries later, as the United States was navigating a post-World War II landscape, the goals for higher education outlined in the President's Commission on Higher Education (1947) echoed a similar focus on democracy and cultivating an educated citizenry. In the latter half of the 20th century, however, colleges and universities across the country seemed to move away from this mission as focus shifted to job preparation and the economic impact of higher education.

In 2012, the National Task Force on Civic Learning and Democratic Engagement issued a national call to action in the form of *A Crucible Moment: College Learning and Democracy's Future*. This document was produced at a time of increased calls for improving college completion and attention to the role higher education plays with career preparation and economic development. Acknowledging these important aims, the task force sought to integrate them with the civic purposes of higher education and drafted *A Crucible Moment* as a catalytic document, designed to reengage American colleges and universities with their roots in citizenship and democratic values. In this charge, community service was introduced as an initial step to address national needs by working in collaboration with others to strengthen communities.

Community service falls on an experiential education continuum developed by Furco (1996) that is designed to distinguish between different types of service programs. Moving left to right across a spectrum from recipient (intended beneficiary) and service (balance of service and learning) to provider (intended beneficiary) and learning (balance of service and learning), Furco identified these programs as the following: volunteerism, community service, service–learning, field education, and internship. Furco's model was influenced by Sigmon's (1994) typology of service–learning that analyzed learning goals in relation to service goals. Giles and Eyler (1994) acknowledged Sigmon's early work with William Ramsey that forged the term *service–learning* in 1967. The underlying foundation for all things related to experiential learning, however, ultimately lies in the writings of John Dewey. Saltmarsh (1996) identified five specific areas in Dewey's work that inform service–learning:

1. Linking education to experience
2. Democratic community
3. Social service
4. Reflective inquiry
5. Education for social transformation

In terms of definitions, some would argue that community service is more often correlated with a court-sanctioned order than with college students engaging with communities in meaningful ways. To further muddy the waters, such concepts as service–learning, civic engagement, and social justice do not necessarily have fixed borders and the nuances of one term often blur into another. For clarity, this chapter will use Jacoby's (2015) definition of *service–learning* to describe student experiences with service and community engagement: "A form of experiential education in which students engage in activities that address human and community needs, together with structured opportunities for reflection designed to achieve desired learning outcomes" (p. 1).

Conscious of the important, but unique, role that Harvard plays in the U.S. higher education landscape, on a visit to Harvard Yard one of the authors of this chapter observed displays of civic engagement ranging from a peaceful protest focusing on Teach for America to impromptu geopolitical conversations over coffee about the visit from the president of Ghana earlier that day. And yet, despite a civic focus that is both ingrained in the spirit of the original legislative act that created the institution and embedded in the present-day mission, as well as significant opportunities to positively impact society, approximately half of Harvard's graduating seniors in 2007 planned to move into lucrative careers in either finance or consulting (Deresiewicz, 2014).

The question that now prevails is whether higher education exists to create a strong society and an engaged citizenry or, conversely, to prepare students for a career. Battistoni and Longo (2006) argued that these two paths can indeed converge and that "workforce development and civic engagement can be complementary visions for the future of higher education" (p. 2).

Service, therefore, offers a unique pathway for students to develop the knowledge, skills, and values for collective action and civic engagement while simultaneously creating opportunities to gain the skills preferred by employers as identified by the National Association of Colleges and Employers (NACE; 2015). This chapter focuses specifically on ways in which students who are involved in service and community engagement experiences can develop the workforce skills identified by NACE.

EMPLOYABILITY SKILLS DERIVED FROM SERVICE AND COMMUNITY ENGAGEMENT PROGRAMS

Verbal Communication

Many universities offer short-term, day-of-service events within the first 6 weeks of college. These limited projects have goals that include introducing service opportunities that connect with the students' previous service experiences, reminding students that they are part of a larger community, and encouraging students to assist in addressing identified community needs. Students participating in short-term service events are urged to make an ongoing commitment to community engagement and develop meaningful relationships while building skills for the future.

For example, Elon University offers the Get on the Bus Program to make it convenient for college students to learn about seven core community partners and volunteer with local nonprofit organizations. During the first 6 weeks of the fall semester, students can volunteer on Friday afternoons by walking up, registering for the program, and boarding the bus. Students volunteer for three hours before returning to campus in the early evening.

Imagine 32 first-year students with limited preparation boarding a bus with other students they probably don't know, venturing into a new community to address complex social issues. It is the responsibility of the student leaders accompanying the group to give participants a brief orientation, discuss the issue they will address, review the agenda for the day, and remind students of appropriate behavior and expectations. Upon arrival at the site, another student leader provides the volunteers with information about the organization's mission and population served and reviews volunteer tasks. On the return trip to campus, student leaders ask for feedback through a written evaluation form and provide information about volunteering at the site in the future.

The verbal communication skills required to create a meaningful and welcoming experience are complicated. The information conveyed on the bus is designed to be informative and concise. The environment of talking to a group on a bus is difficult. Student leaders are asked to convey a warm and welcoming presence and are available throughout the service experience to address any questions or concerns. Depending on the activity and the size of the group, meaningful reflection can be challenging. Student leaders at the site are volunteer/event managers for the day. They must communicate with a large group to engage them in an activity that is short-term and intensive. Student leaders have a total of three 10-minute conversations at the beginning, middle, and end of the program to communicate their message.

The complex nature of volunteer service is a real-world communication challenge. The communication skills required to manage volunteers and events are needed in every volunteer experience.

■ ■ ■COMMON EXPERIENCES

As part of her weekly meeting with her advisor in the community engagement office, Susie identified public speaking as a goal she wanted to hone during her student leadership position. Susie and her advisor identified some opportunities in the upcoming months where she could gain progressive experience practicing her verbal communication skills. Susie gradually moved from chairing a meeting with five individuals, to cofacilitating a training session with her advisor, to designing and presenting her own workshop to a group of 50 student leaders. ■ ■ ■

Teamwork

In describing the effects of service participation on the development of life skills, Astin and Sax (1998) demonstrated the link between service and leadership ability and the skills that contribute to teamwork, such as interpersonal skills, conflict resolution skills, and the ability to work cooperatively. In the past 20 years, the social change model of leadership development (Higher Education Research Institute, 1996) has become ubiquitous in college and university leadership development programs and the ensemble that developed the model articulates that service is a powerful vehicle for understanding and developing leadership. The model describes leadership as a process of individuals and groups working in a community to enact positive change. In addition to a focus on the development of self and community, the model includes a focus on group dynamics, including the values of collaboration, common purpose, and controversy with civility.

The projects and programs that often form the basis for service experiences typically require students to work in teams and to interact with individuals different from themselves. Through opportunities that involve identifying common goals and working toward them by tapping into the assets and strengths of individuals and groups, students engaged in service are challenged to better understand how to work with others and how to use the collective expertise and wisdom of a group to improve a situation. For example, students working alongside other volunteers and leaders in a community organization are often witnessing delegation of responsibility, the fluid dynamic of organizations that rely on volunteers coming into and out of the work setting, and the need for individuals to rely on the expertise and contributions of others. Rare is the setting where trust among volunteers is developed slowly over time; instead, students often experience situations where individuals are expected to quickly organize themselves into teams that complete tasks—sometimes effectively and other times with considerable challenge—to improve their efficiency and output.

Students who lead service initiatives on a college campus are further given opportunities to deepen their understanding of the importance of leadership, teamwork, delegation, and trust as they work with groups of volunteers to implement the programs they are leading. Organizing and leading volunteers, who are often motivated by intrinsic rewards rather than external motivators such as compensation, gives students the opportunity to develop workforce skills in settings where teamwork must be developed rather than mandated.

■ ■ ■■ **COMMON EXPERIENCES**

Sofia, a student executive director of a campus service organization, had this to share in an end of the year reflection:

Teamwork in a service-based environment is unique because each leader is so connected to his or her own social issue, and this passion then energizes the whole team. Each leader brings his or her own strengths to the table, creating a synergy within the group. In my role, I have learned the importance of how forming relationships with those who work alongside you creates a stronger work environment and increases productivity. ■ □ ■■

Making Decisions and Solving Problems

Service experiences have long been cited as contributing positively to the development of problem-solving abilities. This is not surprising when one considers that service programs are a form of cocurricular engagement and curricular pedagogy that is designed to provide a context for the application of knowledge, including the opportunity for students to understand and address complex, often vexing problems. Problem solving and critical thinking was one of the eight outcomes identified by Eyler and Giles (1999) in their frequently cited work, *Where's the Learning in Service–Learning*, an examination of the effects of service–learning that used surveys and interviews with nearly 2,000 undergraduate students. It should also be noted that the development of problem-solving skills through service is particularly strengthened when those experiences are tightly linked with academic material from courses (Gray et al., 1999; Eyler, Giles, Stenson, & Gray, 2001).

Well-designed service experiences give students real-world opportunities to identify the root causes of community challenges and needs, develop and choose between different options to address those concerns, and critique available information and data to determine the most effective solutions. When connected to broad questions that transcend the body of knowledge from a specific academic discipline, the complexity of both the problems and the solutions offers students the challenge of weighing multiple options—each with their own set of advantages and disadvantages—and, often, barriers to implementation in settings that don't accommodate textbook solutions.

In cocurricular settings, students who are leading service initiatives should be encouraged to use reflection, both before and after service experiences, to ensure a similar application of data and information to the problems and questions raised in the community setting. For example, students who are leading a service program that addresses an issue such as hunger and homelessness in the community should be encouraged to engage their peers in conversation about what they experience and to frame multiple possible solutions from their own unique lenses of life experience, college major, or intended area of work. The solutions they discuss can be broad in scope, or they could be specific in addressing situations presented by the site and the work they are doing locally. By focusing reflection on decision making and problem solving, students can ensure that these are not activities restricted to academic contexts, but that transfer to workplace and real-world settings.

■ ■ ■COMMON EXPERIENCES

Daniel, the student director of a service organization, offered the following comments at the end of the academic year:

> Service has afforded me the opportunity to think critically about the social justice issues around me by delving into their root causes and encouraging others to do the same. The intersectionality of these issues has challenged me, humbled me, and inspired me to learn and do more. These are skills that I believe will be transferrable in my life after graduation—not only as a professional, but as an active citizen with values grounded in the well-being of my community.

■ ■ ■

Workflow Planning

Students involved in community engagement have endless opportunities to learn how to effectively plan, organize, and prioritize tasks. Volunteering on-site with a local Habitat for Humanity affiliate, for example, offers students a chance to develop valuable carpentry or painting skills, but also provides a unique lesson in the area of work coordination. In this way, a Saturday morning spent working with a Habitat construction supervisor can become a master class in project management. Volunteers can gain a wealth of knowledge in navigating the challenges inherent in organizing work for and delegating projects to a group of volunteers who may lack experience in framing a house or hanging vinyl siding.

Members of a leadership team for a program designed to address food insecurity gain direct experience in managing projects. On a weekly basis, student leaders in a program like The Campus Kitchens Project use food recovered and donated from campus dining providers and local grocery stores to prepare and deliver meals to community residents in need. The cooking shift leaders are responsible for developing a nutritious menu, repurposing food left over from the previous day's lunch, incorporating donated boxes of pasta from the previous month's food drive, and training volunteers in food safety protocol, with the ultimate goal of preparing a week's worth of nutritious meals in an industrial kitchen.

Experiences through programs such as Habitat for Humanity and Campus Kitchens permit volunteers and student leaders alike to learn about the intricacies of planning, organizing, and prioritizing work. Opportunities such as these can then be further deepened by teaching students about the broader issues of affordable housing and hunger on the local, national, and global levels. Some community engagement programs accomplish this by involving volunteers in pre- and post-reflection activities. The Center for Student Leadership, Ethics, and Public Service at North Carolina State University took this deepening approach to a new level through an alternative service break with a world food policy focus based in Italy. This program engaged students in thoughtful and illuminating conversations with staff from the United Nations Food and Agriculture Organization, World Food Programme, and International Fund for Agricultural Development, in addition to serving meals at the Caritas Termini Station shelter in central Rome.

■ ■■ **COMMON EXPERIENCES**

Anna and Brooke coordinate a nonpartisan student organization with a mission to provide students with the necessary resources to register to vote and learn about issues at stake in upcoming elections. In the academic year prior to the presidential election, they worked collaboratively with a group of students, faculty, and staff to brainstorm ideas and ultimately create an ambitious calendar of events for the upcoming fall semester that included voter engagement and education initiatives. Anna and Brooke had different student organizations and departments cosponsor each event and provided each group of sponsors with the necessary autonomy to provide leadership for that event. This advance work resulted in a smooth series of programs with Anna and Brooke overseeing the entire operation with cosponsors focusing on the details for each event.   ■ ■■

Information Processing

Service is an activity that is often focused on experience and encounter. To that end, the focus on gathering and processing information must be intentionally structured as part of the experience. This often occurs in the context of service–learning, where the service experience is designed to engage students in applying and understanding information about a problem or question in a unique way. For example, data about poverty and its effects may mean one thing in the cognitive inquiry of the classroom setting, but are likely to be understood very differently when viewed through the lens of experience provided in a service setting. For this reason, critical thinking has for decades been cited as an outcome of academic service–learning experiences for students (Astin, Vogelgesang, Ikeda, & Yee, 2000; Eyler & Giles, 1999; Gray et al., 1999).

Although service is often implemented as a strategy to help students process information obtained in a curricular context, the faculty, staff, and students who lead service initiatives should encourage participants to seek out information to help them understand the questions that are raised through programs and experiences. By starting with the experience first and obtaining information next, students will become more skilled in identifying complex problems and seeking out the information needed to develop thoughtful, effective solutions. Reflection that involves experts in the community can further help students understand how to evaluate information for its accuracy, credibility, and usefulness, thus contributing to the development of critical thinking skills often desired in workplace settings.

Although this discussion has focused on using information to solve big questions, the ways student service experiences reinforce information acquisition and processing in smaller ways should not be underestimated. Even the simple tasks of identifying a site for service participation, negotiating transportation, orienting oneself to the work of the organization, and managing the logistics involved will often require students to use information to navigate their community and understand systems and structures. Independence and initiative that are reinforced through the design of service experiences can contribute positively to students' ability to independently obtain and process information for higher order goals and purposes.

■ ■■■ COMMON EXPERIENCES

Cindy was creating a workshop to help prepare student volunteers to work with local community partners. She had heard that a staff member in the community engagement office had recently conducted an impact survey of nonprofit organizations that regularly worked with her university and arranged a meeting with the staff member. During the meeting, the two reviewed the data and discussed areas identified by community partners where students could be better prepared prior to their volunteer experience. Cindy then developed a workshop for the volunteer that directly incorporated the recommendations from community partners.

Quantitative Analysis

The President's Higher Education Community Service Honor Roll is completed by hundreds of higher education institutions annually. The President's Honor Roll asks for detailed data collection on a range of community-engaged work taking place across the college or university. The Carnegie Foundation for the Advancement of Teaching recognizes outstanding community engagement through the Community Engagement Classification. Every 10 years, colleges and universities apply for this prestigious recognition by compiling both quantitative and qualitative data. Even if colleges and universities decide not to complete the application for the President's Honor Roll or the Carnegie Classification, most presidents and chancellors want to know the number of faculty, staff, and students engaged in community-based work. Collecting, collating, and analyzing the data involves individuals from across disciplines and departments.

Increasing numbers of campuses are offering cocurricular transcripts that identify the number of service hours students contribute locally and globally. Students majoring in communication, business, and journalism are applying their academic skills as volunteers to nonprofit organizations. For example, rather than volunteering directly with children in an after-school program, students may use their public relations writing skills to create electronic newsletters, website content, and social media sites for community agencies. They then can analyze how frequently target audiences access the information. Business majors can work with nonprofit administrators to enhance marketing plans and conduct surveys to determine customer satisfaction. Student volunteers can use their volunteer projects in their courses and involve faculty members as consultants on these projects.

Cocurricular service organizations learn about creating and managing budgets through student government allocation processes. Student organization budget proposals often require groups to write and justify a proposed budget and appear before a subcommittee to answer questions and defend expenditures. Once funds are allocated, student leaders must spend responsibly, keep records, complete appropriate paperwork, and complete a budget review at the end of the academic year. For many students, the student government allocation process provides their first experience working with budgets.

■ ■■ COMMON EXPERIENCES

Patrick is the treasurer for an organization designed to help keep students safe by coordinating late night transportation for students on the weekends. A significant amount of his budget was used during his first year on repair costs for the fleet of aging vehicles. Patrick worked with the automotive service manager to analyze a 4-year history of repair costs and mileage for each vehicle in the fleet. Patrick and the manager used the data to identify two vehicles that should be replaced in the upcoming months. He then used this data to prepare a proposal to the student government association to purchase two replacement vehicles. ■ ■ ■

Career-Specific Knowledge

It is not uncommon for faculty and staff working with service and community engagement to hear from students about the impact of their experience on their careers. Students may change a major after an alternative break experience, discover unanticipated skills and interests while volunteering at a service organization for an extended period of time, or respond to questions in an interview and find that the potential employer is more curious about the student's involvement in service than other forms of work experience. Service and community engagement can lead to the acquisition of knowing and development of skills that students can apply directly to their future professions.

Because community engagement work brings students into the community and in contact with different people and contexts, the hands-on nature of the work leads to the discovery of new professional knowledge, skills, and values. For example, future teachers have opportunities to put theory into practice through tutoring children in a Boys and Girls Club after-school program. Aspiring technology sector employees are able to work with a local food pantry to set up and support computer information systems designed to track clients. Graphic design majors can create logos and promotional materials for potential donors in area nonprofit organizations while building their professional portfolios.

Community engagement is frequently described as messy and unpredictable. Students are working with community partners who are dealing with complex social issues with limited resources and clients with many difficult challenges. This work requires an ability to adapt to changing situations and find creative solutions with limited resources. Volunteers must also develop cross-cultural communication skills and competencies while working with people who often come from different backgrounds. These valuable skills transcend career boundaries and can help prepare students for their first professional position. In summary, community engagement is one of the most challenging and rewarding career preparation experiences an undergraduate can have.

■ ■■ COMMON EXPERIENCES

An elementary education major, Michelle took a student leadership position coordinating a tutoring program where students were placed in local elementary schools and after-school programs. Michelle soon noticed that a number of the tutors were having challenges at their sites, primarily due to the fact that these tutors were not education majors and did not have the theoretical or practical knowledge to be as effective as they could be in the classroom. Michelle took the knowledge she had gained in her coursework in the School of Education to design seminars and tools to help prepare non-education majors to be successful tutors. She also helped design a monthly tutor training series featuring some of her faculty members as guest speakers to supplement the resources that she had created.   ■ ■■

Computer Software Skills

Community partners commonly identify a need for more volunteers and employees with technology expertise. Nonprofit organizations frequently don't have access to new equipment or advanced computer training and identify college students as having the necessary computer expertise and knowledge that can benefit their organization. Due to the rapidly changing social media landscape, nonprofit administrators could often benefit from student assistance in using these tools most effectively.

College students are able to set up Twitter, Facebook, and LinkedIn accounts that help nonprofits reach new audiences and enhance their marketing and fundraising efforts. Public relations writing and marketing skills are widely requested and college volunteers utilize their talents by creating PowerPoint and Prezi presentations. There are also opportunities to analyze data from community-based surveys and program evaluations. Students also work with children, job seekers, and seniors to tutor clients in nonprofit organizations in how to use websites to complete homework, search for a job, and stay in touch with family members.

For example, an America Reads volunteer recommended submitting feedback and reflection using a Google form, which creates an Excel document. The document can be used by other tutors as a resource. The community of America Reads tutors can continue to update the document throughout the semester. An America Reads program coordinator explained, "The benefits are three-fold: Tutors have an opportunity for personal reflection, the coordinators are able to check in and manage concerns, and the document serves as a forum for spreading positive practices among the tutors." College students have a level of proficiency with technology that clearly is in high demand by nonprofit organizations.

■ ■■COMMON EXPERIENCES

Camila, an anthropology and public health major, is a student office manager in a community engagement office. One of her responsibilities involves preparing and sending a weekly electronic newsletter to several thousand students, faculty, and staff informing them about opportunities for getting involved with local nonprofit organizations. Camila did not have significant technical skills before she began her position, nor had she ever produced an electronic newsletter. Through this position, she became proficient in using e-mail marketing software, and she now serves as chief editor of the newsletter.

Writing and Editing Reports

Community service programs can provide a venue for students to develop and hone written communication skills. An integrative learning (Huber & Hutchings, 2004) approach to this work means students may learn about the foundations of effective writing in a foundational English course and then apply these skills in a community setting. As a result, a student learning outcome on written communication developed and implemented by a community service program supports and advances a first-year composition course objective of developing a more sophisticated writing process.

The report *College Learning for the New Global Century* (National Leadership Council for Liberal Education and America's Promise, 2008) puts forward a set of essential student learning outcomes informed by the university and business sectors. These outcomes were designed to prepare students for the 21st century in the areas of academics, work, and citizenship. Written and oral communication is identified as a key outcome under the broader heading of intellectual and practical skills. Interviews conducted with more than 300 employers by Hart Research Associates (2010) indicated that 89% of those employers articulated that colleges should place an increased emphasis on the ability to communicate (oral and written) effectively.

Elon University's Alternative Service Break program is an example of how the infusion of writing into a service experience can create a seamless model of engaged curricular and cocurricular learning. The publication *More Than Just a Trip* (Lilienthal & Small, 2015) chronicled the written reflections of participants on fall, winter, and spring break experiences. Student leaders who coordinated programs to locations from New Orleans to Nicaragua—focusing on social issues such as education disparities and environmental sustainability—used the writing process to create, revise, and edit ideas that ultimately emerged as thoughtful writing prompts for participants. These prompts were entered into blank notebooks for participants to respond to during their experiences. This opportunity to connect time spent volunteering with a refugee resettlement agency to content learned in academic disciplines allowed students to use writing not only to explore their commitment to addressing the greater good, but to deconstruct the effectiveness of community solutions used to address the root causes of these issues. This approach, furthermore, has made a valuable contribution to the university's Writing Excellence Initiative as part of the institution's Quality Enhancement Program.

Students can also develop as writers through community work by enrolling in academic service–learning courses in disciplines such as communications and marketing. When a class takes on a local nonprofit organization as a client for a public relations project, students can generate content for a newly created website or brochure. The writing and editing process takes on new meaning as students utilize interviews with agency staff and clients, along with research on an organization's mission and services, to develop text that accurately conveys the philosophy of a community partner to a broad audience.

■ ■■ COMMON EXPERIENCES

Liz, a former Alternative Breaks director, recalled the impact of her service experiences on her development as a writer:

> As a student leader, I have had the opportunity to apply writing and editing skills to submitting grant applications and compiling a university voting guide. These opportunities have allowed me to concisely express a message, clearly communicate with others, and develop organizational skills.

■ ■■

Selling and Influencing

Service can both introduce and reinforce the valuable transformational leadership attribute of creating a shared vision. Kouzes and Posner (2009) identified that being forward-looking was the key characteristic that separated leaders from nonleaders in a *Harvard Business Review* article reporting survey findings from questions posed to tens of thousands of individuals in the workplace.

Community engagement work is often described in terms of a three-legged stool consisting of direct service, indirect service, and advocacy. While students find it relatively easy to involve themselves in the direct service of tutoring elementary school children or the indirect service of donating books to a literacy program, advocacy work often poses a challenge. Advocating for an issue, cause, or piece of legislation is a valuable and necessary skill in the areas of community engagement, civic engagement, and social justice. Volunteering at a local animal shelter to provide basic care for cats and dogs is an important way to support animals on a local level; however, encouraging other students to consider where their food comes from, and become part of a broader movement to treat animals more ethically, or alter their diet away from animal-based food sources uses advocacy to advance a larger cause.

Students on the executive board of Elon Volunteers!—Elon University's largest service organization involving nearly 150 student leaders—are involved in an initiative to deepen the service experience for student leaders and volunteers. This deepening includes reframing the way that student coordinators previously viewed their work in the community, as independent programs, to an issue-based model where programs intersect to jointly address areas such as education, affordable housing, and community well-being. Executive board members are involved in achieving buy-in from coordinators on this new collaborative framework in addition to using this structure to introduce Elon Volunteers! to first-year students through Elon 101 courses.

Furthermore, the executive directors are involved with the task of influencing others to engage in a shared vision of using the newly developed Kernodle Center for Service Learning and Community Engagement curriculum to enhance the student service and leadership experience. Working with fellow students to see the merits of incorporating scholarly readings on the foundations of service–learning and social justice into training programs and committee meetings has taught students valuable lessons about using a range of strategies to influence the thoughts and behavior of others.

■ ■ ■ COMMON EXPERIENCES

Laura is the director of human rights in a large student-run service organization. She inherited a position that had challenges in recent years due to the fact that students often struggled connecting with human rights issues they felt were half a world away. Laura worked with a nonprofit organization that helped support newly resettled refugee families in the local area and agreed to coordinate a new group of students to visit a family once per month. She held information meetings, presented at numerous residence hall floors, spoke at campus events, and had many individual conversations with students to discuss human rights, explain the refugee resettlement process, and convince student volunteers to join her on these monthly visits to support a family who had fled the Democratic Republic of the Congo. Laura soon had a full roster of volunteers who worked together to prepare and conduct English lessons and cultural exchange activities with this family. By putting a face on human rights issues, Amy helped countless students better understand the concerns.

ASSESSING EMPLOYABILITY SKILLS AS AN OUTCOME OF SERVICE AND COMMUNITY ENGAGEMENT PROGRAMS

Research and assessment in service and community engagement is well-documented, especially compared with some other forms of cocurricular engagement described in the other chapters of this book. Resources such as the *Michigan Journal of Community Service Learning*, the International Association of Research in Service Learning and Civic Engagement, the National Service–Learning Clearinghouse, and Campus Compact all offer excellent starting places for practitioners seeking resources to initiate or improve their assessment efforts. It is worth noting that the body of research on outcomes in curricular service–learning outpaces research and assessment in student cocurricular experiences. In addition, the goals and designs for conducting quality research are unique from those used by practitioners implementing robust assessment plans to measure student outcomes or determine the efficacy of programs and experiences.

Recommendations for high-quality research and assessment in service and community engagement are clearly identified in existing literature (see, e.g., Jacoby, 2015; Steinberg, Bringle, & Williams, 2010), but this chapter offers several observations for those who are working with cocurricular experiences and are wanting to focus on employability skills. First, it is important for practitioners to be clear about the intended outcomes of service and community engagement experiences. High-quality assessment starts with developing well-written, concise, measurable statements of intended outcome, which then serve as the basis for data collection, analysis, and action. To assess the impact of service and community engagement experiences on employability skills, the outcomes to be used for assessment must include those skills in explicit terms. Next, assessment efforts should be multifaceted and should follow recommendations for conducting high-quality measurement. While this will likely include a mix of quantitative and qualitative data collection techniques, assessment should also be embedded in the program experiences. For example, Chapter 5 of this book articulates the importance of reflection as both an opportunity to encourage student learning and a form of assessment. Finally, for outcomes assessment to be linked effectively to the development of employability skills, the engagement of community partners (volunteer "supervisors") is important to the assessment process. Just as future employers will determine the effectiveness of their employees through observation, interaction, and experience, so current service site leaders can assess—and teach—important employability skills through their interactions with volunteers on-site. These simple recommendations, combined with existing guidance for good practice in assessment, will lead practitioners to more robust measurements of employability skills developed through service and community engagement experiences, and ultimately, stronger programs to develop these important skills.

CONCLUSION

As illustrated by the examples presented in this chapter, civic engagement and workforce development are not mutually exclusive activities. As students participate in service and community engagement programs, they are not only meeting needs in their communities but also developing skills that will assist them in their future professions. The National Task Force on Civic Learning and Democratic Engagement (2012), in its national call to action, *A Crucible Moment: College Learning and Democracy's Future*, articulated the essential link between the purposes of higher education to equip students for future careers and to prepare them for future democratic participation and civic engagement, stating emphatically, "Many business leaders understand that education for the modern workforce should not displace education for citizenship" (p. 9). Students who participate in service and community engagement while in college should not do so with the impression that their efforts in the civic arena are somehow distinct from those that some may describe as more focused on their professional preparation. As demonstrated here, thoughtful and intentional reflection experiences can help students understand the important connections between the skills they gain through service experiences and those that are most desired by future employers. In this manner, service and community engagement can become an essential activity that helps students weave together a coherent understanding of their college experience—to become better citizens and to prepare for future career opportunities.

REFERENCES

Astin. A. W., & Sax. J. L. (1998). How undergraduates are affected by service participation. *Journal of College Student Development, 39*(3), 251–263.

Astin, A. W., Vogelgesang, L. J., Ikeda, E. K., & Yee, J. A. (2000). *How service learning affects students.* Los Angeles, CA: University of California Higher Education Research Institute.

Battistoni, R. M., & Longo, N. V. (2006). *Connecting workforce development and civic engagement: Higher education as public good and private gain.* Danvers, MA: North Shore Community College Public Policy Institute.

Deresiewicz, W. (2014). *Excellent sheep: The miseducation of the American elite and the way to a meaningful life.* New York, NY: Free Press.

Eyler, J., & Giles, D. E., Jr. (1999). *Where's the learning in service–learning?* San Francisco, CA: Jossey-Bass.

Eyler, J., Giles, D. E., Jr., Stenson, C. M., & Gray, C. J. (2001). *At a glance: What we know about the effects of service learning on college students, faculty, institutions, and communities, 1993-2000: Third edition.* Washington, DC: Corporation for National Service.

Furco, A. (1996). Service–learning: A balanced approach to experiential education. In B. Taylor (Ed.), *Expanding boundaries: Serving and learning* (pp. 2–6). Washington, DC: Corporation for National and Community Service.

Giles, D. E., Jr., & Eyler, J. (1994). The theoretical roots of service–learning in John Dewey: Toward a theory of service–learning. *Michigan Journal of Community Service Learning, 1*(1), 77–85.

Gray, M. J., Ondaatje, E. H., Fricker, R., Geschwind, S., Goldman, C. A., Kaganoff, T., Robyn, A., Sundt, M., Vogelgesang, L., & Klein, S. (1999). *Combining service and learning in higher education: Evaluation of the learn and serve American, higher education program.* Santa Monica, CA: RAND.

Hart Research Associates. (2010). *Raising the bar: Employers' views on college learning in the wake of the economic downturn.* Washington, DC: Association of American Colleges and Universities.

Higher Education Research Institute. (1996). *A social change model of leadership development: Guidebook version III.* Los Angeles, CA: Graduate School of Education and Information Studies, University of California.

Huber, M. T., & Hutchings, P. (2004). *Integrative learning: Mapping the terrain. The academy in transition.* Washington, DC: Association of American Colleges and Universities.

Jacoby, B. (2015). *Service–learning essentials: Questions, answers, and lessons learned.* San Francisco, CA: Jossey-Bass.

Kouzes, J. M., & Posner, B. Z. (2009). To lead, create a shared vision. *Harvard Business Review, 87*(1), 20–21.

Lilienthal, K., & Small, E. (Eds.). (2015). *More than just a trip: Reflections from alternative breaks.* Charleston, SC: Authors.

National Association of Colleges and Employers. (2015). *Job outlook 2016.* Bethlehem, PA: Author.

National Leadership Council for Liberal Education and America's Promise. (2008). *College learning for the new global century.* Washington, DC: Association of American Colleges and Universities.

National Task Force on Civic Learning and Democratic Engagement. (2012). *A crucible moment: College learning and democracy's future.* Washington, DC: Association of American Colleges and Universities.

President's Commission on Higher Education. (1947). *Higher education for American democracy, vol. 1: Establishing the goals.* Washington, DC: Government Printing Office.

Rudolph, F. (1962). *The American college and university: A history.* New York, NY: Alfred A. Knopf.

Saltmarsh, J. (1996). Education for critical citizenship: John Dewey's contribution to the pedagogy of community service learning. *Michigan Journal of Community Service Learning, 3*(1), 13–21.

Sigmon, R. (1994). *Linking service with learning.* Washington, DC: Council for Independent Colleges.

Steinberg, K. S., Bringle, R. G., & Williams, M. J. (2010). *Service–learning research primer.* Scotts Valley, CA: National Service–Learning Clearinghouse.

16

A Flawed Premise
Next Steps

Adam Peck

I t is important to acknowledge that this book is based on a flawed premise. It supposes that curricular and cocurricular learning are separate experiences in college. Keeling (2006) made this point when he wrote, "In our need to put things in categories, we have classified some parts of higher education as curricular, and other parts as co-curricular, but students just call it college" (p. vii). You probably wouldn't expect the final chapter to begin with such an acknowledgement, but the choice to separate curricular and cocurricular learning was made intentionally, and there are good reasons for doing so. By differentiating these experiences and acting as though they are distinct and separate from one another, the authors were able to examine an area of higher education that is often overlooked by those within the field and those who critique student affairs professionals from outside the academy. But at the conclusion of this book, curricular and cocurricular learning must conscientiously be put back together again. The data and thoughtful analysis presented in the preceding chapters show that there are places where classroom experiences can be most useful in developing the skills that employers want, and there are places where cocurricular experiences can potentially fill in the gaps.

Looking at these two aspects of higher education can also help us address an important and sometimes vexing question: How can student affairs professionals provide experiences that connect learning outside of the classroom to learning inside the classroom? In Chapter 5, Darby Roberts shared a quote from former NASPA Executive Director Gwen Dungy (2011) who challenged student affairs professionals to reach beyond vague notions of how their work contributes to students' learning: "For those in student affairs, it's time to stop saying that our programs complement the teaching and learning that occurs in the classroom when at too many campuses student affairs has no relationship with the faculty and no idea about what the student's experience is in the classroom" (para. 11). The belief that experiential education can provide students with the opportunity to apply what they learn is foundational to the educational philosophy of many in student affairs. But how to approach that is a much more complex issue.

The skills identified by the National Association of Colleges and Employers (2015) are often called "soft skills," described as "interpersonal qualities . . . and personal attributes that one possesses" (Robles, 2012, p. 453) that are related to successful employment. These are contrasted with "hard skills," which are "the technical expertise and knowledge needed for a job" (Robles, 2012, p. 453). In order to be successful after college, students need to graduate with the knowledge and technical proficiency to do their jobs (i.e., hard skills) as well as the interpersonal qualities needed to do their jobs well (i.e., soft skills). Academic programs often produce both hard and soft skills. However, a case can be made that as many institutions try to limit the length of academic programs and shorten time to completion, developing soft skills through curricular learning may become increasingly challenging.

Cocurricular experiences can provide the context for students to practice influencing others, organizing complex projects, developing interpersonal competency, and many other desirable skills. Perhaps the work presented in this book can provide a model for producing integrative learning that can maximize the connection between curricular and cocurricular experiences. Additionally, cocurricular experiences can help students to develop skills that are not easily acquired in academic programs. Skills such as decision making, computer skills, or influencing others, which are not necessarily developed universally in various academic programs, can be developed through cocurricular experiences.

The connection between traditional learning outcomes in student affairs and the skills that employers desire also creates some important opportunities. It increases the relevance of these learning outcomes to both internal and external stakeholders. From the college president or provost who may be held accountable for the employment of the school's students, to state law and policy makers whose investment in both public and often private education is based on a belief that the state can see a return on its investment—many of these stakeholders have a strong vested interest in students being prepared for jobs when they graduate. Business leaders expect that colleges and universities will supply them with students who need little additional training to do their jobs. The better stakeholders understand the role that experiential education can play in advancing students' employment prospects, the better the mission and purpose of student affairs work will be understood.

To capitalize on these opportunities, student affairs practitioners must rethink how we approach cocurricular experiences. Educators should consider this important work with the following guidance in mind. We need to map cocurricular learning experiences with the same intentionality with which academic programs are structured. We must agree to a common set of terms to guide our work. We must become experts at using the data we collect to tell our story to both internal and external stakeholders. This guidance will frame the remainder of this chapter.

MAPPING LEARNING EXPERIENCES

Curriculum mapping is a concept that is already familiar to K–12 educators but is gaining popularity within higher education as well. According to Erickson (as cited in Jacobs, 2004), curricular mapping in a primary or secondary context refers to a process by which educators "identify by calendar month topics, skills, and assessments . . . [in order to] identify gaps, redundancies, and misalignments in the curriculum and instructional program and to foster dialogue among teachers about their work" (p. vi). According to Jacobs (2004), "Success in a mapping program is defined by . . . improved student performance in the targeted areas" (p. 2).

In a higher education context, Cuevas, Matveev, and Miller (2010) called the development of curricular mapping "a necessary first step in addressing [the] call for institutions to articulate clear and complementary responsibilities between general education and majors for institution-wide core competencies" (p. 10). Put simply, in higher education, curricular mapping is seen as a way to understand and articulate how students should develop certain skills between their general education requirements and the courses in their major.

In *Learning Reconsidered*, Keeling (2004) illustrated the need to holistically map the learning environment both inside and outside the classroom, writing: "It is quite realistic to consider the entire campus as a learning community. Mapping the learning environment for sites in which learning can occur provides one approach to supporting transformative learning that identifies strength in collaboration—linking the best efforts of educators across the institution to support student learning" (p. 14). While the practice of cocurricular mapping appears to be gaining some traction (as evidenced by web pages of a variety of student affairs programs across the country), student affairs professionals lack a systematized approach to conduct these mapping exercises and few, if any, programs reflect an integration of classroom learning with learning outside the classroom.

If we as student affairs educators wish to play a significant role in student learning at our respective institutions, we must identify the ways in which learning inside the classroom intersects with learning beyond the classroom. These efforts begin by implementing a robust and trustworthy student affairs assessment program. After creating and measuring clear learning objectives for major programs and initiatives, these objectives must be meaningfully linked to the mission and learning outcomes of the institution as a whole. Within this book, many of the authors have expressed that the impact of student affairs must be better understood by both internal and external stakeholders. Connecting the learning outcomes of the programs and services produced by student affairs to the mission and goals of colleges and universities is often the missing link to achieving a broader understanding of the impact of student affairs work.

Yet, even for those student affairs programs that do assessment well, many student affairs professionals find it difficult to understand and communicate the connections between the experiences and the learning outcomes. As a result, these learning experiences are treated as though they are discrete occurrences that have little or no relationship with each other. In fact, many student affairs educators struggle to connect learning experiences within their own programs, let alone connect them to the learning that is happening within the curriculum of the institution.

This book provides a big step forward. The employability skills referenced throughout the book provide a simple way of illustrating how academic and student affairs programs can advance the shared goal of helping students attain career skills. Cuevas, Matveev, and Miller (2010) suggested that the interest in curricular mapping in academic contexts within higher education has been influenced by "the increased intensity of employers' demands for institutions to significantly enhance efforts in facilitating and ensuring student development of transferable general education competencies" (p. 10). This may present an opportunity for curricular and cocurricular learning to align. Because these employment competencies are likely separate from other outcomes they are mapping, student affairs professionals may be able to engage in this concept without asking academic colleagues to reimagine what they have been doing.

Once cocurricular learning has been mapped, it can become a tool for mindfully connecting programmatic outcomes in student affairs to curricular learning. Illustrating how students might progress through these experiences could be the next level. Student affairs professionals need to develop strategies for mapping cocurricular learning, which can help capitalize on the work of academic departments and institutional research to map core and major requirements.

Stephen F. Austin State University has developed a cocurricular mapping program that has been effective in aligning and sequencing students' career-based learning experiences across their entire time at the institution. This program has helped student affairs better plan for student learning, improved consistency across programs, and aided students, faculty and others in understanding how cocurricular learning occurs on campus.

Called JackTracks (so named because the institution's mascot is a Lumberjack), the model resembles the subway map of a major city (see Figure 16.1). The metaphor of a subway was chosen because earlier versions of the maps appeared too linear to accurately capture the multiplicity of ways in which students experience programs. Students may get "on" and "off" of programs in different places, and the amount of time they spend participating in programs may greatly vary as well.

Figure 16.1. JackTracks Cocurricular Learning Map

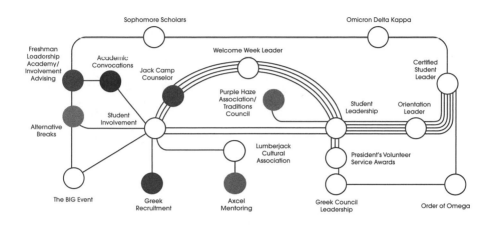

Students may view a master map upon which all major programs of student affairs are listed as stops. Programs that are most typical for first-year students are on the left of the map, and culminating experiences are listed to the right. Additionally, programs have developed learning outcomes that are connected to Bloom's (1956) taxonomy of learning so that as a student navigates the map from left to right, and as the student becomes more deeply involved, the student should encounter more complex versions of the skills acquired. New members will encounter lower order skills, such as remembering and understanding. As they become more involved, they experience intermediate skills such as applying what they are learning and analyzing different learning experiences. When they practice leadership in the context of a given experience, they encounter opportunities that help them develop higher-order skills, such as evaluating complex situations in order to gain new skills and creating new initiatives, programs, or solutions to important issues on their campus. This is laid out for each skill to provide a guide for those who advise these learning experiences. Table 16.1 shows an example for the skill of teamwork.

Table 16.1. **Sample Master Map**

Teamwork: The ability to identify the strengths of those with whom students are working and effectively leverage their skills to accomplish the group's stated goals and objectives.					
Students will learn to identify their own personal strengths and will understand how to seek involvement and leadership experiences that can help them develop these strengths.		Students will apply what they know about teamwork by helping others participating in cocurricular experiences identify strategies for making progress toward shared goals.		Students will actively strive to engage others in the work of their groups, helping them to discover their own personal strengths and providing them opportunities to use their strengths to advance goals that are important to the team.	
New Members		Involved Members		Student Leaders	
Remembering	Understanding	Applying	Analyzing	Evaluating	Creating

Through an approach such as this, student affairs professionals can do more than simply plan the learning objectives of a single program, we can plan for increasingly complex learning through any number of experiences. We can ensure that any students who seek out cocurricular learning, become increasingly involved in that experience, or dedicate themselves to leading important initiatives connected to that experience will be exposed to increasingly higher order objectives.

Foundational to this work is the ability to articulate the kinds of learning experiences we want to map. We must further ensure clear and consistent definitions for each of those outcomes. If the field of student affairs as a whole wants to show improvement in its ability to contribute to students' career-based learning on a broad scale, establishing shared definitions of key terms will be critical. This will be discussed further in the next section.

OPERATIONALIZING TERMS

In Romeo and Juliet, Shakespeare wrote, "What's in a name? That which we call a rose, by any other word would smell as sweet" (Shakespeare, 1599/1992, pp. 72–73). Perhaps this is true. But if we called every flower a rose, or if we called a rose by 1,000 different names, it would be practically impossible to know if a rose was sweeter than any other flower or if we had indeed ever smelled one at all. This may stretch Shakespeare's metaphor beyond its intended proportions, but it does appear to be apt at describing the current state of scholarship and assessment in student affairs.

Historically, much of the early theory in student affairs has been annexed from many disciplines related to our work but not directly connected to it. In a contemporary context, many of the most prominent theorists in student affairs come from the ranks of teaching faculty as opposed to those practicing within the field of student affairs. Perhaps it is the growing responsibility of assessing program effectiveness that makes it difficult for student affairs practitioners to contribute as meaningfully as many would like. Simply put, in many ways, assessment has become the scholarship of the modern practitioner. This is a significant limitation because some of the most interesting findings remain trapped on campus without being shared in a meaningful way.

If we can find a way to agree to an established set of terms and definitions, it will be easier to understand and demonstrate the impact that the entire student affairs profession makes as a whole. This book lays the groundwork, advancing and defining the skills that frame our efforts to clearly define the kinds of employability skills students can gain in college, specifically from cocurricular experiences. These definitions can provide the foundation for making these skills central to the assessment programs of student affairs divisions in the vast array of institutions around the world. By using trusted approaches to collect data on student learning in cocurricular programs, student affairs professionals can begin a grassroots effort to shape how the profession is perceived on college and university campuses. But this is not enough. To capitalize on the full potential of promoting career-ready skills, we must share our information with each other. To that end, Stephen F. Austin State University has created a repository called Project CEO (Cocurricular

Experience Outcomes) to collect and disseminate information on this important topic. Defining terms clearly should allow student affairs professionals to collect data that interconnect across the entire discipline in ways that help demonstrate the contributions of student affairs work to student learning. As we do this, we must find strategies for sharing this information with both internal and external stakeholders.

INTERNAL STAKEHOLDERS

When I speak to groups of student affairs professionals about helping stakeholders understand the purpose of our work, I frequently begin by asking how many of them have a parent, grandparent, or spouse who could accurately describe to others what they do for a living. This usually elicits a lot of laughs and very few raised hands. Among the few who do raise their hands, I frequently counter by asking if that person who could accurately describe what they do had worked or currently works within the field of higher education or student affairs. This statement tends to often encompass the outliers.

How did we allow our work to become so mysterious that those who know us well or work beside us on campus frequently don't understand the impact we make on students? Even the students themselves often seem unaware that we are teaching them. I count this among the greatest advantages of student affairs. As discussed in Chapter 8, the fact that cocurricular experiences are fun and compelling is why students are attracted to them.

How can we demonstrate the impact of cocurricular experiences to our own campus colleagues who may not perceive what we do as connected to student learning in college, or worse, may see us as a potential distraction from learning? This persistent question is difficult to answer. In the book *Contested Issues in Student Affairs: Diverse Perspectives and Respectful Dialogue*, Benjamin and Hamrick (2011) addressed the topic, "How does the perception that learning takes place exclusively in classrooms persist?" They wrote, "More than 15 years after student affairs leaders proposed this shift in perspective [referring to the *Student Learning Imperative*, 1996] student affairs professionals are still met with skepticism or indifference when discussing their contributions to student learning" (p. 24). So how can we change the minds of our skeptics?

The simple answer is data. But it's not the entire answer. Yes, we need to collect better data that show the impact of student affairs in this age of assessment. But how we show this impact to others matters. Since 2014, I have shared Project CEO through my work with colleagues all across the country, in white papers, articles, and in speeches to groups large and small. But it was a video released in March 2015 that made the greatest impact. Titled "Why Involvement in College Matters," within days of being uploaded to YouTube, the video became the second-most viewed video on Stephen F. Austin State University's YouTube channel. It was shared widely on social media and generated considerable discussion at the NASPA Annual Conference that year.

What's more, the video started a conversation on my own campus. Although Stephen F. Austin State University is a relatively modest size (having fewer than 13,000 students), it can still be hard for faculty and academic administration to know about the work of the student affairs department with any level of detail. Sharing the project in such an engaging format helped to spread this news in a way that mattered to faculty members. It also helped that the research presented in the video indicated that students see their classes as their main source of learning—news our faculty wanted to spread. But the research also addressed a persistent myth in higher education that many faculty care about debunking—that college is simply training for a job or career. It is clear that providing faculty members with ammunition to shape their own narrative likely contributed to the video spreading virally.

But what about those who go beyond skeptics to become critics? My advice with regard to this is simple: For right now, ignore them. Former president Bill Clinton popularized a term during the campaign with Kosovo during the late 1990s. He said that the United States wanted to build "coalitions of the willing" (Blumenthal, 2003, para. 4). This is a useful concept in bridging differences. It can sometimes be so tempting to try to sway our harshest critics that we neglect those who share our ideologies but lack the context to understand what we do. If we do our job effectively, we should grow the number of those outside of student affairs who understand and appreciate our work. That pushes more extreme positions farther to the margins. Some choose to stay at these margins, even as conventional wisdom rejects the premises on which these beliefs are based—that student affairs distracts students from curricular learning. Perhaps some opinions will never change, but if we focus on more moderate viewpoints, real change can be achieved.

Last, data are very important, but stories are often overlooked as a means of convincing others. Kouzes and Posner (2002) found the engagement that results from hearing a story tended to keep a listener's interest more than just hearing data. A study conducted by Martin and Powers (1983) confirmed this assumption. They looked at four ways to persuade others when challenging a previously held assumption. The first approach was to use a story, the second was to use relevant and trustworthy data, the third was to use data and a story, and the final approach was to use a policy statement from a senior executive. Their research found that stories alone were the most powerful. We shouldn't interpret this as discounting the role of data. Clearly data have become important currency in higher education. But sharing with our colleagues across the academy real stories of students who have achieved their personal and career goals based on participation in student affairs programs can be a great start. Once those within our organizations understand student affairs work, we can look at ways to share our story with stakeholders outside of higher education.

EXTERNAL STAKEHOLDERS

In recent years, federal and state governments have become harsh and vocal critics of higher education. For example, while the run-up to the 2016 U.S. presidential election revealed a nation and candidates deeply divided on a number of important issues, both major parties seemed to have consensus on one issue: Higher education is too expensive and inefficient.

Ohio Gov. John Kasich advocated for nationalizing the system reportedly in use in Ohio, in which "universities won't get paid a dime unless a student graduates or completes a course," (CNBC's "Your Money, Your Vote," 2016, para. 601) and called for higher education to be divested of what he called "non-academic assets," saying "they shouldn't be in the parking lot business, they shouldn't be in the dining business, they shouldn't be in the dorm business" (CNBC's "Your Money, Your Vote," 2016, para. 603). These performance-based funding approaches have become popular rhetoric among many outside higher education. It makes logical sense to many, that colleges and universities would ensure more students are successful if the schools were paid or incentivized only when a student completed a course or graduated. But that system would also create incentives for colleges and universities to ensure these favorable outputs without improving the outcomes that lead to them. For example, a report created by the Community College Research Center at Columbia University studied community colleges and universities in three states with performance funding (Lahr et al., 2014). It identified a number of unintended impacts such as grade inflation, raised admission standards that excluded at-risk students, and taking much-needed resources away from educating students in order to fund the costs of complying with these standards (Lahr et al., 2014).

Perhaps this assessment is too pessimistic, but it is unlikely that better data or better stories will make a significant difference in the ways in which some politicians view higher education because it is often to their political advantage to see colleges and universities in ways that advance their viewpoint and which fail to acknowledge the culpability they share for rising costs. Neither data nor stories can change that. The desire to see fundamental changes in higher education stems largely from the rising cost of higher education and the inability of many of today's students to afford college without taking out substantial loans. This has undoubtedly been influenced by the divestment in higher education by both the federal and many state governments (Archibald & Feldman, 2011). If state and federal lawmakers played a role in creating the funding crisis in higher education, their analysis of the problem will likely be based on a different causation for the current situation. In response, we might expect them to cite other believable, but inaccurate, causes for the present situation, including the salaries of presidents and senior administration, the number of nonteaching employees, or the number of nonacademic buildings that cater to students.

It is beyond the scope of this chapter or book to solve the financial crisis in higher education, but this example does illustrate the point that refuting claims with evidence may be a beneficial way to tell the student affairs story on campus; however, when telling the student affairs story to those off campus, we may need to show our impact in areas that are less contested.

One way to do this is by recognizing what Kingdon (1995) called "policy windows" in which there is an "opportunity for advocates to push their pet solutions, or to push attention to their special problems" (p. 165). As this quote implies, it is a popular tactic to try to force a policy window open by finding a pressing issue for which the desired goal is the logical solution. When I teach about policy windows, my favorite example is from the musical *The Music Man* (Wilson & DaCosta, 1962), in which traveling salesman "Professor" Harold Hill comes to River City, Iowa, to get locals to start a boys' band (giving him the ability to sell the instruments, uniforms, music books, etc.). He enlists a local confederate to help him identify an issue of concern that can be solved by a boys' band. They quickly identify the new pool hall and its potential negative impact on young men in the community as the problem they wish to address. In much the same way, many who seek to shape policy in a variety of contexts are often looking for ways to shoehorn their priorities into the contemporary political climate.

But not all policy windows need to be forced open; some open all on their own. We are in a time in higher education in which many stakeholders are looking for ways to show business leaders and parents that college can lead to a good job. The connection between participation in cocurricular experiences and the development of career-ready skills can provide a policy window for showing our impact, but only if we speak with one voice. As the idea of developing career-ready skills from cocurricular experiences becomes better known, similar policy windows should open. Leaders in higher education need to be poised to capitalize on these opportunities by collecting their own local data and having those data at the ready when opportunities present themselves.

LOOKING AHEAD

One of the greatest strengths of higher education in the United States is the tremendous diversity that exists within it. But this diversity can also be a barrier. While different disciplines in higher education face common challenges, their perspectives on these challenges can be quite different. This book, however, is a rare case in which a significant cross section of the student affairs profession recognizes the importance of demonstrating the impact that student affairs makes on helping students develop career-readiness skills. The book has benefited from the participation of six professional associations in student affairs and higher education: the Association of College Unions International, the Association of Fraternity and Sorority Advisors, the National Association for Campus Activities, the National Association of Colleges and Employers, NASPA–Student Affairs Administrators in Higher Education, and NIRSA: Leaders in Collegiate Recreation. This speaks volumes to the timeliness of this topic and the deep desire to show the important role that cocurricular experiences play in student learning as a whole.

This book marks the beginning and not the end of this conversation. It is hoped that many in higher education will be inspired by this approach to develop assessment programs that anchor the concepts from this book on their campuses, conduct and disseminate scholarly research, and create approaches for informing both internal and external stakeholders about student affairs work.

REFERENCES

Archibald, R. B., & Feldman, D. H. (2011). *Why does college cost so much?* New York, NY: Oxford University Press.

Benjamin, M., & Hamrick, F. A. (2011). How does the perception that learning takes place exclusively in classrooms persist? In P. M. Magolda & M. B. Baxter Magolda (Eds.), *Contested issues in student affairs: Diverse perspectives and respectful dialogue* (pp. 23–34). Sterling, VA: Stylus.

Bloom, B. S. (Ed.). (1956). *Taxonomy of educational objectives: The classification of educational goals. Handbook I: Cognitive domain.* New York, NY: David McKay Company.

Blumenthal, S. (2003, May 1). Clinton's war: What Kosovo can teach us now. *The Washington Monthly.* Retrieved from https://www.thefreelibrary.com/Clinton's+war%3A+what+Kosovo+can+teach+us+now.-a0101861609

CNBC's "Your Money, Your Vote: The Republican Presidential Debate" (Part 2). (2016, October 29). Retrieved from http://www.cnbc.com/2015/10/29/cnbc-full-transcript-cnbcs-your-money-your-vote-the-republican-presidential-debate-part-2.html

Cuevas, N. M., Matveev, A. G., & Miller, K. O. (2010). Mapping general education outcomes in the major: Intentionality and transparency. *Peer Review, 12*(1), 10–16.

Dungy, G. (2011, December 23). *Campus chasm.* Retrieved from https://www.insidehighered.com/views/2011/12/23/essay-lack-understanding-between-academic-and-student-affairs

Jacobs, H. H. (2004). *Getting results with curriculum mapping.* Alexandria, VA: Association for Supervision and Curriculum Development.

Keeling, R. P. (Ed.). (2004). *Learning reconsidered: A campus-wide focus on the student experience.* Washington, DC: ACPA–College Student Educators International & NASPA–Student Affairs Administrators in Higher Education.

Keeling, R. P. (Ed.). (2006). *Learning reconsidered 2: Implementing a campus-wide focus on the student experience.* Washington, DC: ACPA–College Student Educators International, Association of College and University Housing Officers–International, Association of College Unions International, National Academic Advising Association, National Association for Campus Activities, NASPA–Student Affairs Administrators in Higher Education, & National Intramural-Recreational Sports Association.

Kingdon, J. W. (1995). *Agendas, alternatives and public policies* (2nd ed.). London, England: Longman Publishing Group.

Kouzes, J. M., & Posner, B. J. (2002). *The leadership challenge* (3rd ed.). San Francisco, CA: Jossey-Bass.

Lahr, H., Pheatt, L., Dougherty, K., Jones, S., Natow, R., & Reddy, V. (2014). *Unintended impacts of performance funding on community colleges and universities in three states* (pp. 1–73). New York, NY: The Community College Research Center at Columbia University.

Martin, J., & Powers, M. (1983). Organizational stories: More vivid and persuasive than quantitative data. In B. M. Stew (Ed.), *Psychological foundations of organizational behavior* (pp. 161–168). Glenview, IL: Scott, Foresman.

National Association of Colleges and Employers. (2015). *Job outlook 2016.* Bethlehem, PA: Author.

Robles, M. M. (2012). Executive perceptions of the top 10 skills needed in today's workplace. *Business and Professional Communication Quarterly, 75*(4), 453–465. doi: 10.1177/1080569912460400

Shakespeare, W. (1992). *The tragedy of Romeo and Juliet* (B. A. Mowat & P. Werstine, Trans.). New York, NY: Washington Square Press. (Reprinted from *The most excellent and lamentable tragedie, of Romeo and Juliet,* by W. Shakespeare, 1599, London, England: Thomas Creede.)

Wilson, R. M. (Writer), & DaCosta, M. (Producer/Director). (1962). *The music man* [Motion picture]. United States: Warner Brothers.

Appendix
Employability Skills Rubrics

Compiled by Stan Dura

Teamwork					
Dimension	Performance Indicators*	Performance Level 1	Performance Level 2	Performance Level 3	Performance Level 4
Planning and Execution	Recognizes different team structures (functional, matrix, self-managed, etc.) and associated strengths and weaknesses of them	Unaware of different team structures; assumes the one that is familiar	Somewhat aware of different team structures, but is not aware of the strengths and weaknesses of them or assumes the familiar one is most appropriate	Aware of several different team structures and recognizes several advantages and disadvantages of each	Aware of numerous team structures and the advantages and disadvantages of each
	Involves others in planning and decisions	Excludes others in planning and decisions	Selectively includes others in planning and decisions, provided it is convenient, but may marginalize the input of others when included	Often includes others, even when inconvenient, and attempts to integrate input	Almost always includes others, even when inconvenient, and attempts to integrate input
	Assists in clarifying team goals, roles, tasks, context, resources, challenges, etc.	Does not assist in clarifying goals, roles, tasks, context, resources, challenges, etc.	Assists marginally, sometimes fully, in clarifying goals, roles, tasks, context, resources, challenges, etc.	Often assists fully in clarifying goals, roles, tasks, context, resources, challenges, etc.	Consistently assists fully in clarifying goals, roles, tasks, context, resources, challenges, etc.
	Proposes and executes courses of action and sequencing of activities to achieve tasks/goals, overcome challenges, etc.	Does not propose or execute courses of action or sequencing of activities that advance team goals, overcome challenges, etc.	Proposes courses of action, but does not execute or may have difficulty sequencing activities to effectively help advance team goals, resolve challenges, etc.	Proposes and executes courses of action and sequencing of activities that generally help advance team goals, overcome challenges, etc.	Proposes and executes courses of action and sequencing of activities that consistently help advance team goals, overcome challenges, etc.

Note. The Employability Skills Rubrics build upon the work of the Association of American Colleges and Universities (2014) and the National Association of Colleges and Employers (2015).

Teamwork					
Dimension	**Performance Indicators***	**Performance Level 1**	**Performance Level 2**	**Performance Level 3**	**Performance Level 4**
Coordination	Facilitates feedback processes to detect errors and problems; evaluates and uses feedback received	Does not consider the need to detect problems or errors, or solicit feedback	Considers the need to solicit feedback but not detect errors or problems; uses simplistic means to solicit feedback	Considers the need to solicit feedback as well as detect errors and problems; may use advanced strategies to solicit feedback, but facilitates simple methods to detect problems and errors	Considers the need to solicit feedback as well as detect errors and problems; facilitates advanced methods to solicit feedback and detect problems and errors
	Helps monitor resources, conditions, etc., affecting progress toward goals	Does not monitor resources, conditions, etc., affecting progress toward goals	Minimally monitors obvious resources, conditions, etc., affecting progress toward goals	Monitors obvious resources, conditions, etc., affecting progress toward goals	Monitors resources, conditions, etc., both obvious and subtle, affecting progress toward goals
	Assists in the coordination of tasks and activities	Does not assist in the coordination of tasks and activities	Infrequently assists in the coordination of tasks and activities	Fully participates in the coordination of tasks and activities	Consistently assists in the coordination of tasks and activities
	Recognizes and helps manage team attitudes and behaviors	Does not recognize team attitudes and behaviors	Recognizes team attitudes and behaviors, but does not help manage them or does so only marginally	Recognizes and helps manage team attitudes and behaviors, excepting the more difficult or extended situations	Recognizes and helps manage team attitudes and behaviors, including the more difficult or extended situations
Contribution and Cooperation	Adjusts style to accommodate dynamics and differences between individuals, situations, and team structures	Is not aware of or does not consider the need to adapt due to styles, dynamics, structures, etc.	Is aware of and considers the need to adapt due to styles, dynamics, structures, etc., but chooses not to adapt or adapts in superficial or otherwise ineffective ways	Generally makes reasonable and effective adaptations due to styles, dynamics, structures, etc.	Consistently makes reasonable and effective adaptations due to styles, dynamics, structures, etc.
	Reliably performs assigned tasks and attends meetings	Does not perform assigned tasks or attend meetings	Performs some tasks and attends some meetings	Performs most tasks and attends most meetings	Performs virtually all tasks and attends all or nearly all meetings
	Shares relevant information, including details, opinions, positions, feelings, etc., honestly and transparently	Does not share relevant information, details, opinions, positions, or what is shared is not honest or transparent or is a repeat of others' information, opinions, etc.	Shares relevant information and details openly and honestly, but does not share opinions, positions, feelings, etc., as much; may repeat or agree with others' opinions, positions, etc., to avoid sharing their own	Shares relevant information and details, opinions, positions, feelings, etc., openly and honestly; may withhold stronger opinions, feelings, etc.	Shares relevant information and details, opinions, positions, feelings, etc., openly and honestly, including stronger opinions and feelings

Teamwork					
Dimension	**Performance Indicators***	**Performance Level 1**	**Performance Level 2**	**Performance Level 3**	**Performance Level 4**
	Frequently helps team members with their tasks to ease workload or leverage strengths	Does not help team members with tasks	Helps team members with their tasks when it is convenient or personally beneficial, or to control the product more so than to ease workload or leverage strengths	Helps team members with their tasks, even when inconvenient, more often to ease workload or leverage strengths, but sometimes to control the product	Helps team members with their tasks, even when inconvenient, almost always to ease workload or leverage strengths and rarely to control the product
	Works toward consensus and cooperation	Focuses on authoritative decision making and advancing individual ideas; splits up tasks in ways that emphasize individual work	Generally prefers authoritative decision making or advancing individual ideas, but sometimes attempts to combine ideas to gain buy-in and support; splits up tasks mostly in ways that emphasize individual work, but may involve some cooperation	Often combines and adapts ideas to seek consensus or near-consensus agreement (e.g., voting) on them over authoritative decision making; splits up tasks in ways that require some individual work but also require significant cooperation to complete	Almost always combines and adapts ideas to seek consensus or near-consensus agreement (e.g., voting) on them over authoritative decision making; splits up tasks in ways that require some individual work but also require significant cooperation to complete
Engaging Conflict	Seeks solutions and win-win opportunities rather than win-lose outcomes	Generally does not offer solutions, but may still point out problems; usually seeks to achieve self-interested goals during conflict	Sometimes offers solutions, but solutions to conflict tend to forward their own goals; occasionally seeks win-win opportunities	Usually offers solutions that are often based on win-win solutions	Almost always offers solutions that are based on win-win opportunities
	Openly acknowledges and works through conflict cooperatively	Generally ignores conflict and does not work through conflict cooperatively	Often acknowledges conflict openly and sometimes works through conflict cooperatively	Almost always engages conflict openly and usually works through conflict cooperatively	Almost always acknowledges conflict openly and engages conflict cooperatively
	Recognizes and considers the impact of power, policies, and procedures within conflict	Generally unaware of the impact of power, policies, and procedures within conflict; relies on formal power, policies, and procedures to address conflict	Sometimes recognizes and considers the impact of power, policies, and procedures in conflict, particularly when personally and negatively affected by a power, policy, or procedure; often relies on formal power, policies, and procedures to address conflict, except when alternatives provide a personal benefit	Often recognizes and considers the impact, sometimes even when the power, policy, or procedure benefits them; considers and sometimes engages alternative power, policies, and procedures when available and appropriate	Almost always recognizes and considers the impact, even when the power, policies, or procedures benefit them; often considers and engages alternative power, policies, and procedures when available and appropriate

Teamwork					
Dimension	Performance Indicators*	Performance Level 1	Performance Level 2	Performance Level 3	Performance Level 4
Builds Trust and Commitment	Leads by example: - Trusts, supports, and shows concerns for others - Seeks feedback and others' point of view - Places team goals above own - Adheres to personal and team values, principles, etc.	Consistently demonstrates less than four of the following: - Trusts, supports, and shows concerns for others - Seeks feedback and others' point of view - Places team goals above own - Adheres to personal and team values, principles, etc. - Maintains a sense of purpose and participation in connection to team - Willing to take and share risks with the team - Able to recover from setbacks and overcome challenges - Shares and engages with colleagues on a personal level - Values long-term relationships over short-term success	Consistently demonstrates four or five of the following: - Trusts, supports, and shows concerns for others - Seeks feedback and others' point of view - Places team goals above own - Adheres to personal and team values, principles, etc. - Maintains a sense of purpose and participation in connection to team - Willing to take and share risks with the team - Able to recover from setbacks and overcome challenges - Shares and engages with colleagues on a personal level - Values long-term relationships over short-term success	Consistently demonstrates six or seven of the following: - Trusts, supports, and shows concerns for others - Seeks feedback and others' point of view - Places team goals above own - Adheres to personal and team values, principles, etc. - Maintains a sense of purpose and participation in connection to team - Willing to take and share risks with the team - Able to recover from setbacks and overcome challenges - Shares and engages with colleagues on a personal level - Values long-term relationships over short-term success	Consistently demonstrates at least eight of the following: - Trusts, supports, and shows concerns for others - Seeks feedback and others' point of view - Places team goals above own - Adheres to personal and team values, principles, etc. - Maintains a sense of purpose and participation in connection to team - Willing to take and share risks with the team - Able to recover from setbacks and overcome challenges - Shares and engages with colleagues on a personal level - Values long-term relationships over short-term success
	Self-motivated: - Maintains a sense of purpose and participation in connection to team - Willing to take and share risks with the team - Able to recover from setbacks and overcome challenges				
	Forms positive relationships with colleagues: - Shares and engages with colleagues on a personal level - Values long-term relationships over short-term success				

*Performance levels are absolute, meaning all criteria must be met in that level to achieve it; otherwise, the product is scored at the lower performance level. Products that do not meet the performance criteria for Level 1 are deemed "not evaluable."

Decision Making/Problem Solving				
Dimension	**Performance Indicators***	**Performance Level 1**	**Performance Level 2**	**Performance Level 3**	**Performance Level 4**
Recognition and Analytics	Uses data and considers multiple possibilities, perspectives, moral and ethical codes, and potential outcomes to analyze the context of the problem, decision, etc., using multiple analytical methods (situational analysis, cost/ benefit, SWOT, etc.)	Does not attempt to analyze the problem, situation, decision, etc.	Attempts to analyze the problem, situation, decision, etc., without using a formal methodology, but only selectively or partially considers data and/or other perspectives, morals, ethics, and potential outcomes	Analyzes the problem, situation, decision, etc., and considers data, multiple perspectives, morals, ethics, potential outcomes, etc., using at least one formal analytical method	Analyzes the problem, situation, decision, etc., and considers data, multiple perspectives, morals, ethics, potential outcomes, etc., using multiple analytical methods
	Accurately defines the problem, options, situation, etc.	Does not define the problem, situation, options, etc., or does so superficially	Defines the problem, situation, options, etc., in a somewhat incomplete and/ or ineffective manner	Defines the problem, situation, options, etc., in a relatively thorough and effective manner	Defines the problem, situation, options, etc., in a thorough and effective manner
	Adapts the degree of planning and analysis In decision making based on the degree of certainty and risk	Does not adapt the degree of planning and analysis to fit the context	Adapts planning and analysis, but generally does not consider the degree of certainty or risk in the process	Adapts the degree of planning and analysis based sometimes on the degree of certainty and risk	Adapts the degree of planning and analysis based usually on the degree of certainty and risk
	Considers sources of internal and external bias and evaluates the credibility of perceptions, data, and information	Does not recognize sources of internal and external bias and treats most sources, particularly affirmative or expert sources, as inherently credible	Recognizes some sources of external bias, particularly in terms of inaccuracies and thoroughness, but may not consider bias in data and internal perceptions and understanding; treats most expert and affirmative sources as inherently credible	Recognizes several sources of external and internal bias, including biases in data and personal perceptions, but may treat affirmative expert sources as inherently credible	Recognizes several sources of external and internal bias, including biases in data and personal perceptions, and evaluates sources equitably
Action	Synthesizes information to develop a coherent decision or solution that addresses variable and contextual factors	Focuses on singular pieces of information rather than synthesizing multiple points and/or the decision is incoherent or does not address variable or contextual factors	Attempts to synthesize multiple pieces of information, but it is incomplete and may emphasize some points over others; the decision is coherent but does not address the necessary variable or contextual factors	Synthesizes multiple pieces of information; the decision is coherent and addresses some variable and contextual factors but not all that are necessary	Synthesizes multiple pieces of information; the decision is coherent and addresses all necessary variable and contextual factors

Decision Making/Problem Solving					
Dimension	Performance Indicators*	Performance Level 1	Performance Level 2	Performance Level 3	Performance Level 4
	Decisions are contextualized and made thoughtfully based on personal principles, relationships, criteria, standards, etc. (e.g., ethic of care or justice, fairness, integrity, "do no harm," "good of the many")	Decisions are based on convenience or rules, without considering context, principles, criteria, standards, etc.	Decisions are based on rules, with adherence to rules being the dominant principle/criteria; context, other principles or criteria, etc., may be considered but are otherwise dismissed	Decisions are based on adherence to one or two dominant personal principles and based on context where rules as well as personal principles or ethics of care, justice, fairness, etc., are considered	Decisions are highly contextualized and based on a reconciliation between or synthesis of multiple principles and ethics (e.g., ethic of care or justice, fairness principle, etc.)
	Implements the decision or solution	Does not implement the decision or solution	Implements the decision or solution but only partially or incompletely	Implements the solution completely	Implements the solution completely and evaluates the results
Feedback and Adaptation	Subjects ideas to scrutiny of others and recognizes and integrates useful feedback	Does not share or subject ideas to the scrutiny of others	May share ideas, but selectively so, and does not consider or integrate feedback received	Shares ideas for the purpose of gathering feedback, but may avoid sharing with those perceived as most disagreeable; attempts to integrate useful feedback	Shares ideas widely for the purpose of gathering feedback, and may intentionally target those perceived as most disagreeable; integrates useful feedback
	Incorporates means to generate, collect, and analyze data to evaluate the decision or solution	Does not consider the need to evaluate the decision or solution afterward	May (or may not) consider the need to evaluate the decision or solution, but considers it unimportant or unnecessary ultimately; means to evaluate the decision are either not developed or are superficial in nature	Develops somewhat effective means to collect and analyze data to evaluate the solution	Develops effective means to collect and analyze data to evaluate the solution

*Performance levels are absolute, meaning all criteria must be met in that level to achieve it; otherwise, the product is scored at the lower performance level. Products that do not meet the performance criteria for Level 1 are deemed "not evaluable."

Workflow Planning				
Dimension	**Performance Indicators***	**Performance Level 1**	**Performance Level 2**	**Performance Level 3**	**Performance Level 4**
Plan	Identifies relevant tasks and benchmarks and their relevant timetables and deadlines	Jumps right in before identifying relevant tasks, benchmarks, timetables, etc.	Attempts to identify relevant tasks, benchmarks, timetables, etc., but overlooks important details, resulting in numerous errors and gaps	Accurately identifies relevant tasks, benchmarks, timetables, etc., to a moderate level of detail	Accurately identifies relevant tasks, benchmarks, timetables, etc., to a substantial level of detail
	Recognizes when others need to be involved and/or informed	Fails to recognize that others need to be involved or informed	Recognizes some of those who need to be involved or informed; recognition is influenced heavily by subjective aspects (relationships, ease of contacting, etc.)	Recognizes many or most of those who need to be involved or informed; recognition is equally influenced by subjective aspects (relationships, ease of contacting, etc.) as it is by objective aspects (expertise, quality of work, etc.)	Recognizes most of those who need to be involved or informed; recognition is more influenced by objective aspects (expertise, quality of work, etc.) than subjective aspects (relationships, ease of contacting, etc.)
	Identifies and secures resources needed	Does not consider physical, human, or fiscal resources needed prior to beginning work	Identifies physical, human, and fiscal resources at a basic level, but overlooks considerable details; attempts to secure some but not all of the identified resources	Identifies physical, human, and fiscal resources at an advanced level, and overlooks a small number of details; attempts to secure all of the identified resources	Identifies physical, human, and fiscal resources at an advanced level with virtually no errors; attempts to secure all of the identified resources
	Identifies means to track progress at the relevant scale needed	Does not consider how to monitor progress	Considers how to monitor progress at a very basic level, relying on simple metrics or processes that are mostly ineffective	Considers how to monitor progress and develops simple and somewhat complex metrics and processes that are relatively effective	Considers how to monitor progress at an advanced level where the metrics and processes are complex and highly effective
	Scans and identifies threats to quality, timeline, resources, etc.	Does not consider external and internal threats such as competing projects or responsibilities, resource competition, staff vacations, supply schedules, policy challenges, etc.	Considers external and internal threats at a basic level and identifies the more obvious threats, such as competing projects or responsibilities, supply schedules, large budget gaps, etc.	Considers external and internal threats with some degree of sophistication and identifies obvious and harder-to-see threats, such as policy challenges, technological shortcomings, problematic budget projections, etc.	Considers external and internal threats with a considerable degree of sophistication and identifies both obvious and obscured threats, such as subtle cultural and ideological challenges, systemic features (e.g., delayed feedback loops), etc

Workflow Planning					
Dimension	Performance Indicators*	Performance Level 1	Performance Level 2	Performance Level 3	Performance Level 4
Organize	Establishes communication and documentation	Does not initiate the needed communication and documentation	Establishes one or the other—needed communication or documentation but not both; numerous gaps and errors make efforts somewhat ineffective	Establishes both needed communication and documentation, where one is more thorough and effective than the other; a few errors may be present, affecting effectiveness slightly	Establishes both needed communication and documentation where both are relatively error-free and equal in their effectiveness
	Engages and ensures that key persons understand the purpose, plan, and timeline	Does not make an effort to ensure that key persons understand the purpose, plan, and timeline	Makes a token but ineffective effort to ensure that key persons understand the purpose, plan, and timeline	Makes a moderate and mostly effective effort to ensure that key persons understand the purpose, plan, and timeline	Makes a significant and highly effective effort to ensure that key persons understand the purpose, plan, and timeline
	Assigns accountability for tasks and ensures the documentation of progress	Does not identify who is accountable for what or how to monitor/ document individual progress	Identifies who is accountable for obvious aspects (e.g., specific deliverable) but does not establish a method to monitor and document individual progress	Identifies who is accountable for what, including less obvious aspects (e.g., initiating communication, updating timeline) and establishes a somewhat effective means of monitoring and documenting individual progress	Identifies who is accountable for what, including less obvious aspects (e.g., initiating communication, updating timeline) and establishes a highly effective means of monitoring and documenting individual progress
Prioritize	Evaluates urgency and importance of tasks and prioritize accordingly	Does not consider relative urgency of tasks or does so superficially	Considers relative urgency and importance of tasks, but sticks to a strictly linear or procedural method of prioritizing	Considers relative urgency and importance of tasks, but the priority and urgency are more influenced by procedural or linear processing than by contextual factors	Considers urgency and importance of tasks, and the priority is influenced more by contextual factors (opportunity to consolidate tasks, nonlinear task dependencies, etc.)
	Recognizes when information and/or context changes and adapts priorities appropriately	Does not recognize when information or context changes and does not adapt or makes unnecessary or ineffective changes	Recognizes when information or context changes and makes adaptations that are not effective enough	Recognizes when information and context changes and makes effective adaptations	Recognizes when information and context changes and makes highly effective adaptations
Execution	Executes plans according to priorities	Does not execute plan(s)	Executes plans but ignores or loses sight of priorities	Executes plans mostly in accordance with priorities	Executes plans according to priorities

*Performance levels are absolute, meaning all criteria must be met in that level to achieve it; otherwise, the product is scored at the lower performance level. Products that do not meet the performance criteria for Level 1 are deemed "not evaluable."

Verbal Communication					
Dimension	Performance Indicators*	Performance Level 1	Performance Level 2	Performance Level 3	Performance Level 4
Attention to Audience	Leans slightly toward partner or audience, nods head in response, speaks equally of self and others, encourages other participants to communicate, recognizes and adapts to audience's reactions/ behaviors; manages speaking time between parties	Inconsistently performs these behaviors	Regularly performs less than half of these skills; inconsistently performs the others	Regularly performs more than half of these behaviors; inconsistently performs the others	Consistently performs all of these behaviors
Maintaining Composure	Speaks fluently (avoids pauses, "uh"/"you know" statements, etc.) and confidently, neither too nervous nor overconfident sounding; varies the speaking rate, avoiding extremes; avoids extremes in volume and posture; avoids unintended movement (twitches, tapping feet, hair twirling, etc.); adapts smiling, laughing, and eye contact to fit the context and audience/ recipient	Inconsistently performs these behaviors	Regularly performs less than half of these skills; inconsistently performs the others	Regularly performs more than half of these behaviors; inconsistently performing the others	Consistently performs all of these behaviors
Managing Expression	Enunciates clearly, modulates voice, and avoids overly monotone and dramatic tones; expresses opinions assertively but neither passively nor aggressively; varies facial expressions and avoids blank and exaggerated expressions; uses gestures and humor/ storytelling for emphasis	Inconsistently performs these behaviors	Regularly performs less than half of these skills; inconsistently performs the others	Regularly performs more than half of these behaviors; inconsistently performs the others	Consistently performs all of these behaviors

Verbal Communication					
Dimension	Performance Indicators*	Performance Level 1	Performance Level 2	Performance Level 3	Performance Level 4
Presentation	Provides clear, concise content; core message(s) understood easily; effective use of persuasion, data, storytelling, visual aids, etc.; adapts style and content to meet audience needs and context; avoids overuse of jargon, buzzwords, ambiguous terms, etc.; responds to questions appreciatively and thoughtfully; acknowledges sources	Inconsistently performs these behaviors	Regularly performs less than half of these skills; inconsistently performs the others	Regularly performs more than half of these behaviors; inconsistently performs the others	Consistently performs all of these behaviors

*Performance levels are absolute, meaning all criteria must be met in that level to achieve it; otherwise the product is scored at the lower performance level. Products that do not meet the performance criteria for Level 1 are deemed "not evaluable."

Information Processing					
Dimension	**Performance Indicators***	**Performance Level 1**	**Performance Level 2**	**Performance Level 3**	**Performance Level 4**
Obtain Information	Determines depth and breadth of information needs	Does not consider depth or breadth of information needs before beginning to search or access information	Considers information needs at a surface or basic level before beginning to search or access information	Considers information needs to a moderate level of depth and breadth before beginning to search or access information	Considers information needs to a significant level of breadth and depth before beginning to search or access information
	Identifies, accesses, and considers differences between multiple sources of information (physical sources, online databases, Internet keyword searches, etc.)	Identifies and accesses one or two sources without considering differences between sources (academic journal database, online blog, popular science quarterly, etc.)	Identifies and accesses a limited range of sources and attempts to evaluate differences between sources (academic journal database, online blog, popular science quarterly, etc.) at a surface or basic level (a peer-review journal vs. a product-related website)	Identifies and accesses a moderate range of sources (academic journal database, online blog, popular science quarterly, etc.) and evaluates differences between sources at an advanced level (peer-review process, impact rating, author's credentials, frequency of citation, etc.)	Identifies and accesses a substantial range of sources, all evaluated at an advanced level (peer-review process, impact rating, author's credentials, frequency of citation, etc.)
	Documents sources	Does not document sources	Documents sources with numerous mistakes in terms of accuracy, thoroughness, standards (e.g., APA, MLA), etc.	Documents sources with a moderate amount of mistakes in terms of accuracy, thoroughness, standards (e.g., MLA, APA), etc.	Documents sources with few mistakes (if any) in terms of accuracy, thoroughness, standards (e.g., APA, MLA), etc.
Process Information	Evaluates validity, authority, and relevance of information, considering evidence of validity, authority, and sources of internal/external bias and error (bias or error in cognition, process, source, etc.); the contextual nature of authority; and the constructive nature of knowledge	Does not consider the validity, authority, relevance, or bias pertaining to information processed	Considers relevance, authority, validity, or bias (some but not all) mostly at a basic level (academic journal vs. magazine, etc.)	Considers relevance, authority, validity, and bias mostly at a moderate level of scrutiny (peer-review status, impact rating, etc.)	Considers relevance, authority, validity, and bias mostly at an advanced level (methodological errors, theoretical assumptions, sampling bias, etc.)
	Synthesizes information from multiple sources to identity coherent and compelling points, themes, differences, etc.	Draws information from a single source, or simply patches information from a few different sources without identifying themes, differences, etc.	Draws information from a limited range of sources, and synthesizes information that is basically similar (similar points, conclusions, or criticism, etc.) between sources	Draws information from a moderate range of sources, and integrates basic and complex themes, shared points, differences, etc.	Draws information from a large range of sources, and synthesizes basic and complex themes, shared points, differences, etc.

*Performance levels are absolute, meaning all criteria must be met in that level to achieve it; otherwise, the product is scored at the lower performance level. Products that do not meet the performance criteria for Level 1 are deemed "not evaluable."

Quantitative Analysis					
Dimension	Performance Indicators*	Performance Level 1	Performance Level 2	Performance Level 3	Performance Level 4
Identify Purpose of Analysis	Identifies the nature of the question or problem and how quantitative data can be used to answer or solve it	Does not understand the question or problem, and/ or does not recognize the need or benefit of quantitative data in terms of resolving it	Understands the nature of the question or problem, but does not recognize how quantitative data can help resolve it	Understands the nature of the question or problem, but underestimates how quantitative data can help resolve it	Understands the nature of the question or problem, and recognizes how quantitative data can help resolve it
Knowledge of Quantitative Methods and Procedures	Degree of knowledge is related to quantitative methods and procedures and their application	Knowledge is limited to basic addition, division, subtraction, and multiplication	Knowledge involves the application of some advanced knowledge (algebraic, geometric, calculus, etc.) in addition to division, subtraction, addition, and multiplication	Substantial knowledge related to applying advanced methods and procedures, including calculus, algebra, trigonometry, etc.	Significant knowledge related to applying advanced methods and procedures, including calculus, algebra, trigonometry, etc., as well as substantial knowledge of basic inferential statistics
Evaluate and Identify Appropriate Methods	Evaluates relevant methods, formulas, and concepts, and identifies methods appropriate for the intended purpose	Identifies methods and procedures without evaluating their fit and appropriateness given the context	Identifies methods and procedures, and attempts to evaluate their fit and appropriateness given the context; however, the evaluations are more accurate for low-level procedures and less accurate for more complex procedures	Identifies methods and procedures and attempts to evaluate their fit and appropriateness given the context; evaluations are accurate for low- and medium-level procedures and less accurate for more complex procedures	Identifies methods and procedures and attempts to evaluate their fit and appropriateness given the context; evaluations are accurate for both basic and complex procedures
Execution	Values/variables correctly translated and calculated; formulas and math concepts correctly applied and executed	Extensive errors in the application, translation, calculation, and/ or procedures	Moderate number of errors in the application, translation, calculation, and/ or procedures	Small number of errors in the application, translation, calculation, and/ or procedures	Few if any errors in the application, translation, calculation, and/ or procedures
Analysis and Interpretation	Conclusions logical and reasonable; processes, assumptions, conclusions, etc. scrutinized for errors, bias, etc.	Conclusions are not reasonable or are not congruent with the data; does not scrutinize the procedures, assumptions, etc., for possible errors, bias, etc.	Conclusions are moderately reasonable and congruent with the data; token effort to scrutinize their assumptions, procedures, etc.	Conclusions are highly reasonable and congruent with the data; moderate effort to scrutinize their assumptions, procedures, etc.	Conclusions are highly reasonable and congruent with the data; substantial effort to scrutinize their assumptions, procedures, etc.

*Performance levels are absolute, meaning all criteria must be met in that level to achieve it; otherwise, the product is scored at the lower performance level. Products that do not meet the performance criteria for Level 1 are deemed "not evaluable."

Career-Specific Knowledge					
Dimension	Performance Indicators*	Performance Level 1	Performance Level 2	Performance Level 3	Performance Level 4
Technical Knowledge	Articulates the basic and some specialized knowledge and skills pertinent to their field	Articulates a few, very basic skills obviously involved in the field (e.g., math skills in engineering)	Articulates several basic skills involved in the field	Articulates several basic and a few advanced skills involved in the field	Articulates several basic and several advanced skills involved in the field
Connecting to Curricular and Cocurricular Experiences	Articulates, with compelling details, how curricular and cocurricular experiences helped develop skills	Has difficulty connecting skills to curricular or cocurricular experiences in concrete ways	Articulates a small number of cases where skills were developed in curricular or cocurricular experiences, but has difficulty providing compelling details	Articulates several cases where skills were developed in curricular and cocurricular experiences, and is able to provide compelling details for some of them	Articulates multiple cases developed in curricular and cocurricular experiences, and is able to provide compelling details for many of them

*Performance levels are absolute, meaning all criteria must be met in that level to achieve it; otherwise, the product is scored at the lower performance level. Products that do not meet the performance criteria for Level 1 are deemed "not evaluable."

Computer Software Skills					
Dimension	Performance Indicators*	Performance Level 1	Performance Level 2	Performance Level 3	Performance Level 4
Utilize Functions of Different E-Mail Applications to Create and Edit Electronic Communications for a Variety of Contexts	Basic features: compose, send, carbon copy, change priority/ importance, reply, reply to all, attach items, conduct simple searches, create signature, check spelling, copy/ paste media and links, create a few simple folders	Uses less than half of the basic features regularly	Uses most of the basic features regularly	Uses most of the basic features regularly	Uses all or nearly all of the basic features regularly
	Advanced features: recall, filter, and archive e-mails; embed images and links using html; edit/ view settings; organize multiple folders; create and manage rules; conduct complex searches; delay sending; integrate with other applications using plugins; link e-mail account to a smartphone; create and use contextual signatures, etc.; edit sharing and account management permissions	Uses few if any of the advanced features consistently	Uses less than half of the advanced features regularly	Uses most of the advanced features regularly	Uses all or nearly all of the advanced features regularly
Utilize Functions of Different Calendaring Applications to Manage One's Personal and Professional Time Commitments	Basic features: create new one-off and recurring meetings and appointments, set reminders, create invite text/signature, request and share calendar access, conduct simple searches	Uses less than half of the basic features regularly	Uses most of the basic features regularly	Uses most of the basic features regularly	Uses all or nearly all of the basic features regularly

Computer Software Skills					
Dimension	Performance Indicators*	Performance Level 1	Performance Level 2	Performance Level 3	Performance Level 4
	Advanced features: track and edit meeting attendees, change view settings, check attendee's availability, check location availability, set categories, link calendar account to a smartphone, integrate with other applications using plugins, edit sharing and account management permissions, conduct complex searches	Uses few if any of the advanced features consistently	Uses less than half of the advanced features regularly	Uses most of the advanced features regularly	Uses all or nearly all of the advanced features regularly
Utilize Functions of Different Word Processing Applications to Create and Edit Written Documents for a Variety of Contexts	Basic features: open new; change font size and style; save; change margins; print; insert picture, graph, clip art, screenshot, bullet, etc.; create headers/footers; export to basic formats; use check spelling and thesaurus	Uses less than half of the basic features regularly	Uses most of the basic features regularly	Uses most of the basic features regularly	Uses all or nearly all of the basic features regularly
	Advanced features: mail merge; embed video or online data; automatic text fields; export to multiple formats; integrate with other applications using plugins; track changes; use multiple dictionaries; use symbols to correctly spell foreign language words and unique names; cross reference multiple documents	Uses few if any of the advanced features consistently	Uses less than half of the advanced features regularly	Uses most of the advanced features regularly	Uses all or nearly all of the advanced features regularly

Computer Software Skills					
Dimension	Performance Indicators*	Performance Level 1	Performance Level 2	Performance Level 3	Performance Level 4
Utilize Functions of Different Spreadsheet Applications to Manage Information and Create Relevant Products	Basic features: open new; change font and border size, style, and color; save; change margins; print; insert graph; apply simple equations or functions; data validation; filters; sorting; searching; export to basic formats; check spelling; password protect the file	Uses less than half of the basic features regularly	Uses most of the basic features regularly	Uses most of the basic features regularly	Uses all or nearly all of the basic features regularly
	Advanced features: apply complex data tools, equations, functions, and statistical tools; conditional formatting; connecting data from multiple spreadsheets; complex data tools; export to multiple formats; track changes; integrate with other applications using plugins; password protect specific cells	Uses few if any of the advanced features consistently	Uses less than half of the advanced features regularly	Uses most of the advanced features regularly	Uses all or nearly all of the advanced features regularly
Utilize Functions of Different Presentation Applications to Create and Edit Presentations	Basic features: open new; create new slides; change font size and style; save; print; insert picture, graph, clip art, bullet, etc.; export to basic formats; check spelling	Uses less than half of the basic features regularly	Uses most of the basic features regularly	Uses most of the basic features regularly	Uses all or nearly all of the basic features regularly
	Advanced features: embed live or online video or data, transitions, animations, narrations, export to multiple formats, integrate with other applications using plugins	Uses few if any of the advanced features consistently	Uses less than half of the advanced features regularly	Uses most of the advanced features regularly	Uses all or nearly all of the advanced features regularly
Utilize Functions of Different Specialized Applications (Imaging, Statistical, etc.): Create and Make Edits to Files and Utilize for the Intended Purpose to Generate Products	Basic and advanced features	Regularly uses some of the basic features and few, if any, advanced features	Regularly uses many basic features and some advanced features	Regularly uses most basic features and several advanced features	Regularly uses most of the basic and advanced features

*Performance levels are absolute, meaning all criteria must be met in that level to achieve it; otherwise, the product is scored at the lower performance level. Products that do not meet the performance criteria for Level 1 are deemed "not evaluable."

Selling and Influencing					
Dimension	Performance Indicators*	Performance Level 1	Performance Level 2	Performance Level 3	Performance Level 4
Preparation	Knowledge of product or situation; knowledge of audience and the strategic preparation of supplemental materials	Knowledge of product or situation is limited; need to consider audience is not recognized; need to consider supplemental materials is not recognized	Knowledge of product or situation is adequate but not nuanced; need to consider audience is recognized, but knowledge of audience is limited; supplemental materials are considered but not used	Need to consider audience is recognized and knowledge of audience is adequate; supplemental materials are considered and used in somewhat superficial or partially strategic manner	Knowledge of product or situation substantial and highly nuanced; need to consider audience is recognized and knowledge of audience is substantial; supplemental materials are considered and used in a very strategic manner
Engaging and Relating to Others	Develops personal connection with others quickly; gains others' interest and attention and solicits information/ feedback related to the feelings, interests, and context of others to discern their needs and goals	Appears somewhat detached or doesn't attempt to connect with audience; attempts to gain the audience's attention and interest, but may not be effective and makes few, if any, attempts to solicit information or feedback from audience	Appears personable and attempts to connect with audience but may not be successful; is somewhat successful in gaining the attention and interest of the audience and makes several attempts to solicit information or feedback from audience, but may not be successful	Appears personable and adequately develops rapport with the audience; is moderately successful in gaining the attention and Interest of the audience and makes several attempts, and is somewhat successful in soliciting information or feedback from the audience	Appears very personable and develops a strong rapport with the audience; is very successful in gaining the attention and interest of the audience and makes numerous attempts, and is successful in soliciting information or feedback from the audience
Motivation**	Motivation stems from performance in relationship to goals or competitive performance	Motivation is based solely on financial incentive	Motivation is based primarily on financial incentive, but the competitive desire to do better than others or beat personal goals also influences performance	Motivation is based somewhat equally on financial gain, competition, or surpassing personal goals	Motivation is based primarily on competition or surpassing personal goals
Negotiating Resistance and Conflict	Acknowledges objections and conflict; makes sincere attempts to address objections/ conflict and effectively resolves objections/ conflict	Appears unaware of objections or conflict and/or does not make any attempt to address objections or conflict; is ineffective in resolving objections and conflict, both minor and difficult	Is aware of objections and conflict, but does not acknowledge them directly; attempts to address objectives and conflict passively or indirectly to marginalize, bypass, obfuscate, or dismiss it and Is moderately successful in resolving minor objections and conflict, and marginally successful in resoling difficult ones	Acknowledges objections and conflict but in an indirect or passive manner; addresses objections and conflict directly in a manner that attempts to resolve it, but may still marginalize, bypass, or obfuscate the issue to some degree and is very successful in resolving minor objections and conflict, and moderately successful in resolving difficult ones	Acknowledges objections and conflict directly and openly; addresses objections and conflict directly in an objective and thorough manner that respects the needs and interests of all parties and is very successful in resolving objections and conflict, both minor and difficult

Note. Products that do not meet the performance criteria for Performance Level 1 are deemed "not evaluable."

*Performance levels are absolute, meaning all criteria must be met in that level to achieve it; otherwise, the product is scored at the lower performance level.

**This deals with motivation found to be successful in relationship to sales and persuasion. There are many other sources of and approaches to understanding motivation.

REFERENCES

Association of American Colleges and Universities. (2014). *VALUE: Valid assessment of learning in undergraduate education.* Retrieved from https://www.aacu.org/value/rubrics

National Association of Colleges and Employers. (2015). *Job outlook 2016.* Retrieved from http://www.naceweb.org/s11182015/employers-look-for-in-new-hires.aspx

The Authors

Jan Arminio is professor and director of the Higher Education Program at George Mason University. She received her doctorate from the University of Maryland, College Park. Her scholarship has focused on the study of the integration of new populations in higher education through trustworthy qualitative research methodologies. Examples of her work include the coauthored books *Student Veterans and Service Members in Higher Education* (Routledge, 2015) and *Negotiating the Complexities of Qualitative Research* (Routledge, 2014). She served as first editor of *Why Aren't We There Yet: Taking Personal Responsibility for Creating an Inclusive Campus* (ACPA & Stylus, 2012). Recent articles include "Waking up White," "A Narrative Synthesis of Understanding Addictions, Surrender, and Relapse," and "Synergistic Supervision." She received the 2011 Robert H. Shaffer award for excellence in graduate teaching and is an associate editor for the *Journal of College Student Development*.

Elizabeth Beltramini serves as director of content curation for the Association of College Unions International, where she oversees its content strategy, development, and delivery. Her role includes serving as editor of *The Bulletin* magazine, overseeing digital communications

435

and marketing, and recently developing a documentary for PBS. Additionally, she is a member of the association's management team, advises the Research Program Team, and serves as senior diversity officer. During her tenure at ACUI, she has contributed to numerous books, produced events, and facilitated presentations and workshops. She has a bachelor's degree in journalism from Indiana University and a certificate in Diversity and Inclusion Management from Cornell University.

Jamie Bouldin is director for the Center for Career and Professional Development at Stephen F. Austin State University (SFA). Prior to joining the career services area, she served held a variety of roles, including as an academic advisor in SFA's Arthur Temple College of Forestry and Agriculture, as the assistant director for leadership and service in SFA's Office of Student Engagement Programs, and as a journalist for The Paris News in Paris, Texas. She holds a master's degree in college student personnel from The University of Tennessee and a bachelor's degree in journalism from SFA. She spent 4 years on the National Advisory Council and two terms as national convention program chair for Omicron Delta Kappa, the national leadership honor society, which awarded her the Eldridge W. Roark, Jr. Meritorious Service Award and the Morlan-Bishop Outstanding Faculty Officer Award, as well as inducted her into its Five Star Society.

Daniel A. Bureau is the executive assistant to the vice president for student affairs at the University of Memphis. He has worked in student affairs for 20 years, including 10 years directly with fraternity and sorority life. He continues to serve as a consultant for fraternity and sorority life, particularly through his role as the Association of Fraternity/Sorority Advisors (AFA) liaison to the Council for the Advancement of Standards. He has served in a number of higher education and interfraternal roles, including as the 2004 AFA president. He has contributed to more than 50 publications, including refereed journals and chapters in books and monographs. For his work within fraternity and sorority life and higher education, he was awarded the 2009 Distinguished Service Award from AFA. He received his BA in communications and English from The University of New Hampshire; his MEd in higher educational research, policy, and administration from the University of Massachusetts Amherst; and his PhD in higher education and student affairs from Indiana University.

Toby Cummings serves as executive director of the National Association for Campus Activities. He previously served as president and CEO of various state chapters of the Associated Builders and Contractors. Prior to his career in association management, he worked in higher education for 7 years as the director of student activities at San Juan College in Farmington, New Mexico, and as the director of conferences and special programs for Missouri Western State University (MWSU) in St. Joseph, Missouri. He has a BS in music education from MWSU and completed graduate studies in adult and continuing education administration from Kansas State University.

Jon Dooley is assistant vice president for student life, dean of campus life, and assistant professor at Elon University, where he is responsible for several offices and university initiatives for service learning and civic engagement, diversity and inclusion, and the integration of residential and academic student experiences. His previous administrative experiences at Marquette University and the University of Illinois at Urbana–Champaign focused on leadership education, student activities and organizations, student government, fraternity and sorority life, and student affairs assessment and he has taught graduate and undergraduate courses in leadership, diversity and social justice, and college student personnel administration. He holds a doctorate in educational policy and leadership from Marquette University, a master's degree in counseling psychology from James Madison University, and a bachelor's degree in history and social studies education from St. Norbert College. He is a frequent consultant and conference presenter and is a past board chair for the National Association for Campus Activities.

Stan Dura serves as assessment program manager at Western Governor's University (WGU). Before joining WGU, he held various appointments in higher education, both within and outside the United States, directing student affairs assessment and research programs, teaching and developing curriculum for first-year-experience courses, and serving in academic advising and residence life. He is an active member of the Student Affairs Assessment Leaders, previously chairing its board, and is also affiliated with ACPA–College Student Educators International, NASPA–Student Affairs Administrators in Higher Education, and the American Educational Research Association. He has completed a doctoral program in learning and technology at the University of Nevada Las Vegas (ABD) and holds an MA in student development from Appalachian State University and a BA in psychology from Huntingdon College. He recently published a chapter addressing competency-based cocurricular transcripts in the book *Integrating Curricular and Co-Curricular Endeavors to Enhance Student Outcomes* (Emerald, 2016).

Terrence L. Frazier currently serves as an assistant vice president for student affairs and services at Michigan State University. He is affiliated with and highly involved in numerous professional associations in higher education and student affairs including NASPA–Student Affairs Administrators in Higher Education and ACPA–College Student Educators International, where he serves on the African

American Male and Female Summit faculty. His love for student affairs began on the campus of Ohio University, where he earned a bachelor's degree in elementary education and a master's degree in higher education. He holds a doctorate in educational leadership and policy studies from Iowa State University. In 2012, he received the Outstanding Young Professional Award from Iowa State University College of Human Sciences and was named a Notable Leader in the Nacogdoches, Texas, community.

Robert Frigo is the associate director of the Kernodle Center for Service Learning and Community Engagement and an instructor in the Department of English at Elon University. He holds an MA in Irish literature from Queen's University Belfast, an MEd in student personnel services from the University of South Carolina, and a BA in English from Marquette University. He has published on the use of student development theory with college union student employees and the role of murals in the Northern Ireland peace and reconciliation process.

Kate Griffin is associate vice president for campus success at Campus Labs. She has a wealth of assessment experience through her consulting work with a variety of campuses across North America. She currently spearheads initiatives for Project CEO, a study that focuses on student perceptions of skill development and attainment, especially in relation to cocurricular experiences. Her experience in higher education administration and teaching includes distance education, general education, student academic support services, first-year experience, and new student orientation. She received her undergraduate degree in health and human services from the University at Buffalo and her master's degree in college student personnel administration from Canisius College.

David Hall is the interim assistant vice president of student affairs and director of campus recreation at Springfield College. He received the 2015 NIRSA Regional Award of Merit for outstanding service to the region within NIRSA: Leaders in Collegiate Recreation and the 2014 NIRSA Horace Moody Award for commitment to student development. He holds a doctoral degree in educational administration and leadership from the University of the Pacific; a Master of Science degree in health, leisure, and sports studies from the University of West Florida; and a Bachelor of Science degree in psychology from Virginia Commonwealth University.

Crystal King has contributed to the student affairs field for nearly 20 years, most recently serving as the director of the Carolina Student Union at the University of North Carolina (UNC) at Chapel Hill. Prior to beginning her directorship at UNC in 2013, she served as the associate executive director for the university unions at The University of Texas at Austin. She holds a Bachelor of Arts degree in English from the University of Memphis and a Master of Education degree in college student personnel administration from the University of Texas at Austin.

Mark Koepsell currently serves as the executive director and CEO for both the Association of Fraternal Leadership and Values and the Association of Fraternity/Sorority Advisors (AFA). Prior to these roles, he served 17 years in higher education at three institutions working within student affairs and as a faculty member teaching personal leadership and organizational planning. He also served as an adjunct faculty member for Colorado State's Student Affairs in Higher Education master's degree program. He was awarded the AFA Sue Kraft Fussell Distinguished Service Award in 2006 and was granted the Alumni Leadership and Service Award from his alma mater, Eastern Illinois University, in 2011. That same year, he received the Jack L. Anson Lifetime Achievement award from AFA.

Kevin Kruger draws on more than 30 years of experience in higher education. He joined NASPA–Student Affairs Administrators in Higher Education as associate executive director in 1994 and became its first executive-level president in 2012. He represents NASPA in national forums such as the Washington Higher Education Secretariat, which includes the leaders of approximately 50 higher education associations. He has published and presented nationally on leadership development, the use of technology in student affairs administration, international education, change management, and trends in higher education.

Shannon LaCount is assistant vice president of campus adoption at Campus Labs. Her career in higher education includes 8 years of clinical and classroom teaching experience as an assistant professor in communication sciences and disorders and 5 years as director of student learning assessment at the University of Minnesota Duluth, where she led a campuswide assessment process for academic departments and student life programs. She has served as an advisor for student research, presented at national and international conferences in the areas of speech and language disorders, cultural competence, learning assessment, and scholarship of teaching and learning, and has participated in consultations and professional development events as a Teagle Assessment Scholar with the Wabash College Center of Inquiry. She has a master's degree in speech-language pathology from the University at Buffalo and a doctorate in education from the University of Minnesota.

Alex C. Lange currently serves as the assistant director of the Lesbian, Bisexual, Gay, and Transgender Resource Center and coordinator for organizational effectiveness for the Division of Student Affairs at Michigan State University. Lange's research interests and publications have focused on transgender/gender nonconforming student engagement, socially responsible leadership, and queer student leadership. Lange has been honored as an Annuit Coeptis Emerging Professional by ACPA–College Student Educators International and is an alum of the NASPA Undergraduate Fellows Program. Lange earned a master's degree in college student affairs administration from the University of Georgia and a bachelor's degree in law and American society from the Wilkes Honors College at Florida Atlantic University.

Justin Lawhead serves as the associate vice president for student affairs and dean of students at the University of Memphis. He has more than 20 years of experience in higher education in the areas of student leadership training, program coordination, and advising and assessment. He directs a comprehensive student development program designed to enhance the educational experience for University of Memphis students. His research interests include the impact of social media on identity development and cocurricular contributions to employment competencies. He earned a Bachelor of Arts in political science and Master of Education in educational counseling from the University of Pittsburgh. He earned his Doctor of Education in higher education administration from the University of Memphis by completing his dissertation studying the effects of fraternity and sorority participation on leadership identity development.

Marilyn Mackes is the executive director of the National Association of Colleges and Employers, a position she assumed in 1997. She leads an organization of more than 3,100 employing organizations and educational institutions engaged in the career development and employment process of college students and alumni. In her extensive interactions with recruiting professionals, leaders in business and education, and the media, she addresses such issues as employment and salary trends, benchmarking and best practices, candidate expectations, and developing effective recruiting strategies. As a leader and consultant in the corporate college relations and recruiting field, she has worked with various professional, corporate, educational, and government organizations in the United States and abroad. She regularly conducts media interviews regarding the college employment market and has appeared on *ABC Nightly News*, *CNN Headline News*, MSNBC, CBS, and *The PBS NewsHour*.

Mary Morrison serves as assistant dean of students and director of the Kernodle Center for Service Learning and Community Engagement at Elon University. She has more than 20 years of experience with community service, service–learning, and community-based programs. She coauthored "Differentiating and Assessing Relationships in Service–Learning and Civic Engagement: Exploitative, Transactional, or Transformational," which appeared in the *Michigan Journal of Community Service Learning*. She earned her Master of Science degree in adult education from North Carolina State University.

Adam Peck has served as assistant vice president and dean of student affairs at Stephen F. Austin State University in Nacogdoches, Texas, since 2008 and has been a student affairs practitioner for more than 20 years. He currently is state director of Texas for NASPA–Student Affairs Administrators in Higher Education and president for the Texas Association of College Personnel Administrators. He previously served as chair of the Texas Deans of Students Association. Prior to his current role, he was the director of student life at Saint Louis University, senior student affairs administrator for the Texas Union at The University of Texas at Austin, and director of student activities at McKendree College (now McKendree University). He earned a Bachelor of Arts degree in theater from Lewis University, a Master of Arts degree in speech communication from Southern

Illinois University at Edwardsville, and a Doctor of Philosophy in educational administration from The University of Texas at Austin.

Michael Preston has served as executive director of the Florida Consortium of Metropolitan Research Universities since July 2015, where he works with Florida International University, the University of Central Florida (UCF), and the University of South Florida on collaborative projects designed to increase retention, improve graduation rates, and ensure graduates are career ready. Prior to taking on this role, he served for 4 years as the director of the Office of Student Involvement at UCF, where he oversaw a comprehensive involvement program including entertainment programming, student organizations, volunteer and service programs, and student government. He has worked in higher education for nearly 20 years and is regularly asked to speak and present on such topics as student affairs assessment, personal career development, student engagement practices, and developing student leadership competencies. In addition to his work in student affairs at UCF, he is a faculty member in the higher education and policy studies department, where he teaches on the subject of organization and administration in higher education. He is a graduate of East Carolina University and Southern Illinois University Carbondale and earned his EdD in higher education administration and policy studies at Texas A&M University–Commerce in 2011.

Darby Roberts is the director of student life studies at Texas A&M University. She coauthored *Student Affairs Assessment: Theory to Practice* (Stylus, 2016) and coedited *Learning Is Not a Sprint: Assessing and Documenting Student Leader Learning in Cocurricular Involvement* (NASPA, 2012). She also has contributed chapters to multiple books related to student affairs assessment and student learning. From 2013 to 2015, she cochaired the Assessment, Evaluation, and Research Knowledge Community (AERKC) within NASPA–Student Affairs Administrators in Higher Education and currently is an editorial board member for the *College Student Affairs Journal*. In 2014, she was recognized with NASPA's AERKC Innovation Award. She earned a doctorate in educational administration, a master's degree in human resource management, and a bachelor's degree in business analysis and research, all from Texas A&M University.

Teresa E. Simpson serves the Lamar University Center for Doctoral Studies in Educational Leadership as a clinical instructor and education abroad coordinator. Prior to joining the College of Education and Human Development, she served in various leadership positions for the Division of Student Affairs and has held leadership roles in a variety of professional associations in the field of student affairs, serving as director for career and professional development and interim-director for new student and leadership programs/student life. In conjunction with her supportive role on committees for the National Association of Colleges and Employers, she has served on the board of several regional, state, and national associations.

Gayle Spencer serves as director of the Illinois Leadership Center at the University of Illinois at Urbana–Champaign. She served as the chair of the National Association for Campus Activities (NACA) Board of Directors from 2002 to 2003 and was a member of the Board of Directors from 1999 to 2004. She was the 1999 NACA National Convention chair and chair of the NACA Diversity Task Force. She is currently representing NACA on the Council for the Advancement of Standards for Higher Education Board of Directors. She received the 2015 Founders Award from NACA, the 2005 Western Illinois University Alumni Achievement Award, the 2004 NACA East Coast Higher Education Research Scholarship, and the 2004 ACPA–College Student Educators International Commission for Student Involvement Research Award. She holds a PhD in student counseling and personnel services from Kansas State University, an MS in college student personnel from Western Illinois University, and a BS in business administration from the University of Nebraska at Omaha.

Becky Spurlock serves as the senior associate dean for student life at The University of the South in Sewanee, Tennessee. An active member of NASPA–Student Affairs Administrators in Higher Education, she currently serves on the NASPA Center for Women Advisory Board and previously served on the NASPA Board of Directors. She also held leadership positions within NASPA Region III, including serving as director and awards coordinator. In 2013, she published "Culture of Evidence Rubric" in the book *Building a Culture of Evidence in Student Affairs: A Guide for Leaders and Practitioners* (NASPA, 2013). She has a PhD in higher education administration from Texas A&M University as well as two degrees from Texas State University—a BS in recreational administration and an MEd in counseling and guidance.

Amy Swan is assistant professor of higher education at George Mason University. Her research interests center on students' academic and career development, with a particular focus on experiential and contextual factors that shape students' educational decision-making processes and occupational aspirations. Her work has appeared in *Career Development Quarterly*, the *Journal of Women and Minorities in Science and Engineering*, and the *NASPA Journal About Women in Higher Education*. She hold a PhD in education from the University of Virginia.

John Taylor serves as chief executive officer for the Association of College Unions International (ACUI). He became CEO in 2015, after having worked at higher education institutions for 27 years and serving as an ACUI volunteer for much of that time. During his career, he led unions at Missouri State University and Rutgers University before serving as senior director of auxiliary services and director of university unions at the University of Michigan in 2005. He has a bachelor's degree in history from Rutgers University, a master's degree in higher education and student affairs administration from the University of Vermont, and a doctoral degree in educational leadership from the University of Missouri.

Pamela Watts is the executive director for NIRSA: Leaders in Collegiate Recreation. A former certified public accountant, she joined NIRSA in 2000, and during her tenure with the association she served primarily as NIRSA's second-in-command until assuming the executive directorship in early 2012. She is a certified association executive and, in her role fostering external relationships for the association, currently serves as the chair of the Council for Higher Education Management Association's Steering Committee. She holds a BS in accounting and political science from Regis University.

Steve Westbrook serves as vice president for university affairs at Stephen F. Austin State University. With more than 30 years of experience in the field of student affairs, he has served as a board member and chair of the National Association for Campus Activities and is an executive officer for the Texas Council of Chief Student Affairs Officers. He is also active in NASPA–Student Affairs Administrators in Higher Education and the Texas Association of College and University Student Personnel Administrators. He received his EdD in higher education supervision, curriculum, and instruction from Texas A&M University–Commerce and his MEd in counseling and BA in history from Stephen F. Austin State University.

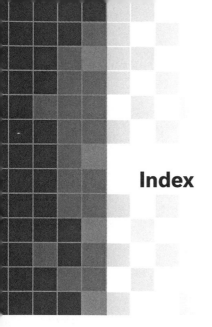

Index

Figures and tables are indicated by f and t following the page number.